AF572746

JOHN FORSTER: A LITERARY LIFE

James A. Davies

John Forster: A Literary Life

1983
BARNES & NOBLE BOOKS
TOTOWA, NEW JERSEY

First published in the USA 1983 by
BARNES & NOBLE BOOKS
81 Adams Drive
Totowa, New Jersey, 07512

Designed by Douglas Martin
Photoset by Wyvern Typesetting Ltd, Bristol
Printed and bound in Great Britain
at The Pitman Press, Bath

Library of Congress Cataloging in Publication Data

Davies, James A.
John Forster, A Literary Life.
Bibliography: P.
1. Forster, John, 1812–1876. 2. Literary
Historians – England – Biography. 3. Authors,
English – 19th Century –
glish – 19th Century –
Biography. 1. Title.
PR29.F67D38 1983 820',9'008 (B) 83-3792
ISBN 0-389-20391-2

Contents

Illustrations

To Jen

Acknowledgments

During the writing of this book I have incurred many debts. I remain grateful to Emeritus Professor Cecil Price for suggesting to me that John Forster's literary career might repay investigation. Too many years ago Professor Price supervised the doctoral thesis from which this book developed; he has given me much help and encouragement. More recently I have benefited from the advice and support of Professor Philip Collins. I am greatly indebted to Dr Aurelia Brooks Harlan for unrestricted access to the Forster material collected by herself and her late husband, J. Lee Harlan, Jr, and for entrusting me with much of it before deposition in the Armstrong Browning Library of Baylor University, Waco, Texas. In its present form this book would hardly have been possible without Dr Harlan's collection, nor, of course, would I have had the privilege of meeting her. The staff of the Armstrong Browning Library, above all its Director, Professor Jack W. Herring, and its Librarian, Mrs Betty Coley, are owed special thanks for their helpful expertise and enthusiastic interest in my work. I shall always be grateful to Professor Robert G. Collmer, then chairman of the Department of English at Baylor University, now the University's Dean of Graduate Studies, for enabling me (with my family) to spend the spring semester of 1981 as visiting professor in his Department. This much facilitated my work on the Forster/Robert Browning relationship. My thanks are due to the present chairman, Professor James E. Barcus, and his colleagues for making my visit such a pleasant one. For invaluable help of various kinds I wish to thank George and Carol Evans, Professor K. J. Fielding, Dr Gertrude Reese Hudson, Professor Sylvère Monod, Mr T. I. Rae of the National Library of Scotland, Mr Graham Storey, and the library staff of University College of Swansea.

The following copyright owners have generously allowed me to quote from manuscript material: Hon. David Lytton Cobbold, Mr Christopher Dickens, Mr John Landor, Mr John Murray, Lord Tennyson, and the Trustees of the National Library of Scotland. I am grateful to the following institutions for permission to utilize their holdings: Armstrong Browning Library, Baylor University; Henry W. and Albert A. Berg Collection, New York Public Library, Astor, Lenox and Tilden Foundations; British

Library Department of Manuscripts; Brotherton Library, University of Leeds; William Andrews Clark Memorial Library, University of California, Los Angeles; The Dickens House; Fales Library, New York University; Folger Shakespeare Library, Washington, D.C.; Free Library of Philadelphia; Hertford Record Office; Houghton Library, Harvard University; Humanities Research Centre, The University of Texas at Austin; Huntington Library, San Marino, California; Kungliga biblioteket (the Royal Library), Stockholm; Manchester Public Libraries; Pierpont Morgan Library, New York; National Library of Scotland; Carl and Lily Pforzheimer Foundation, Inc., New York; Princeton University Library; Tennyson Research Centre Collection, Lincoln (by Courtesy of Lord Tennyson and Lincolnshire Library Service); University of Chicago Library, Department of Special Collections; Victoria and Albert Museum (for Crown Copyright material in the National Art Library, mainly in the Forster Collection).

Chapters Two and Three are based on articles that first appeared in the *Review of English Studies*; the material is used by permission of Oxford University Press. By kind permission of the editor, Chapter Seven includes material first published in *Victorian Periodicals Review*. Parts of Chapters Six and Eleven were originally articles in the *Dickensian*; a version of Chapter Fifteen was published in *Dickens Studies Annual*, VII. Extracts from R. H. Super, *Walter Savage Landor* (New York, 1954), are quoted by permission of New York University Press, those from the Pilgrim edition of *The Letters of Charles Dickens*, vols. I–V (1965–81), Robert L. Patten, *Charles Dickens and His Publishers* (1978), and the Clarendon Dickens editions of *Dombey and Son*, ed. A. Horsman (1974), and *Little Dorrit*, ed. H. P. Sucksmith (1979), by permission of Oxford University Press.

I am grateful to Mrs Rita Williams and the secretarial staff of the Department of English, University College of Swansea, Mrs Vera Coxall and Mrs Kate Loveridge, for expert typing. My thanks are also due to Mr Peter L. Boulton and Mrs Susan Martin of Leicester University Press for much helpful advice. I am glad to acknowledge a British Academy research award that enabled me to visit libraries in the U.S.A. and several grants from the University College of Swansea's Research and Fieldwork Fund.

Without my wife's encouragement and co-operation this book would not exist. The dedication is a hopelessly inadequate expression of gratitude.

James A. Davies, September 1982

Part One Early Life and Influential Friends

CHAPTER 1 *Newcastle to London*

At the age of 48 John Forster wrote of himself in his diary: 'I believe if a man has anything in him it comes out on the whole in the shape & way that nature has appointed.'[1] It may be that innate qualities inevitably assert themselves; certainly the likelihood is increased when external circumstances are propitious. It is hard to imagine an upbringing better designed to develop the qualities that made Forster a vigorous political journalist, a literary reviewer alert to new trends, a revisionist biographer, and a wise adviser to popular writers in a strange new Victorian market-place than was provided by the first 21 years of his life.

The Forsters were Northumbrians. John Forster of Corsenside owned land, was a man of substance, and had three sons. When he died only the two eldest, Lionel and Thomas, benefited. The youngest, Christopher, received nothing. Christopher had two sons, John and Robert, who both became butchers and cattle-dealers in Newcastle upon Tyne. John, for long a bachelor, prospered and, with his stick and courteous manner, was known as 'Gentleman John'.[2] Robert, six years younger, did less well and married at least slightly beneath himself, his wife Mary being, in a nicely-edged Victorian phrase, 'a gem of a woman, although the daughter of a Gallowgate cow-keeper'.[3]

Robert and Mary Forster had four children, two sons and then two daughters. Christopher, the eldest, was born in 1807, lived his life at home as a bachelor and became a marine insurance broker as a partner in Slack & Forster of Quayside, Newcastle. Sister Jane, who was unmarried, lived with him. Elizabeth, also unmarried, eventually became a governess. John Forster, the subject of this study, was the second child and born in Newcastle 'in a little yellow house … in Fenkle Street',[4] on 2 April 1812, when both his parents were in their mid-30s. He was named after his uncle.

Little is known of Forster's father but his mother was remembered by her nephew, James Gilmore, for her kind and affectionate nature: she would provide cast-off clothing for her sister Anne's eight children, the impoverished Gilmore family living on a guinea a week. When the sisters met, as James Gilmore recalled with emotional nostalgia, 'their hearts made their lips come together' and 'tears would follow the kiss that parted them'.[5] The Forsters were better-off than the Gilmores, but whether they were happier is another matter: James Gilmore refers mysteriously to the family's 'trials'[6] and to Mary Forster's 'troubles'.[7] He does not explain what these were.

The Forsters soon left Fenkle Street for nearby Low Friar Street. When John Forster was 16 they lived at 5, Green Court. Each home was in the centre of old Newcastle, then a city of 30,000 people, a jumble of houses, works and potteries, a lead manufactory in Gallowgate (the street where Mary Forster had lived before her marriage), refineries and ironworks, and the river, with its wharves and warehouses at Quayside, never far away. Here and there crumbling reminders of the medieval city still persisted, such as the ruins of the ancient Black Friars' monastery near the Forsters' Low Friar Street home.[8]

The family was Unitarian and attended Hanover Square meeting house.[9] They were members of a minority sect concerned to reject dogma and so with Christianity as a way of life rather than a creed. Unitarians asked only for the acceptance of New Testament beliefs 'such as are intelligible to human reason'.[10] Central to the faith was a rejection of the doctrine of the Trinity, a doctrine that, for Unitarians, inspired only 'a diseased taste for prodigies, fictions, and exaggerations, for startling mysteries, and wild dreams of enthusiasm'. Rather, God was 'the common Parent'[11] and Christ was his son. Unitarianism was thus a reasonable religion and a main consequence of this stress on reason was a strong belief in the individual's own capacity for improvement. It follows that notions of original sin and of essential depravity, as well as deterministic philosophies, were firmly rejected.

From such thinking came the Unitarian passion for education and support for those reformist policies, such as franchise extension, free trade, corn law repeal, that would lead to increased individual responsibility. Unitarians favoured Benthamite ideas and the related notion of 'self-help' which expressed a fierce hatred of patronage; it was later popularized by the Unitarian Samuel Smiles. Here was an intellectual and influential religious group whose members saw themselves as the vanguard of the age. Their worship had only been legalized in 1813, so at the time when John Forster worshipped with his family at Hanover Square during the 1820s their new status combined with their reasonable view of man's capacities to make Unitarians anxious to work for social and moral progress in ways that were law-abiding and socially respectable.

Hanover Square was the centre of Newcastle's flourishing Unitarian community. Its famous minister, the theologian and author William Turner, established one of the first Sunday schools in North-East England, a school that taught not only religious knowledge but also reading, writing and arithmetic. For the adult congregation the chapel maintained a good library in its vestry[12] and was a progressive force in the city.

Forster's secular education was received mainly at Newcastle's Royal Grammar School. Uncle John paid the fees and Forster followed his elder brother, Christopher, into the school at a time of change and upheaval. The headmaster was Edward Moises who, in 1787, had become head of a famous and successful school, offering the traditional classical education. Under Moises the school declined, mainly because of competition from new kinds of schools offering education geared to the demands of industry and commerce until, in 1820, when Forster could have entered at eight years of age, only nine pupils remained. An enquiry followed and changes were made: new masters were hired and the curriculum widened to include not only classics but also English grammar, writing, history, geography and mathematics. Though Moises had little heart for the reconstituted system the school revived through the 1820s. In 1826 there were 80 pupils and 100 in the writing school, paying fees ranging from 5s. to 15s. per quarter. Building extensions were completed in 1827.[13]

Family life that knew monetary pressure, deep emotion, class movement and urban mobility in an ancient but industrialized conurbation, an intellectually progressive minority religion selfconsciously treasuring a new-found social status, an education forced to come to terms with a changing world – here was much that was typical of that collective experience that produced Victorians. Such an upbringing makes us see, particularly, why Forster was such a good adviser to popular writers. He represented a constituency of which he himself had been part. Further, even at this early stage Forster demonstrated significant personal qualities. To quote James Gilmore once again: 'I remember how kind he was to me, when we were "Boys together"; "James" he would say, "I have a new suit of cloath's [*sic*] making, & my Mother says you are to have these, when I get my new ones, come with me to the Tailor's, & we'll learn when that will be." '[14] Forster had, wrote Gilmore, 'the power to turn desirable acquaintances into friends'.[15] He was, at 16, a strong-jawed, kind-hearted adolescent reconciling traditional interests with new enthusiasms; he was 'an intense student of Byron and Scott – an enthusiastic antiquary and collector of ballad poetry, and always seen with a book under his arm'.[16]

Hanover Square chapel had strong connections with Newcastle's Literary and Philosophical Society, founded by William Turner, who still in the 1820s acted as secretary. Here Forster heard visiting lecturers, experienced discussion that could be so lively that periodic appeals had to be made to bury differences and to listen courteously, and had the use of a fine library.[17] At school he distinguished himself in the continuing traditional areas of mathematics and, particularly, classics. He became Edward Moises's 'favourite'[18] and head boy of the school, this last in a line that included Lords Eldon and Collingwood. Forster received, as he himself agreed, 'an excellent preliminary education'.[19]

But, in a world of change, Forster, too, reacted against established procedures. Whilst he studied classics at the Grammar School he began making friends in the local literary world. One was the drama critic of the *Durham Chronicle*, another the slightly raffish William Andrew Mitchell, who held nightly court at Newcastle's Blue Bell, edited the *Tyne Mercury*, and published, monthly, the *Newcastle Magazine*.[20] Most importantly, Forster became interested in the theatre. At the age of 14 he expertly dramatized a version of *Ali Baba*, offering a sketch of the set, instructions about movable parts, and even lighting details ('Blue mediums before the Lamps').[21] By 1827, aged 15, he was a regular theatre-goer.

The theatre was hardly a central Dissenting enthusiasm and the mother of Forster's friend Francis Bennett was quick to supply a tract 'against the stage'.[22] Forster countered with a long letter containing, as he put it with some quantitative understatement, 'a few thoughts in vindication of the stage'. In this he drew on wide reading to present a history of the theatre as part of an argument for its didactic function through the provision of dramatic support for religion and the law. The letter is always vigorous though, at times, optimistically adolescent, as when he writes of the theatre exhibiting 'Truth, pure and incorruptible', to counter 'Bacchanalian joys, ruinous play, a thousand frenzies which idleness begets'. Here, though, is an attractive passion seen again in Forster's notion of the theatre as a national institution fostering 'the *spirit* of a Nation'. Only the stage could do this 'because she *alone* traverses the whole empire of human knowledge ... head and heart'.[23] Whether Mrs Bennett was persuaded is not known; she must, at least, have been impressed.

Practice followed theory. In May 1828 Forster's play, *Charles at Tunbridge or The Cavalier of Wildinghurst*, by 'A Gentleman of Newcastle', received its only performance at the Theatre Royal, Newcastle, for the benefit of the leading resident actor, Thomas Stuart. The play is set in the reign of Charles II and is about the attempts of an aging and impoverished cavalier, Sir Mark Willoughby, to obtain just recompense for himself and his daughter Grace from the king he has helped to restore to the throne. The king's favourite page, Harry Brooke, is in love with Grace and loyal to the king; Brooke has a rival in the rich and villainous Squire Akkerdale. The king refuses Sir Mark's suit and the cavalier makes Brooke choose between court and girl. Brooke's friend at court, the Earl of Arlington, helps resolve this conflict of loyalties by taking Charles in disguise to Wildinghurst where the king sees the error of his ways.

Akkerdale is the dominating character. Much given to gloomy soliloquizing, in dialogue, also, he has a wordy turn of phrase. He is the kind of villain who says to the heroine whom he is seeking to abduct:

> Submit to thy fate and fly with me to a foreign land – a brighter land than this ... where the eye may look bright upon groves of the palm and the cocoa ... where the foot may move over fields carpeted with flowers.

Grace replies, oddly, with patriotism not morality:

> My own country has charms for me – which no other land on earth can present to me. Not the fairest scenes in a foreign clime – not the brightest sunbeam that ever shone upon the richest landscape – would win my thoughts for a moment from the dear land of my deceased ancestors – and of my living father.[24]

That has little effect, but the attempted abduction is thwarted by an honest servant. Akkerdale's subsequent suicide is sufficiently remorseful to become part of the happy ending.

It has to be admitted that this is not great literature. *Charles at Tunbridge* is staple melodramatic fodder the theatrical quality of which is partly undermined by Forster's liking for long speeches. The play is mainly valuable for what it tells us of the young Forster, of his ardently romantic nature supported by his reading of Scott and Byron, his democratizing leanings made explicit in the action of Akkerdale's servant, his view of drama as a didactic force brought out most strongly in the contrast between the decadent wealth of the court and of Akkerdale and the virtuous poverty of Wildinghurst and Willoughby, and in Forster's insistence that a leader must be worthy of his position, and of a strong patriotism that Forster was never to lose. Importantly, the play shows one way in which his Unitarian beliefs received literary expression: the king, in breaking free from the influence of his foppish court, and Akkerdale from memories of a past in which failure in love made him eager for revenge on all women, both discover their true moral selves. Such ideas, though, are more impressive in summary than in their dramatization, despite the fact that Mitchell, who reviewed the play, was sure it had 'great merit'; the blundering production, perhaps fortunately, made it 'impossible to judge correctly'.[25] The audience, at least, received it well.

A few months later, as Robert Grainger rebuilt central Newcastle and a new Clayton Street swept away Forster's 'yellow coloured'[26] birthplace, he left Newcastle for Cambridge. Once again he was financed by his uncle and much was expected of him; yet he stayed at Cambridge only a month and then went to London. He had found his 'expences [*sic*] at the Cambridge University' to be 'very great',[27] perhaps, as Harle hints,[28] too great for Uncle John. He might have been influenced by the fact that Dissenters, Unitarians amongst them, could not take degrees. Whitwell Elwin, writing many years later, considered that Forster left Cambridge because he became more interested in modern than in ancient learning.[29] And Forster himself wrote, 22 years after the event:

> In London the mere merchant and the mere politician have been removed from the liberalising influence of letters; and at Oxford and Cambridge the man of letters, kept apart from the real business of life, has declined into the cloistered bookworm ... Most of the latter class who may have felt a generous aspiration to mix in the struggles of active life, and participate in, or ameliorate, the common destinies of their kind, have been obliged to desert the English Universities at an early period of life.[30]

It may have been, simply, that for a romantic youngster, full of books and theatre, glamorous London proved irresistible. The only certainty about this hazy episode is that, for the second time in his life, Forster flew in the face of convention.

Though not wholly so. In Newcastle his theatrical writings, in themselves a daring venture, reflected and endorsed the ideas of his upbringing; his rejection of Cambridge and the classics was not for metropolitan bohemia but, ostensibly, for a far more respectable activity. Forster found lodgings with a Mrs Gibson, at 17 Penton Place, Pentonville; on 10 November 1828 he enrolled as a law student at the Inner Temple and began attending Andrew Amos's law class at the new University College.

Here was the vibrant alternative to the sectarian, conservative and classical education offered by Oxford and Cambridge. University College was non-sectarian, though with a strong Unitarian element in its founding that may have appealed to Forster, and in its concern to link 'theory and active life'[31] looked to Benthamite ideas of useful knowledge. Amos was Professor of English Law and taught a large class that included Forster, the playwright Gerald Griffin, and Forster's closest friend of those early days, James Whiteside, later to be Chief Justice of Ireland. James Emerson, who became Governor of Ceylon and who was, like Whiteside, some years older than Forster, joined the class later and was his other close companion. Whiteside remembered Forster, with real affection, as 'joyous, generous, sincere ... the uncompromising advocate of all that was just, noble & good'. Yet, in also describing Forster as 'a raw oddly-dressed, energetic, impetuous youth from the provinces',[32] Whiteside makes us see that conflict between Forster's character and its public expression that had important long-term effects. Through Whiteside Forster met Thomas Chitty, the eminent special pleader, and in 1830 the three friends, Emerson following Forster's advice, entered Chitty's chambers as part of their legal training.

His friends were beginning successful legal careers; Forster, too, showed brilliant potential as a practical lawyer, 'so able a pupil as not infrequently to act for a distinguished special pleader'.[33] But, in 1832, he 'flung away his chances at the Bar – for which Mr Chitty never forgave him – and [relied] only upon Literature for his support'.[34] Whitwell Elwin suggested that Forster studied law only to placate his family,[35] meaning Uncle John, who held the purse-strings. If so, this can only emphasize the serious wilfulness of his rejection of a hugely promising career. This rejection, the third unconventional act of his early years, differs almost in kind from turning to local dramatics and rushing from Cambridge to London, more nautical pyromania than the mere burning of boats.

This was particularly true at that time; the London literary world of the 1820s and early 1830s was in a depressed state. The famous crash of Ballantyne and Constable still had its effect and even John Murray was in difficulties. Publishers were cautious, bringing out small editions at high prices. The market, such as it was, reacted adversely to most non-literary events; George IV's death, reform, cholera, were all distractions and bad for business. The deaths of Byron and Scott did not help.[36] Forster's family must have thought him mad, or close to it.

In retrospect we see that Forster jumped, with perfect timing, from blazing boat to passing literary life-raft. The literary world was changing and beginning to expand. The spread of literacy, which owed much to interest in reform and to new printing technology, was giving rise to a mass market never before available to writers. The patron had gone and now the public was arriving. Popular writers would receive bigger rewards and, because of this, would be swiftly professionalized with precise agreements and complex written contracts. Forster, shrewd, devoted to literature, and trained as a lawyer, had an obvious part to play.

That he should have jumped when he did could perhaps have been predicted. Almost his first act on arriving in London had been a literary one: he wrote a review for Mitchell's *Newcastle Magazine*. 'Remarks on Two of the Annuals'[37] is a precociously confident account of *The Keepsake* and *The Anniversary*, most interesting now for its main theme, a concern for the public reputation of literary men. Coleridge, Southey, and Scott, contributors to *The Keepsake*, are criticized for providing items unworthy of their talents, Forster, aged 16, commenting magisterially: 'We do not like to see such men in their undress – in their "night gown and slippers".' Nonentities, like Normanby and Frederick Mansel Reynolds, are attacked fiercely for their coarseness. Particular praise is given to the 'quiet repose and calm beauty'[38] of John Wilson's 'Edderline's Dream', and to Allen Cunningham's poetry and editing, Forster here, as Mitchell pointed out, more 'an advocate than ... a judge'.[39]

Again, at University College, Forster 'attended but never regarded'[40] Amos's law class. Although he passed his examinations and demonstrated his brilliant potential, he reserved greater enthusiasm for the *London University Magazine*, which his class founded in the face of official disapproval, and for 'the Monthly Magazines' which, as Whiteside recalled, he and Forster 'actually devoured'.[41] He obtained from Whiteside an article for the *Newcastle Magazine*,[42] and lent Emerson volumes of Gibbon to further his spare-time task of writing a *History of Modern Greece*.[43] In 1831 the *Englishman's Magazine*, a short-lived but distinguished journal for which Leigh Hunt, Lamb, Hood, Clare and the young Tennyson all wrote, published Forster's short story, 'Prodigious!', a parody of gothic excess in which a monomaniac kills his brother's baby son, hurls the body into a chasm, stabs his father, and then finds all to have been a dream.[44] The same journal followed this with four solid essays on 'Early Patriots',[45] mainly Pym and Sir John Eliot, that are important not only because they provide an early glimpse of a scholarly Forster, but also because, in linking the seventeenth-century struggle between parliament and the king with the reform movement of his own day, Forster demonstrates how his literary interests were fuelled by his political beliefs.

The latter were a passion. He, Whiteside and Emerson were '*always together* ... [and] ... always discussing politics'.[46] So was Professor Amos, who would breakfast at Forster's new lodgings at 4 Burton Street, Burton Crescent, St Pancras, and discuss 'manoeuvres to avoid a dissolution'.[47] Forster attended Parliament and wrote excitedly to Emerson of his (Forster's) support for the ballot.[48] He began a biography of Cromwell.[49]

Literature and politics distracted Forster from the law. He began to cultivate long-term ambitions by starting to collect material for a life of Goldsmith. In the shorter term, in 1832, he published a volume of verse, *Rhyme and Reason*,[50] and was lucky enough to publish it anonymously. The poems are those of a devout, impressionable and widely-read young man. Subjects range from the theological ('A Prayer', 'A Hymn') to the moralistic ('Virtue and Vice'), to 'Evening Reflections in a Country Churchyard', to the patriotic ('A National Song', 'A Naval Song'), the aesthetic (an ode to 'Beauty') and the heavily humorous ('Dialogue Between the Eyes and Nose', 'Riddles'). The poems are over-influenced by Wordsworth and Byron, Gray, Crabbe and Cowper; they reflect Forster's interest in history. Almost all have, most damagingly, a forbidding adolescent gloom and sternness of purpose, as poems in which Forster, aged 19, seems to impersonate a wise but embittered centenarian concerned to

Examine carefully this fleeting life
Where piety and sin exist in strife.[51]

He never again published poetry and never again referred to this volume.

That publication ended his purely creative ambitions at a time when he was making his first steps in more promising areas. For, also, in 1832, Forster persuaded Bulwer, then editor of the *New Monthly Magazine*, to use his journal to appeal for funds for a struggling Leigh Hunt.[52] He made similar arrangements for Sheridan Knowles, until Knowles declined to be helped,[53] and urged J. P. Collier to 'insert a paragraph in the Chronicle ... urging the people to a more generous testimony on behalf of ... Knowles ... than they seem at present disposed to'.[54]

Then came a breakthrough. Almost certainly because of the 'Early Patriots' articles Dionysius Lardner, the literary impresario and Professor of Natural Philosophy and Astronomy at University College, commissioned Forster to write five volumes of Commonwealth biographies, of Eliot, Strafford, Pym, Hampden, Marten, Vane and Cromwell, the latter already started, for his multi-volume *Cabinet Cyclopaedia*. The commission came as Forster, with a piece on Hunt's novel, *Sir Ralph Esher*, began reviewing for the *New Monthly Magazine*. It was followed by the start of his full-time literary career: in the summer of 1832 he became dramatic critic of the *True Sun*;[55] in December he added to this the editorship of Moxon's *Reflector*.[56]

The *True Sun* was a radical newspaper that had links with the underground press. W. J. Fox, the Unitarian minister, was editor and popularizing a Benthamite utilitarianism that looked to social progress via general intellectual emancipation. Journalists had a crucial part to play in mediating 'the chasm between middle- and working-class reformism'.[57] Forster wielded much reviewing power and did so with impartiality: Douglas Jerrold wrote to thank him for praising *The Housekeeper*;[58] Knowles, actor as well as dramatist, wrote angrily, 'repudiating his friendship',[59] when Forster criticized his Macbeth.

The *Reflector* was less successful. Lamb contributed but the journal folded after only three issues, leaving Forster perhaps chastened but certainly, as he told Leigh Hunt's wife, 'much harassed for ready money from the failure of a magazine in which I was concerned and from which I had expected assistance'.[60]

At the end of 1833 Forster had been in London for five years and had earned a living from literature for most of two. He was rising, as Whiteside put it, 'not rapidly but by degrees'.[61] He was not well-off and may have been, generally, more hard-up than comfortable, particularly since funds from Uncle John seem to have stopped. His main income came from the *True Sun*.[62] The rejection of conventional progress, in particular of a lucrative legal career, shortage of money, work for a radical paper, all suggest the start of a life on the left. In fact, Forster seems, in these radical contexts, a man of passionate respectability. His political views reflect this: for example, he was ardent for reform yet, as he told Emerson, prepared to move forward step by step.[63] His support, for instance, of Sheridan Knowles, his concern for the latter's reputation and financial soundness, makes the same point in literary terms.

Forster, wrote Harle, 'determined to write a book and connect himself with the periodical press'.[64] In 1833 he was writing and had connected. The determination persisted and, towards the end of the year, he consolidated magnificently by becoming 'Theatrical Examiner' of the *Examiner*, the weekly that was 'the principal representative, in the newspaper press, of radical opinion',[65] edited by Albany Fonblanque, 'the greatest journalist in England'.[66] At the age of 21 Forster had leapt to the centre of London literary life.

Forster began an *affaire de coeur* with Letitia Elizabeth Landon, 'L.E.L.', whose poetry made her *the* literary lioness of the time. He was establishing himself as a literary figure. Arguably, his most significant actions thus far relate to the help he gave to others, help that included the small services he performed for Emerson and Whiteside, and his support of Sheridan Knowles. For the above account of Forster's early life is not the whole story and the rest concerns four friendships. In 1829, probably at one of Henry Colburn's literary evenings,[67] Forster met Leigh Hunt. Through Hunt and Procter he met Charles Lamb. In 1832 his work for the

New Monthly Magazine led to friendship with its editor, Bulwer Lytton. The following year, at Edmund Kean's funeral, he met the tragedian William Charles Macready.[68] In these friendships we see writ large the impulse to help literature and literary men, the drama and serious actors, glimpsed in those other small services. This impulse dominates the relationships. In return, these four men helped establish Forster; their combined influence dominated and shaped the rest of his literary career.

CHAPTER 2 *Leigh Hunt*

When he met Leigh Hunt, Forster was only 17. Hunt was 45 and worth knowing. He had been the friend and champion of Keats and Shelley, had been close to Byron, to Coleridge, to Hazlitt, Moore, Landor, and the Lambs. In 1801, when Hunt had been 17, he had made his name with *Critical Essays on the Performers of the London Theatres*. He had been founder-editor of the *Examiner* and a fearless radical once jailed for insulting the Prince Regent. Hunt remained a poet and essayist of note, a prolific and respected reviewer and journalist, a popularizer of literature. He was, Forster recalled, 'the first distinguished man of letters I ever knew'.[1]

Naturally and evidently Forster hero-worshipped. Hunt was, he told Hunt's wife, 'a man of very fine genius',[2] and he referred publicly to the friendship as 'a source of profit and delight'.[3] Yet Forster did not so much fall at Hunt's feet as take him by the hand. His admiration and necessary cultivation were expressed in terms of helpful action.

Forster regarded Hunt as a literary martyr, a genius reduced to 'unmerited distress... Mr Hunt has been of late years the object of a persecution almost unparallelled in the history of letters'.[4] Here was evidence of literature's need for better recognition and recompense from the society it served, evidence that made Hunt's poverty one of the main reasons for the 'dignity of literature' movement in which Forster was to play a prominent part. Such sentiments come readily to a 17-year old; more rare was the ability to translate sentiment into practical help and to dominate the relationship. Even rarer was Forster's awareness and acceptance of his hero's faults: Hunt was 'incapable of making a shilling do the work of sixpence',[5] a failing aggravated by his wife's alcoholism and the fecklessness of both his wife and son John; and Hunt himself was not always honest.

So Forster not only took Hunt by the hand, he took him in hand with equal firmness, regulating his conduct ('just remember to come in a short coat',[6] he cautioned Hunt in 1849, when sending a theatre ticket) and trying to regulate his income by furthering Hunt's literary career. Forster's edition of Hunt's *Christianism* appeared in 1832, almost certainly by subscription, in order, as Forster's own preface put it, to show 'the real state of Mr Leigh Hunt's opinions upon a point on which he has been greatly misconceived'.[7] Then followed a series of fund-raising activities including, in 1832, an appeal to the Royal Literary Fund, when Forster acted as intermediary and obtained, for Hunt, a special grant.[8] Such activities often headed off Hunt's imminent financial disasters, and culminated in amateur dramatics with Dickens for Hunt's benefit, and long and eventually successful agitation for Hunt's State Pension. Some sense of Forster's energy and commitment to his friend's welfare can be gained from his early letter to Mrs Hunt:

> I went yesterday... to a man of some eminence in literature to ask his opinion – (without *reference* of course *to your* letter or to any *present application, but only mentioning* circumstances that are generally known) – about the probable success of *a selection from Mr Hunt's works in prose and verse.* He entered into it warmly – thought that it would not only be encouraged by Mr H.'s personal acquaintances but be most acceptable to the public and well fitted for the present time. Now what I would propose to you is this – that you should break this matter to Mr Hunt, and obtain his permission to allow his friends to form themselves into a kind of committee (there are many *men of celebrity in letters* who will gladly join it) for the purpose of issuing prospectusses of such a work, and of obtaining among their friends by personal exertions a list of subscribers. If you can procure his consent to this, the prospectusses might be issued, the (private) committee formed and the subscribers procured in a very short space of time, – Mr Hunt would easily manage to prepare the work, and a Bookseller would be found I doubt not (indeed we have one in contemplation) that would not scruple to give me a handsome sum for the MSS. *provided* the *list of subscribers were handed in to him.* – For myself I can only say that if this meets with your approbation no exertion shall be wanting on my part to carry it into effect – and I have every reasonable hope of perfect success. I shall indeed, with all my personal acquaintance, (and they are very numerous), make the tenure of my further acquaintanceship depend on their enrolling themselves as subscribers to the work.[9]

The edition was published by Moxon in 1832.

Fund-raiser was only one of Forster's roles. He also acted as Hunt's unpaid agent, pushing his work at publishers and negotiating with actor-managers. Thus Forster wrote to J. W. Parker: 'I wish to see you for a few minutes this afternoon as to something which I fancy you might not object to insert in the *next number* of Fraser's Magazine'.[10] Again, a year or so later, in a letter that combined business with a touching description of his friend, Forster wrote:

> Will you kindly submit the enclosed to the Editor of Fraser's Magazine?
>
> It is a little tale told in imitation of Chaucer... and is, I think, very pretty and ingenious, to say the very least of it.
>
> It is by Leigh Hunt; and if approved might be printed with his name.
>
> I need hardly add perhaps that any *honorarium* which the Editor might think it worth (if accepted) would be gladly received by the veteran wit, poet, prose-man, party-man, translator whose life is drawing to a close amid the same studies and enjoyments in which it began.[11]

During the winter of 1849–50 Forster did his best to persuade Samuel Phelps to stage Hunt's play *The Prince's Marriage*.[12] He failed at the last but was then successful in placing it with – but, ultimately, not in getting it produced by – Webster, the Haymarket's manager.[13] When he became editor of the *Examiner* and the *Foreign Quarterly Review* he found books for Hunt to write about, an ironic reversal of fortunes. Forster constantly sought to regularize Hunt's financial position by ensuring him a steady income. He wrote to Chapman and Hall:

> I send herewith (pray forward it instantly to the printers) the whole memoir and all the stories from Boccaccio.
>
> Ariosto and Tasso will follow without delay.
>
> I have promised Mr Hunt that you will let him have the 150£ for this second volume in 3 portions of 50£ each, as he sends the copy of each.
>
> Pray send me, tomorrow, or Monday at latest, a cheque for 50£ for him.[14]

Forster corrected Hunt's proofs.[15] Most importantly, Forster reviewed Hunt's own work regularly and influentially. Indeed, Hunt began to expect such attention and sought to manipulate it: 'Pray be as kind and *un-pain-giving* ... to a set of performers, most anxious to do all they can for your friend, as you can find it in your conscience to be',[16] he begged

Forster before the first night of *A Legend of Florence*. When Hunt complained about his treatment Forster's temper was quickly lost:

> You can point out no book or labour of any kind of yours which has not been noticed by me – as a matter of duty as well as of affection, for my own gratification as well as for yours. I give you the whole sixteen years in which I have been writing for the Exr and challenge you to name a single exception.[17]

It is hard to see why Hunt complained, for Fonblanque, when *Examiner* editor and Forster's employer, was forced to curb Forster's enthusiasm: 'I am as anxious as you are to give the best support to Hunt, but ... I know not how room can be found for the two notices you propose... Both for the variety of the paper & the interests of Hunt it is best that we should have a theatrical notice *only* this week, and a literary one next week.'[18]

The reviews themselves, however, were not uncritical. Forster admired Hunt and could apply the term 'genius' with sincere abandon, but he was well aware of the limitations of Hunt's work. Amid the youthful enthusiasm of 1832 he still noted how Hunt's only novel, *Sir Ralph Esher*, set in the reign of Charles II, came close to the 'insipid and improbable', and criticized it for violating known historical truth: Nell Gwyn's 'boarding-school breeding' was 'preposterous'.[19] Despite the rapturous reception given to *A Legend of Florence* by a first-night audience of Hunt's friends, Forster's review virtually admitted the piece to be unstageworthy: 'There was nothing in the appointments of the play; with one beautiful exception there was not much in the acting; there was still less in what may be called the theatrical movement of the scene; and the situations and conventional effects, were rare.'[20] Forster disapproved of Hunt's account of Congreve: 'We cannot think that Mr Hunt has looked with the kindest eye on some passages of his career';[21] he insisted on the 'modest ... pretensions'[22] of *The Palfrey*; he wrote of *Stories in Verse*: 'Leigh Hunt's only care is to tell it as he feels it ... There are views of the vocation and art of the poet certainly higher than this.'[23]

But Hunt could not have been offended, for such criticisms were more than countered by Forster's general view of Hunt's work:

> There can be no doubt, we apprehend, that Mr Hunt is a man of singular and delicate genius: a poet of great insight and happy fancy, and a prose-writer of varied excellence, ranging from deep pathos to wit and humour of as mercurial and rare a character as any in the circle of English literature. There is scarcely a note on the scale of human interest, which he has not touched with effect.

Here is precise praise, such terms as 'delicate', 'fancy', 'mercurial', 'touched', showing Forster to be soundly aware of Hunt's lightness, liveliness, beauty, and attractive superficiality. Hunt's work, Forster continued, led readers to distinguish between 'the province of falsehood or truth...not so much by pithy maxims and direct precepts, as by producing high examples'. Such examples reflected the dominant tone of Hunt's work: 'he is essentially a lover of quiet, and his illustrations are, for the most part, drawn from subjects connected with gentleness or repose'.[24]

When Hunt's work was less successful Forster undermined his own proper criticism through an appeal to the author's personal qualities. Thus, in the review of *Sir Ralph Esher*, Forster wrote of his friend:

> his writings have been a continual effort to discover all that is good and pleasant in the world about us; and in the midst of anxieties and troubles which have had no parallel, we believe, even in the history of letters, he has supported this virtuous and manly disposition, and inculcated it with a spirit that no calamity has been able to take away.[25]

A Legend of Florence was a 'brave and gallant effort ... to redeem the worldly failure of a life, whose successes, till now, have been all unworldly. Brave men will feel this best, and best know what a large respect is due to it. But it will force respect and praise from every one.'[26] The plight of the author distracted readers from the defects of the works; Forster allowed his critical sting to be drawn by his admiration of and sympathy for literary men. Any adverse change in his view of the latter was bound to lead to a more jaundiced view of the popular literary scene. And so it was, as later chapters will show.

Meanwhile, in the age of enthusiasm, Forster had yet another role to play. Arguably, his greatest influence on Hunt was exerted on the creative process itself, as editor and as private literary adviser. As editor Forster insisted on his right to 'manner it in my own way':[27] 'You sent me a most charming criticism', he wrote to Hunt in 1849, '...Why I took out two lines of it, I will tell you on Wednesday'.[28] As adviser he approached all Hunt's manuscripts in a similar collaborative spirit. Forster received requests for titles, as with *A Book for a Corner*,[29] but was more often concerned with basic problems of composition, such as the structure of *A Legend of Florence*:

> I have serious misgivings about the catastrophe, and should like you to see it more clearly before going further ... For the story of Mary deCastro – that which has invested her name with all sorts of

> tender and awful recollections is in fact *her retaking from the tomb* – therefore it is not as though, in an extremity of alteration at the last, you could dispense with that incident and substitute another ... Not only a fine thing must be the result, but a practicable thing ... [30]

Hunt wrote on this letter: 'Misgivings about catastrophe all since done away', seeming to indicate the effect of Forster's advice. Certainly the printed text of Hunt's play is an improvement on the manuscript version he gave to Forster in which, instead of Guilio the page discovering the empty tomb, as in the final version, Hunt bridged the gap between Ginevra's funeral and her reappearance after 'death' at Agolanti's house with a mainly superfluous cemetery scene featuring a boy, the all-purpose sexton of graveyard drama, and only faint hints at Ginevra's resurrection.[31]

Even 'The Inevitable', the poem 'Inscribed to John Forster' and beginning

> FORSTER whose voice can speak of awe so well,
> And stern disclosure, new and terrible,
> This were a tale, my friend, for thee to tell.

– the tone suggesting a Forster of advanced age and patriarchal demeanour (he was then 37) – did not escape criticism. Hunt wrote to Forster in 1849:

> I was not satisfied with my account of the *Angel of Death* in the blank verses, especially after the wish you expressed that more should have been said of the horror of his advent: so to give myself altogether a fresh feeling on the subject, I have put the legend into a rhyme; of which I beg your acceptance.[32]

Forster replied:

> ... it seems to me the horror of the advent of the stranger should be told – not in *his* external aspects of awe – but in the effects (as yet unknown to the reader – known indeed only to him who is about to die) seen in the restless terror and affright and at length shrinking petition of the Courtier.
>
> In a word it should be internal. Only through the Courtier should it be known. One should not hear without surprise as now (who *can* be surprised at any wish to evade such terror) his wish to be on the remotest mountain of Cathay. Yet that very wish ought to be an awe and a surprise to us ... Only keep this before you – that the

> reader should not know till the grand closing couplet that this was indeed Death's angel. Have I made myself clear, my dear Hunt?[33]

Ainsworth published the poem in the *New Monthly Magazine* of January 1850; the title had been changed from 'The Angel of Death' to 'The Inevitable', and the final text reflects the substance of Forster's reiterated criticism.

During the last decade of Hunt's life Forster tightened his grip on the old man. On occasion he decided questions of *genre*, so that Hunt wrote to Robert Bell: 'My own views tend to a poem of some length ... but Forster has just put me upon shaping something dramatic, which I have begun, for the winter stage.'[34] The result was *Lovers' Amazements*, published in 1851 though not performed until 1858, the year before Hunt's death. In February 1850 even subject matter was supplied, Forster writing to Hunt:

> there is a story told by Jeremy Taylor which I have long wanted you to throw into verse. I think you know it. But here it is. It is the conclusion of his *Apology for Christian Toleration*:
>
> He says that Abraham sat one day at his tent door, according to his custom, waiting to entertain strangers, when he aspied an old man stooping and leaning on his staff, weary with age and travail, coming towards him, who was a hundred years of age. He received him kindly, washed his feet, provided supper, caused him to sit down, but observing that the old man ate and prayed not, nor begged for a blessing on his meat, he asked him why he did not worship the God of heaven. The old man told him that he worshipped the fire only, & acknowledged no other God. At which answer, Abraham grew so zealously angry, that he threw the old man out of his tent, & exposed him to all the perils of the night & an unguarded condition. When the old man was gone, God called to Abraham & asked him where the stranger was. He replied, I thrust him away, because he did not worship thee. God answered him, I have suffered him these hundred years, though he dishonoured me; and wouldst thou not endure him one night, when he gave thee no trouble? Upon which, saith the story, Abraham fetched him back again, & gave him hospitable entertainment *and wise instruction*.
>
> Jeremy concludes with a go then and do likewise, & thy charity will be rewarded by the God of Abraham.
>
> Now, my dear Hunt, I think this a text on which you might preach a divine and enduring sermon in verses worthy of the moral.[35]

Hunt obediently wrote 'Abraham and the Fire-Worshipper' and published it in *Household Words*, Dickens's journal part-owned by Forster. Forster was not only taking Hunt by the hand but coming close to seizing the pen it held.

Of course there were some quarrels, yet Hunt, for the most part, fell fulsomely at Forster's feet. 'I need not repeat to you how highly your gift is valued', he wrote to the young Forster in 1831, after receiving the gift of Steele's *Tatler*, 'I have been carrying it about the house with me, like a child who has a picture-book given it'.[36] By 1835 his reliance seemed absolute: 'I have just heard ... that there is a report that *I* have been writing in a conservative paper! ... Do you think I had better notice it publicly ... Oblige me with a line to say Yes or No.'[37]

Forster's critical advice was understood and appreciated. 'Am astonished at what they would have said to you', Hunt remarked to Forster in a letter about Beaumont and Fletcher, 'had you been at their side, insisting upon advance of story, non-superfluities, etc.'[38] And in 1855 Hunt wrote:

> I agree so much with a great deal of what you say respecting my poetry, at least in regard to such poems as the *Story of Rimini*, that I had fairly given up nine-tenths of that production... I stand by you ... in the main spirit of your objections; have long felt it; and hope to make some little essential salt of extract of myself before I die ...[39]

Diffuseness had always been Hunt's weakness; the successive drafts of 'A Story of Rimini' during the time of the friendship show him cutting and compressing under Forster's influence. That influence was all-pervading: 'When I sent you the MS of the book on Saturday,' wrote Hunt to Forster, 'I forgot, at the last moment, to alter the close of the remarks on De Foe; but not the less was the alteration intended. You were right on the point; and De Foe shall be treated, as he deserves to be, entirely like *De Friend*' ...[40] And: 'On awakening in bed this morning (a fine fresh time for making corrections), I saw instantly that your objection to the word "bass" was right. Be good enough, therefore, to change it to "voice". "I hear the deep voice of a grief divine." '[41]

In 1847 Forster wrote to Hunt about the latter's poem, 'Jaffar', which, like much of Hunt's work at this time, was dramatic in concept, with characters and dialogue, and (a main effect of Forster on Hunt) pointing a moral: 'But are all these vivid little histories of thought and passion to have the dramatic framework in which I had a place I prized so?'[42] Here is the strangest aspect of the Forster/Hunt relationship, the most compelling and unusual evidence of the extent of Forster's influence. For Hunt's eastern anecdotes, including 'Jaffar', 'The Bitter Gourd', and 'The Inevitable', each in first-draft form included both author and Forster in a 'dramatic framework'. One fragment, poem unknown, has survived:

Hunt. Tell me a story, Forster.
Forster. Well, there lived
 A woman once who loathed her husband.
H. Pleasing.
F. Pungent. 'Tis olives for the wine. Well, Hunt,
 She loathed her husband, and she loved her cousin.
H. Happy dog! To be loved of one that loathed.
F. He was, for he escaped her.
H. Pardon me.
 My interruptions were but freaks of comfort.
 I am all ears.
F. The story merits it,
 As you'll allow.[43]

The story then followed. Forster's helping and controlling hand had become almost indistinguishable from Hunt's own.

This last implies mutual absorption, serving to remind us that Hunt, too, was an influential friend. In his first years in London friendship with Hunt not only led Forster to Procter, to Charles Lamb and, *via* the *New Monthly Magazine*, to Bulwer, but also, almost certainly, to Fonblanque, given that the latter edited what was still, for many, '*Leigh Hunt's Examiner*'. Hunt was one of the 'dear friends'[44] associated with the *True Sun* and, again almost certainly, brought Forster on to the paper. More profoundly, as Forster wrote after Hunt's death, 'He influenced all my modes of literary thought at the outset of my life – very probably he led me, at least, confirmed me in Literature as a profession …'[45] Certainly Hunt's was a good example: he took literary criticism very seriously and told Forster so:

> criticism, truly, that is to say, subtilely [*sic*], and searchingly, and judicially so called, with proofs and reasons for proofs (for a critic, you know, is a judge on the bench), it is a very terrible and elaborate matter, not to be expected every moment in hasty articles in newspapers even from the cleverest pens.[46]

Hunt paid close attention to the text and, unusually for the period, used quotations to support points rather than for merely illustrative purposes. He was an attacking critic, quick to find the comic deflator, particularly when reviewing drama. Thus, of the actor Mr Pope: 'His face is as hard, as immovable, and as void of meaning as an oak wainscot',[47] and, of the imitators of Mrs Siddons: 'These ladies use their eye-balls like tennis-balls'.[48] Thus Forster, on Edwin Forrest playing Richard the Third: 'The princely plantagenet ... was ... accomplished by Mr Forrest in all the points of a savage newly-caught from out of the American backwoods'.[49]

Such influence on Forster's critical method was matched by that on Forster's literary tastes. Whitwell Elwin noted, with, for us, odd disapproval, that the young Forster's favourites were Scott and Byron, the romantic and the popular: 'Charmed by obvious qualities, he could not enter into nicer beauties, nor form a critical estimate of merits and faults.' Hunt, steeped in older literature, taught Forster 'to relish subtle graces, and inner deep-seated power more than outward, and sometimes flaunty effects',[50] hence Forster's interest in Milton, in Steele and Goldsmith, and in Wordsworth. Beaumont and Fletcher, Restoration dramatists, Swift, and the eighteenth-century novel, became other shared enthusiasms.

Most important of all was Hunt's effect on Forster's critical principles, on his 'modes of literary thought'. Forster responded to Hunt's view of literature's purpose as pleasure and exaltation,[51] to his idea of the drama as 'the first of moralities',[52] and to Hunt's popular and simplified version of Coleridge on the role of the imagination and the organic nature of literary art. And Hunt insisted on the need to judge plays in the theatre. The implications of such ideas in terms of subject matter, form, structure, use of imagery, style, versification, can be clearly traced through Hunt's work and then through Forster's. What Forster made of such ideas was often expressed in Hunt's own terminology, particularly the terms Hunt used to characterize good poetry: 'strength, sweetness, straightforwardness, unsuperfluousness, *variety*, and *one-ness*'.[53] Hunt's reference to Forster advising Beaumont and Fletcher, already quoted, is a near-instance of such usage, and makes the further point that, during 30 years of friendship, Hunt's work was altered by Forsterian ideas that had begun life as Hunt's own.

The word 'begun' is used advisedly, for the friendship did not create a Leigh Forster who in turn sustained a John Hunt. Hunt's influence on Forster is crucial and demonstrable but equally crucial differences remained. Thus, Forster criticized *A Legend of Florence*: 'But the lover prospers, and Ginevra half sanctions his love ... The effect left on the mind is that of a perplexed moral sense';[54] in 1847 he wrote to Hunt about *Vanity Fair*: 'It is remarkably clever – but my objection to it is, that wickedness has as many winning, pleasant, hearty ways, – as represented in it, – as virtue itself. I really don't know which I'd rather be';[55] Hunt disagreed:

> you cannot yet have given it … [close] perusal yourself, otherwise I am convinced that a critic, so accustomed to receive a total impression from things, would never have felt him to make no difference between bad people & good. His noble & catholic reverse of this, is surely one of his greatest merits …[56]

Hunt's great hero was the actor Edmund Kean; Forster admired Kean but came to prefer Macready. Hunt could suggest that Shakespeare's text might be altered to satisfy contemporary taste; Forster lined up with Lamb and Macready in asserting the absolute primacy of what Shakespeare wrote. For Hunt's 'pleasure and exaltation' Forster substituted clearer moral attitudes; romantic brilliance was replaced by Macreadian decorum and conceptual unity; Forster had a greater respect for the writer, a firmer sense of the text's integrity.

Forster admired much of Hunt's work and felt great affection for the man, the extent of the latter evident in his letter to Hunt before the first performance of *A Legend of Florence*: 'tomorrow is Dickens's birthday! He and I would have had a box together, but for this, for a party was invited to him long ago, and nothing but your play would have kept me from it.'[57] He thought Hunt unjustly neglected and tried to put things right, hence his involvement in the 'dignity' movement. His differences from Hunt (expressing, as they do, a preference for the moderate style and a reverence for the writer as teacher) are manifestations of such involvement. Hunt's influence on Forster is thus felt forcefully even when the two men seem furthest apart.

CHAPTER 3 *Charles Lamb*

By 1831, when Forster was 18 and Lamb 55, they had met and become friends. Lamb was then living in retirement at Edmonton as a distinguished literary man. Like Leigh Hunt he would have attracted Forster because of his links with the recent and glamorous literary past, for Lamb had known the young Wordsworth, had known Southey and Hazlitt; Coleridge had been his 'fifty years old friend without a dissension'.[1] He was a fine critic and a great essayist. His sister was a lunatic and he himself a saddened, garrulous, humorous, and gregarious bachelor who often drank too much.

Drinking and gregarious gossiping suited the young Forster, and Forster suited Lamb, who treated him with a mixture of patronage, affection and reliance. Forster was Lamb's 'dear boy'[2] to whom he would write letters divided into 'Orders' and 'Requests'[3] and urge Forster to 'Scamper off'[4] with a manuscript to Dilke's *Athenaeum* or to Moxon the publisher. But Forster was not simply a messenger boy; he was 'a friend of comparatively recent date, but one with whom Lamb felt himself as much at home as if he had known him for years',[5] whom Lamb would summon with affectionate vehemence: 'Swallow your damn'd dinner and your brandy and water fast – & come immediately.'[6] Forster would sometimes obey and travel out to Edmonton with Edward Moxon, Sheridan Knowles, Henry Carey and, occasionally, with Letitia Landon.

For Lamb Forster did various small services beyond the call of the messenger's duty: he helped arrange publication of Lamb's essays in the *Athenaeum*, was involved in persuading Lamb to write a prologue for *The Wife*, Knowles's new play, was responsible for obtaining theatre 'orders' to save the cost of seats when the great man came to London.[7] But he owed more to Lamb than Lamb ever owed to him, even though a Lamb grateful for small favours once sent Forster a collection of 'Elia' manuscripts. Friendship with Lamb meant, for Forster, acquaintance with the publisher

Edward Moxon, who was married to Lamb's adopted daughter, and through this acquaintance came Forster's links with the *Englishman's Magazine* and with the *Reflector*,[8] both owned by Moxon. These were invaluable contacts providing priceless experience. But, on 27 December 1834, less than four years after first meeting the young Forster, Lamb died.

A few months later Forster wrote about Lamb in the *New Monthly Magazine*, in an article that begins by publishing Lamb's account of his feelings for Coleridge and then becomes an account of Forster's feelings for Lamb.[9] The latter account begins with wistful reference to Lamb's urban upbringing and to his early London associations with the great Romantics. Forster then describes Lamb's work. He was a critic of unique quality, always able to 'show you "fresh fields and pastures new", and these the most fruitful and delightful'. His essays expressed a similar charitable spirit; they were deeply imaginative yet with a deceptively 'social and familiar air'. Such essays were concerned to 'help on the world' by shattering absurdities and exposing 'stale evasions' so that together the essays offered 'a general and honest appreciation of the humane and true'. His other work, *Rosamund Gray*, *John Woodvil*, and the poems, offered 'unequalled delicacy and pathos'.

'But', Forster continues, 'it was not as a Critic, it was not as an Essayist, it was not as a Poet, fervently as we entertained for him in these characters the admiration we have poorly endeavoured to express – it is not in any of these that we felt towards him the strongest feeling of devotion – we loved THE MAN.' He writes of visiting Edmonton, of being welcomed to Lamb's 'little book-clad room', of seeing his tattered books and hearing brilliant literary talk. Forster remembers the Lambs' occasional visits to London and one visit in particular when, Mary Lamb having despatched him to search for 'Charles', he found her brother gazing at his birthplace in the Temple. And then the final days: Lamb's composure the day before he died, his love for his sister which 'accompanied him to his grave'.

Lamb had weaknesses, continued Forster, but these should be excused by a need to counter a depressive nature and 'the great and peculiar sorrows he was fated to experience through life'. Essentially, 'he was the most entirely delightful person we have ever known'. His 'personal appearance was remarkable. It quite realized the expectations of those who think that an author and a wit should have a distinct air, a separate costume, a particular cloth, something positive and singular about him.' Lamb had

> a head of amazing fineness. We never saw any other that approached it in its intellectual cast and formation. Such only may

be seen occasionally in the finer portraits of Titian. His face was deeply marked and full of noble lines – traces of sensibility, imagination, suffering, and much thought.

His character was as fine as his looks; he was a great friend.

This, of course, was hero-worship, expressed in a strained, emotional, revealing, very moving account of the relationship's heart. Here was an idea of Lamb that Forster was never to forget and had much cause to remember. For Mary Lamb lived on to 1847 when, on a hot May day, the mourners, Forster amongst them, met at the house where Charles Lamb had died, to follow his sister's hearse to Edmonton churchyard.[10] Editions of and articles on Charles Lamb continued to appear throughout Forster's lifetime, as did lives and letters, often written or edited by Forster's friends. Forster himself was approached during the 1860s to 'superintend a Selection'[11] of Lamb's works for Moxon. Forster was willing but unable and contented himself with assisting the efforts of others: Talfourd's, Procter's and, in 1876, Percy Fitzgerald's. The assistance itself reflects persisting hero-worship: the provision for Fitzgerald, for example, of documents demonstrating Lamb's generosity to William Godwin, Lamb giving £50 to a subscription to which the wealthy Byron gave 25 guineas and John Murray only ten.[12] The same persistence led Forster to alter one of his letters from Lamb to insert the sentence, 'I send you the last proof not of my friendship'.[13] And Fitzgerald recalled that Forster once burst into tears when reminded of 'poor dear Charles Lamb'.[14] Lamb's posthumous presence provided for Forster not only memories of youthful idealizing but also a permanent romantic image of the literary man that affected profoundly the whole of his subsequent literary career.

Certainly it made him susceptible to Lamb's influence. The latter's enthusiasms were similar to Leigh Hunt's: Goldsmith, Defoe, the eighteenth-century novel generally, Elizabethan, Jacobean and Restoration drama. These all, as will be seen, became Forster's enthusiasms also. Further, Forster himself declared that Lamb stimulated his interest in Landor's work.[15] Importantly, Lamb's ideas dominate Forster's writings on Shakespeare. Forster, it must be stressed, through his association with Macready played a large part in the movement to restore to the theatre Shakespeare's original texts and, through his reviews in the *New Monthly Magazine* and, particularly, in the *Examiner*, publicized influential interpretations of the plays.

As regards textual restoration: Lamb, as has been noted, was unequivocally opposed to any meddling with Shakespeare's work. In 'On the Tragedies of Shakespeare'[16] he attacked Garrick's alterations, Tate's

King Lear (in particular, the 'happy ending', with Lear alive and restored: 'As if the childish pleasure of getting his gilt robes and sceptre again could tempt him to act over again his misused station'), made a general attack on the 'ribald trash', the 'vulgar stuff', of 'Tate and Cibber, and the rest of them', and hit out at 'the vile mixture which Dryden has thrown into *The Tempest*', designed to entertain 'the impure ears of that age'.

Forster followed Lamb and often echoed him. He attacked Garrick's 'many foul assaults upon Shakespeare',[17] Tate's *Lear* as being 'the ignorant trash of Mr. Poet-Laureate Tate',[18] and ridiculed Tate's treatment of Lear at the close of the play, 'giving him back again his gilt robes and tinsel sceptre'.[19] Forster criticized Cibber's version of *Richard III* ('one of the severest reproaches that could possibly be passed upon the profession of the stage, considered as an intellectual art')[20] and Dryden and Davenant's rehash of *The Tempest* ('nauseous or disgusting details').[21]

Lamb's influence on Forster's reviewing can be illustrated by the following parallels:

Lamb	*Forster*
The greatness of Lear is not in corporal dimension, but in intellectual: the explosions of his passion are terrible as a volcano: they are storms turning up and disclosing to the bottom that sea, his mind, with all its vast riches. It is his mind which is laid bare. This case of flesh and blood seems too insignificant to be thought on; even as he himself neglects it. On the stage we see nothing but corporal infirmities and weakness, the impotence of rage; while we read it, we see not Lear, but we are Lear, – we are in his mind, we are sustained by grandeur which baffles the malice of daughters and storms.	(*a*) Our sense of Lear's physical sufferings merges into the sense of his passion and his sublime imagination. Of the condition of his outward man we think not – we reject it, even as he himself rejects it. We wish, as Mr. Lamb has so finely said, in a paper of unparallelled beauty, to see the mind of Lear laid bare – to feel ourselves within it, sustained there by the grandeur that enables *him* to baffle the malice of daughters and of storms. (*New Monthly Magazine*, XLI, 1834, 223) (*b*) For what is the poet's purpose? It is to show Lear … rising up to 'baffle the malice of daughters and of storms' even by the help of that vast wealth and strength of the immortal part of him, which the storm and

	convulsion of his disruptured affections had upturned from unconscious rest in the inner depths of his mind. (*Examiner*, 6 Nov. 1836, 711)
What have looks, or tones, to do with that sublime identification of his age with that of the *heavens themselves*, when in his reproaches to them for conniving at the injustice of his children, he reminds them that 'they themselves are old'.	Lear is old, but the Heavens themselves are old, and in his sublime identification of his own age with their's, we behold the sublime analogy of his sorrows. (*Examiner*, 6 Nov. 1836, 711)
... the plays of Shakespeare are less calculated for performance on a stage, than those of almost any other dramatist whatever ... The character of Hamlet ... [his] profound sorrows, these light-and-noise-abhorring ruminations ... how can they be represented by a gesticulating actor ... ?	We try in vain to conceive of an actor that should present with effect the exact Hamlet of Shakespeare. There is that in it, considered deeply in the closet, with which eye, and tone, and gesture, have nothing to do ... his solitary musings, his silent thoughts, his 'light-and-noise-abhorring' ruminations. (*Examiner*, 11 Oct. 1835, 644)
These tokens of an unhinged mind (if they be not mixed in the latter case with a profound artifice of love, to alienate Ophelia by affected discourtesies, so to prepare her mind for the breaking off of that loving intercourse, which can no longer find a place amidst business so serious as that which he has to do) are parts of his character, which to reconcile with our admiration of Hamlet, the most	(*a*) [Macready's] scene with Ophelia was truly exquisite. It was the realization of Mr. Lamb's opinion, that the scene is a profound artifice of love, an attempt to alienate Ophelia by affected discourtesies, so as to prepare her mind for the breaking-off of that loving intercourse, which can no longer find a place amidst business so serious as that which he has to do. It was indeed not alienation,

patient consideration of his situation is no more than necessary …

but distraction purely, and such it made itself felt by her – not anger, but grief assuming the appearance of anger – love awkwardly counterfeiting hate, 'as sweet countenances when they try to frown'.
(*Examiner*, 11 Oct. 1835, 644)

So to Ophelia – All the Hamlets that I have ever seen, rant and rave at her as if she had committed some great crime, and the audience are highly pleased … whether Hamlet is likely to put on such brutal appearances to a lady whom he loved so dearly, is never thought on. The truth is, that in all such deep affections as had subsisted between Hamlet and Ophelia there is a stock of *supererogatory love* (if I may venture to use the expression) which in any great grief of heart, especially where that which preys upon the mind cannot be communicated, confers a kind of indulgence upon the grieved party to express itself, even to its heart's dearest object, in the language of a temporary alienation; but it is not alienation, it is a distraction purely, and so it always makes itself to be felt by that object: it is not anger, but grief assuming the appearance of anger, – love awkwardly counterfeiting hate, as sweet countenances when they try to frown: but such sternness and fierce disgust as Hamlet is made

(*b*) [Hamlet is] a lover, who finds himself obliged to counterfeit hate in the hope of alienating both himself and his mistress from a passion that had suddenly to both become hopeless … Taken as an artifice of love to wean Ophelia from him, and to stop the continuance of that affectionate intercourse which a supernatural visitation had for ever forbidden in this world, the apparent brutality of the gentle and princely Hamlet throughout the interview is in truth the secret of its most afflicting pathos … The actor may be allowed indeed to counterfeit this affected hate and brutality to Ophelia awkwardly, and the scene will be all the better for it: but counterfeit it he must, or the scene is nothing.
(*Examiner*, 14 Jan. 1838, 20–1)

to shew, is no counterfeit, but the real face of absolute aversion, – of irreconcilable alienation. It may be said that he puts on the madman; but that he should only so far put on this counterfeit lunacy as his own real distraction will give him leave; that is, incompletely, imperfectly; not in that confirmed practised way, like a master of his art …

Malvolio is not essentially ludicrous. He becomes comic but by accident … his pride, or his gravity (call it which you will) is inherent, and native to the man … There was something in … [him] … beyond the coxcomb … the decent sobrieties of the character began to give way, and the poison of self-love, in his conceit of the Countess's affection, gradually to work … ('On Some of the Old Actors', *The Essays of Elia*, World's Classics edn, 1951, 194–7)

Because Malvolio is ludicrous in one scene, should it follow that he must be ludicrous in every scene? … There is many a smile, there is now and then a laugh … but there is grave sympathy, too for the gravity of his wonderful conceit, not without some regret for its utter hopelessness and discomfiture. (*Examiner*, 22 Sept. 1839, 599)

[Fletcher] lays line upon line, making up one after the other, adding image to image so deliberately, that we see their junctures. Shakespeare mingles everything, runs line into line, embarrasses sentences and metaphors; before one idea has burst its shell, another is hatched and clamorous for disclosure. ('Characters of Dramatic Writers Contemporary with Shakespeare', *Lamb's Criticism*, ed. E. M. W. Tillyard (1923), 30)

[Forrest] can never master at a time more than one image, or one passion … in such characters as those of Shakespeare, images or passions cut out separately are nothing; it is only when connected with or opposed to each other that they become indeed affecting and true. (*Examiner*, 12 Feb. 1837, 101–2)

These links with Lamb show Forster upholding at least two fundamental Romantic tenets: the concept of organic form, to which Lamb, like Hunt, subscribed, working within the tradition of Schlegel and Coleridge, and enabling critics to perceive a unity of impression stemming from the reconciliation of disparate elements within a work;[22] and, secondly, the stress on character that was such a feature of Romantic criticism in general and Lamb's in particular.

Elsewhere in Forster's work is further evidence of his affinities with the Romantic Lamb. For example, Forster's approval of Sir Richard Steele's comment that 'it always seems as if Shakespeare were suffering from the events represented, while the rest were merely looking on'[23] brings him close to the Romantic theory of Shakespearian creation, of his characters as 'so many embodiments of Shakespearian selves',[24] derived from within rather than by holding a mirror up to nature. It follows, as it did with most Romantic critics after Schlegel (and this certainly includes Lamb), that Forster had much praise for Shakespeare the man who could embody forth so much of great worth and profundity.

In Forster's writings on comedy Lamb's influence can again be clearly seen. Further parallel passages make the point:

Lamb	*Forster*
We have been spoiled with – not sentimental comedy – but a tyrant far more pernicious to our pleasures which has succeeded to it, the exclusive and all devouring drama of common life; where the moral point is every thing ... We must live our toilsome lives twice over, as it was the mournful privilege of Ulysses to descend twice to the shades. All that neutral ground of character, which stood between vice and virtue; or which in fact was indifferent to neither, where neither properly was called in question; that happy breathing-place from the burthen of a perpetual moral questioning – the sanctuary and quiet Alsatia	He strives to fix, in permanent colours, some of the fleeting bygone follies of mankind ... the dramatist restores to us ... [Beau Nash] ... as he lived, with his tawdry dress and his white hat, putting him on the real scene, with the real associates of his life around him, fearing not to make them occupy what is now rare and dangerous ground (for the stage, now-a-days, must reduce everything either to strict morality or to 'open manslaughter and bold bawdry') – that neutral ground of character that stands between vice and virtue, which is, in fact, indifferent to neither, the 'happy breathing-place from the burden of a perpetual moral

of hunted casuistry – is broken up and disfranchised, as injurious to the interests of society. The privileges of the place are taken away by law. We dare not dally with images, or names, of wrong. We bark like foolish dogs at shadows. We dread infection from the scenic representation of disorder; and fear a painted pustule. In our anxiety that our morality should not take cold, we wrap it up in a great blanket surtout of precaution against the breeze of sunshine ... The whole is a passing pageant, where we should sit as unconcerned at the issues, for life or death, as at a battle of the frogs and mice. But, like Don Quixote, we take part against the puppets, and quite as impertinently.
('On the Artificial Comedy of the Last Century', *The Essays of Elia*, World's Classics edn, 1951, 206–9)

Judged morally, every character in these plays – the few exceptions only are *mistakes* – is alike essentially vain and worthless. The great art of Congreve is especially shown in this, that he has entirely excluded from his scenes, – some little generosities in the part of Angelica perhaps excepted, – not only anything like a faultless character, but any pretensions to goodness or good feelings

questioning', and scorning to mar the truth of his picture by any merely trading convulsion or startling situations. ... [Jerrold] has done right and boldly in leaving these characters as they were. He has effected the purpose of perpetuating manners and society in a certain conventional aspect, and the picture will live. It is not his fault if some of his personages are mere puppets – moral or immoral as the strings are pulled. Such is artificial society ever. We leave the moral Quixotes to fight against them as they may; or we leave them, 'in their anxiety that their morality should not take cold, to wrap it up in a great blanket surtout of precaution against the breeze and sunshine'.
(quoted from Forster's review of Douglas Jerrold's *Beau Nash* in the *New Monthly Magazine*, XLI, 1834, in B. Jerrold, *The Life and Remains of Douglas Jerrold*, 1859, I, 11–12)

Money does not belong exclusively to the artificial school of comedy, nor yet to the sentimental. It has that union of sentiment with artifice which modern manners exact from the stage. In the time of Congreve, when the sentimental comedy was quite unknown, it was the aim of the comic writer, while he obeyed the instinct of his genius to expose the false pretensions of society, to avoid at the same time whatsoever. ... [*The School for Scandal*] grew out of Congreve and Wycherley, but gathered some allays of the sentimental comedy which followed theirs. ... Not but there are passages, – like that, for instance, where Joseph is made to refuse a pittance to a poor relation, – incongruities which Sheridan was forced upon by the attempt to join the artificial with the sentimental comedy, either of which must destroy the other ... Oh who ... would forego ... the escape from life ... to sit instead at one of our modern plays – to have his coward conscience (that forsooth must not be left for a moment) stimulated with perpetual appeals ('On the Artificial Comedy of the Last Century', *The Essays of Elia*, World's Classics edn, 1951, 208–13)

the possibility of direct offence by leaving society no pretensions at all. This was getting into a sort of safe neutral ground of wit. The merits which men had not, were not only denied to them, but also the merits which they had. 'The great art of Congreve', says Mr Lamb, 'is especially shown in this, that he has entirely excluded from his scenes not only anything like a faultless character, but any pretensions to goodness or good feelings whatsoever'. ... Now all comedy since then has been a wavering between these two schools, and the best has been that in which the sentiment was most lightly interwoven with the wit and character. This was Sheridan. But even since Sheridan's time our audiences are more in earnest, and require to see fairer play to the truth as well as the falsehood of the society of which they form a portion. Hence the mixed character of the excellent comedy we are noticing (*Examiner*, 13 Dec. 1840, 790)

But Forster did not simply regurgitate Lamb. His view of Shakespeare differed from Lamb's in two important ways. Firstly, Forster, under Leigh Hunt's influence, was a man of the theatre. Although, like Lamb, he acknowledged the limitations of the stage, agreeing that an 'exact' Hamlet was impossible[25] and, of Lear, that 'the resources of the actor are too limited for the perfect expression of this',[26] yet his argument continued:

> No doubt, at a play it is from other arts than the poet's that what is mainly material should reach us. ... in practice ... all kinds of descriptive and other indulgences have to be brought in aid of the purely dramatic. The result expresses just the concession or

> compromise which the stage requires from the drama, which Shakespeare understood ... and which even such writers as Landor and Lamb comprehend imperfectly when they object to the stage-presentation of *Lear*.[27]

The drama offered a unique experience, part intellectual, part dramatic, 'our fancies reconciled to our waking thoughts',[28] an effect which Shakespeare's plays were designed to create. Though reading had its advantages the disadvantages were correspondingly large: Lamb had dismissed the latter as hardly worth bothering about.

Secondly, though Forster agreed that Shakespeare's characters were profound psychological studies, yet he did not follow the implications of, for example, Hazlitt's statement:

> [*Othello* has] a closer application to the concerns of human life than that of almost any other of Shakespear's plays. ... The pathos in *Lear* is indeed more dreadful and over-powering: but it is less natural, and less of every day's occurrence. We have not the same degree of sympathy with the passions described in *Macbeth*. The interest in *Hamlet* is more remote and reflex;[29]

or Lamb's contrast between 'fine vision' and 'the standard of flesh and blood', or his statement that Shakespeare's plays were 'natural' only in the sense that 'they are grounded deep in nature, so deep that the depth of them lies out of the reach of most of us'. That is to say, Forster did not subscribe to the romantic assertion that since Shakespeare himself was, in Schlegel's opinion, 'a demi-God',[30] or in Lamb's (quoting Jonson) 'the very "sphere of humanity" ', the great tragic characters, the 'embodiments of Shakespearian selves', were much closer to their creator (seen as half-divine) than to any ordinary human being. Forster recognized Lear's grandeur, for example, but was equally, if not more, concerned to stress the human, the more 'ordinary' side of the man. In doing so Forster was, as we shall see, responding to the notion of domesticated tragedy stressed by Hunt and demonstrated by Macready.

More generally, as the passage from Forster's review of *Money* shows, Forster ultimately differed from Lamb in the same way as he did from Hunt. Whereas Lamb saw the moral drama as a decline, concerned only to pamper the 'moral vanity'[31] of the audience, Forster emphasized and supported the drama's didactic function.

To point out differences is not to reduce Lamb's influence on Forster for, paradoxically, even the differences reflect Forster's hero-worship. In stressing the effectiveness of performance Forster was pointing to the drama's importance as an intellectual art; by domesticating Shakespeare he purveyed a Shakespeare more readily approachable by the Victorian mass-readership and theatre audience, the middle and the upper-working classes; in underlining the drama's didactic role Forster made a case for the theatre's respectability. All three urge the claims of literature and the drama to greater dignity and social acceptability, such urging in itself suggesting that literary men and theatricals, past and present, as dispensers not only of entertainment but of wisdom and guidance, deserved enhanced social status. Forster's view of literature and what it deserved, of literary men and what they were entitled to, was influenced profoundly by his posthumous love and respect for that thin-legged, black-clad figure whose talk, appearance and personality captivated Forster when Forster was young and romantically impressionable.

CHAPTER 4 *Bulwer*

When the playwright Westland Marston wrote his memoirs he remembered the effect of Edward George Earle Lytton Bulwer's works on the literary world of the 1830s. 'With us young critics', wrote Marston, 'his epigrams, his rhetorical flashes, and, let it be said, a vein of aspiration and generous feeling ... had made him a favourite.'[1] In December 1831 Bulwer was at a first high peak of such fame and influence. For one month he had been Thomas Campbell's successor as editor of the *New Monthly Magazine* and was swiftly turning it into a vigorous reformist journal.[2] Lady Blessington had befriended him and brought him to her brilliant Gore House *salon*. Since the runaway success of *Pelham* in 1828 he had consolidated with *The Disowned*, fallen back with *Devereux* and risen again, in 1830, with *Paul Clifford*; he was only a few days away from publishing *Eugene Aram*, due to be controversially successful. In April 1831 St Ives had elected him to Parliament as a fervent supporter of reform. He was 28, married to the beautiful Rosina Wheeler; his second child and only son, Robert Lytton, was a few months old. The Bulwers lived in Hertford Street and entertained lavishly.

Yet the literary success, the brilliant social life, masked an unhappy marriage, and a constant shortage of money that forced him to write too much and take on too many commitments. His work, more vulnerable through haste, was attacked, viciously, by his enemy William Maginn in *Fraser's Magazine*. Bulwer's extreme sensitivity to criticism was a major expression of a personality that was essentially, beneath the glamour, diffident and insecure.[3]

Forster was 19 and still studying law. He had done nothing very much by 1831 but he had become Leigh Hunt's friend and had, as has been noted, enlisted the *New Monthly Magazine* and Bulwer's contacts in an appeal for that impecunious veteran. Forster and Bulwer corresponded about Hunt, and then became friends.

The butcher's son from Newcastle and the general's son from the *beau monde* seemed an unlikely team. They did, however, have much in common: an enthusiasm for the eighteenth century, with Forster collecting material for his life of Goldsmith and Bulwer setting *The Disowned* and *Devereux* in that period, for Lamb's work and for Leigh Hunt's. Above all, the friendship began and persisted, with very few breaks, until Bulwer's death in 1873, because each recognized in the other not only integrity but also a serious concern for literature and, importantly, the recurring theme of these early friendships, for the status of literary men. When, in 1831, Forster wrote on Hunt's behalf Bulwer was impressed by such 'evidence of high and pure feeling in this low world of literary jealousy and abuse'.[4] Seventeen years later, reviewing Forster's life of Goldsmith for the *Edinburgh Review*, he laid public stress on Forster's 'strong sympathy with men of letters'.[5] In 1869, in a private tribute, Bulwer wrote glowingly and with the force of the deeply felt, of Forster's fine qualities and practical affection.[6]

As for Forster's Bulwer, two quotations demonstrate a similar notion of his friend evident in the initial assumption that Bulwer would help Hunt and in Bulwer's early expressions of concern for the state of literature.[7] In 1846, during the affair of *The New Timon*, Forster defended Bulwer to Tennyson:

> Yet let me say for him – that he has done many kind great things – and that there is a large piece of his nature infinitely worthier & better than this that has offended here. I have known him do acts of generous & delicate kindness (the case of poor Blanchard was one – he greatly assisted him while he lived) that would have gladdened you.[8]

And, a public assertion, there is a draft account Forster made of an after-dinner speech in which he proposed Bulwer's health:

> Never had he for the moment forgotten the interests of Literature, or of any calling or profession connected with it ... Placed in a condition of independence by his birth and fortune, he had been above the miserable affectation of appearing to *condescend* to letters, as many dignified authors are in the habit of doing. All his life he had been a working man of letters; and had completely identified himself with the efforts and aims, with the toil.[9]

Created by such feelings the relationship generated a deep and general affection apparent in the moving cadences of a note from Bulwer during 1858: 'Old friend, I fear there is something between us. It is not my fault, I am sure. Perhaps it is only Fate's. But can't we root it thoroughly away?[10] It is even more apparent throughout Forster's letters. When Bulwer's daughter Emily died of typhoid fever Forster wrote a letter in which grief was close to the frantic:

> Never have I had such a shock. I have not slept. I have thought of all you have been suffering all the night through. I cannot tell you how deeply I suffer with you ... for you, for poor Edward, I feel the bitterness of grief. My dear Bulwer – we have been long connected, are old friends, and you must let me come and speak to you ... God bless you and support you my dear Bulwer Lytton prays your deeply affected and very affectionate friend.[11]

In 1853, more than 20 years after their first meeting, Forster told him: 'I could never bring myself to think you strange to me. Some of the whitest stones in my memory mark the steps of our friendly intercourse, and I cannot look back into a single year of my life since I came to manhood in which your kindly and familiar image does not stand more prominent than any other'.[12] To the end it was, as Mrs Procter wrote to Mrs Forster, 'so long, so tender a friendship – bound together as they were by similar tastes, and by your husband having been his staunch friend & *wise* adviser for so many years'.[13]

Not surprisingly, such strong basic attachment withstood the inevitable occasional differences. Forster was quick to apologize when Bulwer took offence at his falling asleep during Macready's reading of *Richelieu*, Bulwer's equally swift reply pointing to the significance of his own pained reaction: 'rather that of a friendly feeling hurt than a vain one wounded'.[14] Relations were more strained in 1846 when Forster, as Tennyson's friend also, resented Bulwer's attack on the poet in *The New Timon* and arranged the publication in *Punch* of Tennyson's counter-attack. Forster was justifiably annoyed, for Bulwer had denied to him the poem's authorship.[15] But he was wrong to ferment a public squabble for, in retrospect, Bulwer's lie seems the result of shame, Tennyson's retort hasty and soon regretted.

More important were political differences. Bulwer soon left the radical path and, by 1851, with *Letters to John Bull*, was a true-blue protectionist pamphleteer. During the 1850s his Toryism threatened the friendship. 'I see nothing of Forster', Bulwer complained to Macready, 'He is so political that he always says something to hurt one's feelings.'[16] Bulwer's parliamentary duties, plus office in 1858 as Secretary of State for the Colonies, Forster's editorship of the *Examiner*, then his marriage, then a government appointment as Lunacy Commissioner, all worked against regular contact. There were, as Forster noted, 'great blanks ... in our intercourse',[17] but, as he also noted on a separate occasion, 'seeing so little of you as I now do – I do not think the less of my old friend – for whom nothing can ever abate the grateful regard and affection that lives always in my heart'.[18]

Political differences simmered in 1860 when Bulwer reviewed Forster's work on commonwealth history in the *Quarterly Review*.[19] He objected to Forster's support of the revolutionary Pym and argued that the approach of Pym's contemporary, Falkland, an approach that sought to preserve the monarchy but regulate its power, was much better. Monarchical reform was certainly to be preferred to the civil war that resulted from Pym's actions. Forster was hurt, continued to disagree, but came, slowly, to accept his friend's sincerity and a true difference of opinion.[20] The friendship, strengthened through strain, was never again seriously threatened. For, through the crises, both *desired* to remain friends. And so they did.

For Bulwer the initial fellow-feeling quickly deepened into an affection that included reliance. In those early 1830s he was in desperate need of Forster's 'strong practical sense and sound judgment'.[21] Within a year of their first meeting Bulwer was discussing his work in his letters to his new friend; by 1836 Forster was firmly established as literary adviser. But this 'professional' side of the relationship flourished, one feels, because the central core of personal involvement hardened and strengthened as Bulwer drew Forster into area after area of intimate experience.

In 1836 Bulwer separated from his wife and sought a new London home, Forster acting as Bulwer's agent in negotiations for houses, fittings, and leases.[22] This is striking evidence of Forster's role in Bulwer's financial affairs, a role that led to Forster becoming trustee of the Manors of Knebworth and Mardleybury, handling Bulwer's investments, and, in 1865, lending him money – £1,000 to raise which Forster had to sell stock in the Brighton railway.[23] The house negotiations also point, crucially, to Forster's support for Bulwer during the sad aftermath of the separation from Rosina Wheeler.

From 1836 to Bulwer's death Rosina filled her life with private and public and increasingly unbalanced recriminations and accusations. In 1839 she published *Cheveley*, a novel in which she viciously satirized Bulwer and his circle. Each year found her writing poisonous letters to her husband and, about him, to others until the campaign culminated in her shouting abuse at Bulwer during the Hertford by-election that followed his appointment as Secretary of State for the Colonies.[24]

Though Forster could refer, lightly, to Bulwer's 'terrific wife ... the aforesaid "screamer" of a woman (as the Americans would style her)',[25] he was sincerely on his friend's side. He shared Bulwer's view of the 'whole of these melancholy and disgusting matters',[26] and did his best both to reassure him and to minimize Rosina's impact. To give a major example, when *Cheveley* appeared Forster wrote to Bulwer of Talfourd's reaction and how to respond:

> The style of the thing seems to have inspired him with supreme contempt...The idea of your answering it he scouts and laughs at. Indeed he is right here, in common with F. and myself. You might as well tell the public that your brains had not been blown out ... Under these circumstances I am much disposed to withhold Fox from doing anything in the Chronicle, and to refrain from writing anything myself, as I proposed, in the Courier ... It is setting the papers that have discreetly refrained from notice ... a very bad example.[27]

It is hard, at this point, to resist the 'wheeler-dealer' pun; certainly Bulwer's reputation owed much to Forster's 'fixing' of the press. In the aftermath of *Cheveley* the fixer became sleuth; Forster travelled to Bath on Bulwer's behalf to stay with Landor and pump him and others about Rosina's conduct in that city. But Landor knew little that Bulwer could use against her, gossip about a friendship with a man named Hume being all that emerged.[28]

Given such strenuous metamorphoses it is ironic that Forster was partly to blame for Bulwer's unwise reaction to the fracas at Hertford, the committal of Rosina to an asylum and the unsuccessful attempt to keep her there. For Forster had fanned the flames in earlier letters: 'Her own only refuge', he wrote to Bulwer in 1839, 'is apparent to every one ... a mad house.'[29] But whereas, in 1839, that reflected a friend's indignation, by 1858 and the committal Forster had, unluckily, become Secretary to the Lunacy Commission. Even though he advised Bulwer to proceed with caution he also offered him his knowledge of committal procedures. These last – including, particularly, the obtaining of lunacy certificates from two doctors – were observed, but this did not prevent public accusations that Forster's advice alone had led to the committal. Only a public statement by Robert Lytton, an explanatory letter from his father to the Lunacy Commission defending Forster, and, above all, the release of Rosina, stopped strengthening calls for a public enquiry.[30] Here was a rare instance of Forster's strength of fellow-feeling undermining the prized objectivity of his advice. But the damage to Bulwer was more than repaired by Forster's part in bringing up Bulwer's son.

This subsidiary friendship began in 1839, when Robert Lytton was seven and Forster 27. Forster stayed at Cheltenham with Bulwer and the three made an excursion down the River Wye that, 20 years later, Robert Lytton remembered vividly and affectionately. He was then a diplomat and a poet, writing as 'Owen Meredith' to avoid confusion with his father; the dedication to Robert's poem, 'The Wanderer', recalled the Wye journey and described Forster as

> A staff to stay, a star to guide,
> A spell to soothe, a power to raise.

Here is no exaggeration. Robert Lytton's parents hated each other and lived apart; Bulwer, who had custody, neglected him as Bulwer when young had himself been neglected. As a father, as Forster noted, Bulwer was 'quite helpless'.[31] Forster became Robert's 'beloved friend' and 'dearer than father mother brother sister'.[32] In effect he became guardian, withdrawing the boy from Harrow when Rosina appeared there, choosing his tutors, looking after him during vacations, supervising his reading, buying his clothes, giving him 'treats'. Forster advised him about his diplomatic career, encouraging him, in particular, to accept a post in Washington, and, inevitably, involved himself in all aspects of 'Owen Meredith's' literary career.

This last involvement was typically Forsterian, beginning with observations on the suitability of Robert's subject matter, and the provision of source material. The writing of *Lucile* (1860) found Forster at his most dominant:

> Lytton sent the sections of his manuscript to Forster, who in turn forwarded them to Chapman to be printed off in slips or rough galleys. These were then gone over by Bulwer, who made criticisms and suggestions on the margins in ink. Forster then made his annotations in pencil and then forwarded the proofs to Vienna ... When Lytton had made the revisions recommended, the process was begun anew, until all stood finally approved.[33]

Forster's role was, here again and throughout Robert's career, mainly and ruthlessly that of the creative editor, concerned to eliminate superfluousness and to impose upon the work correctness, general decorum, elegance, proper rhyming, shape. Inevitably, also, Robert absorbed Forster's social views: *Orval* (1868), for example, reflects Forster's liberalism during Robert's formative years.

Having, with Bulwer, knocked the work into shape, Forster applied himself to the task of placing it. Thus in 1855 he brought Robert, with

Clytemnestra, to Chapman & Hall; Forster arranged for later work to appear in *All the Year Round*. After publication he did what he could, but although that included a favourable, though not uncritical, review of *Clytemnestra* in the *Examiner*, and threats to take Robert from Chapman & Hall that modified George Meredith's unfavourable review of *Chronicles and Characters* in Chapman & Hall's own journal, the *Fortnightly Review*, much of Robert's career came after Forster's withdrawal from journalism that reduced his power to fix and manipulate. Nonetheless, by publication time, Forster had given to Robert Lytton's work vast tracts of time and affectionately meticulous attention.

There can be little doubt that Forster's devotion to Robert's welfare was one result of his (Forster's) own childlessness and a powerful desire for children; his devotion was no less genuine, his paternal feelings no less deep, because of that. In return he was loved:

> I have been thinking of many a old wintertime (snowier and yet warmer those old winters seem to have been!) when Xmas books I received from you – & went to the Play with you – and dined with you (do you remember?) in that book-house of yours at Lincoln's Inn, – with that great picture of Macready in Werner looking down at us, and oh for the sound of your laugh, cordial & kind, driving away from me the thought of school & black gowns ... your laugh, what echoes it has still ... *I* remember that it was with you, that I first heard Macready – heard Hamlet – heard Macbeth (– his Macbeth how fine it was!) And Jaques at Arden ... They were episodes in your life, they are the foundations of *my* past![34]

There could be few more attractive pictures of Forster than this. The relationship between the bachelor critic and the neglected son reveals the tender, thoughtful father Forster so often was but never properly became. It is a further pointer, also, to the closeness of the Bulwer/Forster friendship, in some ways the closest of all these literary liaisons. 'So many recollections come back to me',[35] Forster wrote when Emily Lytton died. Son, wife and money were the main hoops of steel that bound him to Bulwer. The intense personal relationship moves in parallel with a literary duet that is both its consequence and its reflection.

This is seen most obviously in the way Forster supported Bulwer in schemes of practical literary help. For, in these, Bulwer was always prominent, from the successful campaign of the 1830s, supported by the *Examiner* for part of the time, to free the press by reducing newspaper tax,[36] to parliamentary agitation for copyright reform. The latter was a desperate need at a time when all rights expired with the author's death – a neat recipe for the pauperization of his survivors – and when there was no protection during the author's lifetime against piracy in the form of abridgment or alteration. Bulwer, with Talfourd, made a series of unsuccessful attempts to change the law, cheered on by Forster's epistolary encouragement and, again, the more public support of the *Examiner*. In 1842 a bill was passed securing copyright for the longer of 42 years or 7 years after an author's death. Eight years later came the founding of the Guild of Literature and Art as a rival to the Royal Literary Fund. Bulwer, Dickens, and Forster played leading parts in this venture, Bulwer giving land for literary almshouses, and a new play, *Not So Bad As We Seem*, in which Forster acted, to help raise money for buildings and for pensions. An Act of Parliament incorporated the Guild in 1854, but also froze its funds for seven years. Though, unfrozen, it came momentarily to life in 1861 when houses for poor writers were built at Knebworth, the enterprise petered out through lack of support. From founding to foundering is a well-known story,[37] here important for its practical demonstration of that common concern for the dignity of literature that first drew together the two unlikely friends.

All aspects of Forster's role in Bulwer's personal life, a role successively and successfully supporting, protecting and sustaining Bulwer's position and reputation as landowner, father, and wronged husband, reflected that concern. Literary men must be seen to be dignified. Forster's part in Bulwer's *literary* career, his practical efforts to improve his friend's financial lot as well as the services he rendered to Bulwer at almost every stage of the creative sequence, had an identical aim. At least as early as 1832, when writing *Rienzi*, Bulwer began discussing his work in letters to Forster. From 1836, when he asked Forster 'to look over the sheets of my tragedy of Cromwell…and to suggest any improvements your taste and experience can offer',[38] to 1870, when Bulwer's dependence on his friend seemed absolute – 'With regard to the MS., return it here and place in pencil marks at all the passages you object to… I will attend to any suggestions you may make, or put aside the MS. altogether'[39] – there were times when Bulwer's only solo activity was the holding of the pen.

Until 1840 (and periodically thereafter) Forster's main concern was with Bulwer's plays.[40] He read them, as he wrote of *Walpole*, 'with the stage before me all thro' ',[41] and with two clearly-defined aims. Firstly, he was concerned to turn Bulwer's dramas into successful theatrical events. To do this he became, as Leigh Hunt had quickly noticed, the masterly editor, the ruthless pruner, the enemy of localized 'effect', seeking a concentrated dramatic rendering through the strengthening of a play's unity.

Two examples make this point in terms of internal coherence. In 'Cromwell', Forster insisted, Bulwer needed 'to connect ... the magnificent Exit of Cromwell in the close of the first act, actively and immediately with the stirring progress of events in the second act' and 'the Episode of Edith as it is in the first act ... with the interest of Cromwell and Claypole at the opening of the fifth act'.[42] A compliant Bulwer was 'much struck by your views'.[43] Further, with *Not So Bad As We Seem*, Forster argued for 'connecting links and strengthening of motives and inducements throughout the 3 first – to the 2 last acts'.[44] Again, Bulwer followed instructions. Similarly within scenes: Forster sanctioned the final scene of 'Brutus' '*provided you can make the part of Brutus strong in it*; my fear is that it would make Sextus so strong as to be in danger of over-riding him'.[45] Equally important was the relationship between character and play: Forster wrote of Hardman, the part in *Not So Bad As We Seem* that he himself was to play, and so a moment when Forster-as-friend resembled Forster-as-flagellant, that he would 'object to *nothing* in the way of reduction or modification which you fancy may improve the general effect'.[46] And, always, the superfluous was eliminated. 'Some pruning must take place as a matter of course', he wrote even of *Money*, soon to become a smash-hit, ' ... the scene of the Butler's pantry seems scarcely called for'.[47] Out it went, as did historical inaccuracy, grammatical errors, slips of the pen, and, in *Walpole*, faulty rhymes.[48]

Any temptation to view Forster only as a 'play-doctor', simply concerned to keep the show on the road to commercial success, is more than countered not only by the principles of moderation and decorum that govern his advice on Bulwer's dramas, but also by the second aim of that advice. The second is a more overt version of the first, a more obvious insistence implicit, of course, in the 'doctoring', that Bulwer's work should conform to a notion of artistic respectability. For example, when Bulwer revised *The Sea Captain* into *The Rightful Heir* he proposed, as a major change in the action, that Violet (Lady Ashdale's ward), in love with the captain (Lady Ashdale's long-lost son), should go mad after believing him to be drowned. Forster reacted swiftly:

> You are to remember that the interest of the audience about her [Violet] in these latter scenes will not be anything comparable to that which centres in Lady Ashdale and her son. My notion therefore is that to substitute a deep dejection for the loss of reason would be natural and right... the force of passion or emotion in a play must in some respects be regulated by the prominence or otherwise of the characters in the interest and attention of the audience.[49]

Here is seen not only the practical man of the theatre, with a shrewd sense of audience reaction, but also an adviser concerned that the play should succeed not through sensational effect but through the balanced dramatic power of the serious drama.

'There is no safer adviser about literary work', wrote Bulwer of Forster, and added, 'especially poetry'.[50] Though now we may agree with J. A. Sutherland that Bulwer produced poetry 'by the yard'[51] Bulwer himself took this side of his literary career very seriously. That a professional writer devoted so much energy to more or less esoteric verse is, in itself, evidence of that seriousness. On such verse Forster lavished an almost obsessive care, writing page after page, letter after letter of detailed criticism. To no other writer did Forster give so much time and attention. He advised on all Bulwer's poetry, advice reflecting similar principles to those seen in action on Bulwer's plays. This is most clearly seen in Forster's work on *St. Stephen's*, revised through the 1850s before publication in 1860.

First entitled *The Orators*, *St. Stephen's* is about parliamentary oratory, an attempt in rhyming couplets to describe famous debaters past and present. Inevitably the poem reflected Bulwer's Toryism, leading Forster to protest, ritually, that Walpole became 'only a humbug'[52] and that Charles Fox and the Younger Pitt were underrated, before he agreed his protests were 'opinions – which I have no business to intrude'[53] and concentrated on *literary* criticism that was invariably accepted.

Forster began by refining Bulwer's aims: 'I would have the poem simply descriptive, and altogether *English*', as it became, and then moved smartly to attack the superfluous, the obscure, and the inelegant. 'I don't *quite* like', he wrote, 'some of the "limbs and flourishes" you have given to it, and would recommend them to be lopp'd.' Bulwer should simplify the opening by removing references to the world's creation and foreign mythologies. Rather, 'the Reformation surely would be a grand keynote to strike – for out of the Reformation proceeded the Great Rebellion'. Dutifully Bulwer cut, stressed the Reformation when 'forth soared Reason from the cells of Rome', mentioned Bacon and Shakespeare and then Cromwell and his contemporaries, before responding to the more detailed points that followed in the same letter. 'Pym is good', wrote Forster, ' – the "large imperfect necessary man", but you have used "broad-breasted" before, and somehow I'd rather you made him – broad-shouldered – considering what he had to bear, Atlas like.' The revision, ' 'Twixt saint and sinner – Atlas-shoulder'd Pym', was essentially Forsterian.

Out went occasional plagiarisms, Forster quick to spot that Bulwer's line, 'Laughter dimpling in the cheeks of home', was one of Leigh Hunt's.[54] Out went faulty syntax:

> 'A regal logic, in its car of state,
> Which did not share, but sweep thro', the debate.'
>
> – your meaning good, but the wording or image hardly allowable. It is the 'car' that sweeps – but the 'logic' that shares.[55]

This became:

> A royal eloquence, that paid in state,
> A ceremonious visit to Debate.

Out went all inelegancies, from the weakly colloquial ('locking the door',[56] 'only cares for dash'[57]) to the simply awkward, the lines, as Forster put it, 'that *clink* as they run'. So out went, 'A house when *emp*ty is ex*empt* from rates' and 'The boisterous laugh they *ne'er* relax to *share*',[58] and others.

As the poem grew Forster settled in:

> Meanwhile I have been delighted with the third part of the Orators – incomparably the most rich and powerful and *complete* of all. I cannot really exaggerate the impression made upon me by the Melbourne and Peel – great part of the Canning and Castlereagh – the Plunkett. And though Burdett is raised perhaps, just as much *too* much as O'Connell is depressed, the writing in both is inimitable – with ease, and mastery of the most admirable kind.
>
> And now for some matters (compared with the General Excellence) infinitesimally small –
>
> I don't like 'enough' *always* printed 'eno' '. It recurs three or four times where the homelier word in common use would be better. 'Rare' occurs twice within a few lines – perhaps 'And what choice attributes etc.' might be substituted in the Canning lines. – I don't object to Palmerston – but if you retain 'aim' I'd close at 'sacrificed a friend'. I doubt if you can properly speak (in the MS couplet in margin) of 'power' that 'rots the links, etc.' (being mere illustrations they do not need to be justified in a note.)
>
> There is no real objection, I think, to the casual mention you make of the living Lawyers, which is merely as a passing illustration: but I would suggest that if you leave it, you ought to add another couplet about Bethel – surely a very conspicuous instance of extraordinary debating power, and one that would take away the party color from an excellent reference to Whiteside and Cairnes.

> As to the rhyme of Tierney – you cannot throw it properly, as I fancy, merely on the last syllable:
>
> Light and yet firm, decorous and yet free
> As matchless once it moved in Tiearnee
>
> – I take it that Tierney would more properly rhyme to a double word, or to such a single one as Kearney or Ferney. I suggest this for consideration.
>
> The close does not strike me as at all questionable – but I don't like the very last lines. 'Relics of august effects' is weak. So is the 'formed' and warmed of the last couplet. I would decidedly close at 'Collected Speeches' – a very good epithet to close at.
>
> Be careful of the names. Follett is two ts. Praed is *Winthrop* ...
>
> But now would you not do well to introduce Macaulay? He'd be a fine topic to do mock justice to ...[59]

The comments range from substance to detail and Bulwer heeded them all. What emerged from the collaborative grinder was a clear, simpler, as Forster would say, more 'English' poem, more correct, more elegant, a poem revised and corrected *for its readers*. Forster's efforts strengthened the essential dignity through which Bulwer's poems sought those readers' approval.

Forster gave as much, if not more, attention to Bulwer's plays and poems as he did to the novels and his approach to the latter confirms his critical consistency. In the interests of factual correctness he guided Bulwer's reading that preceded the historical novels, congratulating his friend, as he did for *Harold*, for managing 'to master all that learning'.[60] He checked the legal accuracy of Bulwer's novelistic doings, as when, for *Night and Morning*, the plot of which depended on the need to prove that a secret marriage had taken place, given the destruction of the parish register, he obtained advice from Chitty that a minister's copy of a register entry did not constitute proof of marriage.[61] Bulwer changed the tale accordingly.

Two examples show, once again, the characteristic Forsterian treatment. He wrote of *What Will He Do With It?* (1858): 'Might it not be well to let all that Lionel reveals of the letters of his churlish kinsman come out in the heat of his own temper respecting them – to *quote* them in inverted commas seems hardly natural in such a dialogue at such a time.'[62] And, of *Kenelm Chillingley* (1873): 'The Kenelm and Tom Bowley scene does not admit of another word. I think it fine and masterly to a degree. Any addition of *detail* would play the deuce with it.'[63]

The desire for direct effect, here the concern to dramatize that owed much to his early work on Bulwer's plays, the associated need to avoid over-writing, this last being Bulwer's persisting fault, are familiar exhortations. An exchange with Bulwer about *A Strange Story* points to the additional abiding preoccupation with the social as well as the artistic reputation of novel and novelist.[64]

A Strange Story was written for *All the Year Round* and published there in 1861 and 1862. Its title hardly exaggerates. For the novel is about the arrival of Margrave, skilled in Eastern magic and owning an elixir of life, in a quiet provincial town where the hero, Allen Fenwick, practises medicine and is in love with the innocent Lillian. Then follows a fantastic tale involving visions and other psychic phenomena, a magical wand, and the attempted abduction of Lillian by Margrave for use as a medium. Fenwick takes Lillian to Australia but cannot escape the climax of occult rituals, Eastern stranglers, Margrave's death, and the elixir's loss. The survivors live happily ever after.

Joseph Fradin[65] has argued that the work should be read as an allegory of the unconscious and the conscious mind; Forster, though he recognized the allegorical intent, not surprisingly soon became uneasy about the material. The first part, describing Doctor Fenwick pre-Margrave, posed no problems, Forster praising, in particular, 'the charm and power' of the opening. When he had 'received and read the numbers of the S.S. up to the 21st portion inclusive' he was less enthusiastic. The psychic phenomena he found improbable and himself ill-equipped to deal with the 'magical subjects': 'as for advising in the present state of the Tale, I *could not* take such a responsibility. I feel myself entirely on ground unknown and unfamiliar to me.' All he could offer was the feeling that 'natural causes or reasoning' would not satisfactorily resolve such a story; a supernatural solution was the only one possible. The letter ended with tactfully ambiguous praise of the 'originality and power of the story'.

Bulwer's reply hardly helped. Though one of his purposes, he wrote, was to show how the seemingly incredible could be rationally explained, yet he did believe in 'persons of a peculiar temperament who can effect very extraordinary things not accounted for satisfactorily by an existent philosophy'. Forster replied with a letter whose rapid transition from the tactful to the near-blunt emphasized the extent of his discomposure. He praised Bulwer's originality and profundity, 'the mere human management of the story I regard as uncommonly good', but continued:

> As to the magical or supernatural part … I think if I had seen it in its original form I would have advised some modification … Honestly …

> when I try to assign possibilities or natural causes for the marvels related – I break down – the typical or allegorical portions will not be seen into in all their emblematical significance – I fear – and the fear I have is that the search for the Life Elixir will be taken simply as a sort of closing romantic fire-work.

Then came the advice of commonsense: 'I am therefore for another closing chapter or book – not of dialogue between Fenwick and Faber, but of half-grave half-playful comment as from some one who has been editing Fenwick's story'. The chapter would point to the allegory, 'so criticizing the whole as to have it in the same sort of doubt as that in which you leave the identity of Margrave'. The narrator and, by implication, Bulwer, would not be seen to believe in the incredible events.

Bulwer did not budge and Forster became more direct:

> Up to a vast deal of your argument as to mesmerism and mesmeric phenomena – I go with you … but … Nothing of what you have suggested explains to me in any degree the Wand, the Clairvoyance, the Luminous Shadow, the Elixir Vitae marvels … Such a chapter as I have suggested could … altogether save, if I may so express it, your own personal dignity … If some such thing is not done, it will be open to any enemies you may have in the press to charge you with grave beliefs in all kinds of nonsense and absurdity that, however ingenious and fanciful the shape you put them in, go far to show that graver matters can be hardly safe in such keeping.

He was most concerned, as he told Bulwer in a further letter, to protect Bulwer's 'dignity amid a world of spirit-rapping and wonder-mongers'.

In the face of such pressure from a friend who seemed to be both an intellectual Beau Nash and a stone-kicking Doctor Johnson, at once arbiter of social respectability and source of commonsense plus literary taste, Bulwer gave way. There was no additional chapter but his attitude to Forster's suggestions that Bulwer should abridge that part of the conclusion that 'lapses too much into the tone of grave and earnest assertion', and that he should consider countering the exoticism by placing greater stress on the sense and commonsense of other characters, was accommodating. 'These I have attended to as well you will see', he wrote on Forster's letter.[66] Bulwer offered insertions in the final chapters that absolved the narrator of belief in those strange happenings, such a sentence as, 'Doubtless the sights and the sounds which had haunted the last gloomy night, the calm reason of Faber would strip of their magical seemings',[67] being of that kind. Similar insertions, casting doubt on supernatural as well as natural explanations, were also made in Chapter 77. All this Forster 'heartily' approved, a harmonious note on which to end an exchange that, as much as any other, demonstrates that Bulwer only accepted Forster's advice when it was intellectually, artistically, and socially persuasive.

Having done his best to help produce works worthy of Bulwer, Forster turned next to marketing them. Bulwer, as Elizabeth James points out,[68] was always the astute businessman. This needs stressing for, even though Forster, from the mid-1830s, acted for him in many negotiations with publishers and actor-managers, he seems never to have been given *carte blanche*. For example, when Forster offered *The Heir of Arundel* to Charles Kean he was instructed by Bulwer to ask for £600. Kean demurred so Forster revised the terms to £400 down plus £200 if the play was a success. In moving even this far he had, as he told Bulwer, 'already exceeded my authority as your friend'.[69]

Bulwer's own astuteness notwithstanding Forster had much to do. Most was done in the 1830s and 1840s: treating with Bentley to repurchase the copyrights of *Paul Clifford*, *Eugene Aram*, and *The Last Days of Pompeii* when Bulwer moved to Saunders & Otley; sounding Colburn about a collected edition before Saunders & Otley did the necessary;[70] and agreeing with Webster, then manager of the Theatre Royal Haymarket and Macready's employer, generous terms for *The Sea Captain* (£600 down plus £100 for 'exclusive town rights'[71] for a year to *The Lady of Lyons* and *Richelieu*, well above the market rate). Although during the 1840s Bulwer employed a solicitor to draw up contracts and dot and cross the legal i's and t's, Forster was still the front-line negotiator, arranging the Saunders and Otley cheap edition, as well as that from Chapman and Hall in 1847, and handling the transfer of Bulwer's narrative poem *King Arthur* from Colburn to Chapman and Hall.[72] After 1850 Forster did less, for Bulwer's popularity was so great as to make negotiations less necessary and Forster himself moved from the centre of literary life; certainly he played no part in Bulwer's astounding contract with Routledge in 1853, when the publisher paid £20,000 for a 19-title collected edition. Forster remained important, however, when Bulwer deviated from his normal writing and publishing practice: in 1869 he suggested a strategy for *Walpole*, Bulwer's rhyming comedy, telling his friend, 'I know Mr Webster so well ... that ... I will have him to dine quietly with me – and will either (as you advise) read him the comedy or tell him what it is, with a scene here and there to show the execution.'[73] A year later he prepared to sound Macmillan about *The Coming Race*, the novel that Bulwer, deceiving no-one but himself, published anonymously.[74]

Though his room for manoeuvre was limited Forster was an indispensable negotiator for two reasons. First, he was tough and worldly; he knew when to crack the whip, as he did over Bentley in 1839 when the publisher tried to wriggle out of earlier agreements: 'It does not suit with my convenience to wait upon you in New Burlington Street. If you do not choose to meet me here, in a matter which is your own concern, it is not likely that we shall meet at all.'[75] He knew, too, the value of strategic prevarication: 'Shall we try the effect of carelessness and delay?'[76] he wrote to Bulwer in 1838, as Bentley, again, stalled over a collected edition.

Second, unlike Bulwer, who could be aloof and was often abroad or politicking, Forster had the intimate understanding of the literary market-place only available to one constantly at work in it. He knew what offers were really worth, what terms could be insisted upon. Thus, in 1849, he reported to Bulwer: 'To Anderson I have offered the two plays for his six months season for £35 apiece – which is £5, only, more than Phelps and Mrs Warner paid, when they paid by the season, for theatres one-fourth the size of Drury Lane. I have not had his answer – but the terms shall not be abated.'[77] Again, when Chapman and Hall brought out the 1847 cheap edition of Bulwer's novels, the form of publication – parts then volumes – and the terms – 1½d. per part, 3s.6d. on average for each bound-up novel – were similar to those received by Dickens for the latter's cheap edition of the same year,[78] so reflecting Forster's knowledge of what popular authors could expect, an expertise obviously gained from his negotiations for Dickens.

The move from lump sum to royalty for collected editions was a move to extract a continuing income from work already done. It plucked the successful author from a career spent labouring against deadlines, from the need to complete a new work before money from the last ran out, and made him, virtually, a salaried professional man. Such a change in status, certainly in part the result of Forster's influence, was arguably one of his main achievements and points clearly to the resemblance between negotiator and adviser: in either capacity Forster was much preoccupied (his activities constantly return to this) with Bulwer's professional dignity and related social status. This preoccupation is seen again, in 1850, in a further expression of his knowledge of the market. 'As to your new novel', he wrote to Bulwer, 'I must, I fear, counsel you against Knight's publishers, if they are a certain Messrs Tallis. For these worthies are hawking publishers, and it really would not do to be dragged through all the hawking and lending and travelling expedients to which they would infallibly subject your name.'[79]

Ultimately it might be argued that Forster's greatest contribution of all, as Bulwer's negotiator, to raising the status of professional letters, was his own business conduct. He was worldly, he was tough, but he was also honourable in a world so full of rogues and sharp practice that he once wrote, despairingly, of 'respectable publishers (if such things may be)'.[80] Whenever possible Forster insisted on agreements that legislated against shabby behaviour; in 1838, when Bulwer moved to Saunders & Otley for his first collected edition, Bentley, at times one of the shabbiest dealers and Bulwer's previous publisher, was made to consent '*not to undersell* the Collected Edition – and *never himself to put forth any cheaper Edition*',[81] and was held back so successfully that Forster was able to assure Bulwer that 'Bentley has not been attempting any more evil'.[82]

Forster and Bulwer *expected* agreements to be honoured and words to be kept. Their rigorous honesty shows in negotiations with Charles Kean about *The Heir of Arundel*, a revision of *The Sea Captain*. Kean gave Forster and a witness assurances that he would take the play. Forster, accordingly, refused 'other parties whom I would willingly have served'.[83] Kean agreed to pay £400 down but argued with Forster about a further £200 'contingent upon the success of the performance'.[84] By chance Kean then met Bulwer, who agreed to reduce the £200 to two separate payments of £50 each. Kean's next step was a sudden request to read the play again. Bulwer had no hesitation: Kean was not keeping his part of the bargain so negotiations were at an end. The play was promptly withdrawn. Forster, supporting Bulwer, voiced a genuine indignation. He would 'never', he told his friend, 'think of the man hereafter without disgust'.[85]

Of the proof-reading that followed marketing Forster did much. In that age of cheap corrections he not only read for printing errors, but, as has been seen with *A Strange Story*, continued his advisory service, very ready – as he wrote of *King Arthur* – to place 'an occasional pencil-mark here and there'[86] or, as with *Caxtoniana*, to recommend more substantial alterations:

> Fearing you may want these proofs, I don't like to retain them longer ... I think the preamble of *Richelieu* in the 'Self-Control' not really necessary to your purpose ... Some omissions might be well also in the *first* of the 'Love' essays ... Those *details* of poetical criteria are not in keeping.[87]

Always, of course, the printer and publisher were accommodating.

Other practical decisions remained. 'You will now be able to consult Mr. Forster', wrote Bulwer to Chapman & Hall about the collected edition, 'as to the day of publication, & decide with him, whether Paul Clifford or Pelham shall begin the set.'[88] Publication or, for the plays, theatrical performance, then followed but, for Forster, this did not mean only the opulent fingering of the presentation copy or the excitement of a box on a crowded first night. It meant, also and mainly, another quick change and the emergence of Forster in his persona as reviewer.

In his notices he had much praise for Bulwer's work – not surprisingly, given his own part in their creation. In *King Arthur*, 'the classical finish of the artist is everywhere felt, even while emotions are portrayed as truthfully as if nature spoke, unfashioned to rule'.[89] *St. Stephen's*, Forster noted in a much later review, was, impressively, in the tradition of Pope and Dryden.[90] A major strength was the clear morality of most of Bulwer's work: 'There is no perplexed moral in *Lucretia*;' he wrote, defending his friend against a critical onslaught, 'and there is never the remotest danger of a false sympathy with crime.'[91] Such an assertion was made, again, of *Paul Clifford* and, yet again, of *The Lady of Lyons*. And Forster was quick to insist that clear morality was not dry didacticism; Bulwer was the true heir of Fielding and Sterne, his work being, as Forster wrote of *The Caxtons*, 'as instructive as it is delightful'.[92] Above all, Bulwer revealed 'the heart of love' beneath the cold and 'grotesque surface'[93] of much of human life – praise that was a sudden reminder of that young Newcastle Unitarian.

Though general praise of Bulwer's work was to be expected it was not fulsome back-slapping but part of a considered verdict. Forster's reviews of Bulwer's work, it must be emphasized, are remarkable for their objectivity. They are often critical, for when Bulwer did step out of moral or artistic line Forster was quick to do his duty. We see this in his review of *Night and Morning* where, in characterizing the murderer, William Gawtry, 'the limits between good and evil are scarcely marked throughout with sufficient clearness and precision' so that Bulwer risked 'the extreme danger of suggesting a false sympathy with crime'.[94] Parts of *Zanoni* were obscure, *Lucretia* had structural defects, *Night and Morning* not only fell off the moral pedestal but suffered also from a lack of central aim, the second part of *The New Timon* failed to sustain the interest of the first and exhibited Bulwer's main faults of diffuseness and the too-glittering style, as did *King Arthur* and *Richelieu*. Of the last Forster was not less than candid:

> In ... the acted play ... we observed it as a fault that the incidents trod too quickly on each other's heels, and finally overcrowded the scene. ... its French vivacity of expression is now and then pushed to a faulty extent, and that emotions, translated too often into pictures, glitter before us with a dash of artificial mannerism.[95]

Even *Money*, highly praised by Forster, was not immune: parts of Act Four asked too much of the actors.

Three examples illustrate Bulwer's revealing response. 'I have just read your notice of *Arthur* in *The Examiner*', he wrote to Forster in 1848, 'and believe me, I feel deeply grateful for it, and sincerely affected by what I consider a real proof of the friendship I have so often tasked. I feel this the more, because I know how many differences of taste there are between us in poetry.'[96] Of Forster's review of *Zanoni*: 'your lengthened criticism is most kind ... How can I expect that there is any man, however friendly, who will see *Zanoni* with the eyes of the author ... ?'[97] Lastly, in the moving tribute to Forster already mentioned: 'He has served more than any living critic to establish reputations ... Me, I think, he served in that way, less than any of his friends.'[98]

Of course there were many ways in which Forster served Bulwer and to the account already given can be added the work Forster solicited for the *Foreign Quarterly Review*.[99] Forster was even able to arrange *Examiner* support for Bulwer the politician; 'even' because that radical weekly usually had little time for Tories. Support was offered through a rather specious distinction between Bulwer's personal qualities and his political beliefs, or through assertions that previous disagreements concerned issues no longer of central importance. The result had too much the effect of presenting Bulwer as a great but greatly deluded human being to be a vote-catcher, but there could be no doubting the support's benevolent intent.[100] In private Forster offered more effective encouragement, as he did in 1858 in dissuading Bulwer from retiring from office because of ill health: 'You are worth fifty Colonial secretaries – and just in the balance against one, the other end may well kick the beam.'[101]

Finally, during the 1840s and 1850s, Forster collected Bulwer's royalties. 'I shall touch up Mr. Phelps before Xmas for his payment to you', he wrote aggressively, 'By this time it must, by my count, and the Surrey Theatre business, be bringing tolerably near £100.'[102] And: 'I expect something from Mr. Anderson for your plays at Durham next season (you perhaps know he has taken the theatre) and I wish you would tell me what *you* think it would be fair to ask.'[103] Sums received were then paid into Bulwer's bank account, in exact anticipation of the modern literary agent.

The serving was not one-way. From Bulwer Forster got entrées into reviewing, with the *New Monthly Magazine* in those early 1830s, and into Bulwer's wide and influential social circle. Most importantly, from the first exchange about *Eugene Aram*, when Bulwer insisted on 'the *duty* of Fiction, in her higher shapes, – to exalt and idealize',[104] Forster's critical principles absorbed his friend's influence. The relationship between the didactic and the pleasurable, the real and the ideal, upbringing and character, the superior power of the dramatic, the depiction of passion, the function of the plot, an interest in the eighteenth century, are areas in which Bulwer's ideas became, or affected, Forster's own. In many cases, as has been seen in the friendship with Leigh Hunt, Forster absorbed his friend's ideas and trained them back on his friend's own work as well as on the work of others.

Any account of the friendship between Forster and Bulwer returns to two central points. Firstly, the close and persisting personal ties between the two men, ties that made Bulwer accept Forster as critic, drew Forster, through respect and affection, to Bulwer's belief in the dignity of literature and the need for an enhanced social status for those who wrote it. Forster's supportive stance in Bulwer's private life, as well as his advice on the manuscripts and proofs – advice that sought to make Bulwer's work more approachable and so to counter Bulwer's near-contempt for much of his mass readership[105] – reflect his concurrence with that central belief. The public critical reviews, in such a friendship the supreme statement – because they criticized and because Bulwer accepted that criticism – of the way literary values, honesty and personal respect ranked above a more superficial notion of friendship's obligations, present no contradiction.

Secondly, only once did Bulwer attempt a literary portrait of his friend. In Hardman, in *Not So Bad As We Seem*, there is much of Forster. Hardman is 'a man who finds everything out', who has 'a hard life of it'[106] because of his services to others, who is liked despite his politics, and has fought his way up through early disadvantages. At the play's end his name belies his behaviour, his pugnacious exterior hides a ready magnanimity. Most significantly, his own belief that he has risen unaided is shown to be mistaken; his friends had helped him as he had helped them. The portrait is affectionate but the point is firmly made: this friendship of opposites and differences as well of similarities and agreements was, above all, a friendship of equals.

CHAPTER 5 *Macready*

Forster's first great theatrical passion was for the acting of Edmund Kean. That took him to Kean's funeral where, as has been mentioned, he met William Charles Macready, Kean's undisputed successor both as leading tragedian and head of the profession. Some months later they met again, after dinner at Talfourd's. Macready liked Forster, and so did Macready's wife and sister.[1] He liked him even more on meeting him frequently in that circle of lawyers, writers and journalists who dined indulgently at each others' homes.

In 1833 Macready was almost twice Forster's age, 40 as against 21, so repeating the strange pattern of Forster's early friendships. Here was another eminent established figure cultivated by and sincerely attracted towards a young man only beginning to make his way. Here, also, was a famous man who, like Hunt for much of his life and Bulwer for part, was driven by financial need, having to rely only on his own wit and skill and so always in some need of those able to further his career. Like Bulwer, Macready was a man ill-at-ease in his world. In Bulwer's case his aristocratic connections were, at the least, unusual in the milling market-place of literary professionalism. In Macready's his background – born into a theatrical family but educated at Rugby by a father concerned to make his son a gentleman and determined to keep him off the stage and heading for the Bar, only to be thwarted by financial collapse – was rare in a theatre more used to recruiting from the feckless and the lowly.[2] Macready was a man of learning and taste whose colleagues, he considered, were very vulgar indeed. It was no accident that Macready, again like Bulwer, had a vanity and touchiness that found constant expression in the theatrical equivalent of Bulwer's obsession with the dignity of literature.

However, beyond the obvious fact that Macready was an actor, there was one important difference between him and Hunt, Lamb, and Bulwer.

Hunt's home life was chaotic, Lamb's that of a saddened bachelor, Bulwer's beyond repair; Macready had a secure and happy marriage, many children, and an ordered and respectable family home in rural Elstree. Such attractions were compelling for the young, child-loving and far-from-home bachelor, and need to be firmly emphasized because the friendship with Macready, like that with Bulwer, was centrally a personal one.

From the first Macready himself received Forster's devotion, the younger man eager for his company and devouring his letters 'with greedy and grateful pleasure'.[3] Forster had, as he told Talfourd, 'great regard and admiration of Macready, for his so many fine qualities and solid excellence of character in every way'.[4] As the *Examiner* put it, in an account of the Astor Place riots inserted during Forster's editorship and with comments almost certainly by him, Macready behaved 'in the natural character as a high-spirited gentleman', being at once 'manly, dignified, and forbearing'.[5] Such devotion was deep but not blind, Forster being well aware of Macready's 'serious faults of manner'.[6] His controlled response to Macready is clearly seen both in that awareness and in his opinion of the famous fight between Macready and the odious Alfred Bunn, then manager of Drury Lane Theatre. He wrote to George Cattermole:

> Macready … was goaded into a severe chastisement of Bunn by a thousand practical insults and injuries, which may extenuate if they do not excuse his lifting his hand against an animal he despises. … Poor Mrs Macready has suffered very deeply, and Macready is mortified in the extreme that he so far forgot himself, though everyone rejoices that he punished the wretch.[7]

Forster here preserves a sense of proper conduct that evaluates, even though he quite understands, Macready's behaviour. Significantly, he is concerned not only with Macready but also with his family.

Forster was a regular visitor to the Macready house and a constant diner at Macready's table. He gossiped with his wife and played cards with her and the eldest children. 'Found Forster at home', wrote Macready typically, 'who had convoyed the family and Mrs. Carlyle to see Madame Laffarge at the Adelphi!!!'[8] 'I wish to see Twelfth Night myself', wrote Forster to Samuel Phelps at Sadler's Wells, with a request for a private box, 'and to bring Mr Macready's son, who has never seen a Shakespeare play.'[9] The extent of the affection Forster lavished on the Macready establishment and, particularly, on the children, is movingly apparent in his response to family sorrow. When illness struck he was grief-stricken to a degree at least as great as when Emily Lytton died of typhoid. He 'lost all self-control'[10] when it took three-year-old Harriet Joanna:

> My darling goddaughter Joan was laid on Monday in the vaults of the Harrow Road Cemetery. All was so gentle and quiet – so simple and deeply affecting – that you could not call it what goes by the name of *funeral*. Her dear father and myself were there alone. If you had witnessed the manly, affectionate spirit he has shown through all this heavy trial, you would love & admire him even more than you do.[11]

Ten years later, with Mrs Macready confined for yet another child, it was Nina's turn. Forster sent a water-bed, clotted cream, and a 'sweet, consolatory' letter. 'Dear kind Forster … my best friend,'[12] Macready repeated to his diary and named the new baby Jonathan Forster Christian Macready. Eight years on and the family was decimated. 'Poor Macready', wrote Forster,

> he left us only a fortnight since, after we had laid in Kensal Green Cemetery by the side of poor Mrs Macready, and Joan, and Nina, and Walter, and Henry – the loveliest, prettiest, most gentle & loving, most accomplished, – oh Browning I cannot tell you what dear little Lily Macready was! 'Little' I call her – but she was so tall – and the handsomest of all. She was only 16. She was the pride of the whole house.[13]

In 1860, eight years after his wife's death and aged 67, Macready remarried. His second wife, Cecile Spencer, was 23. Browning was again Forster's confidant and was told not only the startling news but also the bride's background. The latter account, with its reference to her being 'one of a large family, whom the father's death turned on their resources', hints at fortune-hunting. Forster continued: 'The incident has been as great and as *sudden* a surprize to me as it could possibly have been even to you. Nor can I reconcile myself to it. It seems to carry poor old Elstree and Clarence Terrace farther than ever away from me.'[14] Unwisely Forster allowed Macready to know his feelings. As he wrote, regretfully, to Browning: 'in consequence of some excited declaration against the marriage of his son William … I was obliged to reply to an appeal with certain intimations from myself that I found it really *not possible* to suppress.'[15] He had not meant to cause offence but he succeeded too well and the friendship ended abruptly.

The marriage flourished and produced a child. In 1863, after three years of estrangement, an unhappy Forster admitted his error to Dickens and the latter, who had greeted the marriage enthusiastically and remained the closest of Macready's friends, recognized his friend's sincerity. 'He spoke with emotion and feeling', Dickens reported to Macready, 'and evidently on no impulse, but in pursuance of a set purpose.'[16] Dickens persuaded Macready out of an understandable reluctance and reconciliation followed, never again to be required.

The estrangement took place long after the end of Macready's career but Forster's disappointment, both at the shattering of the sentimental memory of family life until then preserved in Forster's own emotional aspic, and at the violation of his notion of Macready's respectability, suggests how strong must have been Forster's attachment to Macready during the latter's acting and dramatic prime. In that earlier period, despite his awareness of Macready's faults, such as the violent hastiness shown in the Bunn affair, Macready, in his personal life, was, for Forster, essentially and invariably a happily-married gentleman. The part Forster played in Macready's career during its last and greatest third can again and again be seen to reflect and support an idea of Macready the professional close to that of Macready the man.

Initially, Forster was valued for his theatrical gossip; he was, as Macready noted, 'quite an enthusiast'[17] and seemed to know everything about the work of rival managers and companies, and the movements of actors, as well as less valuable but no less interesting scandal and malicious rumour, for instance, the Talfourds' jealousy of Bulwer,[18] or the '*affaire de coeur* between Ellen Tree and Mr. C. Kean'.[19] Forster's role as informer should not be despised; its most important element, awareness of new writings, certainly paid off handsomely. He helped bring to Macready plays by Bulwer, Sheridan Knowles, Browning, and Talfourd, and not only introduced new work but also evaluated their possibilities and strove, with actor and author, for effective revision. As has been seen, the Macready/Bulwer/Forster triangle is a detailed and typical example of advice and collaboration that Forster also let loose on work by Westland Marston, Darley, Griffin, and James White. Forster's tight editing to produce a concentrated dramatic effect, already documented in terms of Bulwer's plays and to a lesser extent in terms of Leigh Hunt's, would have been his main contribution. Talfourd's *Ion* and *The Athenian Captive*, Griffin's *Gisippus*, Darley's *The Plighted Troth*, White's *The King of the Commons*, Marston's *The Patrician's Daughter*, as well as Browning's work and most of Bulwer's, were ambitious blank-verse plays to which Forster was almost certainly attracted because of his interest in Elizabethan and Jacobean drama which was so much encouraged by Hunt and Charles Lamb. The verse, and the presence of heroes of dignity and fine feeling, together made suitable vehicles for the mature Macready style and the over-ripe social selfconsciousness of the eminent tragedian. Arguably, Forster's greatest influence on his friend was on his choice of plays, and so the boosting of Macready's confidence in his own similar convictions. A second way in which such influence was exercised was *via* the advice Forster offered on suitable parts. This is most clearly seen in the closing months of Macready's career when Forster was responsible for the inclusion of Richard II, a new role for his friend, amongst all the old favourites.[20] Again, when Macready thought of Joseph Surface to end the first half of his farewell performances and then had second thoughts, 'thinking, on reflection, Joseph Surface might be *beneath my position*', Forster decisively gave his opinion, '*on good grounds*, against acting the *School for Scandal*'.[21]

Plays, of course, need theatres. Macready obtained them either as actor-manager, in which venture he was much encouraged by his friends, with Forster in the van, or as employed actor. As regards the former, Forster's part in the business dealings, the leasing of theatres, the hiring of personnel, cannot be established in any detail. What can be stressed is the, as it were, general encouragement offered by Forster to his friend. Macready was urged to 'take up the gauntlet for *the Art*';[22] as Forster wrote to Fox when Macready approached his first London management at Covent Garden, a move seen by his friends as close to founding a first national theatre: 'But is not this step of Macready's brave and well? He has evidently great faith in the result – though the fatigue & responsibility and Mrs Macready's fears weigh upon him a little.'[23] For Macready as actor, Forster negotiated with London managers. Significantly, the examples come from the 1840s, emphasizing Macready's ever-increasing reliance on Forster as the friendship proceeded. And behind Forster's help was his insistence, with W. J. Fox and others, that 'the most probable means of re-establishing the high drama again in London'[24] should be urgently explored.

Thus in August 1845 Macready, following a tour of America and appearances in the provinces, responded to such encouragement by looking for a metropolitan venue. He briefed Forster to negotiate with Webster for a season at the Haymarket Theatre. Forster asked for £100 a week for 16 weeks, Macready to act on three nights a week; he mentioned Charlotte Cushman as a possible leading lady. Webster's counter-offer was £100 a week for eight weeks if Macready could recruit Miss Cushman. Forster's reaction was swift and Macready wrote approvingly that he had 'declined the proposal without seeing me'.[25] Maddox, who managed the Princess' Theatre, was next. He accepted Macready's terms and Macready accepted Forster's advice to forgo £5 per week as part of the deal.[26] Macready opened at the Princess' in October 1845 in a season of Shakespeare.

Four years later, with Macready again out of town, Forster began negotiations with Charles Manby, Benjamin Webster's business manager, for Macready's farewell London performances at the Haymarket.[27] Two seasons were planned: October to December 1849, and April to July 1850. Forster asked for £40 per night for three nights per week plus an extra £30 if an additional night per week was required, for two ten-week seasons. Manby's reply was £100 per week for three nights plus £20 for the extra night, and an insistence on two eight-week seasons, this last because the Keans needed part of the season to perform Douglas Jerrold's new play. Forster's decision was unequivocal: 'With many thanks for your prompt attention to what I placed before you, I decline yr offer. Mr Macready is gone to Eastbourne – but if he had been in town I should not have thought it necessary to submit the proposal to him.'

This drew a quick note from Manby agreeing to Forster's nightly terms but stressing again the problems arising from the theatre's engagement with the Keans. Forster confirmed the terms with a letter from Macready and then compromised by agreeing to the shorter seasons. He went on to suggest that Manby might regret the reduction for, in the past, managers had tried belatedly to extend Macready's seasons because of public demand, only to find that the tragedian's commitments made extension impossible. The latter would again be the case:

> I am convinced that the eagerness to welcome Mr M. back to the stage is much greater than at his reappearances from his *first* visit to America (when such great results were obtained); and that the circumstances of his *farewell performances* added to the other, will secure much greater results in the present instance. I throw this out for your own sake, not for his!

There was need for a good leading lady ('remember that if you fail in a good Queen for Hamlet, & a reasonably good Lady Macbeth, two of the strongest plays are made comparatively worthless') and there was further need, on Manby's part, not to exaggerate the expense of the season's costumes. Few of the productions were new; as for *Lear*, 'a very very small outlay would be needed – not much for Julius Caesar (which would include Virginius & Gracchus) as well as both Brutus & Cassius – and there will be but one expense for Henry 8th & the scene of Henry IV (which he proposes to play on the same night)'. Good actressess were obtained, including Mrs Warner as Lady Macbeth, and doubtless the management dared not fail to watch the pennies. The terms remained the same. What Forster's letter demonstrates, above all, is that he was prized as a negotiator because of his whole-hearted and expert commitment to the cause of his 'client'. Following the letter a meeting was arranged between Macready and Webster in Forster's rooms and Macready opened at the Haymarket on 8 October 1849.

The death of Nina, Macready's eldest daughter, meant the postponement of the second farewell series; it eventually took place from October 1850 to February 1851. Even the necessary announcements were closely supervised by Forster, who fulminated against unauthorized alterations and insisted that control of all publicity material should remain in Macready's own hands. 'You will understand why I wrote', he said to Manby. 'That the matter of Mr Macready's engagement & farewell should be thoroughly understood, is – before everything else – Mr Webster's interest, & that of the theatre.' Forster, for Macready, was anxious that the public should not be deceived by playbills and newspaper announcements that confused, perhaps deliberately, Macready's *final appearance* in a part with the *final series* in which he would play that part several times. Here, right at the end of Macready's career, with both his and Forster's auspicious eyes cast on retirement's financial necessities, is a commendable concern for the proprieties far greater than that for the quick return.

When negotiations were complete the plays, and Macready, came to rehearsal. Forster attended assiduously, as did other members of Macready's circle, Dickens particularly, and Talfourd, Browning, and Bulwer. Macready was a martinet, his rehearsals both tense and eruptive. Forster was hardly an oil-pourer. He tactlessly prompted[28] the hot-tempered star and even, as Hall recalled,[29] corrected Macready's pronunciation of Shakespeare. Forster's custodial attitude to Macready is clearly seen, though its only recorded effect, following the prompting, was restricted to the actor's personal diary.

More acceptable was Forster's support of Macready in action and his clear understanding, because actively involved and encouraging, of Macready's aims. These aims were three-fold and had a single source. As manager he did much to improve the comfort and social respectability of the theatre, his most dramatic and effective move being the exclusion of prostitutes from the main areas of Covent Garden and Drury Lane theatres, avoiding the legal problem of being unable to refuse paying customers by admitting whores only to a neglected gallery. Forster explained the exclusion from Drury Lane in a letter to *The Times* written by himself but signed by Macready.[30] Though, as Macready himself recognized in his farewell speech, he failed in his 'ambition to establish a theatre, in regard to decorum and taste worthy of our country',[31] it was a brave and protracted attempt and one that was not without longer-term influence.

Not only did Macready wish to bring back to the theatre the educated and cultured classes but they were to see, amongst other suitable offerings, 'the plays of our divine Shakspeare [*sic*] fitly illustrated'.[32] Macready continued the earlier efforts of Kemble, Planché, and Madame Vestris, to restore accurate Shakespeare texts to the stage in settings and costumes that were historically correct. In this he had much success and lasting effect, his greatest triumph being the restoration of *King Lear* 'as Shakespeare wrote it', and the sweeping away of Nahum Tate's 'disgusting version',[33] with happy ending and no Fool, that had dominated the stage since the late seventeenth century.

Macready was no major originator but, at the least, an intelligent consolidator. As producer he developed Vestris's tentative movements towards realism through unified effect and careful staging and, as actor, sought to integrate the part into the ensemble, often, as with King Lear, through the domestication of his role. He brought to his general task fresh notions of sincerity and overall grasp. Macready's work as manager, custodian of the true bard, and as actor/producer, all reflect his concern with dramatic behaviour fittingly unobtrusive and artistic, a theatrical decorum that was a professional expression of the social unease that ruled his private life.

Forster's support was of two kinds. Firstly, there was much of what could be called basic moral support, such as the appearance, with Macready's circle, in the dressing-room after the performance to provide the first reaction to the night's endeavours that was much needed by Macready and much relied upon: after *Macbeth* 'Talfourd, Forster, and Wallace came to my room, not one had a word of comfort or congratulation',[34] or, after *Hamlet*, 'Forster came round and discoursed very coolly on the evening's effects'.[35] Usually Macready had and deserved admiring friends; they were rarely sycophants.

Secondly and more importantly, Forster supported Macready in reviews and articles that were sympathetic, enthusiastic, sometimes hero-worshipping, but also alive to faults and limitations. Thus, in his reviews of Macready in Shakespeare – reviews strongly influenced, as has been seen, by Lamb's writings – Forster offered clear appreciation of Macready's theories in practice. For example, he praised the attempt to produce *Coriolanus* in historically realistic style and seized upon the moral effect: 'To what infinitely higher purpose is the moral grandeur of the place and of the men, set off by a comparatively rude and barren city!'[36] As for the production of *King Lear*, Forster saw this as a move from that version by Tate that had made much sentimentally trivial, and 'polished all that remained into commonplace', to a fine vindication of 'the higher objects and uses of the drama'. The production was 'the only perfect picture that we have of *Lear* since the age of Betterton'.

But even when the production commanded approval Forster could still be critical of Macready's own performance. Even his Lear was not immune: parts of the heath-scenes 'wanted more of tumultuous extravagance, more of a preternatural cast of wildness. We should always be made to feel something beyond physical distress predominantly here.'[37] As Macbeth Macready, like all his predecessors, 'cannot master it.... The fault of the performance, we should say, generally was this: – that where it was imaginative, its imagination seemed to result from passion; while, where it was passionate, its passion was not the result, nor did it seem under the control, of imagination.' Some moments 'fell flat'[38] because Macready sacrificed poetical beauty to a delivery that was almost off-hand; that is, he sacrificed it to notions of realism. A similar point was made about Macready's Hamlet: 'If we might hazard an objection to a performance so truly great as this, it would be to the delivery of the celebrated Soliloquy on Death, as too quiet and deliberate.'[39] As Othello, to offer another version of that same insistence, Macready, in the early scenes, could not find 'the quiet and graceful self-possession, the measureless dignity, and those touches of happy yet mournful pathos'[40] brought out by Edmund Kean. Each example shows Forster aware of how theories of acting can limit dramatic effect; each example is a revelation of Forster's critical integrity that makes us accept as more than bias his general enthusiasm for Macready's talent. Given Macready's pre-eminence that enthusiasm was hardly misplaced, but many of Forster's reviews provide evidence that it was not, as Rowell unfairly suggests, undiscriminating.[41] G. H. Lewes's objection to Macready's Shakespearian heroes that they were 'domestic rather than ideal, and made but slight appeals to the larger passions',[42] Marston's comment that Macready's Macbeth was 'too obviously reasoned out',[43] may well be more overtly critical but, as contemporary reactions, are not different in kind from Forster's awareness, at particular moments, of the limitations set by Macready's theories and of the effectiveness of the low-key.

It may be thought remarkable that Forster's critical sense persisted for, personal ties apart, Macready as actor was Forster's standard. His success was due to 'thought and study more and more carefully regulated...

increasing poetic appreciation, and ... a larger knowledge of life.' Macready had

> the power of grasping at once the various truths of one of Shakespeare's characters with the as various forces necessary to its full expression ... He never played a part without leaving us a clear and definite notion of what he conceived the writer to have meant by it ... He viewed character as a whole, seeking always to explain by that means its apparent inconsistencies, and to reconcile its harmonies and discords.

Forster was ready to admit that 'in dignity and grace of person he is said to have been surpassed by Kemble', and that 'in flashes of passion Kean excelled him', yet 'we greatly prefer the steady and severe intelligence which, in making an artist master of his emotion, makes him also master of his design'.

Further, 'when Mr. Macready had to write or read a letter on the stage *he did it*, and was not content with the mumbling or scribbling affectation of *seeming to do* either; but ... it may stand as a sort of general type of the truth and sincerity which ran through every part of his acting'.[44] Here Macready moved almost beyond pretence, almost beyond acting, to a form of identification that stressed, as Downer puts it, 'an inner realism of feeling, employing ... emotional memory ... And the emotions of his private life were the tools of his public performance ... Macready, to perform to his own satisfaction, must *be* the thing he represented'.[45] As Forster put it, many years later, 'The foundation of all good acting, in both comedy and tragedy, is the power of feeling earnestly.'[46] He was able to advise Macready on suitable parts because his knowledge of the actor's fine personal qualities, as father, husband, man, made him able to judge which parts would require the expression of those very qualities.

Macready's productions illustrated the principles that governed his acting and were praised accordingly. Unity of conception was the main aim. Forster contrasted 'the old manner of doing'[47] *The Merchant of Venice*, all subjugated to the star as Shylock, with Macready's insistence that the Jew's importance must not overwhelm the other parts. The same approach was made to *A Winter's Tale*: 'the inferior actors shewed a palpable desire to identify themselves with their parts and form portions of the design of the play'.[48] All, including 'the resources of scenery and the various means of scenic illusion', should be unified and harmonized. Forster, using Macready's production of *Gisippus* as his example, stressed the need for such resources to 'embody the idea of the drama. If this is lost sight of for an instant, – the greater the splendour, the greater the mistake.

If this is steadily kept in view ... the greater the justice that will be done not only to the genius of the poet but to the high and instructive purpose of the stage.'[49]

That last phrase recalls the recurring main theme of Forster's writings on his friend: the role of the theatre, the function of the drama. The young man in Newcastle who had written, in his 'Vindication' letter, of 'the great influence which a well-regulated theatre might have on the *spirit* of a Nation',[50] found it easy to admire Macready's achievements. Under him, wrote Forster, the theatre was 'an unfailing resource of noble and instructive entertainment',[51] it was 'not simply...a place for pleasurable excitement or vulgar wonder, but for steady and solid instruction'.[52]

In an important response to Macready's career, written in 1837 as Macready became manager of Covent Garden Theatre, Forster described English theatre history as a constant battle between good and evil. In the Restoration period Betterton and Cibber restored 'decency and decorum', despite the efforts of 'sordid adventuring speculators'. Garrick's time saw him, as manager of Drury Lane, sweep away 'every trace of diseased taste in the public. His reforms extended to every department of the Theatre', even to the notoriously profligate green room. But reform was short-lived and, after Garrick's death, licentiousness returned. So to Macready who, in his own day, 'has taken upon himself the arduous but hopeful task of endeavouring to rescue his own profession from the disgraces brought upon it by reckless adventurers; and that he proposes to achieve this by offering a manly and instructive entertainment to the people, and doing his best to replace the stage in its old and natural position, at the head of the intellectual arts'. Macready, as a second Garrick, was opposing himself to the obnoxious Alfred Bunn at Drury Lane: 'The people are invited to Covent Garden as to a place which they may visit without a blush or self-reproach', it having become 'an instrument of civilization and refinement'.[53]

When Macready retired, in 1851, Forster reviewed his career as an undoubted success story. Macready had given far-reaching services to 'public decency and morals', so that to his efforts were owed 'the proof that a rational and delightful amusement may exist without the aids of puffing or prostitution, that to boast about the noblest dramatic literature in the world need not imply the starvation of every one whose bread depends upon it, and that to act Shakespeare is not of necessity to maim and mutilate him'.[54] All was underlined, at the farewell banquet, in Forster's praise of Macready for having 'made his theatre a place of perfect decorum, and pure and refined enjoyment'.[55]

Such strong principles informing and animating Forster's reviews of

Macready also explain his criticism of Macready's rivals. Even the attacks on Macready's American rival, Edwin Forrest, delivered with an edgy mockery learned from Leigh Hunt, are not to be understood as the prejudices of a friend. Forster wrote of Forrest's Lear:

> The 'Darkness and Devils', etc. was a mere succession of fierce tones interrupted by the most mistaken and misplaced tenderness; and the 'Blasts upon thee', with its frightening threatening of the Curse, was delivered so slowly, and the speaker, at its close, had settled into such comparative calmness, that the Curse itself, suddenly following, appeared to have sprung on the instant from a bad and merely violent impulse of passion. Let the reader observe that this is a trick resorted to by Mr Forrest as often as he can make it practicable, and that it is decisive of the commonplace actor. He severs abruptly the natural relation of two speeches to each other, with a view to producing sudden and violent effects.[56]

He wrote of the same actor's Othello:

> The performance was made up of an infinite variety of parts, through which there was no unity. They were never, as by the imagination or kindled fancy of a man of real genius, flung into a state of fusion. In a word, for this is the only conclusion we can come to, Mr Forrest had no intellectual comprehension of what he was about.[57]

In both cases the objections are to Forrest's ill-conceived departures from the Macreadian norm of unified effect. The same point can be made of a generous review of Charles Kean's Hamlet, in which Forster gave high praise to Kean's talent and potential only to criticize him for over-acting in aid of localized effect.[58]

Occasionally Forster attacked fellow-reviewers; one outburst against *The Times*, in 1834, made Macready, who feared retaliation, cry uneasily to his Diary, 'Save me from my friends!'[59] Once again such attacks were not simply partisan. As Downer points out,[60] Macready's association with Forster, the drama critic of the radical *Examiner*, sometimes made him a target for the Tory press and so much in need of support. Such counter-attacking was only one of several post-performance and post-reviewing services done for his friend. The others were even more acceptable and included what was virtually a press-cutting service, the arranging of social engagements – such as Macready to speak at the dinner for Talfourd when *Ion* was performed, to take the chair at the General Theatrical Fund dinner of 1847, to be guest of honour at dinners before departing for an American tour and following his farewell to the stage – and the enlarging of Macready's social circle to include Dickens, Bulwer, Lady Blessington and her Gore House *salon*.[61]

It hardly needs pointing out that what Forster did for Macready was all of a piece and so, in itself, a shining example of that unity of conception prized by the actor. The search for plays and roles of suitably forceful gravity, the hard bargaining in support of a professional independence, the public championing of moral improvement, of a respectable theatre, of an intelligently dignified style that rejected 'show' and embraced reasoned effect, all reflect Forster's abiding concern, during Macready's career, with the dignity and status of the acting profession in its theatre, a dignity to be derived from a private life that was truly gentlemanly. It scarcely needs to be stressed that what Forster did for Macready the actor resembles what Forster did for Bulwer the writer. In both cases he did what he did partly because of the pressure of their example upon him.

Macready was the most selfconscious, the most socially sensitive of all actors, a man who refused to allow his family to watch him perform until Forster persuaded him to relent during the farewell series. Forster was devoted to him but the devotion had, at times, to be dogged. For, though Macready of course found Forster an invaluable friend and adviser, very often he responded to him with a peevishness hard to confine to a private diary. If the *Examiner* failed to mention a performance, if Forster's advice did not suit, if he took little notice of a Macreadian request (as when Forster refused to be lenient with Edwin Forrest), if he praised a rival such as Charles Kean, Macready as diarist was a forceful fulminator. When he praised a rival play by Sheridan Knowles Forster became 'a mere hooter-on of any successful person.... a poor-talking, low-minded man. "Never more be *friend* of mine." Keep his acquaintance I may, but I strike him out of the list – the very little list of *friends*.'[62] On other occasions Forster was considered indiscreet or the provider of bad counsel. Macready was very ready to write of his friend in a manner that made the famous diary seem much in need of asbestos covers. Yet there were comparatively few serious quarrels until the long estrangement when Macready re-married.

The actor's behaviour to Forster throughout the friendship expressed a basic and paradoxically friendly antagonism. What concerned Macready was the impression Forster made on the world. He sought for Forster the gentlemanly style that Forster sought for Macready on-stage and cursed Forster whenever the latter failed to find it. He often lamented Forster's lack of 'the fine tact of good breeding',[63] as when Forster fell asleep during the reading of *Richelieu*, or was guilty of gross language, conceit, short-temper, dogmatic assertions, or the hundred and one possibilities liable to be discovered by the abnormally sensitive. Macready, so concerned and so much older than Forster, considered himself to be the young man's mentor: 'I must explain to him the causes of my coolness for *his own sake*',[64] he wrote in 1846, when Forster had offended through a too abrupt refusal of a dinner engagement. '*How am I to help* such variations of temper and feeling?' he asked himself desperately two years later, when Forster 'did not seem in the best humour'.[65] Macready proposed Forster's health at dinners, commended him to the world as one of the 'uniform and earnest supporters of the cause of the drama';[66] his dramatic realism, domestication of tragedy, notions of sincerity and concept of unity, strongly influenced Forster's critical thinking. Nothing surpassed the effect on Forster of frequent exposure, in public and private places, to this admired actor who was at once immensely talented and intelligent, conscientious to a fault, greatly embittered and, above all, obsessed with ideas of fitting conduct, social status and his art's dignity.

1. 'John when a boy'
(Fales Library, New York University).

2. Forster in 1830, aged 18
a portrait by Thomas Warrington and Daniel Maclise
(by courtesy of the Victoria and Albert Museum).

3. Forster in 1840, aged 28
a sketch by Daniel Maclise
(by courtesy of the Victoria and Albert Museum).

4. Forster in middle age
(The Dickens House).

5. Forster in later life
a *carte de visite* photograph by Elliott & Fry
(by courtesy of the Victoria and Albert Museum).

6. John Forster
(Armstrong Browning Library, Baylor University, Waco, Texas).

7. Mrs John Forster, *née* Eliza Ann Crosbie
(Armstrong Browning Library, Baylor University, Waco, Texas).

8. Nos. 57 and 58 Lincoln's Inn Fields. No. 58 is on the right (by courtesy of the Victoria and Albert Museum).

9. Palace Gate House, Kensington
a photograph taken during Forster's residence there
(reproduced from R. Renton, *John Forster and his Friendships*, 1912).

Part Two Man of Letters – i The Literary Life

CHAPTER 6 *Literature's Friend*

When W. Lockey Harle, who spent his life in Newcastle and became Sheriff of the city, wrote in his memoir that 'John Forster owed everything as regards formation of character to the town of Newcastle',[1] he offered more than chauvinism. Forster's upbringing gave him a love of family life and a deep affection for 'ever-remembered and never-to-be forgotten friends'.[2] Importantly, and the most obvious pointer to the quality of that early life, it developed his capacity, inherited from his mother, to express strong feeling without inhibition. Whatever were the 'troubles' and 'trials' of Gilmore's enigmatic note, and social tension and straitened means must surely have been included, Forster at 17, when he left Newcastle for Cambridge, was certainly not the product of an oppressively narrow approach to children.

Chance, in the shape of his uncle, gave Forster a fine classical education that inculcated scholarly propensities at first expressed as boyish antiquarianism. His parents' religion exposed him to Unitarian belief in innate goodness, the value of education, the power of reason, and a concern to preserve a newly-won respectability. The 'Lit. and Phil.', with its demanding, questioning, and properly disrespectful approach to new ideas and theories, completed an institutional trio well able to encourage the intellectual progress of a gifted boy.

Family life was a constant. Its context was change: a recently-legalized faith, a reconstituted grammar school, fresh ideas, new addresses in a city itself reflecting the moving age through wholesale demolition. The effects upon Forster were two-fold. Firstly, life in Newcastle gave him enduring qualities of honesty, duty, loyalty and integrity, that concern to further 'all that was just, noble & good' noticed by Whiteside when in Amos's law class. Secondly, to such qualities he added a passionate responsiveness to new opportunities in a changing world. When he defended the theatre as a force for national moral good, central principles of his upbringing were seen in action, whilst his interest in the theatre was *in itself* evidence of independent thinking. His rejection of Cambridge for London was the rejection of one respectable training, in the classics, for another, in the law. Rejecting law for literature, though a more extreme move, was in the end similar in kind: Forster took his values with him. It was particularly appropriate that he should become a critic concerned to judge new works in terms of established standards, that he rejected literary bohemia and began, immediately, to work for the greater social acceptability of literary men. Forster was partly the daring rebel but he was mainly the radical conservative.

As Whiteside's comment shows, Forster's London friends were quick to see his virtues, but even his friends, let alone his enemies, were also aware of his northern accent, rawness of manner, and oddness of dress. He was a butcher's son from a provincial city who, through intelligence and his uncle, had escaped a life like that of his brother Christopher's, a slow settling into clerkdom on Tyneside wharves. His social disadvantages and the narrowness of that escape gave Forster a desperate ambition that made him push and strain and antagonize, but never to compromise his principles.

On the contrary, when he arrived in London he demonstrated a careless integrity. His first review, for the *Newcastle Magazine*, that lambasted luminaries, attacked the 'noble condescension' of aristocratic contributors and the 'indelicacy' and 'dullness' of *The Keepsake*'s editor, Frederick Mansel Reynolds, showed an utter disregard for the susceptibilities, not to mention the powers of patronage, of such metropolitan sophisticates – granted that they were hardly regular readers of Mitchell's magazine. Forster's major concern in that review with the public reputation of writers is another early pointer to the theme that, with an appropriate Macreadian variation, links and dominates his first four important friendships.

It must be emphasized that these were not the opportunistic contacts of a young man on the make, but true relationships despite the differences in age. These differences (Forster was 9 years younger than Bulwer, 19 than Macready, 28 than Hunt, 37 than Lamb) may well have intensified affinity. Though there were obvious benefits to be gained from friendship with the famous, those seem less important than the fellow-feeling that in all four cases at times came close to love. And that Forster, in the first flush of London living, should attach himself to older men, to those four and to others such as B. W. Procter, James Whiteside and James Emerson (respectively 25, and in both latter cases 8, years older) points clearly to a basic loneliness that later events were to aggravate. Yet the friendships did not simply counter Forster's predicament. He needed them to express the urge to serve that was central to his open-heartedness, to his desire to improve and to support that his Unitarianism had heightened. Forster needed to be befriended *and* he needed to be a friend.

Through these early friendships Forster had access to family life, as Robert Lytton's surrogate father, and as an ever-welcome member of Macready's household. The eagerness with which he seized these chances shows the nature of his London loneliness. Further, and crucially, his four friends themselves provided a substitute family, a reconstruction in a sense of the life he had lost on leaving Newcastle. Lamb and Macready were substitute parents, Bulwer a brotherly equal, Hunt, in practice, a 'younger' and feckless child. They all purveyed a romanticism, stressing sincerity and emotional truth, that in itself encouraged the expression of feelings. Also, they combined to influence Forster's concern with literary dignity and social status, as a quartet perfect for the purpose. Lamb, soon dead, persisted as the idealized memory of what a literary man should be; Bulwer and Macready were both obsessed with the problem of 'dignity' and prickly with social selfconsciousness; Leigh Hunt was the great example of the predicament from which literary genius had to be rescued. As family, pressure group, and composite example, the four eminent figures formed a complex of relationships that drew from Forster a profound involvement, friendship expressed as emotional and professional kinship. As he began his professional career he burned with caring zeal to improve the lot of literature.

Upbringing and friendships together created a Forster seemingly full of confidence and drive. He was secure in his religious faith and not afraid to show it. 'Only one Sunday more', he wrote from out-of-town to W. J. Fox, whose services he attended, '& I shall be listening *once* more to the purest thoughts and great religious morality left to this latter Easter of ours.'[3] And to Mrs Cattermole, when invited to attend her son's baptism: 'May he prove worthy of the name – and of that title to a treasure in the skies with which it will invest him.'[4] He later added a Cattermole child to an ever-lengthening list of godchildren in the families of Dickens, Macready, Elwin, and Henry Morley. He was a constant self-improver: 'I dine here at home', he wrote to W. J. Fox, '– fall asleep for an hour after dinner – wake up and read Milton's *Paradise Lost* – which I am going through for study sake!'[5]

Forster was pious and studious, but he was also intensely gay and above all gregarious. In Burton Street he entertained frequently; in 58 Lincoln's Inn Fields, where he rented one large room in 1834, dinners were sent in from a nearby hotel, accompanied by lavish amounts of wine.[6] Eating out was equally convivial: 'I have the bill here to show you', Forster wrote ruefully to Peter Cunningham, 'if you wish to know how many bottles of wine we dispatched in an incredibly short space of time – !'[7] Holidays were high-spirited jaunts; Maclise recalled that Forster at Tintagel, oblivious of steep cliffs and dangerous paths, 'in the manner of a tricksy spirit & stout Ariel actually danced up & down before me'.[8] At one of Procter's parties Forster performed a comic dance in the role of Cupid,[9] at Macready's he swept Jane Carlyle off her feet and into the dancing.[10] Strenuous leisure was a safety-valve, much needed to prevent moments when vehemence turned to violent anger, as when Forster's argument with Douglas Jerrold about acting ended with scuffling, a chase, and the hurling, by Forster at Jerrold, of a full water-jug.[11]

This explosive passion co-existed with much kindness, particularly to children. Forster would dress as a magician's assistant (to Dickens's magician) in 'blazing red' and 'jolly mask'[12] for Twelfth Night celebrations, or become president and supplier of a balloon club for Dickens's family.[13] Gibbs, the 'reading-boy' for the *Examiner*'s printers, remembered how thoughtful Forster could be, how he banned a bully from his office because Gibbs's hair had been pulled. Though he seemed fierce he was 'the last man to think of'[14] dismissing any of the younger staff.

That tender heart had romantic inclinations. He wrote teasing letters to the wives of friends, as to Mrs Blanchard about her devoted husband: 'You must no longer call that little perfidious S. L. B. "Jack" or Sam or any other such familiar and loving name, for he is wholly unworthy of you ... I have just detected him in writing to a lady whom he terms "My dearest Eliza". I have done the duty of a friend – my heart bleeds for it, but ... Comment were useless.'[15] Horne noticed him as something of a lady's man, with a gentle and tender manner towards them.[16] Thackeray wrote in his diary, in a manner not wholly satirical, of an excursion on the river: 'Forster was prodigious in his banter and talk to the ladies perfectly confounding them with the power and splendor of his oratory'.[17] Above all, there was 'L.E.L.' with whom friendship for a while became love.

Letitia Elizabeth Landon – the fact can almost be anticipated – was ten years older than Forster. Writing as 'L.E.L.' she was an established literary figure when Forster met her. Her poetry, five volumes of which had appeared during the 1820s, had led some to mistake her for a second Byron; she wrote criticism for the *New Monthly Magazine*, was a pillar of the *Literary Gazette* as a protégé of its editor, William Jerdan, knew Bulwer well and was close to Laman Blanchard. She was no beauty: in her looks as in her work she was more elegant goose than graceful swan; but her surviving correspondence does offer some clues as to why Forster was attracted. Letitia Landon had an interest in private theatricals, encouraged aspiring writers, had an all-embracing literary enthusiasm, and on the appropriate occasion a briskly businesslike approach that must have appealed to her admirer:

> I enclose the lines for Tivoli – and shall be obliged by proofs of my contribution as my M.S. has been hastily written, and is not at best very plain.
>
> With regard to what you say respecting the remuneration for these pieces, I shall certainly observe silence; but without being mercenary, it was absolutely necessary for me to state these terms, and further to request a check by return for the amount, as I must for various reasons pass it through the hands of my publishers, to show them I have acted on the same principle to all the annuals.[18]

The friendship flourished; Forster squired her to the theatre and took her to visit the Lambs.[19] At this time he was by no means negligible as a beau but was, as W. J. Fox wrote, 'a tall, ardent, noticeable young fellow'.[20] Lady Blessington liked him 'exceedingly...he is very clever, and, what is better, very noble-minded'.[21] Dark, with thick hair and intense eyes, already the friend of the famous, Forster swung through literary London with the poetess on his arm.

She was not there for very long. In November 1833 Forster told Macready that he had been 'on the point of marriage with Miss L—'[22] when he had heard rumours of her scandalous conduct. He pressed a rumour-monger, Alaric Watts, for an explanation, was dissatisfied with what he heard, and then confronted 'L.E.L.' herself. She was appalled both at the rumours and at Forster's attitude. After the meeting she wrote two letters, one of them to Bulwer, always a close friend. To him she vigorously protested her innocence and equally vigorously declared her determination to break with Forster:

> If his future protection is to harass and humiliate me as much as his present – God keep me from it ... I cannot get over the entire want of delicacy to me which could repeat such a slander to myself ... I am sure we never could be happy together. He is clever, honourable, kind; but he is quite deficient in the sensitiveness to the feelings of another which is to me an indespensable requisite. I bitterly regret what has passed and any pain my determination may inflict upon him ...[23]

Her second letter, to Forster, was even more emotional:

> I can find nothing to justify my being the object of such pain; but that is not what I meant to say. Again I repeat that I will not allow you to consider yourself bound to me by any possible tie. To any friend to whom you may have stated our engagement, I cannot object to your stating the truth ... The more I think – the more I feel I ought not – I cannot – allow you to unite yourself with one accused of – I cannot write it. The mere suspicion is dreadful as death.[24]

This decline into melodrama may mark a lack of frankness, the letter an attempt to retain her fiancé by seeming to sacrifice herself for his sake. What is certain is that, whether sincerely or as part of a misconceived strategy, 'L.E.L.' did the breaking-off in the face of 'notes'[25] from Forster asserting, as 'Father Prout' considered many years later, that 'he was perfectly willing to carry it out',[26] to go through with the marriage. In the event, and perhaps, for 'L.E.L.', with unexpected alacrity, Forster accepted the force of her argument and withdrew from the engagement. Only then did he learn more about the rumours: that there purported to be documentary evidence of an immoral liaison with William Maginn, that she had propositioned Daniel Maclise, and even associated, compromisingly, with Bulwer. But though Macready reported to his Diary with vehement solemnity, 'She is fallen!',[27] it has never been clearly established either what was true or what Forster discovered to be true. All that can be said is that her literary career was never again so buoyant, that in June 1838 she married George Maclean, governor of the Gold Coast, returned with him to Africa, wrote cheerful letters home about continuing her literary career and about the problems of housekeeping at Cape Coast Castle ('if any one would steal the plate – which must be cleaned – and the mahogany table – which must be polished – I should be very comfortable'),[28] and died of poison in October 1838, either by accident, or by her own hand, or by another's. At the time of her death she was 36. The affair lingered on into the 1840s, in the occasional magazine article and in the correspondence of surviving friends. As late as 1866 'Father Prout' was recalling, rather confusedly, the whole sad business and protesting her innocence,[29] as her friends always did.

For Forster affectionate remembrance persisted. In 1845 the *Examiner* reviewed Hawthorn's *Journal of an African Cruiser* and extracted a description of her grave with a reference to unfounded rumours about the way she died.[30] Three years later, during Forster's editorship, he added a footnote to Dickens's review of W. Allen's *Narrative of the Niger*

Expedition: 'Most English readers will be as unwilling as the manly writers of these volumes, to leave one spot at Cape Coast Castle, without a word of remembrance.'[31] In the same year he wrote to Leigh Hunt of Jane Carlyle's friend, Geraldine Jewsbury, that she was a 'young girl wonderfully like poor Miss Landon in manner & appearance'.[32] As the years went by, particularly given Forster's capacity for potent nostalgia, as seen for instance in his reaction to Macready's second marriage, the dead poetess buried in a far corner of the Empire served to remind Forster of lost romantic hope. Until 1856, as his friends settled and their families increased, Forster remained a bachelor. Occasionally a suppressed sexuality emerged semi-facetiously: 'Say, at 5 oclock:' he wrote to Ainsworth, arranging to dine, 'for I will take you to see a *wonderful* actress and most fascinating woman (with whom your unhappy friend is over head & ears in love)'.[33] A more revealing reaction, one redolent of Forster's emotional and physical frustrations, was his response to the appearance of Mrs Manning at her public execution:

> Since this letter was begun I have seen the Mannings hanged! I never witnessed such a sight which I think a man ought to undergo once, for his soul's sake – as he goes through meazles for his body. You should have seen this woman ascend the drop, blindfold, and with [a] black lace veil over her face – with a step as firm as if she had been walking to a feast. She was *beautifully dressed*, every part of her noble figure finely and fully expressed by close fitting black satin, spotless white collar round her neck low enough to admit the rope without its removal, and gloves on her manicured hands. She stood while the rope was adjusted as steadily as the scaffold itself, and when flung off, seemed to die at once. But there was nothing hideous in her as she swung to and fro afterward. The wretch beside her was as a filthy shapeless scarecrow – she had lost nothing of her graceful aspect! ... this is heroine-worship, I think![34]

Immunization, if such it was, proved ineffective: a month later, Forster added:

> After I wrote to you about that extd criminal – the woman Manning, I heard what fell from her as she stood on the drop. 'Mind you do your work well!' she said to the hangman as he adjusted the rope. 'Nothing, but to thank you for much kindness' she said to the parson, as he advanced to ask if she had anything to say, hoping she might *then* confess. Then – when he had retired – she called to the surgeon, who had led her (blindfold) up the

> scaffold, and said these words – the last she spoke on this earth. 'I am poorly, at present; I trust to you that it shall not be made known.' It was true – and she had obtained a clean napkin not 10 minutes before she ascended the drop. A sensitive cleanliness of body seems to have been her passion – and the doctor who exd [examined] the bodies after death, and who said he had never seen so beautiful a figure, compared her feet to those of a marble statue.[35]

He was attracted towards Mrs Gaskell's friend, Emily Winkworth,[36] and at some point before 1856 proposed to and was refused by Dickens's sister-in-law, Georgina Hogarth,[37] with whom for the rest of his life he remained a close friend.

Forster's failure to marry, given his love of family life and of children, compounded that basic loneliness behind his friendship with older men. He remained solitary, for most of his time, and far from home. Mitchell wrote occasionally, introducing visitors from Newcastle and asking for news.[38] Forster kept in touch with Mrs Blackett, a family friend.[39] Elder brother Christopher made the odd visit. And, one by one, the family died. Forster's father, always a shadowy figure, went as early as 1836, when Macready commented that Forster 'did not seem much distressed'[40] and certainly did not rush home. On Christmas Eve 1844 Christopher died suddenly in a Newcastle office and a grieving Forster, though in poor health, left quickly for the Newcastle funeral. He was much put down and on his return to London drew from Dickens the emotional assurance that 'you have a Brother left. One bound to you by ties as strong as ever Nature forged'.[41] In 1852 Forster's mother, then well into her 70s, was the next to go, and followed a year later by two further blows. In August 1853 his uncle died: 'My best friend all through life. I hope I have not ill repaid his kindness to me. A true good man', Forster wrote in his diary.[42] A month later came the turn of his sister Jane: 'I have had another great sorrow since we met', he told Bulwer, '– the sudden death of a very dear sister in painful circumstances – attacked by this frightful pestilence of cholera. I knew nothing till all was over.'[43] By 1855 only Elizabeth, the governess, remained alive.

Forster himself was in poor health. Even in the 1830s some felt he might not live long. Though he could joke about minor ailments, as when he told W. J. Fox of being 'tortured nigh to madness with a toothache which ambitiously aspires to the dignity of a sort of tic doloureux', others became impossible to laugh away. Rheumatism caused him much pain and at times prevented him writing or feeding himself; his social progress was littered with cancelled engagements. In 1846 work on the *Daily News* left him looking 'very ill'. Five years later ill health helped force him to withdraw from provincial performances of *Not So Bad As We Seem*. The following year, 1852, he was confined to bed with 'inflammatory rheumatism'. Rheumatic fever immobilized him for two months during the winter of 1853. In the early 1850s that rheumatism, combined with bronchitis, began to drive him from London: he stayed at Brighton in September 1852. After five months' illness, in 1853 he was '*at the Garth Hotel on Hampstead Heath* ... I drove about so much, to try & invigorate myself with country air'. Dickens perceptively linked Forster's ill-health and his loneliness: 'Poor Forster ... I wish to God he would marry somebody and not be ill by himself in that howling Mansion.'[44]

Money was never plentiful. Until 1847, when he became editor of the *Examiner* for £500 *per annum*, Forster's main income came from reviewing for that journal: 'The Exr money was the living money – the publisher paid it weekly £4 – then £5, then £6 ... often & often was this sum or a portion of it anticipated in advance of the Saturday'.[45] From 1850 he received, on average, a further £210 *per annum* from his share in *Household Words*.[46] Forster was never poor during his career as a journalist, but neither was he ever comfortable.

Nor was he socially at ease. In 1834 the Garrick Club committee censured him for reporting the club's private functions. 'He seemed annoyed at his own defect of judgement', noted Macready. The following year, at the club's annual dinner, he drank too much and was violently sick in Talfourd's pocket. He was prone to serious gestures of comically respectable piety, as when, at rehearsals for the stage adaptation of *The Battle of Life* in 1846, he provided refreshments for the cast and with food left over instructed his servant 'to find out very poor women and institute close enquiry into their life, conduct, and behaviour before leaving any sandwiches for them'. In politics his general moderation could be punctuated by a radical outburst, as in 1848, when he wrote exuberantly to Leigh Hunt, 'What events in France! ... Vive la République!' Yet contact with aristocratic society, such as his friendship with Lord Nugent, and his appearances at the Gore House *salon* of Lady Blessington and Count D'Orsay, could dazzle him. 'Called on Forster', wrote Macready in 1836, 'whom I found full of Eton and aristocracy.' The well-known story of D'Orsay at dinner, the dilatory waiter, and Forster the host's cadenced order, 'Gracious heaven! waiter – a slice of cold butter for the flounders of the Count', is an obvious expression of public nervousness.[47]

As might be expected, such unease inspired defensive manoeuvres. One such was his decision to be called to the Bar in 1843. There were other reasons for this, as will be seen, but one was certainly social. As Philip Collins puts it, 'The title of barrister was, among other things, a certificate of gentility.'[48] Forster never practised but constantly used the title: his biography of Goldsmith was by 'John Forster, Barrister-at-Law', his book-plate was inscribed 'John Forster of the Inner Temple'. Equally defensive is his letter to Bulwer early in 1850:

> Many thanks for your kindness about the portfolio – but how to get the arms coloured without applying to Heralds Office, and how to dare face those Garters and Griffyns and Lyons with so limited a claim to a pedigree as mine – the Lord only knows. Supposing I sent the Bugle and Flag (the old Forester and Borderer arms – to which I believe my right is perfectly established) and left the colours to the artist? If he made me 'azure fretty argent' or 'bugle horns sable garnished', or exactly the reverse of the colours they would in nature, I fancy it would be all right!![49]

Forster's concern here was with his book-plate, which incorporated the arms and the strangely appropriate motto, 'Follow Me'. The excitable tone betrays slight embarrassment, the insistence his social determination.

His uncertainty was most often expressed by an attempt to dominate. All did not react as considerately as Tennyson, in begging Forster not to be offended at not being told of the poet's marriage,[50] or as genially as Thackeray who, when telling Mrs Procter of a mutual friend's loss of money, added, 'Forster knows nothing of this – and I do not think we any of us dare suffer a loss without his knowing of it'.[51] A friend like Macready recognized Forster's virtues and clearly understood why he acted as he did; he wrote, shrewdly, in 1840: 'Forster ... assumed a supercilious tone before people to give the idea that he was the patron, or *padrone*'.[52] Other friends, such as Robert Browning and Dickens, reacted to Forster's high hand with violent anger and dreadful quarrels. Those who were not friends were swift and eager with snobbish ridicule and vicious envy. Forster had the true friend's gift of making many enemies.

One such was suitably inspired by Forster's behaviour at the Garrick: R. H. Barham's annotations on the members' list recalled 1835 and Talfourd's provision of a post-prandial pocket. He wrote opposite Forster's name:

> A low scribbler without an atom of talent and totally unused to the Society of Gentlemen. He narrowly escaped expulsion from publishing an account of a dinner at the Garrick in a Newspaper to which he was a Reporter. The Committee wrote him a letter on the

> occasion expressive of their disgust which would have caused any other man to retire. About a year after he got beastly drunk at the anniversary Club dinner, and was sick in Serjeant Talfourd's pocket. Tom Duncombe got drunk at the same time but behaved so differently that Poole observed one was the real Gentleman drunk, the other the Spewrious Gentleman drunk.[53]

Poole, for whose financial benefit Forster later acted with the Guild of Literature and Art, attacked again two years later with an article in *The Times* that satirized Forster's critical style. For others he was 'J. Forster, the butcher-boy'. J. P. Collier, looking back through his letters from Forster, inserted malicious endorsements: 'This was when he only assumed equality' (1832), 'This was when he was assuming the superior man and patron' (1841), and, the Forster-haters' refrain, 'Forster at this period ... took upon himself the character of *patron* – the butcher's son who had come to London so poor and so pitiable' (1846). The American press described him as 'the toady of Sir E. L. Bulwer and Mr. Macready'. As late as 1862 the wits at *Punch's* table talked of him as 'a snob – never at ease among gentlemen ... JL would like to show him beside butcher's block crying Buy Buy!!'[54]

In 1848 came James Prior's onslaught. Twelve years previously he had published a biography of Goldsmith that had been attacked by Forster in an *Examiner* review. Now, as Forster published *The Life and Adventures of Oliver Goldsmith*, Prior wrote alleging plagiarism and made the allegations public in the correspondence columns of the *Literary Gazette*.[55] The charge was effectively rebutted. Forster had used some of Prior's factual discoveries but as part of an original interpretation: the new biography took as its theme the necessary 'dignity of literature' and used Goldsmith's impoverished progress to make an impassioned plea for the better treatment of literary men. A second letter from Prior repeated the charge and then revealed the real source of his animosity. Prior insisted on the superiority to Forster's of previous lives of Goldsmith, the best being that by Mitford, 'a scholar and a gentleman'. Forster's book, he continued, was merely an expanded notice originally refused by the *Edinburgh Review*, and its success, through plagiarism, was due to blatant 'puffing' by the press on behalf of one of its members. If such behaviour was encouraged, wrote Prior, 'we shall be obliged to add a new class to the order of literary men, and the *swell mob of the press* become as notorious as the swell mob of another description'.[56] The dispute lasted into the 1850s; when Forster's second and extended edition appeared in 1854 Prior was again roused and Forster aggressive: 'But be his temper as "gentlemanly" at present as Beau Brummel's own', he wrote to Peter Cunningham, 'I am afraid I shall ruffle it not a little'.[57] The simple snobbery, mainly, plus some jealousy, behind most attacks on Forster are understandable, though no less cruel for that. Prior's reaction demonstrates that Forster was additionally disadvantaged through his choice of profession. Newspaper writers were low, scholars were gentlemen. Forster's scholarly aspirations were thus also social. Inevitably they aroused the mindless fury of the traditionalists.

John Forster was a man whose natural passion, energy, and principled gregariousness were often constricted, during the period to 1855, by loneliness, poor health, lack of means, social unease, and the assaults of hostile contemporaries. During his early years in London his close friendships with Hunt, Lamb, Bulwer, and Macready, allowed him to escape these constrictions by giving him much-needed opportunities to express pent-up affection, tenderness, and care. The main friendships that followed, with Robert Browning, Landor, Dickens, and, especially, with Thomas Carlyle, provided similar compensation. But that first quartet, and to some extent the later associations, also nurtured almost to obsession that concern with the status of literature given him already by the upbringing that fostered, in particular, his innate conservatism, desire for advancement, and impulse to serve. And though the eight major friendships are special, intense, large-scale instances of near-obsession in action, they did not fully satisfy that overwhelming impulse. Rather, in this period, it overflowed into a general concern for the whole estate of literature, a concern that informed activities so multifarious that it is difficult to believe Forster to have been one man and not a team. Forster was Literature's Friend. His fierce concern for its well-being, which of course included his own, made him give himself freely. In return he expected, from all *literati*, sound principles and a shared professional love.

CHAPTER 7 *Friendship's Variations 1834–55*

Central to Forster's friendship was hospitality at 58 Lincoln's Inn Fields, where, during the years after 1834, he gradually extended his quarters. He rented two additional rooms at the front, in one of which he built up his collection of books. At this stage it was a splendid working library, Forster buying what he needed to further his constant study of literary history and commonwealth affairs, until 'every inch of wall grew covered with books – later on the little passage also – then the small bedroom & two rooms taken on third floor for Bedroom & Bathroom these also were filled'.

Thus surrounded, he began each day with a cold bath, and breakfast of tea, a hot roll, new laid egg and piece of bacon. On Saturdays and Sundays he would receive at breakfast anyone known to him or who had letters of introduction, and among those who came were not only his close friends – a group that included those major figures already mentioned, and W. J. Fox, T. N. Talfourd, Douglas Jerrold, and the artists George Cattermole and Daniel Maclise – but also almost every other literary figure in England and America. Most brought their problems; as Rawlins recalled, Forster 'was always being consulted by some one or other as to books for review or publication – or as to Dramas for the Theatres – any author in difficulty as to a publisher or manager seemed to come to Lincoln's Inn as a matter of course'.[1] They came to an adviser who was honest, worldly, trained as a lawyer, and toughly committed to their well-being. What Forster did for close friends is described in other chapters; what must be stressed here is that he brought the same painstaking enthusiasm to the problems of less intimate friends and acquaintances.

One such was B. W. Procter, friendly from Forster's first days in London. Forster helped provide material for Procter's *Life of Kean*, and worked on *Ion* and *The Athenian Captive*. When *Examiner* editor, Forster gave Procter reviewing work and published many of his poems.[2] He helped Peter Cunningham, in another early and long-continuing friendship, to correct proofs, as he did in 1850, probably for the second edition of Cunningham's *Handbook of London*, and supplied additional material. 'I am sorry you have not let me help you more', he wrote with masochistic benevolence in 1853.[3] Sheridan Knowles came frequently from the early 1830s. Forster advised during the writing of his plays, as he did on *The Bridal* in 1834 and *Woman's Wit* four years later, when he also provided the title; he recommended them to Macready, arranged terms and negotiated benefit-nights.[4] He did similar work for Douglas Jerrold who, from 1834 onwards, asked Forster to place his work with publishers.[5] Lady Blessington was yet another seeking assistance: Forster introduced her to Chapman & Hall, advised her when she negotiated with them, and offered frequent advice on her work. He found her contributors for the 'Annuals' she edited, and helped her become 'Society' correspondent of the *Daily News*.[6]

In 1843 Thomas Hood resigned the editorship of the *New Monthly Magazine*, only for its publisher, Henry Colburn, to insist on Hood's contractual obligations to continue as a contributor. Hood asked Forster to represent him and though Forster's meetings with Colburn failed to release Hood they drew from Colburn very generous terms for Hood's future work.[7] Three years later, in 1846, Forster was acting for James White, the clergyman-playwright. For him Forster arranged terms with Samuel Phelps for White's tragedy, *Feudal Times*, and a year later had similar discussions about White's play *John Savile*; he was less successful in pushing *The White Rose* in the same direction.[8] Neither could he interest Phelps in a play by G. H. Lewes, through he did find work for Lewes with Richard Bentley.[9] That was in 1848, the year in which he also met Geraldine Jewsbury, who looked like 'L.E.L.', Carlyle noted the attention Forster paid to her first novel, *Half-Sisters*: 'He read it through, cut objectionable things out of it, prepared it with much pains, as one could see, for the press, and it got read and talked about in London drawing-rooms.'[10]

Forster was as concerned with minor writers as with the major figures. No-one could be more minor than Geraldine Jewsbury, except perhaps Sir Frederick Pollock's eldest son, whose translation of Dante Forster took to Richard Bentley,[11] or Lord Denham, whose work Forster placed with Chapman & Hall:

> I was in town as usual on Friday and thought it worth while to call on Chapman & Halls to ask if they would publish it. *They will do*

> *so at their own risk*, giving Lord Denham half the profits; and will produce it in the best way possible – for I made a point to stipulate all that, as to paper, type, etc. They would place it in Bradbury & Evans' hand to print.
>
> Now I do not know if this would be worth Ld Denham's while, but it strikes me as a better & more dignified plan than that of receiving a sum of money (which would be necessarily small) for an Edition... They (C. & H.) would do in all respects what might be desired as to form, price, advertisements, & so forth ...[12]

The letter has interest as a further example of Forster's part in changing publishing practice from lump-sum payments to forms of continuing income, but it is more valuable here in demonstrating why Forster was so prized as an adviser and agent with an expert knowledge of publishing and a willingness verging on the reckless to give his time and attention. Henry Morley, who became a close friend and succeeded Forster as *Examiner* editor, was a further beneficiary. Forster brought him on to the *Examiner* in 1850, put his articles in order, taught him his journalistic trade, helped him prepare his 'Nursery' papers for publication, found him a publisher, and himself revised Morley's *The Defence of Ignorance.* 'Forster', wrote the grateful Morley, 'is a first-rate man, generous and high-minded.'[13]

Such relationships with this gaggle of minor writers and enthusiastic amateurs are, we can be certain, only the known and documented selection from an even more crowded life. They are simple instances of Forster's open-heartedness. More complex, because more revealing of the 'high-mindedness' of Morley's comment, of the strong principles ordering his friendships, are links with three writers of far greater substance: Tennyson, Longfellow, and Mrs Gaskell.

Forster met Tennyson in 1839,[14] having been his early and understanding reviewer[15] and having corresponded with him when raising a subscription for Leigh Hunt.[16] Thus all had begun with Forster's admiration of Tennyson's work, an admiration given full, and near-fulsome, expression in a letter from Forster written seven years later: 'You ... have given me so much pleasure – who are indeed a part of the pleasure of my life (how little in all!) which alone is constant & unfailing.'[17] In this extract Forster's pleasure in the poetry shades into his pleasure in Tennyson the man and so reflects the friendship's progress. Forster admired the poetry and wrote about it in reviews that always encouraged but were never uncritical. He was, for example, alive to the self-indulgence of Tennyson's early work and commended his move to sharper, more publicly acceptable work in *Poems 1842*. The theme of Forster's reviews is

Tennyson's capacity to be 'the poet of our time', to be, in a sense, the Macready of poetry, and certainly an 'unacknowledged legislator'. 'Why does he not assume his mission?'[18] Forster asked in a review of *The Princess*, when criticizing part of the subject matter. Tennyson, generally, took note: 'We have heard of ... Alfred Tennyson being found with a copy of *The Examiner* beside him, labouring to modify expressions which had incurred its formal censure',[19] wrote Francis Espinasse. And the poet frequently sought Forster's opinion.

Out of such mutual respect emerged mutual regard. Whenever he came to London Tennyson called on Forster and became a frequent dinner guest; Forster did the occasional small favour, such as paying Tennyson's rent,[20] and had a part in Tennyson's private life. Though there is a comic side to the well-known incident of Forster taking offence at Tennyson marrying without telling him, that offence does indicate the extent to which he felt he was in Tennyson's confidence. The care Tennyson subsequently took to keep Forster in touch with family developments confirms their intimacy. This side of the friendship is another instance of Forster's need for vicarious domestic entanglements, and a further example of a friend prizing his concern: Tennyson was 'grateful' for Forster's company following the stillbirth of the Tennysons' first child.[21] A letter from Forster in 1854, referring to Tennyson's wife and marriage, not only shows how, for Forster, envy was absent and lack and longing fuelled friendship, but also demonstrates his depth of feeling for the Laureate:

> Hold me in your love and remembrance, my dear A.T., for you & she are much in mine. In the midst of this whirling life I lead here I have sense enough to feel how much better is the life you lead, and thoroughly to rejoice in the happiness which the wisest act of your life has secured to you.[22]

The affection and trusting respect returned by the Tennysons is nowhere better seen than in the period from 1846 to 1854, when Tennyson wrote many occasional poems that needed prompt placing in the journals. Thus, in 1846, when Bulwer anonymously criticized Tennyson in *The New Timon*, Tennyson forwarded to Forster a counter-attack, 'The New Timon, and the Poets'. Forster, despite his friendship with Bulwer, sent the poem to *Punch*. He did so for a number of reasons. One, almost certainly, was because Tennyson asked him to place it. Others are given in Forster's review of the second part of Bulwer's poem:

> There is an attack on Alfred Tennyson's poems in this part. We are sorry for it, in a writer who has given us pleasure; because not to

> appreciate the thoughtful music of Tennyson, is not to be capable of a rare enjoyment ... We would not recal [*sic*] Mr. Tennyson's pension, if we could; we believe it a deserved tribute, and warranted by some peculiar circumstances ...[23]

The 'peculiar circumstances' included the well-known details of Tennyson's ill-health, family problems, and financial difficulties; Forster may well have felt Bulwer to have misrepresented Tennyson's position. But Bulwer's attack was most resented by Forster because it was an attack on literary quality. Such resentment made him further the publication of Tennyson's counter, partly by acting, typically, as go-between for the poet and for *Punch*'s editor, Forster's friend Mark Lemon. Thus Forster wrote to Tennyson on 18 February 1846:

> I enclose the proof. The poem will appear in next week's *Punch*. Send me the proof back with your corrections – by next post.
>
> You will see a query at the last stanza but one. It is suggested by *Punch*'s Editor, who thinks the touch of rouge not in keeping with the rest. Perhaps those four lines *might* be modified or omitted. But the matter is left wholly to you ...

The same letter continued with further explanation for Forster's support:

> My share in this [the poem's publication], dear Tennyson, is explained by the first note I wrote you. I think it an act of Justice – one of those solemn & terrible expiations with which personal likings or dislikings have really nothing to do. I should never have ceased to reproach myself, if I had attempted to obstruct its publication. I should have felt myself a constant traitor to you – who have given me so much pleasure ... Have I any right to arrest what is lifted in Self Defence by one whom I love & honour as I do you?[24]

Letter and review make the same central point: Forster ranked his friendship for literature above that for any individual writer.

The following year Forster became editor of the *Examiner*. During his editorship he published six poems by his friend. 'To —',[25] is an attack on prying literary biography possibly occasioned by Lord Houghton's *Letters and Literary Remains of Keats* (1848). A group of four poems – 'Britons, Guard Your Own', 'The Third of February, 1852', 'Hands All Round', and 'Suggested by Reading an Article in a Newspaper'[26] – were inspired by the *coup d'état* of Louis Napoleon and the House of Lords' refusal to organize militia in case Louis attacked Britain. They are cutting, aggressive, slightly hysterical poems full of anti-Catholic feelings, appeals to America to rise against tyranny, and to the press to be properly responsible by making 'opinion warlike'.[27] In 1854 came 'The Charge of the Light Brigade'[28] and its celebration of heroism.

Editorial correspondence was handled by Emily Tennyson and the occasional correction left to Forster. 'May we beg if the accent in Paerio be on the i "wrong'd" may be erased',[29] Mrs Tennyson wrote of 'Hands All Round', and Forster confirmed the correctness of Tennyson's pronunciation. He played a greater part in agreeing the final version, in the *Examiner*, of 'The Charge of the Light Brigade', and began by answering affirmatively the essential question raised by Tennyson's wife: 'Alfred has just bid me say he begs you will by no means put the ballad in if you do not think it good'.[30] The decisions that followed made the poem, to some extent, Forster's as well as Tennyson's. 'If you think that Stanza crossed out "Half a league, half a league" would begin the poem better than the present beginning will you put it please?'[31] wrote Emily Tennyson. The 'present beginning'

Into the jaws of Death
Rode the six hundred,
For up came an order which
Some one had blunder'd

was thus replaced by the effective vehemence of the now-famous opening that had been the opening in an earlier draft.[32] The following day Tennyson sent a 'final' version with a postscript from his wife asking Forster whether an explanatory note should be printed with the poem. Forster approved, and inserted: 'Written after reading the first report of the *Times*' correspondent, where only 607 sabres are mentioned as having taken part in the charge.' Two days later came the final 'final request': 'I have corrected "Flash'd all their/Flash'd all at once" wh. you can adopt if you have time, & if you approve it'.[33] Forster had and did. The poem was published and, amidst much criticism, both of its subject matter and of its style, Forster remained certain of its worth. He wrote movingly to its author:

> How I value this noble ballad, I need not say – how proud I am to print it first, & that my old friend sent it to me, I *must* say. I hear little of you, but again & again I think of you, & never have I done it so often as of late – never, with a throbbing heart, have read of those fights & heroes at Alma, Balaklava, and Inkermann, that I have not been eager for *you* to celebrate them – the only man that

> can do it up to their own pitch – the only 'muse of fire' now left to us that can of right extend to the level of such deeds.[34]

All that remained to be done, during 1855, was to arrange for copies of the poem to be distributed to the troops abroad. This, as his final task, Forster did.[35]

Dickens met Longfellow in America during 1842, as Longfellow prepared to visit Europe, and invited him to stay at Devonshire Terrace later that year. Dickens returned to England with a volume of Longfellow's poems for Forster to read.[36] Forster met the poet in October 1842, entertained him, and accompanied him, with Dickens and Maclise, to the theatre to see Macready, through London's slums, through Kent, and to Bath to visit Landor.[37] Longfellow remembered all with affection,[38] and was himself remembered with Forsterian open-heartedness: 'I think of you often, often stretch my hand out to you across that waste of waters, often recall those few delightful days which gave me a friend I so much esteem and whose thoughts I am glad to keep so much about me'.[39] The last phrases have familiar significance: Forster's admiration of Longfellow's work was the source from which the personal friendship flowed. The two exchanged books: *Poems on Slavery* for Forster, *The Life and Adventures of Oliver Goldsmith* for Longfellow in 1848. Each encouraged and complimented the other. Forster did so in *Examiner* reviews and, describing Longfellow as 'unquestionably the first of her poets', exempted him from a general attack on 'American Poetry' in the *Foreign Quarterly Review*.[40] In 1851 Longfellow asked Forster to arrange terms with his London publisher, David Bogue, for *The Golden Legend*. To Longfellow's satisfaction Forster was able to transmit £100 to his American friend.[41]

Mrs Gaskell first entered Forster's life in 1847 when a mutual acquaintance, William Howitt, showed him the manuscript of volume one of *Mary Barton*, which Forster immediately recommended to Chapman & Hall.[42] It was then called 'John Barton' and Forster was doubtless instrumental in the change of title: the removal of a murderer from the centre of attention accorded perfectly with Forster's desire for clear-cut moral effects. With the book a great success Mrs Gaskell came to London in the spring of 1849. There she was lionized, Forster entertained her to dinner and introduced her into his circle. Mrs Gaskell, married to a famous Unitarian minister, was herself, like Forster, a Unitarian. Her father, William Stevenson, was from the North-East; as a girl, from 1829 to 1831, she had lived in Newcastle at the home of William Turner, Forster's old minister at Hanover Square chapel. They thus had much in common and found each other to be congenial acquaintances. Forster, she wrote, was '*very* fat and affected, yet *so* clever and shrewd and good-hearted and right-minded'.[43] They met, during her visits to London, until the middle 1850s, with Forster indulging her, and his own, spirited socializing:

> Mrs. Gaskell (the author of Mary Barton) is come up from Manchester on her way to Paris – and I have put up a little dinner here *at punctual 5* tonight, preparatory to a visit to the Lyceum – when the party will be, Mrs G, Mrs Dickens, Dickens, Miss Hogarth, *and Mr Cunningham*, if he will come at 5.[44]

They were regular correspondents.

With hospitality and friendship came practical help. Forster obtained a signed volume by Tennyson for Mrs Gaskell's Manchester friend, the radical poet Samuel Bamford, a grant from the Literary Fund for an aged Knutsford authoress; he published in the *Examiner* extracts from Mr Gaskell's lectures on dialect that were appended to the fifth edition of *Mary Barton*.[45] In 1851 he advised Mrs Gaskell about a price for her latest work, at a time when she became increasingly dissatisfied with Chapman's treatment of her; Forster reminded her how well *Mary Barton* had sold and counselled her: 'Assuming these facts I do not think £250 a fair offer ...'[46] By the following year he had assumed his familiar and seemingly inevitable role: the manuscript of *Ruth* was sent directly to him and he not only arranged its publication by Chapman & Hall but also did the proof-reading. Mrs Gaskell, merely the author, could only write wryly to Eliza Fox that Chapman had told her 'that Mr Forster had given him the MS. of Ruth and that the first 2 vols. *were printed*; all complete news to me!'[47] When *North and South* was serialized in *Household Words* Forster was sou[illegible] Dickens became critical Forster was qui[illegible]tily and earnestly go on with this story w[illegible][49] another instance of Forster's critical integrity outweighing friendship's claims.

In *The Life of Charles Dickens* Mrs Gaskell has two significant mentions, as 'very original' and as the author of 'delightful'[50] work. Since 1856, when Forster married, until her death in 1865, they had lost touch and it is significant that he remembered her as an author. For Forster helped her and became her friend, during the first years of her literary success, because of the nature and quality of her writing. He wrote to her of *Morton Hall*:

> Anybody but you would have made the tragedy of it unbearable but you have the art of softening this, of relieving it by little homely

> touches, and putting such a tender sweetness into it, of setting round and neighbouring it with so much quiet good-hearted humour.[51]

We might be reminded of Forster's praise of Macready's Shakespeare; in this respect the extract demonstrates the consistency of Forster's thinking. That notwithstanding, the letter is a typical example of Forster's wholehearted approval of her work seen throughout the correspondence. Thus, of *Ruth*, the theme of which – that of the seduced girl for whose predicament society is most to blame – moved into areas fraught with contemporary danger, Forster wrote: 'Well done!... I am not quite sure either if it is quite dignified in a hardened critic to confess that he has had neither more nor less than a good cry over these final chapters.'[52] 'It is a true book', Forster wrote a month later, 'beautifully thought out and written out to the end, and will do infinite good to all who by such means are capable of receiving it.'[53] When the *Cranford* papers appeared he pursued Mrs Gaskell with admiration: 'I have read your Cranford papers with delight'[54] and 'Indeed this little paper is a piece of reality which delighted me in reading',[55] are representative compliments from letters that comment on scenes and characters, and stress, above all, Forster's emotional response to their tenderness. His *Examiner* reviews of Mrs Gaskell's novels are controlled and public versions of his letters' sentiments. Forster's relationship with Mrs Gaskell is a further example of friendship developing from prior critical approval.

'Forster', wrote Thackeray, satirically and, in a sense, truthfully, 'is the greatest man I know. Great and Beneficent like a Superior Power... whenever anybody is in a scrape we all fly to him for refuge. He is omniscient and works miracles.'[56] The truth of that is certainly borne out by the stream of writers, major and minor, who brought along their problems, or who, like Emerson in 1848, and Charles Lever in 1854, came simply for hospitality, for what Longfellow called the 'brave world in No. 58, Lincoln's Inn Fields ... the fire-light, wine-light, and, friend-light indoors'.[57] Forster's home became a famous place, at once private club, library, consulting rooms and tourist attraction. Described as Tulkinghorn's chambers in *Bleak House*, ornate with plaster allegory, it assumed for some, as it did for Robert Lytton, the compelling glow of a magical cavern. 'He must see the rooms in Lincoln's Inn Fields',[58] wrote Longfellow of Thomas Appleton, soon to be his brother-in-law. Emily Winkworth wrote to her sister that 'Lily is going to dine with Mr. Forster at his chambers, and how these chambers are in the Middle Temple, a most charming place fitted up with the most beautiful editions of the most beautiful books and engravings, and easy chairs and thick carpets'.[59] In such surroundings, however uneasily financed, Forster crouched, to mix a changed metaphor, dynamo-like at the hub of London literary life. Maclise's famous drawing of the reading of *The Chimes* offers vivid illustration of his role: Forster sits outside the main circle of listeners, a background presence of burly-shouldered forcefulness who not only arranged the occasion but had also helped in the writing of the text.

At 58 Lincoln's Inn Fields Forster practised friendship as others, elsewhere, practised medicine or law. He was a good friend not only because he was a principled one – it can again be stressed that he worked to advance only those for whose work he had genuine admiration – but also because he possessed considerable helpful power. Much of this latter came of course from his reviewing and editing, but some came from his work as literary adviser to Chapman & Hall.

Here he had great authority. Dickens introduced him during the late 1830s and 'it was not long before Forster was acting as literary adviser to the house, swinging into the office as though the whole place belonged to him, and carrying off the proofs of half the publications, to read at leisure in his chambers'. He was, as a later managing director also noted, 'of all the counsellors and literary advisers who have helped the firm… undoubtedly the most influential'.[60] Certainly that firm never glittered so brightly as it did during the period of Forster's association, publishing work by Dickens, Thackeray, Carlyle, Mrs Gaskell, Trollope, Landor, Robert Browning and Robert Lytton, several of whom Forster brought to the firm. The publishers benefited from an enlightened approach to the reading task, one that rejected the then common tendency to reduce acceptable fiction to two types, the fashionable novel and the romance.[61] Under Forster's guidance the list divided

> into two channels, one directed towards the goal of building up a tradition of sound literary taste, and the other bound, as far as fortune will allow, towards that sort of popular success which would fill the coffers … During the late 'forties and early 'fifties of the last century these two streams of energy kept their courses bravely side by side.[62]

The extent of Forster's authority is best demonstrated by a reference to a work without commercial possibilities, Lord Nugent's *Some Memorials of John Hampden* (1854): 'I made Chapman give £100 for it towards the pining "estate" of my poor friend', Forster told Peter Cunningham.[63]

But that his friendship was essentially disinterested can be seen from its range. It extended beyond the active and the famous to areas that could yield no associative kudos and in which Forster operated like a General Booth of book and stage. He worked to help the destitute, as a member of a committee to benefit the actress Ellen Tree, and as treasurer of a fund for Charles Pemberton, the actor, then ill, for whom he also donated two guineas.[64] When Edward Elton, another actor, drowned at sea leaving seven orphan children, Forster joined a committee that raised over £2,000 and obtained Miss Burdett Coutts's assistance for the children's education.[65] 'L.E.L.'s' widowed and near-destitute mother was another for whom he worked, for an appeal in 1840 initiated by Bulwer.[66] Above all was the sad case of Laman Blanchard, the one-time friend of 'L.E.L.', a former editor of the *True Sun*, and a member of the *Examiner* staff. On 15 December 1844 his wife, to whom Forster had once written that teasing letter, died after a long illness. 'I must do his work this week – poor fellow', Forster wrote to Leigh Hunt; 'He feels his loss very, very deeply.' Two months later Blanchard committed suicide, leaving four young children. Immediately Forster took the lead in opening a subscription list. It began slowly before he obtained £100 from the Literary Fund and was able to report that the appeal 'goes on much better – indeed *well* ... A kind person sent me also 20 guineas the other day. Wilson (of the Globe) sent me £10 ... And indeed it goes on with perfect success.' To raise more money Forster prepared material for a memoir of Blanchard written by Bulwer and published the following year with a selection of Blanchard's papers. Enough was raised, in all, to educate the children and to find them situations. 'What a terrible history that was!' wrote Dickens, of the tragedy; 'Forster did himself enduring honor [*sic*] by his manly and zealous devotion to the interests of that Orphan Family.'[67] Forster did so, as Dickens knew, despite wretched health and the sudden death of his brother Christopher.

Yet Forster's sad contemporaries received no more charity than did refugees from literary history. He helped Carlyle raise money for Mrs Begg, the destitute sister of Robert Burns, publicized the desirability of preferring Robert Southey's clergyman son, helped obtain a state grant for a descendant of Daniel Defoe and, with Dickens and Carlyle, prised from Palmerston a £100 donation for Johnson's hard-pressed god-daughter and her sister and then raised enough money to buy them an annuity.[68]

The charitable impulse made him a supporter of institutions at the fringes of his concern, such as the General Theatrical Fund, the News-vendors' Benevolent Institute, and the Printers' Pension Society. Forster frequently spoke at their dinners.[69] The commemorative spirit made him an indefatigable organizer and attender of functions that celebrated his friends' various excursions, Dickens's return from America, for instance, Macready's retirement to Sherborne, the silver jubilee of W. J. Fox's ministry at South Place Chapel, when Forster wrote the address, and the retirement in 1850 of a fellow-editor, William Jerdan of the *Literary Gazette*, for whom Forster arranged a retirement testimonial.[70]

The same spirit fuelled his 'bardolatry'. Forster belonged to the Shakespeare Club, which met weekly at the Piazza Coffee House, Covent Garden, for conviviality and discussions of Shakespeare. In these last he spoke, 'very well'[71] at times, until in 1839 when proposing a toast at the annual dinner he was barracked, lost his temper, and then led a walk-out from which the Club never recovered.[72] In the following year the Shakespeare Society was founded as a subscription club for Shakespeareana. By 1852 Forster was a member of its council and helping to choose works to publish.[73] In 1848 a campaign began to raise money for the purchase and preservation of Shakespeare's house at Stratford. The scheme, concerned to sustain the memory of the past's greatest writer and to benefit a needy contemporary by installing one as house-curator, had great appeal for Forster, particularly because Sheridan Knowles was an early choice for the position.[74] Funds were raised partly by Dickens's 'splendid strolling', that touring company of amateur actors which raised £1,500,[75] and partly by public appeals made by the London Committee chaired vigorously by Forster. He kept a strict eye on the accounts, offered detailed corrections of the texts of appeals, and led agitation for a parliamentary bill to make the house the nation's responsibility. Forster negotiated with Lord Manners, the Chief Commissioner of Woods and Forests, and all progressed successfully until thwarted by a change of government and then by Forster's own ill-health.[76]

The scope of Forster's concern cannot fail to impress but its *ad hoc* nature made it a less than adequate solution to the problems of literature or the trials of the theatre. Throughout the period, Forster also worked for a permanent improvement in the profession's condition. Implicit in his friendship for literature was a desire to reduce that friendship's importance.

A minor example is his part in the founding of the London Library, an institution particularly helpful to literary scholars because from it they could borrow books to read at home. Preliminary meetings took place in 1840; by 1846 Forster was helping to choose the books before continuing as an active member of the Committee.[77] He was involved in the agitation for a new law of copyright that preceded the Copyright Act of 1842, a major matter.[78] In that same year, continuing concern with international copyright found Forster organizing petitions in support of Dickens's American campaign for an international agreement to prevent literary piracy.[79] In 1843 Forster subscribed to the Association for the Protection of Literature that had, again unsuccessfully, the same aim.[80]

A further endeavour was the establishing of the Guild of Literature and Art that was for Forster, of course, closely bound up with his friendship for Bulwer. Money for the Guild was another reason for the 'splendid strolling' that began in 1845 and embarked, in philanthropic asides, on such causes as Southwood Smith's nursing home, an appeal for Miss Kelly, the aging actress and impresario who had been a friend of Charles Lamb, and testimonials for such feckless and/or struggling writers as Leigh Hunt, John Poole, and Sheridan Knowles.[81]

Forster threw himself into amateur drama with customary completeness, playing Kitely in *Every Man in His Humour*, and leading parts in Fletcher's *The Elder Brother*, adapted by himself, *The Merry Wives of Windsor*, and *Not So Bad As We Seem*, plus a small part, the Intendant of Police, in the farcical afterpiece, Peake's *Comfortable Lodgings*. In 1847, with another troupe, he was given the tragic part of Don Ruy Gomez in Hugo's *Hernani*, played in aid of the distressed Irish and Scots. He was in demand because he had much talent.[82] Even Macready, who invariably cast a dropping eye on the amateurs' activities, thought Forster to be 'very fine' as Kitely, 'given that he was an amateur', and considered, perhaps grudgingly, after seeing *Hernani*, that Forster, with a little practice, would make 'a very reasonable actor'.[83] For he brought to his acting the capacity for involvement that distinguished all his various activities: Mary Cowden Clarke, who once played Tib to his Kitely, remembered how he grasped her with such force that she was almost flung to the boards.[84] He also brought a fine, expressive voice. Horne thought him to be 'the best reader of dramatic poetry, especially of the eloquent or pathetic kind, I have ever heard in my life'.[85] For Fox's daughter he was

> without exception the very best reader I ever heard … If any author was anxious to make a particularly good impression with his new play or poem on a select audience, it was Mr. Foster [*sic*] who was begged to read it aloud. He used no action whatever in his reading, and, with the exception of his eyes, which flashed and glowed under heavy beetling brows, he depended entirely on the modulation of his voice.[86]

Even Whitwell Elwin's minor objection, that Forster had 'a slight inclination to be too emphatic, the usual fault of those who feeling beauties strongly are anxious to convey them to the full',[87] reinforces a central point: that the eager escape into dramatic relationships, the identification with literary situations, were expressive counters to

Forster's basic loneliness. His thespian excursions also offer a striking example of Macready's influence: Forster modelled his acting style on that of his friend, and even his off-stage manner – the florid gesture, the obsession with status seen, for instance, in Forster's insistence on having the best dressing-room[88] – was like that of the eminent tragedian. The imitation certainly had its comic side but, like the amateur acting itself, it also reflected serious adherence to Macreadian beliefs in dignity and place.

The Guild of Literature and Art had been founded as an alternative to the Royal Literary Fund. When the Guild's funds were frozen by Act of Parliament its supporters turned back to the older institution.[89] In 1855 Dickens, Forster, and C. W. Dilke made a concerted attack on the Royal Literary Fund's extravagance and on control being in the hands of rich and often aristocratic literary dilettantes. There was need for a new charter to place the Fund 'entirely in the hands of literary and scientific men'. Such agitation resulted in a special committee that included Dickens, Forster, Dilke, and Thackeray.

The committee, being strongly against 'flunkeyism and worship of rank', suggested a new charter allowing the committee itself to administer the Fund, and the award of loans and annuities to needy writers, rather than gifts, so as to avoid the stigma of 'charity'. Forster sat on a sub-committee that sought to make the Fund fit for 'the followers of Literature as a liberal profession' and made radical recommendations: the Fund property should be sold or converted into a lecture centre or literary club, a 'Hall or College' should be built, and leading writers should be made 'associates'.

At a special general meeting in June 1855 Dickens spoke passionately for the reforms. Bulwer promised money, Forster spoke on the legal aspects of gaining a new charter. But a large majority voted against and the would-be reformers retired to regroup.

The squabble was both professional and social. It was also internal in being between different kinds of literary men rather than between the literary world and a wider, disdainful society. It is a reminder that when Forster worked to improve the financial, artistic, and hence social position of literary men and their theatrical counterparts he so often worked against treason from within, from exploitative publishers, unscrupulous managers, patronizing and gentlemanly dabblers, even, as will be seen, from writers of substance who affected to misunderstand their colleagues' social longing. All, in their various ways, sought to restrain the rise of the full-time writer or theatrical from hack or near-vagabond to middle-class and affluent professional. All, in so doing, ensured that hostility became one of the main functions of Forster's friendship for literature. He was most hostile to two kinds of treason.

Firstly, he was quickly and fiercely roused by personal and professional carelessness. This is best illustrated by Forster's friendship with William Harrison Ainsworth. They met during 1834, when Ainsworth was immensely popular, and for the next five years he was, Forster recalled, a 'friend now especially welcome'.[90] Ainsworth thought Forster to be his 'most intimate friend',[91] who supported him in business dealings with publishers and in reviews in the *Examiner* and elsewhere. For example, Forster represented Ainsworth in negotiating terms with Bentley for *Crichton*,[92] and then gave the novel favourable reviews both in the *Examiner* and in *The Metropolitan Magazine*. Ainsworth had expected such notices: he wrote to Macrone, in November 1836, that Forster would provide 'a bang-up article in *The Examiner*'.[93] Forster's reward was a tribute in *Crichton*'s preface that strains the use of 'fulsome':

> Mr. Forster is a subtle analyser of character – a profound and philosophical thinker ... It is a high privilege to enjoy the friendship of one whose name will be, hereafter, an earnest of some remembrance by posterity. This privilege I can boast; and may assert with Charles Nodier, who, speaking of his friend Dumas, puts forth his claim to immortality ... '*Je suis l'ami de Forster*'.

for which he was roundly and deservedly attacked by *Fraser's Magazine*.[94] At the close of 1836 Ainsworth introduced Forster to Dickens; the three became boon companions and a 'Trio Club', later a 'Cerberus Club', with engraved wine glasses and much socializing.[95] In 1839 they visited Manchester, Ainsworth's home city, to attend a dinner to mark the publication of *Jack Sheppard*.[96] It was the high point of the friendship.

That same year Dickens was in dispute with Richard Bentley, seeking to renegotiate part and repudiate part of his contract to edit *Bentley's Miscellany* and contribute to it *Oliver Twist* and *Barnaby Rudge*. During the dispute, which ended with Dickens relinquishing the editorship, agreeing new terms for *Oliver Twist* and, effectively, postponing the writing of *Barnaby Rudge*, Forster had urged the impatient Dickens to stand by legal agreements, however inadequate the terms now seemed.[97] Ainsworth followed Dickens as *Miscellany* editor and was offered a similar contract: the editorship and the contributing of two serials. He turned to Forster and received forthright advice:

> I write you one hasty but most earnest entreaty, *not to sign any such agreement* as that you described to me last night.

> I foresee the result if you do. *You will be in Bentley's power.* I implore you not to do it. You deceive yourself. Most men do. But why have men friends if a friend should not, at such a moment, interfere to avert the ill consequences of such self delusion, so miserably common to all of us ... Remember what I told you yesterday – that you are now in a better position than Bentley. *You can get all you wish from him, & hold a superiority over him*, if you do not wilfully & willingly put yourself beneath his feet.[98]

Possibly Ainsworth was offended by Forster's peremptory tone; certainly he ignored Forster's advice. Further, he put pressure on him to review in the *Examiner* the last number of the *Miscellany* to be edited by Dickens. Forster, reviewing, looked forward to Ainsworth's editorship and contributions and then attacked Bentley for inserting pirated material and indulging in 'cheap self-advertisement',[99] this last referring to Bentley's address to the readers announcing Ainsworth's appointment. Ainsworth then showed the review to Bentley and led him to believe that in the dispute with Dickens Forster had encouraged his friend to break contracts. An angry Bentley stopped advertising in the *Examiner*, and postponed the publication, which Forster had arranged, of plays by Landor. Forster then retaliated by breaking off an agreement with Bentley to write a study of the Queen Anne period. As he told Bulwer: 'I refused to sign the agreement then in my possession with *his* signature, and, too glad to get rid of all connection with the rascal, returned him the money he had advanced to induce me to go on with it'.[100] The money, £150, was paid promptly and angrily as Bentley pursued Forster with the impersonal impudence of his solicitors.[101]

Fences were mended in part when Ainsworth obtained a letter from Bentley seeking to exonerate him (Ainsworth) from implicating Forster.[102] Seven months later came Forster's attack on *Jack Sheppard* in a long *Examiner* review that criticized the novel for its bad moral influence and mounted a fierce onslaught on 'puffing', on 'the paragraphs that with such nauseous repetition have drugged every town and country paper',[103] and on Ainsworth's approval of the many stage piracies of his successful novel.

From this the friendship never properly recovered. Reconciliation of a kind came at the close of 1840, following Ainsworth's invitation to Forster to the dinner celebrating the completion of *The Tower of London*. By 1842 Forster was asking Ainsworth to call: 'I like the notion of your story. Come & tell me about it – & about your magazine'. Forster was quick to offer help when Ainsworth's mother died during that same year. But in 1843, though they were still meeting, Forster was contrasting their present relationship with earlier 'days of confidence'. Two years later he complained to James Crossley about not seeing him when Crossley came to London: 'I relied, as I should have known better by former experiences than to do, on Ainsworth's assurance that we should meet'. After this there was little of moment, and Ainsworth's removal to Brighton ended regular contact.[104]

Ainsworth was bitter about the fading of friendship. Forster, he considered, was '*not* the friend of men of letters, unless they could serve him'.[105] But the events of 1839 are a better explanation. Ainsworth's shoddy behaviour, then and subsequently, was not in itself sufficient to put Forster off. The persisting friend of the unreliable Leigh Hunt and, as will be seen, the wild and whirling Landor, was no fragile blossom. But the writings of both Hunt and Landor had qualities that encouraged such friendly persistence, whereas *Jack Sheppard* revealed the essential vulgarity and ambiguous morality of Ainsworth's work. Forster's friendships usually sprang from critical approval; they never survived the strong whiff of literary meretriciousness.

Secondly, and equally treasonable, were public attacks on their profession by its distinguished members. A simple example is Lockhart's 'invidious and secretly malignant article on Southey... in the *Quarterly Review*'[106] in 1850, castigating Southey as part of a general attack on literary men. Forster, then *Examiner* editor, countered in a pugnacious front-page leader.[107] Literary fame, he asserted, was the only enduring one: 'Is it Johnson or Lord Chesterfield who *now* stands waiting in the ante-room?' Forster followed Carlyle, in *Heroes and Hero-Worship*, and the polemical Shelley, in arguing that the highest objects were best promoted by literature and that 'Great writers who understand their vocation are entitled to speak as the world's unacknowledged legislators'. As for Southey, the *Quarterly* had criticized his religious beliefs, republican tendencies, and lack of principle in accepting fees from the *Quarterly* whilst complaining privately about its editor. The last charge was true, Forster admitted, but the *Quarterly* had been Southey's only effective outlet. And all that should be said about the other objections was that

> No man ever passed through a long life, almost always in the public eye, with a character more manly, honourable or unstained. For the opinions of his extreme youth we believe them to have been in reality a departure from the natural habits and dispositions of his mind. They were less what we should now call liberalism or republicanism than a wild and frantic objection to all institutions. Of his genius there can surely be no question.

Literature was defined in utilitarian terms, the professional practice of literature was treated with understanding, the mature Southey was carefully separated from subversive radicalism. The whole, sincerely presented, was an acceptable package for Forster's respectable readership.

More complex is the case of Thackeray. Their acquaintance began at a Garrick Club dinner in 1834;[108] they dined together at intervals through the 1840s and early 1850s, and were particularly solicitous when either was ill. In 1849 Forster's prompt action in bringing Doctor Elliotson may well have saved Thackeray's life,[109] and, with *Henry Esmond* and *The Newcomes* still to appear, that act was arguably Forster's greatest service to literature. At other times there was warm feeling, as when Thackeray wrote from America: 'This isn't a letter. Only a shake of the hand across the Atlantic.'[110] Forster did the odd favour for him, such as inviting Thackeray to contribute to the *Foreign Quarterly Review*[111] and, with the novelist in America, relaying manuscript corrections to his publishers, Bradbury & Evans,[112] but never became a close associate let alone an adviser. For though Forster on occasion liked the man he did not like the man's views. The dual response was reciprocated: 'I like him though I despise him',[113] wrote Thackeray, and, again, 'There's no mingling our two sorts comfortably together.'[114] There was some professional jealousy – Forster became editor of the *Foreign Quarterly Review* after Thackeray had asked for the job;[115] but the tension resulted from Forster's objections to Thackeray's work and, above all, to Thackeray's attitude to the struggles of his profession. The obvious difference between Thackeray and Ainsworth was that Thackeray was no opportunist but a figure of towering genius and undoubted sincerity.

He was also a gentleman and secure in his social position; the 'dignity of literature' movement reflected the aims and desires of those, like Forster, who were neither. From within his inherited bastion Thackeray wrote disparagingly of his fellow-writers, as with his parodies in *Punch* that included a vicious one of Bulwer during 1847. He sniped at Forster as Tom Boxer, 'Mr. Congreve's man', in early editions of *Henry Esmond*, and later as 'Addison's man' in *The Newcomes*, and in bulbous caricatures circulated among his friends.[116] Most offensively of all he laughed publicly and tastelessly at the 'dignity' movement. For example, when he reviewed the Forster-instigated memoir of Blanchard written by Bulwer, Thackeray used the review to argue forcefully against the memoir's plea for more state aid for literature,[117] so enraging Blanchard's friends.

When *Pendennis* came out in 1850 Forster's dispute with Thackeray became public and personal. On 3 January a leader in the *Morning Chronicle* attacked the novel for fostering prejudices against literary men and continued by deploring the literary profession's low status. It followed Thackeray, however, in rejecting the idea of state patronage. Two days later came Forster's reply in the *Examiner*.[118] He insisted that art, literature, and science were as important to the state as 'services done by professors of arms, law, divinity, and diplomacy' because, 'for enlightenment and refinement the industrial class are in a great measure dependent on the literary'. Literature's claims were thus 'not beggars' petitions, but demands for justice' and it was deplorable that 'even men of genius' should deride its practitioners. Rather, ways should and could be found to raise the latter's status and to enable them most to benefit the nation:

> There are many modes in which men of science and literature can render available services to the State – as the teachers and managers of educational institutions; as curators and directors of public museums, libraries and gardens; as members of scientific associations, supplied by the State with funds for the prosecution of experiments and observations.

And supplied also, Forster explained, with ample free time.

This vision of an all-pervading civil service stirred Thackeray into sending a reply to the *Morning Chronicle*.[119] Headed 'The Dignity of Literature', it answered Forster's charges by asserting that the literary profession was *not* held in low esteem, literary men should silently assume that they *were* gentlemen, *Pendennis* did not attack *all* the literary profession but only the worst members. Forster came again:[120] it was never clear in *Pendennis* that the *whole* profession was not being attacked, Thackeray was in any case too ready with sarcasm and ridicule, Thackeray wanted literary men to accept 'all the honours, places, and prizes they should get' but could not see that 'it is bad economy to save a pension that might enable the student to pursue inquiries free from privation and care, by paying probably a larger stipend for having the State-business bungled'. Forster's own plan proposed that literary men should be found *suitable* positions. It also proposed, Forster repeated, that they should be suitably rewarded; at present the 'First Draughtsman at the Admiralty' received £50 a year more than professors of literature, and writers were grouped on the pension list with royal coachmen.

In 1851 Thackeray's lectures on English humorists and Forster's reviews of them again inflamed the continued unease of their relationship. Forster disagreed with Thackeray's presentation of Swift as insincere and over-secretive and thought Thackeray wrong to praise Addison's egotism. A reconciliation during May 1851[121] ended critical reviewing until Thackeray's final lecture with its closing reiteration that the literary profession was *not* despised by society, that concern about status was a fuss about nothing. Forster's review referred only in passing to 'some vehement sallies of doubtful doctrine and more than doubtful taste',[122] but a week later he wrote another hostile *Examiner* leader[123] that hit hard and in many directions. Thackeray's sincerity was not in dispute: 'We cannot doubt his regard for his calling, or his wish to see it properly esteemed.' But he should see that the state treated it unjustly, especially when one considered, for example, 'the exaggerated appreciation of military talents'. Thackeray could not argue that 'literary talent being given, the social position of an author has been always proportionate to his morality', when his own social esteem seemed unaffected by the writing of novels in which the bad achieved more than the good. In Forster's opinion how authors really stood in the world's eyes was clearly shown by the law of copyright. Whereas the nobility, whose 'social dignity' was often the reward for some long-gone and worthless deed, were allowed to pass on fortunes to their descendants, writers, the 'truly great', could only give their heirs seven years' benefit of their labours. 'Are we not justified', Forster asked '... in refusing to admit that literature and science have yet obtained their true position in this country?'; until writers stopped attacking each other and presented a united front they would get nowhere. Thackeray, in his own words, then 'slapped Forster's face (epistolarily) in a rage after 2 years treason'[124] and the acquaintance never again stumbled near friendship.

Paradoxically, Forster's quarrels with Lockhart and Thackeray are a climax to his career as literature's friend. His leaders made explicit what was implicit in each of his innumerable supportive gestures. Such writings are aggressively defensive statements permeated with concern for colleagues, self, and lettered world – with Forster speaking, as it were, on behalf of that world – that explain why Forster had given so much of his life to literary friendliness. Yet, like most embattled encyclicals, Forster's in those early 1850s were more the product of uncertainty than of professional confidence.

Two seemingly unrelated events point to an explanation. One, already described, was his call to the Bar in 1843, recorded in his diary with the comment: 'It is a date which I hope (ah. not vainly!) may one day be of some importance to me.'[125] Ten years later, as chairman of the London Shakespeare House Committee, ill-health prevented him conducting negotiations with the government. 'My dear Fellow, what is to be done?' he wrote from Hampstead Heath to his committee-man, Peter Cunningham, 'I am very unwell, very very lame – and have fairly taken flight here ... I do not propose to return again until I am able to walk. It may be a month

– it may be more!'[126] Shortly after this he resigned from the chair.[127] In the first case, being a barrister did not only have social value but 'also qualified its holder for certain lucrative "pickings" ';[128] Forster's diary note makes plain that, even at the age of 31, he had already opened an opportunistic eye. Secondly, when continued ill-health began to sap energy and disrupt duty that eye focussed on possible government appointments. B. W. Procter had long been a member of the Lunacy Commission; Fonblanque, whom Forster had succeeded as *Examiner* editor, had left to become a statistician in the Board of Trade. Any editor of an influential weekly with a distinct political position would have useful parliamentary contacts. Forster began to look to them for less onerous and, perhaps, more lucrative work. As circumstances pressed he looked more keenly.

By the late 1840s Forster had discovered the limitations of friendship, whether for literary men or for the whole world of popular literature. His unhappy letters to Tennyson reveal this poignantly. His bad health intensified his loneliness and that deepened further as friends retired, as Macready did to Sherborne, or died. Lady Blessington went in 1849, in debt and in exile, the glittering D'Orsay followed in 1852, then Talfourd in 1854. Forster wrote sadly to Mrs Cunningham: 'How the *next* world gets peopled with our friends as we go on in life – and less unfamiliar, and more prepared, for the visit we must one day pay to it ourselves!'[129] Others matured as family men whilst Forster remained imprisoned in bachelorhood. 'L.E.L.' had found no successor and his most serious attempt to find one, Forster's proposal to Georgina Hogarth, had ended in amicable failure. In 1850, when Bulwer invited him to Knebworth, Forster's reply demonstrates his strength of longing: 'Would I *were* there – in that quiet farm-house near – with a nice wife and my books about me! I'd give up ambition.'[130] Significantly, his longing was not only for hearthed bliss but for the quiet life of the domesticated scholar.

Until 1855 this was an ever-strengthening interest, owing much to his friend Carlyle's opinion of popular literature and example as a historian. 'Forster was always reading – always taking notes',[131] reported Henry Rawlins, and a main early result was the five-volume *Lives of Eminent British Statesmen*, a volume a year from 1836 to 1838, with two volumes on Cromwell in 1839. The set was reprinted in 1840 as *The Statesmen of the Commonwealth of England*, with a long prefatory essay, 'A Treatise on the Popular Progress in English History'. During 1842 and 1843 he contributed a series of essays on ancient philosophy to the *Foreign Quarterly Review*: erudite and authoritative, they are lingering evidence of the quality of that early Newcastle schooling. Then in 1846 came 'his first great success'[132] with an essay on Defoe in the *Edinburgh Review*.

Other essays followed, in both the *Edinburgh*[133] and the *Quarterly*, a move from weekly to quarterly reviewing that reflected both social and scholarly ambition. In 1847 Bulwer even sounded Macaulay, though unsuccessfully, about Forster as a possible successor to Napier as editor of the *Edinburgh Review*.[134] Seven years later in 1854 came his edition of Evelyn's Diary; its modernized spelling, additional notes, and such changes as 'a fresh examination of the orginal manuscript had rendered essential to its correctness and completeness',[135] cost Forster 'an immense deal of labour & pains'.[136] Most revealing of all are the two editions of Forster's biography of Goldsmith. The first, echoing *Oliver Twist* in the learned raciness of its title, *The Life and Adventures of Oliver Goldsmith* (1848), was scholarly in essence, had been constantly rewritten during the 1830s and 1840s, but was aimed at a popular market. The second edition, called, more primly, *The Life and Times of Oliver Goldsmith* (1854), was enlarged to two volumes mainly through the inclusion of much source material and footnoted references, and was a ponderous demonstration of Forster's eighteenth-century scholarship.

Such interests developed their own friendships, including that with Carlyle. One was with James Crossley, the Manchester bibliophile and antiquarian, a partner in Harrison Ainsworth's father's firm of solicitors. Forster and Crossley corresponded from 1837, met occasionally, lent each other rare books and exchanged arcane information. Forster involved Colburn in the publication of Crossley's edition of North's *Diary*, and promised a review of his friend's edition of Potts's *Discovery of Witches*. Crossley came to represent the erudite audience whose respect Forster increasingly sought: 'I should like you of all men to like what I have written', Forster wrote on his paper on Steele.[137] G. L. Craik, later Professor of English in Belfast, was another friend of that kind, as were Alexander Dyce, the editor of Elizabethan and Jacobean drama, Lord Nugent, the commonwealth historian, and Panizzi, with his invaluable access to the bibliographical treasures of the British Museum. In 1854 came friendship with Whitwell Elwin, the Norfolk clergyman and editor of the *Quarterly Review*. 'I shall always esteem your letters', Forster wrote to him, 'the beginning I hope of a long and steady correspondence.'[138] 'I cannot tell you how pleased I was with Mr. Elwin',[139] he confided to Peter Cunningham. Within a year Forster was helping Elwin with his biography of Richardson, and had become a contributor to the *Quarterly Review*.

The scholarly life – even, simply, leisured reading – had always been hard to reconcile with the demands of Forster's towering friendships and the many tasks of his literary life. It was completely at odds with his journalism and, particularly, with his editorships. For two years during the

1840s he controlled the *Foreign Quarterly Review*, and he spent ten increasingly irksome months during 1846 in following Dickens as editor of the *Daily News*. Above all, as drama critic, literary critic, Fonblanque's deputy, leader-writer and, officially editor from 1847 until 1855, Forster's energies were sapped and his life controlled by 'the relentless *Examiner*'.[140] 'Perhaps you have no care for politics', he wrote to Longfellow, '– happy man that has no need to care for them! Now for some six years or so I have had to think of little else – so exclusively have they engaged me. Yet I am only happy when I can creep into some quiet literary corner.'[141] He was, he told Bulwer in a note that almost certainly marks slow movement over the years to the political right, 'weary of writing from week to week against my political friends'.[142] He was weary also of being a week-end scholar and trying to cram all else, the work of several ordinary lifetimes, into the period from Tuesday morning to Friday night.[143] But leisure needed means and Forster had few. That this was so after a quarter of a century of frantic literary endeavour made him deeply aware of missed opportunities. In 1849, after attending a lawyers' dinner, he recorded sadly that his host 'made me serious by recounting all I had lost in turning aside from the bar'.[144] Two years later, after dinner at Pollock's, his reactions sank nearer the desperate: 'Ah, a pity I did not follow it', he wrote of the lucrative law, 'I feel that every day'.[145] Desperation intensified his search for a government post and Lord John Russell, whose policies the *Examiner* had long supported, agreed to help.[146] In December 1855 the Secretaryship to the Lunacy Commission fell vacant. Interest, including that of Bulwer, was immediately brought to bear on Lord Shaftesbury, the Commission's chairman. Forster became Secretary to the Lunacy Commission at a salary of £800 *per annum* and ceased to be editor of the *Examiner*.

CHAPTER 8 *Withdrawal and Return*

At the age of 43 Forster was no longer a professional man-of-letters, but his new work he thought to be not unsuitable; he had, he considered with defiant immodesty, 'every legal and metaphysical qualification'[1] for the post of Secretary. Such a post was itself of recent origin, for the Lunacy Commission was a main result of the Lunatics Act of 1845. Shaftesbury, as chairman, led a group of five laymen, three medical Commissioners, and three legal ones, serviced by Forster and two clerks.[2] He was Secretary for six years, until 1861, and even though his duties made fewer physical demands than had the late nights and deadlines of editorship, it was far from being a sinecure. The Lunatics Act required frequent inspections by Commissioners of all mental hospitals and licensed houses, and insisted not only on reports of such inspections but also on the documentation of all Lunacy activities. All admissions, deaths, discharges, and licensing of institutions had to be notified to the Commission. During the 1850s the number of main asylums rose from 24 to 41 and the number of patients more than doubled, so that the small secretariat came under ever-increasing pressure. At times, and frustratingly, Forster found himself having to deal with the calls of his literary friendships in odd moments snatched from meetings.[3]

After only three months as Secretary came a further, and startling, development: Forster announced his engagement to Eliza Colburn, the widow of Henry Colburn the publisher. His friends were shocked into facetiousness. 'After I knew it (from himself) this morning', wrote Dickens, 'I lay down flat, as if an Engine and Tender had fallen upon me.'[4] In September 1856 Whitwell Elwin came up from Norfolk to conduct the ceremony and the happy couple left for a two-months' honeymoon in the Lake District. 'I have taken a house in Montague Square (No. 46)', he told Bulwer before leaving, 'and (upon my return) poor old Lincoln's Inn

Fields, where I have lived for three-and-twenty years, will hereafter know me not!'[5]

It was at Henry Colburn's home in Bryanston Square that Forster had, almost certainly, first met Leigh Hunt during the late 1820s. The publisher had, as Forster told Peter Cunningham, 'in former days been often kind to me', so much so that, in 1854, Forster had agreed to the onerous editing of Evelyn's *Diary*, the copyright of which Colburn owned, as a return favour.[6] Colburn had owned much more, for a career of sometimes disreputable manoeuvring and blatant 'puffing' of his titles had made him a rich man. In 1841 Eliza Crosbie, the daughter of a Royal Naval captain, became his second wife and when he died on 16 August 1855 Colburn left her £10,000, the house in Bryanston Square, its contents, which included valuable books, and copyrights that were later to realize a further £14,000.

In 1856 the wealthy widow was 37, seven years younger than Forster. In the words of her nephew, Richard Renton, she was '*Petite*, dainty in form and feature',[7] a description confirmed by Boxall's sketch of 1860, and with mildly fragile health, a catcher of colds, a sufferer from headaches, a loser of sleep.[8] She was, Renton considered, 'the most charming, the sweetest-natured woman it was possible to conceive';[9] Robert Lytton told Browning that he liked her '*very* much too. She is thoroughly good, and unobtrusively so.'[10] Certainly she was kind-hearted but could be too talkative: Jane Carlyle complained that she 'gabbles like a mill-clapper when she has any ideas'.[11] But, despite such occasional complaints, her friendship with Carlyle's shrewd and demanding wife is important evidence that the new Mrs Forster was more than a pretty, though sickly, face.

That friendship was a 'feminine' one, with a regular correspondence comparing notes on illnesses, arranging luncheons and visits, and discussing servants and household affairs, in which Jane Carlyle respected her friend's good sense and powers of organization. She also dominated her: in 1864, with Jane Carlyle in Scotland, Mrs Forster's supervision of Cheyne Row's redecoration was accompanied by Caledonian instructions that were detailed and peremptory:

> I have written to Mr C to tell him you would be down upon him with a paper-hanger! So as soon as perfectly convenient, you will perhaps be so kind as call at Cheyne Row, and explain to the maids about clearing out the first floor, – remembering always that they are to be addressed as perfect idiots; and ascertain from *them* and Mr C *when* the Man may come. And oh please get the man to be

> speedy so that Mr C may not be fidgeted with him too long. And oh tell the maids, when the rooms are done they must not go rubbing against the clean paper with their dirty crinolines! – It won't be necessary to paper *behind* the large Picture, which would involve *its* being taken down – Bid them cover it with a sheet.[12]

Despite the dominance, or perhaps because of it, Jane Carlyle prized the friendship. When a blundering servant wrongly denied her to the visiting Mrs Forster strong and sincere apologies quickly followed: 'I am so afraid you wont come again till you are entreated *to!* ... Please *do* come again!'[13] The nature of the affinity was hinted at in a later letter written by Jane Carlyle when an ailing Mrs Forster left for out-of-town convalescence:

> I expect you to return without that tired look which I understand so well! and with your eyes as bright as the[y] are by nature. And then I shall expect you to drive very often to Cheyne Row, and let us try to Cheer one another up a bit. Hang it! Why mightnt we go sometimes with a mutual carpet bag, and spend a day and night at some way-side Inn, when we feel to need 'a change' from our own comfortable homes, and men-of-genius Husbands![14]

That Jane Carlyle considered Eliza Forster to have a marriage as sad and dominated as her own is implicit in this letter's sense and cadences. It is, from Jane Carlyle's point of view, one explanation of her friendship with another childless wife. As an account of the Forsters' marriage it is misleadingly subjective.

On honeymoon Forster was emotional and disorientated. He wrote, from Ambleside, to Elizabeth Barrett Browning, of

> a somewhat important event in my life of which you have heard, and which you, I well know, will rejoice to be told has made me very very happy.
>
> Since that day we have been in every part of this wonderful country of lake, stream, & mountain – which, if you & Robert have not thoroughly explored, you *must* some day – and might the Fates be only so propitious as to give you for fellow travellers a certain old and dear friend and *his* life-companion!

Forster ended: 'I shall not return till the close of the present week',[15] then wrote 'we' across the 'I' with revealing realization. For though Forster from the first, as Jane Carlyle knew, dominated his wife, recalling Stanfield's humorous description of Mrs Colburn as fiancée – 'She has no blood Sir in her body – no color – no voice – is all scrunched and squeezed together ... while Forster Sir is rampant and raging, and presenting a contrast beneath which you sink into the dust'[16] – and Forster's own implicit comment on marriage expressed through his italicizing of lines from one of Birch's letters to Landor – 'an excellent wife is seldom made perfect to our hands, but is in part *the creation of the husband after marriage, the result of his character and behaviour acting upon her own*'[17] – he was wrenched from seemingly-confirmed bachelorhood and succumbed uneasily to his new state. From 1856 Forster's life changed profoundly through the not unfamiliar combination of lunacy and matrimony.

In the early years of the marriage such change was not immediately apparent. Though Macready had long retired, Forster remained preoccupied with the literary and personal affairs of Leigh Hunt, Bulwer, Landor, Carlyle, Dickens, and, to a lesser extent, of Robert Browning in Italy. He still performed tasks for Tennyson: in 1858, when Tennyson wrangled with Moxon & Co. over an illustrated edition of *The Princess*, Forster represented the Laureate in acrimonious negotiations. Tennyson, antipathetic to such editions and annoyed at Moxon's new management's suggestion that he owed the firm money for unsold copies of previous editions, gave Forster a 'Statement of Facts' with which to negotiate. In the event Tennyson conceded the new edition, but received the publisher's apologies and signed a more favourable contract.[18]

Forster remained a prominent critic of the workings of the Royal Literary Fund and in 1857 he was part of yet another attack on its constitution. Dilke and Dickens led the charge and Forster supported them with a speech that attacked patronage and, in particular, the 'fawning, fulsome, and sycophantic' behaviour of Prince Albert at previous annual dinners. For this, Forster's behaviour was criticized by the *Literary Gazette*, and the reformers were heavily defeated. During the following year a pamphleteering attack, again by Dilke, Dickens, and Forster, was easily beaten off.[19]

Minor skirmishes remained. In March 1859 Forster, acting through Dickens, anonymously offered his collection of manuscripts to the Fund, together with an endowment of £10,000, provided that the Fund would accept the central recommendations of the 1855 charter committee.[20] That offer was rejected, as it had to be, given that the Fund's committee knew full well the donor's identity. Forster, annoyed, 'determined...to have no more to do with the Literary Fund',[21] a feeling accentuated when, at the 1859 annual dinner, Thackeray spoke against the reformers and for the correctness of the Fund's decision to reject Forster's generosity.[22] In January 1860 Bulwer made a final gesture in support of his friend when he refused to chair the annual dinner.[23] By 1862 he had relented and only Forster remained in fighting mood, still feeling, ineffectually, that his offer should have been accepted because it would have made the Fund 'a real and ennobling, not a false and dishonouring, help to men of letters'.[24] As for the Guild of Literature and Art, the Royal Literary Fund reformers turned back to it in 1861, when its funds were unfrozen. Houses were built at Knebworth for retired artists and authors, donations were made to the needy. But for most potential beneficiaries such help was unwelcome patronage. Only a few mediocrities took advantage of it and the Guild, never vibrant, was a sad disappointment to its founders.[25]

Other familiar activities continued to claim Forster's time. He remained an occasional contributor to the *Examiner* and, during Henry Morley's editorship, was allowed to vet proofs of reviews of his friends' work.[26] He was still an active philanthropist, as trustee of a fund for Douglas Jerrold's daughter after the death of her father,[27] and as a supporter of a subscription for the poetess Marguerite Power.[28]

Douglas Jerrold's death in 1857 is one pointer to the sea-change occurring in Forster's literary life. 'Poor Jerrold!', he wrote to Peter Cunningham, 'What a shock his death has been to me.'[29] It was the first of a series that thinned the ranks of Forster's friends before the mid-1860s. Leigh Hunt died in 1859, an event that reminded Forster poignantly of early days and aspirations; Elizabeth Barrett Browning, whom Forster had helped from time to time, died in 1861, bringing Robert Browning back from Italy but not to as busy a friendship with Forster as hitherto. Thackeray went in 1863, drawing from Forster a moving tribute in the *Examiner* that sought to distinguish between the novelist's seemingly cynical public persona and his inner, tender-hearted nature. W. J. Fox followed in 1864, with Forster writing an admiring gravestone inscription that stressed Fox's unremitting work for 'the Advancement of the Working Class from which he sprang'.[30]

As for Forster's surviving relationships, inevitably some changed as time passed. In 1858 Landor, beset by scandals, was packed off to die in Italy. There he lived six more years, during three of which he was estranged from Forster following the latter's refusal to reprint the 'Defence' Landor had written against the Yescombes, who had previously, and successfully, sued him for obscene libel. Reconciliation was effected only during Landor's last year of life.[31] With Macready, in retirement at Sherborne, Forster quarrelled in 1860 when Macready remarried, and that breach took three years to repair. From Dickens Forster was never estranged but he now saw less of him as Dickens saw more of Wilkie Collins and became embroiled with Ellen Ternan.

Slowly Forster began to withdraw from areas of popular literary life. Despite his continuing connection with the *Examiner* he could refer to himself, in 1857, as a 'retired newspaper veteran';[32] by the early 1860s he had little general influence, being unable, for instance, to secure many notices for Robert Lytton's *Lucile*.[33] By 1862 all connection with the world of journalism had become tenuous: when W. C. Hazlitt asked him for help to become a journalist Forster could not oblige and readily admitted that 'this department of literature has been almost revolutionized even in the short time that has elapsed since I had connection with it'.[34] In 1856, Forster ended his association with *Household Words* by relinquishing his one-eighth share in the project; in any case, he disliked Dickens's sub-editor, W. H. Wills, and felt insufficiently consulted.[35] In 1857 Forster read the prologue to *The Frozen Deep*, in a performance at Dickens's Tavistock House home, as his last contribution to amateur theatricals.[36] Four years later, in 1861, he resigned as Chapman & Hall's literary adviser after almost a quarter of a century with the firm. George Meredith succeeded him.[37]

Forster's acceptance of the Secretaryship had drawn varied responses from those who knew him. 'I am delighted to hear of ... (it).', Thackeray told Whitwell Elwin, 'it does good to the whole literary profession.'[38] Emily Tennyson's tone was very different:

> We don't know whether it is matter of congratulation to you, this appointment; but we are sure it is matter of congratulation to the appointment and so since you have identified yourself in a measure with it you are at all events doomed to a portion of congratulation greater or less. But we hope it is really pleasant to you, that so we may be glad for you without any drawback.[39]

Such caution and what surely was, on Thackeray's part, ironic glee, indicate the extent to which that appointment had surprised Forster's world. Having argued long and publicly that literary men should not be undiscriminating place-seekers, Forster, under pressure, had joined those he had attacked. And as a further irony his marriage now allowed him to benefit from money made from Colburn the publisher's reprehensible practices. There is no evidence that Forster was troubled by either anomaly and there is no doubt that this withdrawal during the years from 1855 to 1864 reflected an increasing, though not, of course, absolute, disaffection towards literature. This last began with the sense of literature having failed him socially and materially that led him to the Lunacy Commission, and continued with a loss of enthusiasm for new publications: 'Generally books are very dull', he told Bulwer, '... the best book I have read is a version of the Odyssey by a young man named Worsley.'[40] The private lives of Landor, Dickens, and, for a while and for Forster at least, Macready, did nothing to sustain that ideal view of literature and literary men cherished and defended since Forster's Newcastle schooldays.

Forster was moneyed, married, and working for the government. The money was handled, at times, with the wariness of one born to riches. Even Peter Cunningham, a friend since Forster's earliest days in London, had a request for help courteously refused and received only sternly businesslike advice:

> let me take the privilege of a very old friend to say to you ... that difficulties of this kind are not *best* met by occasional loans & advances. They only hamper one more – if the outlook beyond them is not quite clear. Why not ask Dickens & myself (if you will trust me) & any other friends you have confidence in, to look into the whole matter for you, & see how far it is possible that such further anxieties might be spared you.

Yet, generally, Forster spent money freely; in changing to a grander way of living he had no problems of adjustment. He was now able to indulge occasional artistic impulses: able, for instance, to visit Manchester in 1857 for an art exhibition, and in 1861 to consider visiting Vienna to see Robert Lytton; and able, using Peter Cunningham, to buy manuscript material at auction. He treated his wine-merchant with an insistent and affluent precision: 'Tell me at what price you can let me have a really fine claret – not a loaded wine, but a pure after dinner wine of the finest vintage & flavor [*sic*].' In 1862 came the supreme expression of his materialistic translation: 'I am building a house at Kensington', he wrote to Bulwer, 'which has now risen to its third storey and looks very formidable'. Because of this, expenditure for a time pressed upon income, so that Forster could describe himself to Bulwer, with understatement and perhaps some irony, as 'a man of moderate means and liberal desires'. By 1863 building was finished and Palace Gate House, Kensington, became John Forster's last home. Built by Cubitt 'from designs supplied by Mr. Forster himself', and on land for which Forster had paid £4,000, the house had a magnificent oak-panelled library with gallery.[41]

Here, in the brief mid-1860s, after the 'unspeakable confusion'[42] of their first weeks in their new home, the Forsters entertained frequently. Forster's rude dominance was well known; he had always been an autocratic host, on one famous occasion even reproving his guests for smoking without permission.[43] Now, with a new grandeur, he would 'wipe his shoes' on his guests, shouting them down with cries of 'Intolerable!', 'Don't tell me!', 'Incredible!', 'Monstrous!'[44] His servants were cowed but, at the same time, devoted to him: his butler, when told that his home was on fire, served dinner in nervous silence before asking Forster for permission to leave.[45]

There is no doubt that Forster's behaviour reflected a continuing sense of social insecurity. In his Kensington mansion Forster was not less concerned with status and reputation than he had been at Lincoln's Inn Fields. And necessarily so: as late as 1857 the *Literary Gazette*, in reporting the Royal Literary Fund affair, had sounded the familiar strain in concluding that 'educated men cannot fail to resent the pretensions and bad taste of such speeches as those of Mr. Dickens and Mr. Forster'.[46] Sadly, Forster's concern also reflected that growing disaffection towards parts of his old life: whereas he had once been proud to be a literary journalist now he was offended at W. B. Jerrold's description of him as 'long the literary and dramatic critic' of the *Examiner*, and protested that, for much of that time, he had been the paper's editor and political writer.[47] Further, and fuelling such disaffection, was the persisting feeling of chances lost and wrong turns taken. 'Talking in the old strain', he wrote in his diary of a dinner with Chitty, 'of the £5,000 a year I might have been making at the Bar'.[48] The rationalizing that followed was not altogether convincing.

Forster's new affluence, in making him conscious of the uses of wealth, intensified the melancholy of such moments. That melancholy was not lessened by deteriorating health. In 1857 he was racked with rheumatism: 'I have never had a cessation of pain in my arm', he told Peter Cunningham in a letter of New Year's greetings, '– have had to interrupt a series of 24 uninterrupted Xmas days during which I have dined at Macready's table – and have passed perforce a very lenten Christmas.'[49] No improvement came in 1858. In 1859 he was so ill that in July Carlyle persuaded him to leave hot London for rural recuperation.[50]

The state of Forster's health made his work for the Lunacy Commission more onerous. As Secretary he was, he wrote in 1857, 'constantly & continuously occupied in a way that you would hardly believe'.[51] Even when out of London he had to keep in touch, and so was committed to much 'journeying to and fro, and the inevitable business which always lurks in waiting'.[52] In addition, the work was not wholly congenial to a man with Forster's artistic feelings, as Carlyle quickly recognized:

> To you no office is of the least practical moment, yields neither distinction, nor real profit of any kind, – nor does your pleasure lie,

> I think, in that direction, tho' probably some vague notion of 'duty' may, as habit no doubt does. I beg you reflect seriously on this![53]

Despite such problems Forster remained as Secretary for five years and then began agitating for a Commissionership. 'I never let Brougham go', he told Percy Fitzgerald, 'I came back again and again until I wore him out. I forced 'em to give me this.'[54] He became a Commissioner of Lunacy on 19 February 1861.

Commissioners had three main functions: inspecting, licensing, and reporting. Forster, as one of the legal Commissioners, had, with a medical Commissioner, 'to visit each hospital once a year, each licensed house in the metropolis four times a year, and each licensed house in the provinces ... twice a year'. Such visiting involved much travel, the Commissioners moving through England and Wales on fixed circuits, each of three or four weeks' duration, and during most of the year. At each institution they inspected buildings and records, had special powers to visit gaols, workhouses, and single lunatics 'received for profit' and had the authority to discharge patients. In London they could license institutions, and copies of licenses awarded by provincial magistrates had to be sent to them. The Commissioners themselves reported three times a year to the Lord Chancellor's office.

For Forster the post's attractions were status and, mainly, a salary of £1,500 a year, almost double that received as Secretary and a necessary supplement to his wife's money. But it was not the best occupation for a man whose middle age was increasingly melancholic and depressed, a man who, as has been stressed, had a kind heart and deep feelings. For such a person the work could be satisfying but was often deeply affecting. He wrote to Carlyle from Abergavenny in 1861:

> There is an excellently managed Asylum here to which a fair quantity of land is attached – and here we played cricket and bowls yesterday with parties of the patients, assisted by the Medical Officers and a good homely kindhearted Chaplain ... who has made the precious discovery that to take a real interest in these poor creatures, and induce them to join in games & amusements, & any kind of occupation, is worth a million preachings & sermons. – I turned out to be a very good bowler, and covered myself with laurels.
>
> All the incidents in this strange new life are not quite so agreeable, however. At a grand asylum near Bristol the other day, a poor fellow burst into tears as he caught sight of me, and called out my name. He had been a fellow-student with me in Amos's

> law-class centuries ago. Ten years since, when I last saw him, he was one of the most promising of all the young Chancery lawyers and had written a very learned book on the Succession to Real Property. About nine years since, he told me, he fell down one day on the floor of the Rolls Court, and rose with one side paralysed. It was very sad – the petitions to help in such cases (which are not to be helped) are so painful.[55]

Feelings (and health) notwithstanding, Forster's duties had to be performed to the letter, and so could impinge on social life and freedom of manoeuvre: 'At present unfortunately I am unable to leave town, even for a day'; he wrote to Mrs Tindal in the spring of 1862, refusing an invitation, 'and before the close of next week, I go on visitation into Lancashire.'[56] The following winter found him 'hurried and harried night and day'[57] as he was 'incessantly, and much against the grain, at work to get the quarter's visitations into the quarter'.[58]

Yet his health deteriorated, and Lunacy business increased, only gradually. Throughout the first years of his new life there was still energy and time for other interests beyond Forster's continuing though, ultimately, fading literary ones. In 1859 he helped form a 'Committee for the Neapolitan Exiles' to assist the 'brave and noble' refugees forced to flee from an oppressive Italian government.[59] The following year he helped arrange and then subscribed to a 'Testimonial of Admiration to Garibaldi'.[60] In 1862 he was an epistolary applauder of the American North, writing to Spring Rice of 'the recent Federal successes in Maryland. Nothing for a long while since has been so thoroughly satisfactory to me – Join with me, my friend, in a cheer for McClellan.'[61] At home he supported electoral reform: 'All my experience of giving people the franchise ... is that it sobers not maddens them. But I suppose I am in a minority about it.'[62] In such gestures, whether aid for the oppressed or tacit support for slaves and the voteless, are glimpses of the younger Forster raised as a Unitarian and working for the radical press. But, whereas his desire to help on his fellows had earlier been mainly in the service of professional literature, now it expressed itself more frequently in terms of general humanitarian action and political opinion.

Above all there was scholarship, the pursuit of which had, of course, been a main reason for his withdrawal from much of his old life. In his study at Montague Square and then in his magnificent library at Palace Gate House, surrounded by a superb collection of seventeenth- and eighteenth-century pamphlets, tracts, manuscripts and rare books, including an incomparable selection of autograph and printed Swiftiana, built up since his earliest London days and augmented by Henry Colburn's own collection, Forster turned first to the literary history of the previous century. In 1855 he had started work on a study of Swift, meant initially as a paper for Elwin's *Quarterly Review*. Forster then agreed to edit Swift's works for John Murray and to use the study as an introductory outline of Swift's life and career. The project was well advertised and drew in so much new material that the original paper was now projected as a full-scale biography, the appearance of which would precede Forster's edition of Swift's works.[63] Through the late 1850s the collection of material, and basic biographical and editorial work, made progress.

It was, however, frequently interrupted by other scholarly work. In 1858 Forster published *Historical and Biographical Essays*, extended versions of his *Edinburgh Review* and *Quarterly Review* papers on Steele, Defoe, Churchill, and Foote, together, significantly, with two new historical studies: 'The Debates on the Grand Remonstrance' and 'Plantagenets and Stuarts'. The significance of these last two essays is that they demonstrate Forster's return to his first love, seventeenth-century history, that, years before, had produced *Lives of Eminent British Statesmen*. Then, Forster had been fascinated by the conflict between Parliament and the king, or as Fonblanque put it, when admiring Forster's work, with 'that period from which we date our liberties'.[64] The *Lives*, concerned as they were with the gaining of, comparatively speaking, a more democratic freedom, had been a natural product of the reformist 1830s. It seems appropriate that Forster's return to the same area should take place in the decade preceding the second Reform Bill of 1867.

In 1860 came *Biographical Essays*, a revised edition of the papers on Defoe, Steele, Churchill, and Foote, and, as a further indication of Forster's change of direction, an *Edinburgh Review* paper on Cromwell. The essays on Defoe and Churchill were reprinted separately in 1862. In the following year appeared a fourth edition of Forster's biography of Goldsmith; with Procter he edited a selection from Robert Browning's poetry. These were asides from the main thrust of Forster's scholarly enterprise that began the 1860s with two volumes of history: *The Arrest of the Five Members by Charles the First* and an extended version of the historical essays of 1858, *The Debates on the Grand Remonstrance* with an essay 'On English Freedom Under the Plantagenets and Tudor Sovereigns'. In that same year, 1860, Forster's scholarly reputation was sufficiently formidable to allow Brougham to consider him for an honorary degree at Edinburgh University.[65]

Already he was at work on a major enterprise. Under Carlyle's influence, and so from a political stance far less radical than that of the

1830s, he began to recast and reinterpret the *Lives of Eminent British Statesmen*. First to appear, in 1864, was *Sir John Eliot: a Biography*, extended to two volumes; publication of that found Forster already at work on a new life of Strafford. He was jealous of his standing, and could still lack confidence. He wrote to Bulwer in June of that year:

> A copy of Eliot lay upon your table last night – the first volume partly perhaps almost wholly cut open – the second with the leaves in a virgin state – *uncut altogether* ... I confess to the weakness of not liking that strangers, friends of yours, should measure the attractiveness of my Big book by the progress you have been able to make in it. It was a 'd——d good-natured' remark of that kind which drew my attention to it last night.[66]

Yet, even for Forster 1864 must have seemed a reassuring year: on May Day, at the Royal Academy's annual banquet, Forster had responded to the toast, 'The Interests of Literature', and, in July, he accepted an Honorary Doctorate from Trinity College Dublin. His health was worsening and Lunacy business irksome, but, in the summer of 1864, at 52 years of age and happily married, Forster enjoyed general prestige and scholarly recognition, had projects in hand and tasks ahead. Then, in Florence, on 17 September, in his ninetieth year, Landor died.

The old man had left in the press an edition of *Imaginary Conversations* and Forster's first task was to supervise its posthumous publication. This he did and then turned to face the dreadful consequence of being Landor's only possible biographer. For a younger, fitter Forster had promised to write his friend's life and with that in mind had acquired over the years many of Landor's copyrights and large quantities of personal papers. Now the time had come to perform the task and, for Forster, the moment was hardly opportune.

This is not to say that in the mid-1860s Forster was in a state of geriatric collapse; there is much evidence to the contrary. He still made the occasional philanthropic sortie: when Alaric Watts died Forster worked to help the widow of the former journalist remembered for his part in the 'L.E.L.' affair. He remained an active supporter of the London Library, a committee member into the 1870s. He sustained his surviving major friendships, as well as that with Longfellow. For the latter, in 1868, he negotiated terms with Routledge for *The New England Tragedies*. When Routledge suggested two possible methods of payment, either £1,000 in four half-yearly payments of £250 each, the first to be paid on publication, or £400 on publication and then ten annual payments of £100, Longfellow accepted Forster's recommendation that the first method should be adopted. Proof-reading followed, with Forster's substantial help. And to such old friendships Forster added a new one with Percy Fitzgerald. 'I have a real regard for you – *I like you*', he wrote, revealingly, in 1865, 'and that you have no surer way of making me happy & obliged than by coming to see me. Do you know what Wallenstein says of Max – "For oh! he stood beside me like my youth".' He was even more enthusiastic about Fitzgerald's wife, for whom Forster facetiously professed infatuation: 'As for that other Her', he wrote to his young friend, 'well, best say as little as may be – to you, at least: with whom (even in my present good humour) I yet cannot entrust the message I *so long* to send.' Forster encouraged Fitzgerald's literary career, helped him with his biography of Sterne, urged him to write comedies, corrected his style, and consoled him when reviews were bad.[67] Through the Fitzgeralds Forster could recall early years of literary promise and, from the security of middle-aged matrimony, could revive the bachelor's right to succumb to charms and to free flirtation. That is, for Forster the friendship was the result of psychological need, the literary element now seemed almost unimportant.

A few radical embers still smouldered, as when, invited but unable to attend the banquet for Dickens before the novelist's final American tour, he made forceful complaint about the division of the list of stewards into those with titles and those without.[68] He blazed more strongly in his political opinions and, here, could seem at times an exasperated reactionary who owed much to Carlyle:

> I am sick of the Reform Bill, and the Compound Households, and the right of women to vote, and the right of Irishmen or Yankees to commit treason without peril to their necks, and the right of Beales to this Park, and all other corresponding Rights of Man ...[69]

Yet, despite such persisting feelings and fire, part of a letter to Bulwer, from Banstead in 1868, shows clearly how Forster had changed:

> I am here, in a fairly pretty house, with a keen pure dry air blowing freshly round me, and a magnificent Beech with a hundred feet of shade in middle of my lawn – under which I can muse and meditate I know not what of 'trifles and song'.[70]

Forster was 56 but, though the moment seems idyllic, the tone and, particularly, the cadences of the sentence's close, with its hinted dying fall, suggests a much older and wearier man. As Dickens told Macready later that same year: 'he has got into *an old way* which is not wholesome. He has lost interest in the larger circle of tastes and occupations that used to girdle his life'. Dickens blamed the company he kept ('those Commissioners are a duller set of fellows than he was ever used to consort with')[71] but that was far too simple. What Forster had become in 1868 was the result of a whole series of adverse circumstances.

Crucially, the decade saw a rapid deterioration of Forster's health. Bronchitis and rheumatism came with increasing frequency until Forster himself had to admit that his health was 'much broken'.[72] In 1867 gout was diagnosed. Later in the year, whilst on a Lunacy circuit, he 'fell suddenly ill – a violent & continuous pain in my right side ... It is an attack of congested liver' connected, so the doctors thought, with both his bronchitis and 'suppressed gout'.[73] The following year he had 'a most troublesome eruption all over me, which has made me wretched with the continual irritation of it for more than a month. I suffer dreadfully.'[74] In 1869 he feared 'gout in the stomach ... his health is very precarious, and he is always more or less ill, all through the winter'.[75] More and more he was confined to bed, or confined indoors.

Because of his health his Lunacy work became a trial; from the mid-1860s onwards Forster's letters refer to it with anguish and desperate complaint. 'I wish', he wrote to the faithful Bulwer in the cold February of 1865, as Forster set off on a northern circuit lasting three weeks, 'I were going in the other direction – and, instead of taking business with me, could leave it all behind me.'[76] The Commissionership's legal requirements now became a treadmill: 'My health has been very indifferent indeed lately', he told J. H. Burton, but there was 'the necessity I am under of completing much arrear of work within the few days left of this year, which the statute requires to be done.'[77]

Two more deaths grieved him greatly. In 1866 Jane Carlyle lunched at Palace Gate House, left on a spring afternoon, apparently in good health and spirits, and died in her carriage on her way home. 'No one who knew Mrs. Carlyle', wrote Forster, 'could replace her loss when she had passed away.'[78] In 1868 Mrs Forster went to Newcastle to bring to London Forster's sister Elizabeth, once a governess, now an invalid.[79] Two months later, on Christmas Day 1868, he wrote to Browning:

> I laid yesterday in the grave the last relative I have on earth except my good kind wife – who has now been in bed many days worn out with watching and sorrow. My dear sister had to undergo long and terrible suffering, which she bore with patience and submission surpassing belief – and I am left now to think of all her noble qualities, which she could not conceal in that hour of trial, with the unavailing anguish that attends the thought that I ought better to

> have discerned and valued them while yet they were not gone from me for ever.[80]

Five months later, in May 1869, Lunacy work took Forster to Newcastle for the last time. He wrote a short, desolate note to his wife: 'Arrived safely, my darling – and walked sadly before dinner round this once familiar place – nothing that I can associate with my boyhood remaining now ... and all those I knew dead and gone –.'[81]

The 1860s also witnessed the further deepening of Forster's disaffection towards most contemporary literature. The latter had become less important to him, a change clearly and sadly seen in his encounter with Swinburne during 1866. They met at Knebworth, where Swinburne was Bulwer's guest, at a time when *Poems and Ballads* was being reviled for immorality. It was a charge with which Forster tended to agree: 'I suspect he has discovered that the Indecency *does not sell*',[82] he commented sourly to Bulwer when Swinburne later changed style. Yet in 1866 for Bulwer's sake, he induced the *Examiner*, then edited by Henry Morley, to praise that offensive poetry. In the interests of friendship literary principles could now be compromised. And that basic disaffection was felt even towards his own one-time province: Forster took morbid delight in telling Carlyle of a reviewer of Latham's new edition of Johnson's *Dictionary* who denounced Johnson's preface in the belief that it was Latham's. It was, Forster wrote sarcastically, typical of 'the "high and palmy state" of criticism in the present day'.[83]

From the first days of his marriage, in 1856, until 1864, the escape-hatch of historical scholarship had always been open. It had slammed shut when Landor died. From 1864 until the publication of *Walter Savage Landor* in 1869 Forster's working alternative to the pressures of ill-health, uncongenial employment, family bereavement, and the fading of literature's attractions, was the awful complexity and psychological anguish of Landorian biography. There were, of course, the towering problems of writing the life of an 89-year-old. More taxing to the spirit was the need to recreate the friendship's dreadful transition from the strong affection and admiration of the 1830s to the scandals and quarrels of Landor's last years. For such re-creation made Forster think less of Landor and struck a strong blow against that long-cherished and rosy view of the literary character. Further, the exigencies of his Commissionership forced his biographical efforts into an exhausting routine. He wrote to C. E. Norton:

> I regret to say that I have such unexpected difficulties in the way of completion of the book – that, with my official labours beside, I

> fear sometimes that I shall break down. I am obliged to work at night – and very late, which I have not done for years – I am very miserable with it all.[84]

He was returned, in a sense, to those editorial labours for the *Daily News* and, particularly, for the *Examiner*, from which he had long ago schemed to escape. The past was not simply recalled but in some ways re-enacted, almost as if Forster had become the weary victim of a subtly sadistic time-machine.

Completing the biography did not free Forster from Landor, for there still remained the tortuous task of editing the works. And the publication of the biography almost coincided with the death of Alexander Dyce, Forster's 'poor dear old friend ... so good, so scholarly, & gentle'.[85] Forster was his executor and Dyce left an edition of Shakespeare requiring Forster's editorial care. Nevertheless, and despite continuing Lunacy work, in 1869 Forster tried to turn back to rewriting *Strafford* and to the long-projected biography of Swift. But that scholarly interlude was all too short for, on 9 June 1870, there fell the far fiercer blow of Dickens's death.

Forster was travelling the western circuit and the news reached him at Launceston. He went swiftly to Gadshill and saw the body before burial. He wrote movingly to C. E. Norton:

> until yesterday I have been myself little able to write. I broke down on Wednesday last, and had to take to my bed, which I only left on Sunday ... I saw him on Saturday morning ... I had never seen so sweet and calm an expression on his face as when I kissed it in his coffin.
>
> To you only I say this, my dear Norton. I have not been able, nor shall be, to have speech on these matters with any one. And to you for the present I will only further say that nothing in future can, to me, ever again be as it was. The duties of life remain while life remains, but for me the joy of it is gone for ever more.[86]

His first duties were as executor, urgently required to realize the estate to provide for Dickens's family. Such duties were, as Mrs Forster saw, 'very pressing and harass him very much',[87] and the Lunacy treadmill did not stop for grief. Dickens's funeral had not long passed when, as Forster wrote graphically to Carlyle, during an official asylum visit, an

> assault was made upon me, by one of a very dangerous class of men – an insane Indian soldier whose delusion was that I had ordered his food to be poisoned. I had reason to complain of the authorities

> & attendants of the Asylum – but the terrible suddenness of the frenzy was some excuse. I suffered very much, but everything was done promptly to alleviate all that – and there is now no external mark of the injury.
>
> Unfortunately however there was 'effusion' in some of the small vessels of the eye & brain – and I have ever since had the sense of a film or veil passing almost continually over the left eye (the opposite side to that on which the blow was struck) –
>
> All engagements I had were of course abandoned, and every night since I have sat without candles – and for the most part with eyes closed. I *think* I am, during the last two days, a little better – the film being less frequent ... but ... it will be some weeks before the discomfort passes away –[88]

'Had it been an *inch* higher', wrote Mrs Forster to a friend, 'it would have been fatal. – His face was bruised, cut & swollen, but he is now looking more like himself, but he is excessively weak and ill.'[89] In his splendid home, grieving in the dark, Forster's psychological and physical fortunes reached their lowest point. Lunacy business pressed, as did the demands of his surviving friendships: during the year, for example, he worked with John Murray to obtain a canonry at St Paul's for Whitwell Elwin, until Elwin changed his mind.[90] Above all, Dickens's death forced upon Forster a second distressing biographical burden.

By October 1870 he was at work; as he told Carlyle: 'I am at intervals turning to the inexpressibly sorrowful task of looking over poor Dickens's letters. Whether anything will come of it I do not know.'[91] By the end of the year progress seemed unlikely: he was again too ill to meet J. H. Burton and suffered 'from illness which almost wholly incapacitates me for work which the statute nevertheless insists on being done within the year'.[92] 'The joy is gone out of my life', he wrote to Bulwer, 'but I struggle on just as I can, with no certainty from day to day.'[93]

At the end of 1871, having qualified for a pension, Forster thankfully resigned his Commissionership. One by one almost all his friends died. Fonblanque went first, in 1872. C. E. Norton's wife followed during the same year, drawing from Forster a compassionate letter to the widower: 'The pain at my heart is such as to make almost unendurable the anguish of silence.' In 1873 it was Bulwer's turn, 'a terrible blow to me', then 'poor dear Macready', and then, in 1874, 'dear good Procter ... A kinder heart never beat'.[94] Forster's health continued to worsen and the 1870s witnessed a desperate search for a congenial climate: the Forsters tried Worthing in 1870, Bournemouth in 1871, Epsom in 1872, Torquay constantly, Hastings and Seaton in 1874, Romsey in 1875. All was to little or no avail. He developed kidney trouble and was rarely free from coughing and bronchitis. In 1873 he was too weak to write and, thereafter, was confined indoors for longer and longer periods. In the spring of 1874 he had 'acute bronchitis – coughing incessantly – day and night – and terribly weak and exhausted... Mrs. Forster said she never saw him so weakened by any previous attack'. Carlyle was 'in serious alarm'. During his last months Forster lived 'in continual suffering...shut up at present from every one' and coughing 'his lungs away'.[95] He thought little of most new literature and read it hardly at all. His views on the state of his former first love, the theatre, were summed up in a late letter to Percy Fitzgerald: 'I should like very greatly to hear what you say to Mr. Irving's Hamlet – the account of which in the *Times* made me sick to think that a man (Crawford I presume) who has really seen good acting & fine actors, should be capable of such rubbish!!'[96] And, to the end, Forster retained enemies stirred into maliciously jealous comment by his rise to affluence. Seymour Kirkop, once Landor's painter friend, thought Forster to be a 'vulgar swell'; for Ruskin's friend, John Brown, Forster was 'a "heavy swell" and ... always ... to me offensive'.[97] Yet such social enemies without were as nothing to the physiological within.

Such an account of the years from 1870 is, perhaps predictable but is not the whole story. The rest includes further literary achievement that began with the completion of *The Life of Charles Dickens* by the end of 1873. Despite his troubles Forster continued his second brave excursion into the past that was even more painful than had been his first return with Landor. For Dickens had been his closest friend and even though Dickens had, comparatively speaking, drawn apart from him during the friendship's later years, Forster's devotion had persisted. Now, as with Landor, the reliving of much of the relationship led Forster to think less of Dickens, and less of literary men. Once again he faced what he found with heroic honesty and sought, desperately and perhaps despairingly, to reconcile the demands of truth with the pressures of publishing at a time when Dickens's family watched, libel laws warned, and his own health and grief made work impossible. He was rewarded and possibly partly consoled by the book's reception: 'a wonderful success', wrote Robert Lytton, 'fourteen thousand of the first, and twelve thousand of the second volume sold already'.[98] A major revision remained before the second, reconstructed edition of 1876, the year in which an abridged version of *Walter Savage Landor* also came out, as volume one of Forster's multi-volumed edition of Landor's works. Only months before, in 1875, Forster had at last published the first volume of *The Life of Jonathan Swift*, a short-lived return to objective scholarship after 11 years of sad nostalgia among the memories and documents of his former literary life.

His publications are in themselves evidence of the man's dogged courage at a time when even putting pen to paper could be a wearying and painful act. Most impressive of all, in these final years, is the way Forster emerged even from terrible adversity as an attractive and humane figure. Nowhere is this better seen than in the progress of his marriage.

Eliza Forster continued, herself, to enjoy poor health. She was plagued by neuralgia, by colds, sore throats, and abscesses. But her warm feelings helped sustain Forster, as did her anxiety to share and enjoy her husband's interests: she read Carlyle, enjoyed calm excursions around Shakespearian places, and settled willingly to the 'quiet & homely' life forced upon her incapacitated husband. To the end Forster continued to patronize her as 'the small one' and as his 'poor little Madam', but he patronized with tenderness and, despite his own troubles, was never less than considerate of her welfare. In 1869, in Manchester on Lunacy business, he wrote to Carlyle: 'I have had to work under difficulties and disablements of which I have thought it best to say nothing to the small wife at Kensington – I'll go home, well, if I can'. If she was unwell when such business took him from her Forster would anxiously despatch her to Warwickshire to recuperate with Landor's surviving family at Tachbrooke. When she had a fall at Seaton and suffered 'a little strain and stiffness of shoulder & side', he was all concern and much relieved at her lucky escape from serious injury. All in all, even though it seems inappropriate to describe the relationship as one of fierce passion or deep love, it was certainly a marriage of affection and happiness from which Forster drew much strength, and which brought out his finer qualities.[99] Its great lack, of course, was children, and to the end Forster sublimated that need in kindness to his god-children. 'He gave me a Christening Cup', wrote Henry Forster Morley, 'and later a half-hunter gold watch. When I married he gave me a Piano.'[100] In 1872 Forster did not forget to congratulate the young man on success in the London matriculation.[101]

Very occasionally, Forster revived his interest in new literature: he enjoyed *Through the Looking Glass* and told the author so,[102] he looked forward to reading *Middlemarch*.[103] But, apart from Carlyle and the work of Forster's dead friends, he now preferred travel books,[104] a sadly ironic choice for an increasingly immobile reader. In 1872 came a rare glimpse of old ideas and vigour: at the Royal Academy's annual banquet, as a distinguished sixty-year-old man-of-letters he responded to the toast of 'Literature'. In his speech he remembered the dead and recalled the eighteenth-century origins of the Royal Academy, 'and thus to associate with itself for ever such memories as those of Johnson, Burke, and Goldsmith'. He ended by returning to the theme that had shaped his own literary career, his concern with literature's rewards. Literary men were 'quite ready' for such rewards to be better. He sat down to 'loud cheers'.[105]

Such interest, as has been said, had become occasional. More significant, in those last years, were Forster's surviving friendships, and particularly those with Percy Fitzgerald, the same mixture of magisterial advice and facetious flirtation, and with Carlyle. The latter was a second major consolation throughout Forster's decline. It kept alive Forster's interest in politics that, in turn, sustained other friendships, such as that with Lord Shaftesbury, with whom Forster discussed the state of government throughout the 1870s with a vehemence and with views that were themselves Carlylean.[106] He had little time for Gladstonian liberalism: 1871 was the '*most contemptible session of parliament* entered upon any kind of record'.[107] When in 1870 the Franco-Prussian war brought the downfall of Louis Napoleon, the derivation of Forster's accents was unmistakeable: 'Let us continue', he wrote to C. E. Norton, 'in the faith which this Gigantic Nemesis encourages us to hold, that there is really and truly, Bishops and Popes and other Portents to the contrary notwithstanding, a divine overlooking Power to bring wretchedness and falsehood to account even in this poor trumpery world!'[108]

His letters to Carlyle drew from the wretched Forster a persisting humour that has to be admired. From Knebworth Forster wrote to his friend:

> I in the wildest manner rejoice at thus announcing to you that I have done and do No Work; that I have not been (as yet) reading in any rational book; that even my last volumes of Frederick remain unopened; and that all my intellectual provender has been 'Under the Limes', a story in two volumes by a daughter of Sir Henry Taylor's, which seems to be only distinguishable from other stories of young ladies of the present day by the fact that it is decent. But though it has 'no offence in the world', it has apparently as little meaning.[109]

From Melchet Court near Romsey, where he had gone in poor health to seek relief from a London summer, he wrote satirically: 'The house is on too big a scale for my notions of comfort and home... I find it to be no inconsiderable journey to get from one side of my bed to the other – and, in the days when I *could* sleep, I should have tumbled asleep between pillow and pillow!'[110] Forster could even exhibit a talent for self-mockery wildly at odds with any Podsnappic stereotype. For example, his friends knew well – and circulated the anecdote with some glee – that an exasperated cab-man had once described Forster as a 'harbitrary cove'; Forster wrote to Carlyle's niece, Mary Aitken:

> I wonder you'd write such a thing – with the Bird of Wisdom sitting & overlooking you – as that your uncle has 'no sort of command' over me, when you know very well it is he, not I, to whom 'harbitrary cove' is alone applicable! However I did not take up the pen to write that but to say that the next time you come with your uncle to this door and don't enter it – I shall – well I won't say what I'll do – lest I should unconsciously reveal that the direful force of circumstances might disclose another 'harbitrary cove' finding the h.c. alluded to in a former passage.[111]

Friendship brought out the best in him and the aging Forster valued it more and more highly. As he told Percy Fitzgerald: 'What a comfort it is for us all that friendship is so much better than literature.'[112] But in the final weeks, even that could not resist darker, stronger pressures: 'I have been very ill', he wrote to Carlyle, 'and so continue, though with some alleviation of suffering during the last three days. What is to become of me, I do not know; but I find it to be an ill sign that my courage is leaving me!'[113] His state was summarized in a bleak note from Mrs Forster:

> My husband is unfortunately too ill to write, and the hour you name is one when his cough is always troublesome to him. If however you will come tomorrow evening at a ¼ past 5 – I will in any case see you, and he will see you if he possibly can.[114]

To be isolated in illness, and unable even to hold a pen, was a sad fate for so gregarious a literary man. Three weeks later he was dead.

Part Three Man of Letters – ii
Four Friendships

CHAPTER 9 *Robert Browning*

Forster was Browning's contemporary at University College, London. He read law and Browning studied languages. In 1833 they both attended Edmund Kean's funeral. Forster's prominence at college and the way he seized his chance to meet Macready at Kean's funeral reflected his obtrusive and necessary ambition: he needed a career and had to help himself. Browning, on the other hand, although he began his college career from lodgings in Bloomsbury, quickly returned to Camberwell and his financially comfortable parents. He lived in confident expectation of literary success but his first publication, *Pauline*, in 1833, was hardly noticed and later regretted.[1] Neither at Gower Street nor at Kean's funeral did they seek each other out. They met, eventually, at Macready's Elstree home on New Year's Eve, 1835.[2]

According to report Forster greeted Browning with the question, 'Did you see a little notice of you I wrote in the *Examiner*?', referring to his review of *Paracelsus*.[3] This may be apocryphal; what is certain is that Forster was beginning a relationship unique among his major friendships. When he met Hunt, Lamb, Bulwer, Macready, Landor, and Carlyle, they were established and influential figures; when he met Dickens the latter was reaping the rewards of early success. Browning was unknown and unsuccessful, Forster already well known as a feared weekly reviewer. It was a situation calculated to encourage Forster's urge to dominate and desire to patronize. But Browning, though he was ambitious, did not need to write to live and had a clear sense of his own genius. Forster encountered a fierce and often inflammable mixture of professional concern, amateur status, and artistic integrity. Sweetness and light were hardly central to this friendship.

To *Paracelsus* Forster had given a long and balanced review that opened assertively: 'Since the publication of *Philip Van Artevelde*, we have met with no such evidences of poetical genius, and of general intellectual power, as are contained in this volume.' He was fascinated by Browning's interest in psychology, in rendering a mood itself, rather than through 'the operation of persons and events', within an ostensibly dramatic framework; he commended the morality of Browning's poem, its assertion that 'mere pride of the understanding, or the sternness of the will, may never, and should never, avail against the affections of the heart'.[4] Forster publicized enthusiastically, with extensive quotation, as well as inducing his friends, W. J. Fox in the *Monthly Repository* and Leigh Hunt in his *Journal*, to provide further favourable notices.

After meeting Browning Forster wrote a second review in the *New Monthly Magazine*. This stressed *Paracelsus*'s dramatic qualities: 'Passion is invariably displayed, and never merely analysed ... Mr. Browning has the power of a great dramatic poet; we never think of Mr. Browning while we read his poem; we are not identified with him, but with the persons into whom he has flung his genius.' Browning, argued Forster, passed the 'essential dramatic test' in that, when reading *Paracelsus*, 'in the agitation of the feelings, sight is given to the imagination'.[5] Here was new and exciting hope for the ailing English theatre.

Browning was always grateful for this early support; the second review, in particular, helped influence him towards the theatre. But even in those first friendly moments lay the seeds of later dissension. 'Its author is a young man', Forster concluded in that first review; '... we may safely predict for him a brilliant career, if he continues true to the present promise of his genius.'[6] In the second review are references to 'the imagination of this young poet' and the conclusion that 'here is a young poet ... a great poet'[7] who should be supported. Forster, though the same age as Browning, was not deterred from vigorous and potentially disruptive patronage.

This is not to say that Forster, with a liking for the work, was not sincerely attracted to the man. For Browning quickly became Forster's '*all-in-all*'[8] and, increasingly, was involved by him in the world of their mutual friend Macready. Browning was much impressed by Macready's acting, and Macready, pressurized by Forster, who was quick to familiarize him with Browning's work, had hopes that the poet 'had awakened a spirit of poetry whose influence would elevate, ennoble, and adorn our degraded drama'.[9] Browning began an abortive tragedy on Narses,[10] before further involvement with Forster stoked his theatrical ambitions.

On 4 May 1836 appeared the first volume of Forster's historical series, *Lives of Eminent British Statesmen*. This, part of Dionysius Lardner's *Cabinet Cyclopaedia*, contained biographies of Sir John Eliot and Thomas

Wentworth, Earl of Strafford. For Forster it was a difficult year: Browning recalled his poor health[11] and Macready's *Diary*, in recording no meetings with Forster between 27 February and 15 April, also suggests this. The death of Forster's father must have been a further disruptive factor, despite Macready's reference to Forster's indifference.[12] In the event Browning helped Forster write Strafford's life.

Today it seems impossible to establish precisely the respective contributions of the two collaborators but the following sequence can be offered with some confidence.[13] Forster collected materials and began the writing. This is incontrovertible: Browning began helping Forster only when problems arose during the rush to completion. He took possession of Forster's manuscript and materials and produced a full draft. Internal evidence for this is abundant: there are far too many passages not only unForsterian in style but of a brilliance that can only be Browning's, and such passages occur from the earliest parts of the book. Three examples can stand for many: 'Whenever an obvious or judicious truth seemed likely to fall in his way, his pen infallibly waddled off from it',[14] wrote Browning of King James only a few pages into the work. Forty-five pages later is found:

> Infinitely and distinctly various as appear the shifting hues of our common nature when subjected to the prism of CIRCUMSTANCE, each ray into which it is broken is no less in itself a primitive colour, susceptible, indeed, of vast modification, but incapable of further division.[15]

And, towards the end: 'Still, with the increasing and imperious urgency of the need, towered ever proudlier the inexhaustible genius of Strafford.'[16] One can only ask, with Professor Monod, 'And will a single reader ascribe to any one else than a poet'[17] these or other similar extracts?

But it also seems certain that Browning's version was not the final text. For throughout the work and even in those parts most distinguished by Browning's fine style and psychological insights come Forsterian reactions to and reservations about his friend's interpretation of Strafford's character. That is to say, Forster who, after all, was the historian, read carefully and revised the manuscript that Browning delivered. This is best seen in insertions that seek to modify Browning's more sympathetic account of Strafford's career. For example, a reference to Strafford's brave behaviour at his trial ('the earl calmly turned back to his judges, and with uncomplaining composure conferred') is followed by what is clearly Forster's interjection: 'Noble and touching as this is, let the reader re-member, as he reads it, the case of Mountnorris ... It is mournful to be obliged to add that, it is chiefly the genius of a great actor that calls for admiration in this great scene.'[18] Again, to an attack on King Charles for deserting his strongest supporter by weakly signing the Bill of Attainder that was effectively Strafford's death-warrant Forster responded: 'Sufficient has been said to vindicate these remarks from any, the remotest, intention of throwing doubt on the perfect justice of that bill of attainder ... As to Strafford's death, the remark that the people had no alternative, includes all that it is necessary to urge.'[19]

Forster considered the published text to be his own: he presented Browning with a copy inscribed, 'The author to his dear friend, Robert Browning'.[20] But what is most important, here, is not the exact nature of the collaboration but the effect it had on Browning's career. In the first place it is a truism that Browning's poetry is much concerned with conflicts between individuals and oppressive authority. His nonconformist upbringing, liberal tendencies, and interest in Shelley lie behind that concern. That he should immerse himself, when young and impressionable, in a period of history dominated by the clash between people and tyrants, makes the link with Forster importantly catalytic. Secondly, having been pressurized by both Macready and Forster to write for the theatre, through his work on Strafford Browning found his first play. Forster's influence was most potent when he himself lay ill and incapable.

The collaboration was never publicly acknowledged during the lifetime of either man. It existed as a shared secret, a persisting link through the friendship's many vicissitudes, recalled by both in later life.[21] But it placed Forster, as the authority receiving unacknowledged help, at a disadvantage. And Browning possibly resented his own treatment, his draft not only unacknowledged but also altered to fit Forster's preconceptions about Strafford's character. Elizabeth Barrett's indignation, 'I forgot again your Strafford – Mr. Forster's Strafford, I beg his pardon for not attributing to him other men's works',[22] seems a response to Browning's own strong feelings. Further, on the endpaper of his presentation copy Browning inserted two quotations. The first was from *Cymbeline*:

> *Posthumus.* I do believe
> (*Statist* though I am none, nor like to be)
> That this will prove a war.

The second was from *Hamlet*:

> I once did hold it, as our *statists* do
> A baseness to write fair.[23]

The second perhaps refers, ironically, to Forster's revisions that certainly did not improve the work's stylistic qualities. Both quotations convey explicitly Browning's distaste for his early historical venture.

That venture found Browning a brilliant stranger in Forster's world. The role was repeated when Browning wrote his play, for Forster was both an important drama critic and Macready's valued associate. He and Macready understood the theatre as Browning did not; the latter came to them, initially, in a mood of enthusiastic compliance and swiftly produced a draft of *Strafford* for Macready to read.

But Macready became increasingly doubtful about the play's dramatic qualities. Without consulting Browning he sent for Forster and actor and critic together began work: 'We went over the play ... altered, omitted, and made up one new scene; we were occupied from eleven till four o'clock; the day entirely surrendered to it.'[24] They remained dissatisfied and Macready asked Browning for more rewriting. Browning was offended and was at first unwilling to change 'the conduct of the play'; he and Forster 'had rather a warm altercation'.[25] They clashed again when Browning remained reluctant to make further necessary alterations. Macready and Forster, as experienced theatricals, were properly apprehensive of the play's chances; Browning, with a blithe conceit, believed *Strafford* to be a work of quality. In the event, through Macready and Forster's efforts the play had a mixed reception and made 'a grand escape'.[26] Macready gave it five performances before dropping it from his repertoire.[27]

Browning was not pleased at Macready's less-than-ecstatic reaction. More tension came with Forster's review which opened by stressing Browning's potential:

> This is a work of a writer who is capable of achieving the highest objects and triumphs of dramatic literature. They are not achieved here, but here they lie, 'in the rough', before every reader. *Strafford* suggests the most brilliant career of dramatic authorship that has been known in our time. We are not sure that it will be realized ...

Forster then referred frankly to Browning's shortcomings: he had 'suffered himself to yield too much to the impulses of the pure poetical temperament in delineating the character of Strafford. He has gone too subtly beneath the broad masses of light and shade which hang over the history of that great and unfortunate man.' Browning was too sympathetic to Strafford in a play about 'the triumph of patriotism over the antagonist principle of tyranny'. Good dramatic chances were lost, the main one through Browning's decision to exclude a scene from the final trial.

Macready, despite being described as 'not nearly so fine as he is wont to be',[28] thought Forster's review to be 'kind and judicious'. But Browning did not and hurt Forster with 'expressions of discontent at his criticism'. To Macready Browning sent a churlish note and the actor, not without reason, smouldered in his diary: 'It is very unreasonable and indeed *ungrateful* in him to write thus.'[29]

In the sequence of events from the Strafford biography to Browning's play Forster had helped Browning, had patronized him, and had certainly wounded his vanity. Browning, initially, had helped his friend, and had behaved very badly with a confidence becoming conceit. Browning had ventured into history and into drama, areas where Forster was in command and Browning disadvantaged. As Browning turned more and more to poetry the positions became reversed: it was now Forster's turn to peer into a world he did not wholly understand. What continued is what was central to this early sequence, the basic affection for Browning and regard for his work that made Forster, on occasion, over-concerned.

The 'Strafford' collaborations were never repeated. Browning continued to write plays for Macready but Forster was less closely involved in Macready's rejection of *King Victor and King Charles* and *The Return of the Druses*. In 1841 Forster persuaded Macready to read *A Blot in the 'Scutcheon*,[30] shared his doubts about its dramatic viability, and asked Dickens for a third opinion. Dickens delayed a year, then responded very favourably. But Forster never told Browning,[31] probably because, as the play was being prepared for the stage, Macready was again finding Browning hard to handle. This time Browning went too far. The lead in *A Blot* was to be taken by Samuel Phelps, then in Macready's company. Macready, seeking to boost the play's chances, studied Phelps's part and proposed to Browning, with the players present, that the actor-manager should himself take it over. Browning refused; Macready was deeply offended. The friendship ended and so, for all practical purposes, did Browning's hopes for the stage.[32]

Until 1846 and Browning's departure for Italy with Elizabeth Barrett his friendship with Forster staggered along. Forster occasionally acted as literary agent: he persuaded Longman to publish *Strafford*[33] and Ainsworth to place *Sordello* with Macrone.[34] And from time to time he drew from Browning unusual work. In 1836 Browning recalled 'helping Forster to write an article for the "Examiner" ... F. being ignorant of Italian but desirous of doing a service'. The article reviewed the work of Carlo Pepoli.[35] In 1841, in Forster's rooms, in response to his description of Maclise's new picture, 'The Serenade', Browning wrote the descriptive lines that became the opening of 'In a Gondola'.[36] Most importantly, when

Forster became editor of the *Foreign Quarterly Review* he obtained from Browning a review of a new biography of Tasso that quickly became the now well-known 'Essay on Chatterton', an important demonstration of Browning's handling of historical sources.[37] Forster's editorial indulgence was never more valuable.

Such particular services were accompanied by accumulating social enrichment: Browning, through Forster, was drawn into London literary life to become the friend of Dickens, Moxon, Hunt, Landor, Bulwer, Talfourd, Procter, and many, many others. All, services and socializing, took place against the volatile background of Forster's reviewing.

Sordello apart, during this period Forster reviewed all Browning's publications in notices crammed with extreme reactions. Praise was often fulsome. *Pippa Passes* was lauded for its 'entire sincerity' and for demonstrating how humility could influence the world and so express the 'fulness of divine life'. *Dramatic Lyrics* showed Browning's mastery of 'the art of versification', his 'flow' and 'music'; *Dramatic Romances* had 'melodious transitions... most poetical and most musical varieties'. *Luria* was praised for its 'ease and simplicity'.[38]

Yet such praise lay alongside furious criticism. In the Phene/Jules scene in *Pippa Passes*:

> with some few exquisite exceptions, the language is so fitful and obscure, the thoughts themselves so wild and whirling, the whole air of the scene so shadowy and remote, that, with its great blots of gorgeous colour too, we are reminded of nothing so much as of one of Turner's canvasses – pictures *of* Nothing, as someone has called them, and remarkably like.

In the same review Forster took a belated swipe at the unreviewed *Sordello*, its unfortunate author succumbing to 'the temptations which too easily beset a man's pride in his own originality; the enticing and most dangerous depths of metaphysics'. A year later Forster swiped again: 'if poetry were exactly the thing to grind professors of metaphysics on, we should pray to Mr. Browning for perpetual *Sordellos*'. In the generally favourable notice of *Dramatic Romances* is a sharp paragraph insisting that 'Mr. Browning's metaphysics ... retarded his advance'. As for *Luria*:

> it has Mr. Browning's defects. Too much philosophy for passion, and too much passion for philosophy, are the Scylla and Charibdis through which this admirable writer and true poet winds too often a dangerous and difficult way. 'The Sirens wait him singing song for song'; the music near and from afar blend confusedly; and the poet

misses his way in the straits of metaphysics, the metaphysician in the vortex of poetry.

Two further extracts sum up. *King Victor and King Charles*, wrote Forster, showed 'the wayward perverseness of a man of true genius'; when reading *Colombe's Birthday*, concluded Forster viciously, 'we abominate his tastes as much as we respect his genius'.[39] The former shows the polarizing of views that structured whole notices; both, and particularly the latter, clearly demonstrate what Browning certainly felt, that criticism is more memorable than praise.

Browning remained grateful for Forster's early support: in 1842 he gave him the manuscript of *Paracelsus* inscribed 'John Forster, Esq. (my early Understander) with true thanks for his generous & seasonable public confession of faith in me'.[40] In *Sordello* he based Naddo on Forster and though here there is *some* tension, with Naddo described as

busiest of the tribe
Of genius-haunters –

as the man who urged that poetry should be 'Based upon common sense', there was, on Sordello's part, much respect for and reliance upon Naddo's literary advice:

Eat fern-seed
And peer beside us and report indeed.[41]

But Browning, hardly placid, was equally infuriated by Forster's attacks: that on *Colombe's Birthday* caused a month-long estrangement.[42] Elizabeth Barrett's arrival in 1845 did not help. In 1844 Forster had reviewed her *Poems* and, though he had praised her as 'an undoubted poetess of a high and fine order as regards the first requisites of her art, imagination and expression', he had attacked several poems for their 'erroneous, perhaps not thoroughly healthy predilection' for risky sacred subjects and for demonstrating their author's inability to know 'what to keep and what to reject'.[43] That rankled, as her letters to Browning make plain. Elizabeth Barrett came to think better of Forster's work, even, on one occasion, describing him as 'the ablest of English critics',[44] but was more often properly sceptical of Forster's understanding of Browning's work: 'There can be nothing in common between you',[45] she told her husband-to-be.

Forster objected to Browning's friends,[46] and was furious when Browning married secretly.[47] In 1839 Eliza Fox was asked to settle a dispute; in 1845 Browning wrote wearily: 'we will go on again with the friendship, as the snail repairs his battered shell'.[48] The reviews stabbed, nagged, and patronized, Elizabeth Barrett stood by with hostility that was willing and supportive. Reconciliations were, then, always effected eventually.

From 1846 until 1861 the Brownings lived in Italy and made few visits to London. During the period Forster performed only occasional services for his absent friends. In 1848, when Phelps revived *The Blot in the 'Scutcheon* at Sadler's Wells Forster went twice and arranged a complimentary review in the *Examiner*.[49] With Procter and Talfourd he helped prepare the collected edition of Browning's poetry that appeared in 1849.[50] In 1850 Forster was 'caring for Ba's new Edition'.[51] Browning once asked him for information about publishing in America,[52] but there was no regular business correspondence; Forster never became Browning's literary agent or adviser, as Browning's letters to Chapman & Hall make clear.[53]

There was some personal contact, at times warmly emotional, in a three-sided exchange. Forster admired Elizabeth Barrett Browning as 'a woman of such unquestionable genius', argued with her about Italian politics, and expressed his 'true admiration' of her literary achievements. To her went his honeymoon letter with its ardent desire that the two wives might meet.[54]

To her husband Forster wrote of Dickens's doings and of the scandals involving Bulwer's Rosina. He responded to Browning's letters with typical open-heartedness:

> With what true delight my heart then responded to your continued friendly remembrance of me ... There are no friendships like old friendships, my dear Browning – and of all my old friendships there is none that makes such constant and peculiar appeal to me as yours.[55]

In 1860 Forster sent his newly-published *The Arrest of the Five Members*, a work which 'I am now bringing out which will even further remind you of our old studies together; & old times.'[56]

During Browning's last four years in Italy Landor was there also in his final exile. He was estranged from Forster, who begged Browning to look after the old man. Browning, with an ailing wife and limited means, was concerned about this additional and unpredictable responsibility. Forster's letters became frequent as he first reassured Browning that either Landor's family in England, or he himself, would cover living costs, and then, each quarter, forwarded to Browning the family's £50 for Landor's upkeep. All the while he protested his concern for that aging but still irascible character: 'I have never swerved from him for an instant in all our intercourse – nor even entitled myself (though I have had now & then to undergo it) to a moment's forfeiture of his best good will', Forster insisted in 1859.[57]

During this period, Forster's letters drew equally warm responses from Browning. In 1853, with Forster ill and needing constant attention, Browning wrote, with boisterous compassion: 'You inveterate Forster – *marry*, will you? How else will you get a son whom people shall look to, for your sake, and then like for his own ... And let my son be friends with yours.' A year later, after reading the *Examiner*, he wrote with nostalgic affection: 'I am truly happy that the "large composition" I have been used to admire has done itself justice – the Pym-like build of you, which made chairs creak and floors groan when we turned over books together in the *Strafford* crisis'. And to Forster he sent a long and detailed account of Elizabeth Barrett Browning's death, the 'manly, true and honest letter, I think: increasing one's love for Browning'.[58]

Until 1856 Forster continued to notice Browning's volumes. The collected *Poems* of 1849 were praised generously: Browning had 'already done enough to secure a distinguished place in English literature'. Yet, with his undoubted strength, the 'principle of undying vitality in all his compositions', basic faults persisted: 'a vast deal of obscurity, of false philosophy, of ungainly and jerking expression'.[59] A year later Forster also found much to praise in *Christmas-Eve and Easter Day*, but he also, again, found room for the patronizing forecast: '(Browning) will yet win and wear his laurel, and be admitted for what he truly is, one of the most original poets of his time'.[60] In such remarks that future tense had become more cudgel than friendly encourager.

Forster's final review of Browning was of *Men and Women*. Here, he insisted, was much work that was 'as genuine poetry as any that has been written in our time'. Yet

> there are too many pieces in the volumes to which the objection of obscurity in the meaning, and of a perverse harshness in the metres, may be justly urged. It is Mr Browning's old fault. Since his first poem was published twenty years ago, when we were the first to promise him the reputation he has won, this journal has been incessantly objecting to it.[61]

Browning had improved but Forster remained disappointed. And he remained uncomprehending. He had long sensed a great poetic talent but could neither reconcile its achievements with his conventional aesthetic standards nor make any impression on the way Browning wrote. Because he cared greatly about both man and work he had expressed that disappointment in terms of critical antagonism.

Forster's reviews caused long-nursed wounded feelings in the Browning household. In October 1855, when both husband and wife were in London for the publication of *Men and Women*, Forster had a curious exchange with Elizabeth Barrett Browning about his long-gone failure to review *Sordello*. He wrote to her:

> I send a little book which I want you just to look at before you go ... It contains Sordello and I wish you to see ... that my objections ... do not arise from the inability to understand & enjoy (with the due amount of study & patience) – but from the earnest desire I have that a labour should not be imposed as the condition of a pleasure. I fancy it may even please you to see, by glancing through these marks of mine, how honestly I seem to have read to the close, and how much I found that was beautiful & noble ...[62]

Such defensive insistence meant that Forster's failure was continuing to offend, even 14 years later. Certainly the Brownings had not been placated by his subsequent mixed reviews. The tense undercurrent surfaced again shortly after *Men and Women* appeared: Robert Browning wrote from Paris to Chapman & Hall that he had been reading reviews, 'the "Examiner" being the best... The serious notices are to come, it is to be hoped.'[63] Lingering hostility was never more evident.

From 1846 until 1861 Browning made few visits to England. On his first, in 1851, Forster gave him a dinner at Thames Ditton.[64] In 1855 not only was Forster obliged to defend himself against *Sordello*'s champion but had a slight brush with Browning when he (Forster) and Sir Charles Duffy accused him of prejudice against Roman Catholics in 'Bishop Blougram's Apology'.[65] A startled Browning took his surprise back to Italy. Certainly they were never better friends than when they were safely apart.

In 1861 Browning, now a widower, returned to live in London. Forster helped him find a house and gave advice about Pen's education.[66] During the early 1860s Browning dined occasionally with Forster in groups that often included Dickens and Carlyle.[67]

In 1862 Forster gave his last major service to Browning's literary career when, with B. W. Procter, he prepared *Selections from the Poetical Works of Robert Browning*, the first edition of its kind. Forster's was the dominant editorial voice: he overruled Procter's suggestion that only short poems should be included.[68] The *Selection* printed long passages from *Paracelsus*, an extract from *Sordello* that may well have been penitential, scenes from all the dramas, including the abused *Colombe's Birthday*, and from *Christmas-Eve and Easter Day*, together with a wide-ranging sample from *Dramatic Lyrics* and *Men and Women*. The preface at last threw aside equivocation to hail Browning as 'among the few great poets of the century', and was shown to Browning before publication.[69] Browning himself published a complementary selection at the same time. Both sold well and, together, mark the beginning of his rise to fame. In that same year appeared the dedication of Browning's *Collected Works* to his 'old friend John Forster ... their promptest and staunchest helper'. Forster responded with 'thanks – "glad and grateful" as the heart can make it ... do you not know how proud and glad I feel, that our names may thus be found together by the future and for generations of readers that will most surely be yours'.[70] Two years later Forster was made one of Browning's executors. In 1864 it seemed that the friendship had entered a new and harmonious phase.

But both, in their middle age, were obstinate, hot-tempered, and not a little vain. Browning became famous and well-regarded, Forster wealthy and irritated by illness. The friendship, in its closing years, reverted to type. It swung from violent quarrels through lengthening estrangements to emotional reconciliations.

During the later 1860s, when a long silence followed a quarrel, it was Browning who made the first healing move through condolences on the death of Forster's last surviving sister. Forster was moved to reply:

> The only things of the past that now seem real to me are old friendly feelings – and I need not say how many of these I connect with you and with yours – with your kind mother and father, whose faces are as present to me while I write as the recollection of their kindness always is – and with her, ever dearer to you, who was ever good and generous to me ... With such grief at my heart, and at this season of peace and good will, the letter I received three days ago has made it appear to me possible that at least such kindly relations may be renewed with its writer as will admit of our meeting not quite as strangers in future.[71]

They met again. Forster praised 'The Ring and the Book': 'Pompilia' he found to be 'profoundly affecting'.[72] He interceded with Browning for Julian Fane when the latter's *Edinburgh Review* article, vetted by Forster, appeared with editorial alterations that strengthened criticism and removed some praise.[73] On Christmas Day 1869 Browning and Carlyle were the Forsters' dinner guests.[74]

Such friendliness only postponed the inevitable. During the early 1870s they clashed in company about a lady's veracity. Browning, angered beyond reason by Forster's scepticism, seized a decanter and had to be forcibly prevented from throwing it at Forster's head.[75] Not until 1875 did they resume contact: when Forster read the newly published *The Inn Album* it 'brought back 40 years ago' so that, as he told Browning: 'I yield to an impulse too strong to resist, and send a word (requiring no notice from you) to say how profoundly it has moved and affected me ... I am still yours with the affection of that old gone time'.[76] And Browning replied:

> My very first critic, so you remained, to my apprehension, the best – the most competent, although not, perhaps, to me the most impartial. ... It would be strange indeed if I were not proud at in any way pleasing you in my last work. ... I am happy you recall our old days and conversancy – my own friendship was too vital to succumb at the interruption of *that*. Nor have I at all doubted of your good will to me.[77]

Two months later Forster was dead; and Browning glad, as he told George Grove, that the friendship had been renewed.[78]

In that final phase literary disputes were replaced by personal clashes. When together for any length of time each acted as a profound irritant on the other, only for estrangements to foster affection that compelled further contact. All the while they respected each other's talents but, all the while, Forster failed wholly to comprehend his friend's originality. Much of the friendship's tension stemmed from that failure yet, despite it, at crucial moments in Browning's career Forster's influential reach far exceeded his literary-critical grasp.

CHAPTER 10 *Walter Savage Landor*

Forster's relationship with Landor began with Charles Lamb. As Forster recalled, many years later, 'One of the last things said to me by Charles Lamb, a week or two before his death, was that only two men could have written the *Examination of Shakespeare* – he who wrote it, and the man it was written on; and that is exactly what I think.'[1] Landor's fanciful history, *The Citation and Examination of William Shakespeare*, first appeared, anonymously, in 1834, when Landor was 59. Forster was 22 and the *Examiner*'s new drama critic; on 30 November 1834, as a result of Lamb's communicated delight and Forster's consequent knowledge of authorship, Forster made one of his first appearances as 'Literary Examiner' with a four-column review of Landor's work. It was a review coloured by Forster's new and flushed enthusiasm: 'Its wit and pathos', he wrote of the *Citation*, 'its humour, fancy, and imagination, are only made subservient to the most exalted expression of morality.'[2] Other journals were lambasted wholeheartedly for ignoring the work or for criticizing it.

During the year that followed such support would have been further encouraged by Landor's consolatory lyric, 'To the Sister of Charles Lamb', which he contributed to *Leigh Hunt's London Journal*[3] some months after Lamb's death. Yet though that poem would have been read by Forster with intense interest the *Examiner* was mainly responsible for preparing the ground for friendship. Landor was a regular reader; in the spring of 1836, in two reviews of *Pericles and Aspasia* he found himself described by Forster as 'among the greatest writers of modern literature' for his 'scholarship and genius' and for the 'lofty' subject[4] and 'perfectly dramatic'[5] quality of his new volume. Landor was not used to such laudatory reviewing, made yet more acceptable because appearing at a time of great personal crisis during which he had separated from his wife and left his family in Italy. But, even if life had been generally sweet, only a man of stone was proof against Forster's ardent praise. Landor was hardly that.

They met on 26 May 1836, at the celebratory supper for the first night of Talfourd's *Ion*. At this first encounter Landor's liking for Forster was a tribute to the younger man's essential attractiveness and not at all to do with gratitude: Landor believed Fonblanque to have been his reviewer[6] and did not learn the truth until he called on Forster four days later. Although, then, this revelation was a useful adhesive, it was not the only one. Landor found a young and impressionable enthusiast who was much concerned, as always, to support a neglected writer of quality. Forster saw a man of 61, of 'distinguished bearing'[7] and fascinating face, a glamorous figure who had known Leigh Hunt and Hazlitt in romantic Italy, was a friend of Wordsworth, of Coleridge, and of Southey, and who had been close to Charles Lamb. He found a fine talker, his conversation full of literary references, firm opinions, a long life's anecdotage, and much else that was congenial. The two men shared a love of art, the classics, things Cromwellian, Keats's poetry, and the dramas of Sheridan Knowles. Above all, Forster found a man who took literature seriously and had a long-standing interest in the critical activity. Further, as one whose life, private and professional, was in perpetual disorder, Landor was obvious material for Forster's organizing friendliness, even though he was old enough to be Forster's grandfather.

At the friendship's centre was the *Examiner*. Forster used it to publicize Landor's work and did so in two ways. Firstly, he continued to review Landor's work regularly and generously. During 1836 he wrote about Landor in the *New Monthly Magazine*,[8] but the *Examiner* notices were more important. They insisted upon and developed three main points: Landor's work would last, it was for a discerning minority, and his genius was essentially dramatic. As the reviews repeated, his 'reputation will live in the glad and proud appreciation of future days and be a grave reproach to the indifference of our own',[9] his work was 'a building to which the wise will resort in many generations to come', he was 'not a writer to propitiate any large class'.[10] The dramatic quality was everywhere, in the 'imaginary conversations' and in the closet-dramas. 'Nothing can be more dramatic than the means employed; nothing less theatrical than the results arrived at', Forster wrote of *Andrea of Hungary* and *Giovanna of Naples*. The reviews also contain much praise of Landor's scholarship, wit, 'pure' style, and classicism.

But Forster was not uncritical. As early as 1839, in that same review of *Andrea of Hungary* and its companion drama, Forster admitted that they had a 'fair portion indeed of Mr Landor's faults – abrupt and disconnected thoughts; occasional sallies of wilfulness; expressions that now and then verge on the borders of coarseness'.[11] In the collected *Works* of 1846 there was 'occasional wilfulness, intemperance, and violence'.[12] In 1851 came a forthright attack on *Popery: British and Foreign*: 'We cannot close pages which contain such writing as this, without regret that they should be disfigured by a few sentences here and there having apparently more of personal spleen than of any higher feeling in them.'[13] Later that same year the *Examiner*, then of course under Forster's editorship, published a sonnet to Landor urging him to more temperate writing, with equally pointed editorial comment: 'All deprecate his indiscriminating commination of everything and every man not actually embattled on the side of constitution and republics.'[14]

Secondly, Forster made the *Examiner* an outlet for much of Landor's work and for his fiercely expressed views and opinions. From August 1836, when it printed the 'Imaginary Conversation' between Lord Eldon and his son Encombe, until the end of Forster's editorship in 1855, the *Examiner* published many of Landor's lyrics, further conversations, and extracts from several of his other prose works. In addition it printed innumerable 'letters to the editor' that included 13 on church reform during 1837, and many others over the years on subjects ranging from conduct of the clergy and clerical grammar to Canada, Lord Brougham, Eastern politics and the fine arts.[15]

Landor's views, whether expressed in letters or in the extracted literary work, sometimes accorded with those of the *Examiner* itself. Occasionally he could be used as an authority: in 1849 his letter on the fall of Rome to the French was quoted extensively in an *Examiner* leader.[16] His next letter, savagely attacking the Pope for encouraging French conquest, offered further support.[17]

But this was not always the case. Later in 1849, for example, in the aftermath of the Mannings' execution, the *Examiner* argued strongly for an end to public hangings.[18] This drew a letter from Landor protesting against all capital punishment and advocating 'imprisonment, hard labour, and scourging'.[19] Eighteen months earlier, in a topical 'Imaginary Conversation' between Thiers and Lamartine, Landor not only attacked the French government but also asserted that there was now 'a Guizot administration in England. The same reckless expenditure, the same deafness to the popular reclamations, the same stupid, self-sufficient, subservient, and *secure*, majority in parliament.'[20] That government was a liberal one headed by Lord John Russell and strongly supported by the *Examiner*. Indeed, in that same issue the leader contrasted stable, progressive England with the revolutionary ferment on the Continent:

'And why? because [the government] has been compliant, because it has been elastic, because it has conformed and adjusted itself to the wishes and opinions of the country ... Queen Victoria's is happily a light bridle-hand.'[21] The gap between Landor and journal could not have been wider and drew the editor's wry but firm comment on his contributor, 'some of whose opinions in the paper the reader will find not a little at variance with our own'.[22] Very occasionally the *Examiner* simply did not publish, as with a second conversation-piece between Eldon and Encombe, or was glad to divert the offering. Forster wrote to W. J. Fox:

> Landor has been reading of the attacks of some rascally French writers (where writers are more rascally than among us, he says) on the little Queen – and has fired up thereat in the shape of these lines – some of them extremely powerful. They are a little too long for us – and perhaps, for us, a little too strong. I wish you would put them into the Chronicle.[23]

Occasional rejections and diversions notwithstanding, Landor was a regular contributor to the *Examiner* for 20 years. During that time there was one significant gap, a period of 18 months in the early 1840s when Landor, then in his mid-60s, travelled much and wrote hardly anything. In 1843 Forster became editor of the *Foreign Quarterly Review* and started Landor writing again by commissioning a series of essays on classical poets. Three were published. The first, on Catullus, rambled incoherently, the second and third, on Theocritus and Petrarch, were tightly organized and brilliantly written. A second period of silence, so far as the *Examiner* was concerned, lasted from November 1844 until May 1846, but at that time Landor, with Forster's help, was much occupied with proof-reading and further writing for the collected edition. During Forster's *Examiner* editorship, from 1847 to 1855, Landor contributed to almost half the weekly issues; in 1849 alone he contributed ten poems and 23 letters. The poor quality of the Catullus essay suggests the extent to which Landor needed the *Examiner* connection. He needed to write regularly and, more importantly, he needed to write for publication. Most importantly of all, he needed a publisher, here Forster at the *Examiner*, and a context, here the requirements of a weekly journal that knew its readership and had limited space, that would discipline and control him. The *Examiner* welcomed him in reviews and with space, but not unconditionally. It used a rein that could be tightened and came as near as was possible to imposing a shaping routine on Landor's literary career. That it did not succeed in the long term is mainly because when Landor grew old he became less and less controllable. In 1851 he complained to Forster that all his contributions were not being published. 'Beginning of his discontents',[24] Forster wrote on the letter that was itself an indication of the importance Landor attached to his links with the journal. Well before those links weakened they had established Forster, albeit temporarily, as controller of Landor's career.

The abiding *Examiner* connection quickly forced a sense of Forster's authority and usefulness even upon a writer as wilful and recalcitrant as Landor. It facilitated Forster's transition to general literary adviser. He was soon at work on Landor's dramas, suggesting Act divisions for both *Andrea* and *Giovanna*, subjecting them to rigorous editing and, so far as he could, insisting on the requirements of the stage. He was a good teacher, as is evident from *Fra Rupert*, the third play of the trilogy and 'the most dramatic of the three ... with greater vigour of treatment with characters more broadly contrasted'.[25] Forster showed it to Macready who admitted that it took 'stronger hold of him than either of its predecessors'.[26] Though, to Forster's disappointment, all three dramas stayed obstinately in the closet, within it his advice made them more lively and coherent.

As for Landor's poetry and prose: 'I am acting religiously on F.'s advice', he wrote to Lady Blessington, 'I pluck out my weeds all over the field, and leave only the strongest shoots of the best plants standing.'[27] Leigh Hunt, for one, would have recognized that advice and Landor, like Hunt, accepted it readily. On other occasions Forster was equally successful in excluding problematic work by Landor but was not always successful in retaining his goodwill: he forced Landor to exclude an attack on Wordsworth from the collected *Works* and angered him seven years later by removing an essay on Eliza Lynn from *Last Fruit Off an Old Tree* even after it had been set up in galleys.[28] The friendship lapsed for four years when, in 1859, he and the publisher, John Nichol, offended Landor by deleting references to the Yescombe affair from a new edition of *Hellenics*.[29] Landor strongly resisted Forster's onslaught on his spelling. Landor wished to revise orthography, to write phonetically, as with 'red' for 'read', and 'whipt', 'stript', 'blest'. In Forster's words, because of this there 'arose conflicts that ended sometimes doubtfully, but always peacefully. Against his intended reformation of spelling I waged a successful war.'[30] Forster won but Landor never gave in. Even after publication he cherished hopes of revised editions: following the appearance of *Last Fruit Off an Old Tree* (1853) Landor, at 79, corrected the whole volume in great detail to reflect his eccentric principles,[31] but the new version was never printed. Forster's great service was to establish Landor as a lyric poet of stature: many of the shorter poems that Forster insisted on him including in the *Works* of 1846 are of high quality and three-quarters had never previously been published.[32]

Forster did not win *all* the struggles. Though at one stage during the assembling of the collected *Works* he was given *carte blanche*, being left, as he was told, to 'put ... into the two volumes all you think worthy of a place in them',[33] Landorian *carte blanche* seemed always provisional and Landor successfully opposed Forster's attempts to exclude all 'imaginary conversations' with political themes.[34]

When the work had reached an uneasy stability Forster's procedure was often a simple one: he sent the manuscripts to Bradbury & Evans to be set up in print and then began negotiations with publishers. These last he conducted with authority, for one expression of Landor's gratitude was the assignment of copyright. In 1844 Forster acquired not only the copyright of the 'Imaginary Conversations' but also that of Landor's main publications from 1820 onwards, as well as work then uncompleted. Forster later added the copyright of *Last Fruit Off an Old Tree*. In the event, authority was less valuable than persuasiveness, for representing Landor was very different from cracking the whip for best-selling authors like Bulwer or Dickens. Landor had often paid to have his works in print and Forster at least relieved him of that: when he acquired Landor's copyright he agreed to stand the 'trouble and expense' of publishing the collected edition. There was often 'trouble', usually from Landor, and 'expense' was often a possibility: *Poemata et Inscriptiones* sold only one copy. Forster's incentive to find risk-bearing publishers was, thus, very great and his efforts invariably successful.[35]

In 1838, Landor's plays, *Andrea of Hungary*, *Giovanna of Naples*, and *Fra Rupert*, were given to Richard Bentley. 'Whatever the Sale may be', Forster wrote to the publisher, with an optimistic appeal to his better nature,

> – and I have no doubt it will be such as may at least hold you harmless – it will at *all* events not be an unpleasant matter of reflection with you to have given to the world the masterpieces which these tragedies are – of such a writer as Landor.[36]

The first two plays became victims of Bentley's dispute with Dickens and Forster when the publisher, in petty revenge for Forster's part in Dickens's withdrawal from the editorship of *Bentley's Miscellany*, delayed their publication and ceased to advertise them. Though they eventually appeared their chances, such as those were, had been harmed, and by that time an angry Forster was determined to look elsewhere. The *Works* of 1846 were brought out by Edward Moxon, a long-standing friend of

Forster's through their links with the Lambs. Moxon published *Poemata et Inscriptiones* (1847), with its single-copy sale, *The Hellenics* (1847), *Last Fruit Off an Old Tree* (1853), and *Imaginary Conversations of Greeks and Romans* (1853). During this period Forster also arranged with Longmans the publication of Landor's political pamphlet, *Imaginary Conversations of King Carlo-Alberto and The Duchess Belgioioso.* Chapman & Hall, for whom Forster was, of course, literary adviser, published *Popery: British and Foreign* (1850), and *Letters of an American* (1854), this last as part of their Railway Library. *Antony and Octavius* (1856) went to Bradbury & Evans during the period in which they became Dickens's publishers as well as printers. The list is a clear demonstration of Forster's power and influence. That it is not a complete list of Landor's publications during the period of their friendship is a pointer to Landor's contrariness: for example, even though Forster helped him bring out *Last Fruit Off an Old Tree* and a new edition of *The Hellenics*, Landor himself had given both to the Edinburgh publisher, John Nichol. In 1853, angered by delays in publishing *Last Fruit*, Landor tried for American publication without Forster's knowledge. When an American selection appeared two years later Landor thoroughly approved, despite the blatant infringement of Forster's copyright that hardly helped the latter's quick temper.[37] For no other service did Landor owe Forster as much as he did for the placing of his work, yet, even here, displeasure and disputes lurked ominously at the fringes of their common concern.

Placing was one matter, publication was another; between the two fell the shadow of the proofs. Landor's papers were particularly foul, his approach disorganized; he was a compulsive corrector and continuous inserter. Two examples help make a basic point. 'You will call me fastidious as well as troublesome', Landor wrote to Forster in 1839, 'when I beg of you to alter (in the words about Canning) "the pen of an English epigrammatist" for "the *quill*" and "Vanquisher of the eastern world and *Protector* of the western".'[38] Secondly, in 1848 Landor offered warm praise of Forster's biography of Goldsmith and continued,

> And now you might reward me for my gallantry by correcting two or three faulty verses to Lamartine as follows.
> v.6 Prime actor on the grandest scene.
> & Grow envious of exalted worth
> 12 For foes were many, friends were few
> 22 With potent speech thy tears forbad
> 32 Is not to prune the deadly tree
> Do not forget to send me a dozen slips containing this Epistle.[39]

As the final reminder makes clear, 'To Lamartine' was a contribution to the *Examiner*.[40] Both letters are requests for simple corrections to short pieces. But Landor asked or, rather, demanded of Forster the same attention to *all* his works, no matter how long and complex the latter were. Forster wrote, with despairing recollection, of preparing the 1846 *Works* as Landor wrote new poem after new poem, 'struck out amid the wearisome correction of proofs',[41] sent correction after correction, and continued to argue with Forster about the use of reformed spelling. *Poemata et Inscriptiones* created even greater difficulties; Forster wrote:

> I have had as many as half-a-dozen letters on the same day correcting in as many ways a correction found at last to be itself not necessary ... He was always inflicting a needless trouble on himself and on me, and pleading still that each should be the last.[42]

With the proofs for *Five Scenes*, which appeared during 1851 in *Fraser's Magazine*, Landor reduced Forster to bewilderment through constant emendation, the mislaying of parts, the sending of passages for which Forster could not find a place, and the inability, when questioned, to give Forster coherent placing instructions.[43] The best example of the demands he made upon his friend is, again, Landor's post-publication correcting of *Last Fruit Off an Old Tree*: if Landor had had his way Forster would have been given the task not only of supervising revised spelling, but also of ensuring that the next published text incorporated 'hundreds of corrections of literals and punctuation, substantial alterations and additions, several passages ... deleted, and the order of the poems ... drastically rearranged'.[44] This was all too typical. As Landor acknowledged so apologetically, 'I do read with my mind, rather than with my eyes ... What infinite trouble have I given you, my generous, indulgent Forster'.[45] The letter correcting 'To Lamartine' shows Landor at least trying to sugar the pill. But apologies, self-awareness, and moments of rare conciliation did not change his ways. Forster was all too often not so much the mender and cleaner of 'inky fishing nets'[46] as the patient unraveller of potent entanglements hurled at him, all too skilfully, by an aging but still spritely gladiator.

Unravelling done and publication achieved, Forster turned to reviewing. He worked hard to interest other journals in Landor's work, one result being Douglas Jerrold's review of the collected edition in his own *Shilling Magazine*,[47] as well as providing his own regular support. Given Forster's role in the pre-publication process the balance and comparative objectivity of his notices are a striking indication of his friendship's sincerity. Only once did he overstep the mark and that most prestigiously. In 1846 Forster persuaded Macvey Napier, then editor of the *Edinburgh Review*, to insert in the *Edinburgh* a review of the collected edition.[48] The notice was very favourable and drew a swift and hostile response from Thomas Longman who knew that Forster, as copyright holder, was reviewing his own property. Napier protested, Forster had the grace to squirm.[49] Here is a rare instance, at this stage of Forster's career, of friendly enthusiasm bypassing his socio-literary antennae.

It is perhaps surprising that such bypassing did not happen more frequently, for Forster had much respect and affection for the old man. He remembered him as 'genial, joyous, kind, and of a nature large and generous to excess'.[50] Nowhere could there be found 'a more pervading passion for liberty, a fiercer hatred of the base, a wider sympathy with the wronged and the oppressed'.[51] He sent Landor books, visited him in Bath and entertained him in London with excursions to art galleries.[52] In 1855 Forster pleased Landor greatly by arranging a visit to the Crystal Palace where through Forster's friendship with Paxton the fountains were set playing in his honour.[53]

Forster's liking for Landor's work that led him to an equally intense liking for the man in turn fired further concern for the former. He sought to improve and to change Landor's writings. Under his tutelage and, to repeat, particularly through the *Examiner* connection, Landor became more self-critical and was encouraged to be more self-disciplined. He pruned and revised; he developed, even at that late stage, as a lyric poet. He was sometimes saved from his own extreme opinions, usually through Forsterian veto. Behind such pressures lay Forster's obvious desire to make Landor's work more socially respectable as well as more aesthetically pleasing, as yet another expression of Forster's belief in the 'dignity of literature'. However, though that desire was partly satisfied through textual change and omission, the man himself proved somewhat less malleable.

Landor thought much of Forster. He was, he considered, his best critic, though run close by Landor's brother Robert.[54] He admired Forster's own volumes, not only the early commonwealth history but also Forster's *Goldsmith*, which he read quickly and passionately, thinking parts to be 'very nobly written' and responding to Forster's account of Goldsmith's death with admiring marginalia: 'Well said my good John Forster!'[55] That private response was obviously sincere: no less so, though public, was his poem 'To John Forster', included as the final lyric in the 1846 edition and reprinted by Forster, with unconvincing reluctance, in his biography of Landor:

Forster! whose zeal hath seiz'd each written page
That fell from me, and over many lands
Hath clear'd for me a broad and solid way,
Whence one more age, aye, haply more than one,
May be arrived at (all through thee), accept
No false or faint or perishable thanks.
From better men, and greater, friendship turn'd
Thy willing steps to me. From ELIOT's cell
Death-dark; from HAMPDEN's sadder battle-field;
From steadfast CROMWELL's tribunitian throne,
Loftier than king's supported knees could mount;
Hast thou departed with me, and hast climbed
Cecropian heights, and ploughed Aegean waves.
Therefore it never grieved me when I saw
That she who guards those regions and those seas
Hath lookt with eyes more gracious upon thee.
There are no few like that conspirator
Who, under prétext of power-worship, fell
At CAESAR's feet, only to hold him down
While others stabb'd him with repeated blows;
And there are more who fling light jibes, immerst
In gutter-filth, against the car that mounts
Weighty with triumph up the Sacred Way.
Protect in every place my stranger guests,
Born in the lucid land of pure free song,
Now first appearing on repulsive shores,
Bleak, and where safely none but natives move,
Red-poll'd, red-handed, siller-grasping men.
Ah! lead them far away, for they are used
To genial climes and gentle speech; but most
CYMODAMEIA: warn the Tritons off
While she ascends, while through the opening plain
Of the green sea (brighten'd by bearing it)
Gushes redundantly her golden hair.[56]

The opening risks presenting Forster as agile office-boy but does place significant emphasis on the practical help through which Landor felt his works to be secured for posterity. Forster is complimented on his own achievement as historian of the commonwealth and, possibly, on his own classicism. Landor almost certainly also had in mind Forster's appreciation of Landor's own classical accomplishments, referred to here with typical lack of modesty. Central to the poem is the poet's sense of Forster's support, placed in grateful and graceful contrast with a world savage and 'repulsive' in its incomprehension. The poem explains a great deal about the friendship: when he came with youthful praise and help and stayed to offer more, Forster tapped a vein of deep feeling in the older man. Landor, despite disclaimers, longed for general recognition and Forster found him some.

But gratitude did not remove all problems for, in one important way, Landor was unchanging: in his dealings with the literary world he was the archetypal gentleman-amateur. Landor considered publishers to be tradesmen and tried to treat them accordingly.[57] Sometimes he paid to have his work published; almost always he refused to write for pay. Throughout his career he donated his profits (there were usually none) to worthy causes as diverse as Grace Darling, Sicilian revolutionaries, and an impoverished Bedfordshire clergyman. When Saunders & Otley lost £150 on *Pericles and Aspasia* Landor, to Forster's unconcealed astonishment, insisted on repaying them.[58] When an admirer, noting his frequent contributions to the *Examiner*, appeared to think he worked as a journalist, Landor was deeply offended.[59] Friendship with Forster, whose every action sought to 'professionalize' the literary Landor, may have inspired gratitude but was also a frequent source of tension.

This last was not helped by Landor's wilfulness: in this connection a warning bell sounded as early as 1839 when Forster enlisted Landor in support of Talfourd's bill to extend the period of literary copyright. Landor was a willing recruit but could not be restrained from writing to the *Sun* to advocate rights in perpetuity.[60] He was always hard to handle, as that and the constant literary arguments emphasize. As he grew very old even trivial matters aggravated him: 'What has Bath to do with me?' he asked Forster fiercely, when the latter once called him 'the lion of Bath'.[61] That was a salutary response, a reminder that Landor considered his best work to have been done, years ago, in Italy, and that Forster knew Landor for only the last 28 years of a life lasting almost 90. Yet, though it was too late for teaching new tricks, during the years of the friendship to 1856, through a combination of literary advice, practical arrangements, occasional censorship, and the whip-cracking of a forceful copyright holder, all reflecting an authority that owed much to the *Examiner* connection, Forster imposed a pattern of sorts upon Landor's chaos. In any fundamental sense Landor was never professionalized, but he did become – was forced to become – comparatively respectable.

It seems no accident that, in 1856, Forster's withdrawal from the *Examiner* and his subsequent preoccupation with a new wife, new work and a moneyed respectability, coincided with the disintegration of Landor's life. With the last control gone senility burgeoned. Its effect upon Landor's last years in Bath has been exhaustively documented by R. H. Super[62] as a sad and pathetic sequence involving an old man's infatuation for the young Geraldine Hooper and a dubious friendship with Mrs Yescombe, another Bath neighbour, whom Landor suspected of having improper designs upon young Geraldine, himself, and his money, and whom Landor libelled first in pamphlets and then in indecent poems in *Dry Sticks*.

In 1857 the Forsters visited Bath to see Landor and to tour the area. Forster found the pamphlets written and distributed, a libel action being contemplated, and Landor's legal affairs in the hands of Taylor & Williams, a firm of local solicitors. Forster forced Landor to sign a retraction only for the old man to be infuriated by Taylor's own later addition in which Landor promised not to repeat such conduct. In less than a week he began pestering the Yescombes with insulting and indecent letters. *Dry Sticks*, when it followed, compounded his offences.

In 1858 Mrs Yescombe sued for libel. Taylor & Williams, fearing the worst, advised Landor to transfer his estate to his niece Kitty and to flee the country. Kitty took Landor to London to seek Forster's advice and spent a few days at Montague Square. There it was decided that Landor should go to Italy and Forster busied himself to arrange a crossing to Boulogne where Landor would await the arrival of one of his children from Fiesole.

Super takes a dim view of Forster's conduct. He argues that Forster was a barrister, a man of the world, and that he must have known that Landor and his niece had been badly advised by Taylor & Williams:

> Landor could not be brought personally into the courtroom by the Yescombes, he would not be sent to jail, and if a verdict should be given against him the transfer of the annuity could certainly be overthrown by the Yescombes and there would be no saving to the estate. The old man's removal from the few friends he loved and his modest contentment was cruel; the journey he was being sent on was dangerous for one of his age; and there was no reason to suppose that there would be any comfort at its end – indeed no one had yet determined where Landor was to make his home on the Continent. The flight was outrageous, and Forster knew that it was.[63]

There is some truth in this, though there are mitigating circumstances. Firstly, though Forster was a qualified barrister he had never practised; it cannot be assumed that he knew more than a practising solicitor seemed to know about the laws governing libel and consequent claims upon estates. It could be argued that, at the very least, he should have consulted one of his many lawyer friends, but that he did not may have been due, partly, to the fact that he had much else on his mind. Not only was Forster in the midst of his Lunacy Secretaryship but he was much distracted by the problems of Bulwer Lytton. During the very week in which Landor and Kitty descended upon Montague Square Bulwer took the 'unwise & imprudent' step of seeking to commit his long-estranged and unbalanced wife, Rosina, to an asylum. 'What has most harassed me during this week', Forster wrote desperately to Robert Browning, 'has been this unhappy business of Bulwer's wife.'[64] It can be mentioned, further, that Landor's relations, who included solicitors in Rugeley, appear never to have complained about or remonstrated with Forster regarding Landor's departure. On the contrary, Forster's long-standing links with Landor's family continued and Mrs Forster began warm friendships with Kitty and with Sophy Landor that lasted far beyond Landor's death. Forster himself blamed Taylor & Williams both for 'driving your uncle into perpetual banishment', as he wrote to Sophy Landor, and for their subsequent advice to compromise over the payment of damages.[65] He counselled delay, though that, three years of it, only increased eventual costs.

Forster never saw Landor again. Even if his part in exiling his friend is hardly as clear-cut as Super insists, there can be little doubt that the old man's capacity for causing embarrassment came to outweigh Forster's regard for his writing. But whether or not Forster heaved a sigh of selfish relief when Landor left for Italy, after the departure he continued to try to help his friend. For exile was quickly followed by the trial; its inevitable verdict against Landor led to widespread newspaper attacks. Forster, now a man of waning influence, managed to silence some.[66] He felt Landor to have been badly treated and badly defended: 'I can understand an advocate throwing up his brief ...', he wrote as part of a persuasive letter to Leigh Hunt's son, Thornton, then editor of the *Leader*, 'but I cannot understand his retaining it & throwing up his client.'[67]

Settled again in Italy, Landor continued to write and to prepare a new edition of *The Hellenics*. He was 84 and cantankerous. The *Hellenics* were delayed mainly because of the need to censor the text, in particular for Forster to remove, without Landor's permission, lines on the Yescombes that may well have been actionable. That censoring, plus Forster's refusal to make public a statement by Landor defending himself against the court's verdict, infuriated Landor and ended the friendship.[68]

Little more remained, either of the friendship or of Landor's life. The estrangement lasted from 1859 until December 1863. During that time

Landor worried about the split, as is evident from the helpless vehemence of an epigram of 1860: '"Will the old fool never have done?" cries John Forster. "Not yet", cries the old fool.'[69] But as time passed he became increasingly bitter about his former friend whom he referred to as 'John Fals-stuff'.[70] Landor turned to Arthur Walker, an acquaintance of Landor's sons, and sought to make him his biographer by sending him the contents of his writing-desk.[71] All the while Forster corresponded regularly with the Brownings, who took responsibility for Landor in Florence, and sent out the quarterly allowance supplied by Landor's family.[72]

In 1863 Landor read an extract from a proposed biography of himself to be published by Newby. It was, he considered, full of 'abuse and falsehood'. By this time Walker's inadequacy as Forster's replacement had been conclusively demonstrated. That inadequacy forced Landor to write to Forster begging for further friendship and the resumption of biographical responsibilities: 'How often', wrote Landor flatteringly, 'have I known you vindicate from unmerited aspersions honest literary men!'[73] Bundles of letters and private papers followed swiftly. Reconciliation thus effected, Landor lingered only a few months before his death in 1864, Forster being left with the works to edit and the life to write.

A final glimpse of the friendship is provided by William Allingham, who reported in his diary:

> Landor used sometimes to write most unreasonable and exasperating letters to Forster, and one day that I was with Forster and he had been talking of Landor almost with indignation, he suddenly exclaimed 'If he were standing here before me – I'd hug the old man!'[74]

The saddest aspect of the relationship is that, for both, the longer it continued the more difficult hugging became. For Forster particularly, though he never wholly lost his affection for his aging friend, to keep him at arm's length became a more desirable posture. In the friendship's later years and for Forster as biographer even that was sometimes too close.

CHAPTER II *Charles Dickens*

When Forster met Charles Dickens at Kensal Lodge, home of their 'common friend Mr. Ainsworth'[1] during the closing days of 1836 he was already a man of standing and reputation in literary London. Most importantly, by 1836 his intense concern for the dignity of literature and the drama had not only been well nourished and firmly shaped by the combined influence of Hunt, Lamb, Bulwer, and Macready, but was also in action in his new friendships with Browning and Landor. Forster's first contact with Dickens's work, before the two had met, is a further expression of what had quickly become his central obsession. In his *Examiner* review of *The Village Coquettes*, Hullah's operetta for which Dickens had written the words, Forster attacked the unseemly conduct of both leading actor and author:

> at the fall of the curtain, Mr. Harley came forward, and asked the audience 'if it were all right?'. They made a great din – we presume in acquiescence – and he then proceeded to beg favour for the piece, in that whining, half-apologetic, all-familiar strain, now so very common on our stage.... and a disgusting farce was kept up between the favourite actor and his patrons ...
>
> ... then the audience screamed for Boz! Now we have a great respect and liking for Boz; the *Pickwick Papers* have made him, as our readers are very well aware, an especial favourite with us ... Bad as the opera is ... we feel assured that if Mr. Braham will make arrangements to parade the real living Boz every night after that opera, he will insure for it a certain attraction.[2]

Dickens had lived permanently in London since 1822. His rise to prominence is well known; when he met Forster he was half-way through the *Pickwick Papers*, had completed the opening parts of *Oliver Twist* and had contracted to edit *Bentley's Miscellany*. He had become 'one of the most promising literary young men of the present day'.[3] 'Have you seen the *Examiner*?' he wrote to Hullah about Forster's review; 'It is *rather* depreciatory of the Opera, but ... so well done that I cannot help laughing at it, for the life and soul of me.'[4]

Apart from that indication of a shared sense of humour the two, at that first meeting, had in common such mutual friends and acquaintances as Ainsworth, Douglas Jerrold, and Henry Colburn, and links with the law that included Dickens's desire to be called to the Bar. Both had worked for the *True Sun* and so had the same radical political contacts. Both were used to irregular hours and to working under pressure; both were lively men, passionate about the theatre, keen on drinks and company and excursions, on being intensely gay, relaxing violently, responding vehemently. Forster the comic dancer and water-jug thrower reacted readily to Dickens's 'unwearying animal spirits'.[5]

But one common experience that they would certainly not have discussed at their first meeting was their comparatively humble origins. Dickens's secretive attitude towards the Marshalsea and blacking-warehouse period is common knowledge; Forster, who was to write grimly that 'Men who have been at the galleys ... are not wise to brag of the work they performed there',[6] was not so successful in concealing the facts of his childhood nor in restraining his anger when taunted by his enemies. Yet for both a major consequence of their early days was a relentless pursuit of literary fame and associated material reward, in which Dickens sky-rocketed upwards and Forster rose by degrees and *via* his wealthy marriage. It is no accident that some of the most perceptive pages in the *Life*[7] are those assessing the effects of Dickens's childhood, the way the adult Dickens was 'often uneasy, shrinking, and over-sensitive', that he was, at times, 'even hard and aggressive; in his determinations a something that had almost the tone of fierceness; something in his nature that made his resolves insuperable', for Forster had the same determination, the same furious energy, and his own symptoms of social unease. Even if the effect of his early friendships was to be set aside Forster himself was an obvious and eager recruit for any movement in support of the dignity of literature.

So too was Dickens who, in 1836, was already exhibiting a concern similar to Forster's when he dedicated *The Village Coquettes* to his leading man, J. P. Harley: 'That you may long contribute to the amusement of the Public, and long be spared to shed a lustre, by the honor and integrity of your private life, on the profession which for many years, you have done so much to uphold.'[8] As we have seen, Forster thought less of that lustrous theatrical, but in general attitude and expectations Dickens's words could well have been Macready's about himself, or Forster's about Macready.

The meeting with Forster was for Dickens the beginning of a relationship in which these feelings were worked upon by a Forster ever conscious that the status and standing of the literary profession was derived from the behaviour and productions of each of its members.

Yet Forster should not be seen, simply, as a combination of Professor Higgins and Victor Frankenstein; his concern for Dickens's dignity was inspired by a sincere liking for the man. This last is very evident in Forster's account of that first meeting, recollections that are an odd mixture of anatomical details and moving phrases as Forster wrote with Maclise's portrait before him and remembered Dickens when young.[9] Such affection is evident also in the *Life* which, up to a point, furthered the cause of literature in society by portraying Dickens as embodying almost all the qualities prized by the Victorian middle classes: determination to surmount all obstacles in a progress from rags to riches, 'the marvellously domestic home-loving shape',[10] the hearty and cheerful extrovert, the common-sensical Englishman. To be sure, Forster went on to face frankly the darker aspects of Dickens's character that came to dominate his biography but the popular image of the novelist was, he believed, a true reflection of the *essential* Dickens, that which lay below the mixture of good and bad actions making up Dickens's external life, a permanent inner core of good qualities the perception of which made Dickens Forster's friend.

Forster gained little, in a practical way, from his friendship with Dickens. He occasionally received 'kindly counsel',[11] owed his post as Chapman & Hall's literary adviser to his association with Dickens, and began his connection with the *Edinburgh Review* by being introduced by Dickens to its editor, Macvey Napier.[12] His position on the *Daily News* and his small profit on his investment in *Household Words*[13] were other tangible benefits. Yet Forster principally needed his friendship with Dickens as a counter to the deficiencies of his own life, in particular the loneliness of his bachelor state, aggravated by ill-health. Whilst his friends married and brought up families, whilst his parents, brother and sister died in far-off Newcastle, Forster spent much of his late 30s and early 40s lying bed-ridden and alone in his stylish chambers in Lincoln's Inn Fields. Friendship with Dickens gave Forster access to seemingly innumerable children, to well-ordered family life and irrepressible companionship; all this in central London. To a lesser extent there was reflected glory, considerable power and much deserved credit to be gained from being so close to the most popular writer of the day. That this also meant much to Forster is evident from the *Life*.

To account in this way for Forster's relations with Dickens is to indicate their essentially straightforward nature. Dickens's relations with Forster, however, were far more complex. For, unlike Forster, Dickens gained much from the friendship as far as practical affairs were concerned. Especially, Dickens found in Forster a friend who could be entrusted with specific business responsibilities. That specificity needs stressing because Dickens so often relied upon others, such as the solicitor, Thomas Mitton, a friend from Dickens's earliest days in London, for much financial advice, for the vetting of private accounts, even for direct relief from pressing monetary needs. For legal advice and professional procedures, such as the drafting and signing of contracts, Dickens usually turned to Mitton, or Talfourd, or Frederick Ouvry. Forster, however, negotiated with publishers on Dickens's behalf, and only occasionally did other related things, such as inspecting publishers' accounts during Dickens's absences abroad[14] or holding a power of attorney when Dickens visited America in 1867.[15]

Dickens, like Bulwer, did not allow Forster a free hand. Their business relationship has been succinctly described:

> John Forster served as Dickens's unofficial literary agent from the days of *Pickwick* onward. But for the most part Dickens's publishing contracts were the product of his own determination, enforced, if necessary, by cajoling, threats, and a battery of legal and financial representatives.[16]

Forster, of course, was one of the latter. He was typically in action during the first six months of their friendship when Dickens asked him to see John Macrone to object to the planned publication of *Sketches by Boz* (originally published by Macrone) in a format similar to that of *The Pickwick Papers*, then being brought out by Chapman & Hall. That plan, Dickens considered, sought to improve sales of the former by capitalizing, to Macrone's advantage alone, on the rising sales of the latter. 'I need not tell you', he wrote to Forster, 'that this is calculated to injure me most seriously.' Dickens's letter can be quoted at length as an example of the precision with which he briefed his friendly representative:

> I heard half an hour ago on authority which leaves me in no doubt about the matter (from the binder of Pickwick, in fact) that Macrone intends publishing a new issue of my sketches in monthly parts of nearly the same size and just the same form as the Pickwick papers.
>
> I need not tell you that this is calculated to injure me most seriously, or that I have a very natural and most decided objection

to being supposed to presume upon the success of the Pickwick, and thus foist this old work upon the public in its new dress for the mere purpose of putting money in my own pocket. Neither need I say that the fact of my name being before the town, attached to three publications at the same time, must prove seriously prejudicial to my reputation.

As you are acquainted with the circumstances under which these copyrights were disposed of, and as I know I may rely on your kind-feeling, may I beg you to wait upon Macrone, and to state in the strongest and most emphatic manner, my feeling on this point. I wish him to be reminded of the sums he paid for these books – of the sale he has had for them – of the extent to which he has already pushed them – and of the very great profits he must necessarily have acquired from them. I wish him also to be reminded that no intention of publishing them in this form was in the remotest manner hinted to me, by him, or on his own behalf, when he obtained possession of the copyright. I then wish you to put it to his feelings of common honesty and fair-dealing whether after this communication he will persevere in his intention.

I feel it necessary to add – not as a hasty threat but as my deliberate and well-considered determination – that if this new issue does appear, I shall advertize in all the Newspapers that it does so – not only without my sanction, but in opposition to my express request; that it is of no advantage whatever, to me; and that I most earnestly and emphatically entreat all my friends and supporters to abstain from purchasing it. Wherever he advertizes the work, I will advertize this statement.

I have only to add that in case you should be met with the assertion that the preparations he has made have involved him in great expense already, and that this is a reason for his persisting in his design, Chapman and Hall, knowing my feeling on the subject are ready and willing to buy the copyrights, and to consider this circumstance in settling the amount of the purchase money.[17]

In the event Macrone agreed to sell the copyrights to *Sketches by Boz* to Chapman & Hall. He asked £2,000, at which Forster was appalled. But Chapman & Hall accepted and obtained Dickens's agreement by convincing him that as an equal partner in the venture he would profit from an issue in monthly parts under their own imprint; and though as an equal partner Dickens would be responsible for a half-share of the copyright price that, Chapman & Hall assured him, would be deducted from his profits. Before a final commitment Dickens tried to consult his disconcerted adviser, but Forster was not available so Dickens went ahead. It is impossible to quantify the damage that might have been done to the sales of *Pickwick* had Macrone issued *Sketches*, but in terms of financial return from the latter it is hard to argue against Forster's concern: in 1841 the legal description of Dickens's copyrights referred to him having only a '*contingent* interest'[18] in his half-share of *Sketches by Boz*, suggesting that he still had not cleared his debt to Chapman & Hall; later profits on the volume were negligible.

Forster played a full part in Dickens's well-known dispute with Richard Bentley. Having contracted with Bentley to write two novels, to edit Bentley's *Miscellany* and to be its regular contributor, Dickens, represented throughout by Forster, moved to increasingly advantageous financial positions: the price of *Barnaby Rudge*, one of the two promised novels, was much increased, and the other, *Oliver Twist*, allowed to become Dickens's *Miscellany* contribution, before another agreement allowed *Rudge* to follow *Twist* in the *Miscellany*. Further, although the first agreement gave Bentley possession of the *Rudge* and *Twist* copyrights, Dickens emerged from the whole dispute knowing that half the copyright to both would revert to him after only three years. In 1840 Forster again acted for Dickens in negotiations to move, wholly, from Bentley to Chapman & Hall and a more financially beneficial relationship.

Forster, again working to a detailed brief, agreed terms with Chapman & Hall for *Master Humphrey's Clock*. Following preliminary negotiations he and Dickens met Chapman & Hall in July 1839 and not only agreed terms for the *Clock* but also a bonus payment for *Nicholas Nickleby*'s good sales. That bonus was £1,500, which pleased Dickens very much. In October Forster witnessed the *Clock*'s final agreement. On 30 May 1840 a further meeting took place in Forster's rooms and he took detailed minutes to form the basis of a new agreement. *Barnaby Rudge*, that increasingly valuable yet still unwritten novel, was to succeed *The Old Curiosity Shop* in the *Clock*, for which Dickens would receive £50 per instalment, half the profits, and own half the copyright. However, when Chapman & Hall had bought out Bentley's interest in Dickens they had paid £2,250 for Bentley's remaining stock in *Oliver Twist* and to induce him to surrender his claims to any of Dickens's work: that £2,250 was to be taken from the £3,000 Chapman & Hall had agreed to pay Dickens for the copyright to *Barnaby Rudge*. The new agreement for *Rudge* meant that Dickens was no longer owed the £3,000. The £2,250 that Dickens still owed the publishers was now to be paid out of *Rudge*'s profits, so that the publishers, though they had paid Bentley that original £2,250, were now no longer sole holders of *Rudge*'s copyright. They asked Forster to arrange security for the £2,250 and some legal assignment to them of Dickens's copyrights pending sufficient profits from *Rudge* to enable full repayment. Forster agreed to ' "a lien in the nature of a mortgage" '.[19] This Dickens did not give but eventually and under pressure from the publishers' lawyers he agreed to sign a bond, write a letter of commitment, and take out a life insurance policy for £2,000. Good relations between Chapman & Hall and an offended Dickens were only with difficulty restored.

Following the completion of *The Old Curiosity Shop* Forster, in August 1841, presented to Chapman & Hall Dickens's proposals to take a year off financed by a further loan of £2,000 from the publishers; this was to be repaid out of the proceeds of Dickens's next novel, to be written after the break, in the copyright to which they would have only a half-share for which they would have to make additional payment. In the end Chapman & Hall agreed but, overruling Forster's objection, they forced into the agreement for what became *Martin Chuzzlewit* a clause allowing them to deduct £50 per month from Dickens's share if profits seemed insufficient to repay Dickens's debt to them. The objection should have been heeded. When *Chuzzlewit*'s prospects seemed to be poor Hall proposed invoking the deduction clause and this time so angered Dickens that he began looking for new publishers.

Here was Forster's next task. On Dickens's behalf he approached Bradbury & Evans and ended the novelist's association with Chapman & Hall, for whom Forster continued to act as literary adviser. On 1 June 1844 Forster and Dickens met Bradbury & Evans to draw up an agreement. Against the security of life policies and for a quarter-share in his work for the next eight years Dickens received £2,000 to finance a year in Italy and possibly a further £1,800 in 1845. In return he agreed only to write a Christmas sequel to *A Christmas Carol* for 1844 and became vaguely committed to starting a magazine. Thus Dickens went to Italy almost unencumbered for the first time in his career.

What has been said of Bulwer can be said of Dickens also: as his fame grew his agreements with publishers became increasingly advantageous to him and his need for a forceful negotiator to subdue recalcitrant firms became proportionately less. Forster became useful for occasional sticky tasks: in 1859, for example, he handled Dickens's break with Bradbury & Evans (that included the winding-up of *Household Words*) and his return to Chapman & Hall; and during the 1860s when Dickens contracted to write *Our Mutual Friend* and *Edwin Drood* he was appointed to determine the publishers' compensation if Dickens died before completion.

Given his friendship with Dickens, that final role is a clear indication of Forster's reputation for fairness and honesty, qualities that together with a lawyer's mastery of his brief and a forceful personality made him an invaluable representative, especially for Dickens, whose strange nervousness about business transactions was demonstrated in 1841 when he wished his publishers to finance his year off in America. As he wrote to Mitton: 'When I had got into my head the enormous advantages of such a step ... I walked off to Forster, and said "Now will you in my presence say to Chapman and Hall for me after dinner today (as I am not a very great demonstrator when my own affairs are at issue) what I am going to tell you ..." ' Forster did so, 'extremely well'.[20] When Dickens had decided to leave Chapman & Hall for Bradbury & Evans he wrote to Forster: 'And do, my dear fellow, do for God's sake turn over about Chapman and Hall, and look upon my project as *a settled thing*. If you object to see them, I must write to them.'[21]

Such reliance upon him hardly undermined his influence upon Dickens. Forster's brief was given but was bound to reflect his own views, in particular those on the rightful rewards of literature. Forster's reaction to the price put by Macrone on the *Sketches* copyright is one example of such views in action. Another is the way that, during the dispute with Bentley, Forster kept querying agreements that Dickens had already made: thus when, on 17 March 1837, Dickens extended his editorship of Bentley's *Miscellany* Forster suggested looking again at the earlier contract for *Twist* and *Rudge*. It was renegotiated later that year, much to Dickens's advantage.

Richard Bentley's publishing practices were not conducive to the dignity of literary men: his agreements were rarely generous, he was prone to interfere with his writers' work, and he 'puffed' shamelessly. Forster's negotiating style was much affected by this: he cracked the whip with severity. Beginning with the assertion that Dickens was 'the greatest master of prose fiction in this or any other language',[22] Forster's tone was at best peremptory. 'Is it exactly prudent to use the expression "forthwith" respecting the appearance of Barnaby in the Miscellany?'[23] he demanded in 1838; he and Bentley should meet, Forster later insisted, 'because it may possibly save some unpleasantness to us all'.[24] Such a tough attitude helped persuade Dickens to harden the bargains Forster drove for him, a state of affairs that did not escape the publisher's notice: Edward S. Morgan, Bentley's chief clerk and accountant, rightly believed that Dickens's 'feeling of discontent so pertinaciously exhibited was to be attributed to the meddling agency of some person by whose advice Mr. Dickens allowed himself to be swayed'.[25]

This influence apart, Dickens's literary finances were transformed by Forster's particular concern with the value of copyright. Robert L. Patten again makes the point:

> under Forster's prodding Dickens was, in the winter of 1857–8, vigorously working his copyright. He had arranged for the first quality edition of his works, brought the Cheap edition up to 1853, contracted for French rights, issued texts of his readings, and in general brought Bradbury and Evans into a large number of new projects.[26]

What Forster was urging, of course, was that Dickens should increase his earnings from work already done. This was achieved and when it is recalled that Dickens quickly moved from selling copyright to retention of much of it plus profit-sharing it can be seen that in the last third of Dickens's career he was, in effect, both salaried and in receipt of the literary equivalent of an investment income. In his early years Dickens 'behaved outrageously'[27] in seeking financial advantage, in later life he achieved the financial status, and so, in some respects, the life-style, of the professional man of good family, with what he earned being buttressed by what he already possessed. That social progress had commanded Forster's utmost support and reflects his central obsession.

With agreements signed Dickens began writing and Forster stood by. He himself described his next task, without exaggeration:

> There was nothing written by him ... which I did not see before the world did, either in manuscript or proofs; and in connection with the latter I shortly began to give him the help which he publicly mentioned twenty years later in dedicating his collected writings to me.[28]

Forster quickly read the manuscript of each instalment and corrected obvious mistakes, such as the misnumbering of chapters in *Barnaby Rudge*,[29] before sending it to the printer for setting-up. The usual procedure can be briefly outlined. Proofs were sent to both Dickens and Forster. Dickens made necessary cuts, alterations and insertions, before sending his set to Forster. The latter then copied Dickens's corrections into his own set, 'making a few stylistic alterations himself, and adding heavily to CD's very sketchy punctuation'.[30] Two comments by modern editors are relevant:

> Forster seems to have been furnished regularly with proofs and to have corrected punctuation, going beyond this only with permission

> … [There is] … a strong possibility that, even where there is no evidence of such permission, substantive alterations by Forster have the author's approval.[31]

and: 'Most of Forster's corrections concern punctuation.'[32]

Any attempt to assess Forster's direct effect on Dickens's work must begin with the central implication of the preceding paragraph: Forster's editorial endeavours were as carefully controlled by Dickens as were his business activities on Dickens's behalf. Further, it is one of the sad ironies of Forster biography that adequate documentation of the kind, for example, available for his relationships with Bulwer and Leigh Hunt, does not exist for that with Dickens. Though Dickens's proofs are often corrected in Forster's handwriting only in a few instances do we know the extent of Forster's always limited authority.

One such instance is Forster at work on *The Old Curiosity Shop*, when Dickens allowed Forster to reduce the 39th part, Chapters 62 and 63, to the required length. Forster cut two long passages from Chapter 62, each foreshadowing Quilp's eventual death by drowning, and Dickens, accepting that neither was strictly necessary, commented, 'it will come well enough without such a preparation, so I made no change'.[33] Others are from *Barnaby Rudge*. 'Don't fail to erase anything that seems to you too strong',[34] wrote Dickens about Chapters 17 and 18, and Forster made several significant cuts from the dramatic confrontation between Mrs Rudge and her husband. They included:

a. I am desperate, I warn you
b. (her hands) held up at arms' length towards Heaven
c. By this right hand, whose history you know, and by this devil's seal stamped on me, you remember when, I will!
   He pulled his slouched hat from his brow, and pointing, as he spoke, to the gash upon his cheek, replaced it, and sat awaiting her
d. and towered above him as though she could have crushed him in her passion[35]

From Chapter 25 Forster cut one dreadful passage:

> ye limners of God's attributes who can devise no fitter crown for Mercy's head than wreaths of ever-burning fire; ye fashioners of a false cross from twisted thunderbolts and scourges.[36]

Dickens wrote approvingly: 'It was too bad of me to give you the trouble of cutting the number, but I knew so well you would do it in the right places.'[37]

'File away at Filer, as you please',[38] he wrote from Italy to Forster in London during the composing of *The Chimes* in 1844. His adviser filed sparingly, removing only Filer's comment that Will Fern 'by going to prison oftener than his turn, ... kept twenty-seven deserving people out'.[39]

In August 1846 Dickens sent Forster amended proofs of the first number of *Dombey and Son* and wrote: 'In case more cutting is wanted, I must ask you to try your hand. I shall agree to whatever you propose.'[40] Forster condensed prolix humorous dialogue in Chapter 1. In Chapter 2 he made three substantial deletions: a heavy-handedly humorous description of how Biler got his name, replaced by Forster's short but apposite parenthesis in the chapter's penultimate paragraph; reflections on selfishness and its connection with Mr Dombey that impeded the narrative flow, were implicit in Mr Dombey's actions and were to be used, more appropriately, in Chapter 8; and a short passage ('Thence he passed to the contemplation of the future glories of Dombey and Son, and dismissed the memory of his wife, for the time being, with a tributary sigh or two.') that obscured the cutting irony of the paragraph it ended. For good measure Forster also altered some impieties: 'Devil' became 'very Deuce' and 'But my God' an unexceptionable 'But'. Also in *Dombey and Son* is a further small example of Forster 'going it alone'. In the proof of Chapter 37, in Part 12, Dickens wrote of Edith: 'Entrenched in her pride and power, and with all the obdurancy of her haughty spirit summoned about her ...'; Forster deleted 'haughty', presumably because the earlier presence of 'pride' made the later word redundant.

We can be certain that these few examples are the small tip of the large iceberg of authorized intervention. We might also be safe in concluding, even from such small-scale evidence, that Forster's proof-work was not simply, or mainly, motivated by practical considerations of available space. The *Dombey and Son* deletions point to Forster's eye for artistic effect and insist on his concern for correctness. This last the other examples extend into a general notion of decorum. The deletions from *The Old Curiosity Shop* and *Barnaby Rudge* are all of melodramatic over-insistence or other kinds of sensationalism. Further, we see these deletions as revealing Forster's basic beliefs: the 'devil's seal', the notion of widespread depravity also implicit in the filed-off Filer comment, let alone melodrama *per se*, were all anathema to the rational Unitarian, as well as to the man concerned for the reputation of literature.

Perhaps even more important than his controlled editing was the main result of his constant and close involvement with all that Dickens wrote: the ideas and suggestions he offered to his friend. They began as early as *Oliver Twist*, when Forster helped persuade Dickens to redeem Charley Bates.[41] They continued with the heroine of *The Old Curiosity Shop*: '[Dickens] had not thought of killing her', wrote Forster, 'when, about half way through I asked him to consider whether it did not necessarily belong even to his own conception'.[42] That death, Forster considered, was 'a kind of discipline of feeling and emotion which would do me lasting good, and which', he told Dickens, 'I could not thank you for as an ordinary enjoyment of literature'.[43] Dickens responded warmly: 'When I first began (on your valued suggestion) to keep my thoughts upon this ending of the tale, I resolved to try and do something which might be read by people about whom Death had been, – with a softened feeling, and with consolation.'[44] Arguably, this was Forster's most famous or infamous intervention.

Forster deterred Dickens from introducing into *Barnaby Rudge*, 'as actors in the Gordon riots three splendid fellows who should order, lead, control, and be obeyed as natural guides of the crowd in that delirious time, and who should turn out, when all was over, to have broken out from Bedlam'.[45] He persuaded Dickens to omit a chapter of *American Notes* that sought to explain and defend Dickens's views of that country;[46] he prevented Dickens from writing a defence of the American chapters in *Martin Chuzzlewit*,[47] and from using 'Your homes the scene. Yourselves the actors, here!', as that same novel's motto.[48] In 1844, as Dickens wrote *The Chimes*, Forster raised objections and Dickens responded: 'As you dislike the Young England gentleman I shall knock him out and replace him by ... A real good old city tory'; this involved the removal of some few hundred words satirizing the 'Young England' movement led by Disraeli (whose *Coningsby* was in part a manifesto), which advocated an idealized feudalism as the solution to working-class problems of the 1840s.[49]

Much of *Dombey and Son* was written whilst Dickens lived abroad, and so Forster's advice is better documented.[50] Five instances, of varying importance, can be cited here. Firstly, when Dickens, having over-written the first number, proposed transferring its final chapter, the present Chapter 4, to the second number, Forster raised strong objection that as a consequence the interest of that first number would be weakened. Chapter 4 introduces Solomon Gills and Walter Gay and hints at romantic possibilities for the latter and Florence Dombey. Dickens readily and sensibly accepted the force of Forster's response: 'I have no doubt you are right', he wrote, 'and strength is everything'. As has been seen, he then asked Forster to play a major part in the necessary cutting.

To the second number there were more objections, again accepted. Out went a reference to Miss Tox killing bugs:

> In any part of the house, visitors were usually cognizant of a prevailing mustiness; and in warm weather Miss Tox had been seen apparently writing in sundry chinks and crevices of the wainscoat with the wrong end of a pen dipped in spirits of turpentine.

And out went Walter Gay's description of 'Carker the Junior' and of the 'extraordinary interest' the older man took in him, the passage omitted almost certainly because not only did the 'mystery' distract from the scene's main purpose of developing the Florence/Walter relationship but also, in linking Walter with an older man who had fallen, it would be at odds with Walter's triumphant progress. Forster insisted upon that last notion, objecting further to Dickens's plan to exhibit the boy's career as a salutary lesson, 'to show how the good turns into bad, by degrees', and Dickens again acquiesced.

Fifthly, concerning Edith, in Chapter 46 Forster advised upon 'a nice point in the management of her character and destiny'. 'I have no question that what you suggest will be an improvement', replied Dickens, 'The strongest place to put it in, would be the close of the chapter.' From Dickens's additions to the close it can be inferred that Forster suggested clarifying Edith's motives for encouraging Carker as part hatred of him and part desire to humiliate her husband.

Finally, two later interventions: Forster suppressed the over-farcical treatment of Mr Dick in *David Copperfield*, partly by replacing that unfortunate's obsession with 'the date...when that bull got into the china warehouse' with the now familiar reference to 'King Charles's head',[51] and he induced Dickens to modify his treatment of Skimpole in *Bleak House* to reduce the resemblance to Leigh Hunt.

What emerges is that Forster's well-developed commercial sense is virtually indistinguishable from the practical expression of his principles. Killing Little Nell was an aid to sales, a development of the novel's earlier thrust, and a strengthening of didactic intent. Restoring Chapter 4 to the first part of *Dombey and Son* helped capture readers and, in countering the essential bleakness of the opening chapters, reflected Forster's Unitarian-inspired optimism. The pruning of excesses, the removing of impieties, the countering of gloom, the concern for narrative development and for the usefulness of fiction, all leavened the Dickensian mixture in the interest of the broader social acceptability of literary men, this last being demonstrated more overtly in Forster's advice about 'Young England', Dickens and America, Skimpole, and the need to avoid too great a familiarity with houses full of bugs.

As literary agent and as literary adviser Forster was Dickens's 'right hand and cool shrewd head'.[52] He was equally invaluable when Dickens's work was ready for reviewing. He wrote occasional notices himself, but was most useful to his friend in providing space in the *Examiner* for notices that almost certainly were often written by others. From 1836 until 1856 the *Examiner* was edited, successively, by Fonblanque and Forster, and Fonblanque also was a friend of Dickens. During the whole of that 20 years Forster was either 'Literary Examiner' or editor. It can be taken for granted that reviews of Dickens's work would have met with the management's approval. Indeed, there is some evidence of a controlling hand in the appearance of recurring concerns in the numerous reviews.

One such concern was to publicize through extensive quotation: the great length of several of the reviews was due to the inclusion of long and appetizing extracts and more were often used as column-fillers in other parts of the paper. Here was the evidence in support of the reviewer's insistence upon Dickens's literary and social respectability. That insistence was effected in the first place by giving Dickens a great and glorious literary pedigree. In an early review of *The Pickwick Papers* he was coupled with Defoe and with Fielding,[53] reviews of *Nicholas Nickleby* described him as 'the indeed worthy companion of the GOLDSMITHS and FIELDINGS'[54] and then added Richardson[55] to the extending pantheon. *Barnaby Rudge* brought in Hogarth,[56] *David Copperfield* almost everybody: in the latter work Dickens exhibited the 'broad and genial humour of which Fielding's Parson Adams, Smollett's Humphrey Clinker and Matthew Bramble, Stern's Uncle Toby and Mr Shandy, Goldsmith's bashful heroes, and Addison's Sir Roger, are such genuine and delightful emanations'.[57] And, for good measure, the same notice provided a comparison with Scheherazade. Dickens joined old and new: 'a superior insight into the general principles of character joining itself to the old and exquisite representations of local peculiarities and humours'.[58] The result was a 'strong power of reality' that was never 'vulgar or low'[59] and in which clear moral distinctions were always apparent: 'Vice loses nothing of its grossness, and virtue nothing of its triumph.'[60] That result was a firm expression of the writer's own character: through his work Dickens appeared as 'a man who believes and practises what he says',[61] and as a man who seemed, as the reviewer of *The Chimes* asserted rhapsodically four days before the Christmas of 1844, 'a very product of the season ... He has its life, spirits, and humour ... He has its seriousness, piety, and true religion ... He has its imaginative as well as kindly thoughts.'[62] Further, and importantly, Dickens in his work took up a political/cultural stance very acceptable to an *Examiner* that at least recalled its own radical, Benthamite roots. Dickens was 'the combiner of severe utilitarianism, with the laughing and tearful sympathies that are least looked for in its company';[63] a man who, in *Hard Times*, 'because he knows that facts and figures will not be lost sight of by the world, he leaves them, when he speaks as a novelist, to take care of themselves, and writes his tale wholly in the interests of the affections and the fancy',[64] and who, in *Pictures from Italy*, stressed the 'common-life aspects of Italy'[65] to produce an unusual travel book of democratic spirit.

The reviews were not uncritical; they pointed firmly to occasional inconsistencies, exaggerations, faults in construction, failures in characterization; 'correctness' and 'moderation' were always in the reviewers' minds. But faults were wholly subsumed in strengths, in particular within the central effect of the author's character in action. Dickens gave 'a direction to the popular tastes which before was not felt, and popular fiction shows everywhere the impression of his genius'.[66] The didactic force of the fiction was to be commended for, as Forster himself wrote of *The Chimes*, Dickens was 'giving to thousands of hearts new and just resolves'.[67] In a review of *Oliver Twist* appeared a summarizing sentence that linked literary advance, social progress and moral force: Dickens, wrote the reviewer, was 'young, popular, prosperous, *and doing good*'.[68]

In the closing years of Forster's association with the *Examiner* new notes were sounded. There was a growing stress on the increasing unity of successive novels, on greater artistry and seriousness of purpose, first apparent in *Dombey and Son* where, the reviewer insisted,

> we would say that with no abatement of the life and energy which in his earlier works threw out such forcible impressions of the actual, we have in a far higher degree the subtler requisites which satisfy imagination and reflection ... But we are not certain if the appeal thus made is not to deeper sympathies than, in the swift and cursory reading which is one of the effects of serial publication, are always at hand to respond to it.[69]

Further dissatisfaction with serialization's exigencies came with *Bleak House*, as a major consequence of the reviewer's praise of Dickens's 'complete and masterly'[70] unification. Both instances comprised a new version of the ubiquitous desire for dignity: since the greater artistry increased the moral effect which demonstrated the author's admirable character, a more worthily appropriate method of publishing was now needed. Such notes continued to echo insistently through the earnest but drabber notices of the *Examiner*'s post-Forster period.

Dickens owed much to the *Examiner*. Not only did it review his works but it also publicized his philanthropic ventures by reporting his speeches. It opened its columns to him; Dickens became an occasional reviewer and, particularly during Forster's editorship, a frequent contributor of articles that often, as with his articles on sanitary reform during 1849,[71] rehearsed themes and concerns to be developed in the novels. Further, as has been clearly shown, 'Dickens used his work for the *Examiner* as a try-out or training-ground for *Household Words*'.[72] The latter began in 1850 with a reversal of roles: with Dickens as editor Forster became an occasional contributor as well as the holder of a one-eighth share in the journal and a great help in setting it up. He discussed the venture with Dickens, sought out staff – including W. H. Wills – and introduced contributors. In addition to occasional articles he also helped compile the journal's monthly supplement, the *Household Narrative of Current Events*.[73]

Forster widened Dickens's social circle, and played leading roles in the 'splendid strolling'. When these peripheral activities are added to Forster's central work as agent, adviser, and controller of reviews, it must have seemed from Dickens's point of view, that Forster could only have been replaced by a combination of Man Friday, Maxwell Perkins, and the Inimitable Jeeves.

For all this Dickens was suitably grateful and he lost no opportunity of telling Forster so.[74] Frequent thanks for services rendered, for Forster's 'warm, unflinching and friendly exertions',[75] were often accompanied by or interspersed with expressions indicative of much deeper, more personal feelings. As Dickens wrote in the first year of their friendship: 'It shall go hard, I hope, ere anything but Death impairs the toughness of a bond now so firmly riveted.'[76] And when sending Forster a present of a silver-mounted claret-jug: 'My heart is not an eloquent one on matters which touch it most, but suppose this claret-jug the urn in which it lies, and believe that its warmest and truest blood is yours.'[77] Again, when Forster's only brother died: 'you have a Brother left. One bound to you by ties as strong as ever Nature forged. ... I read your heart as easily as if I held it in my hand.'[78]

When they were apart Dickens's letters continue this theme. 'I can't go to bed without writing to you from here',[79] he wrote from Ballechelish in 1841. 'How I miss you!'[80] he wrote from America and, also from America:

'You are a part, and an essential part, of our home, dear friend.'[81] To C. C. Felton:

> If I could but tell you how I have set my heart on rushing into Forster's study (Forster is my great friend ...) ... you would almost think I had changed places with my eldest son, and was still in pantaloons of the thinnest texture.[82]

Dickens here seems a man who wore his heart more on his hat than, even, on his sleeve, but in the final analysis there can be no doubt about the sincerity of such feelings. He remained friends with Forster for 33 years and behind the sometimes effusive expressions lay much shared experience of holidays, bereavements, and events both professional and domestic. But here the complications begin for there is little doubt, also, that the extracts quoted are at odds with some of Dickens's other reactions to his friend.

A strange and early instance of the latter occurred hardly three months into the friendship. In the thirteenth number of *The Pickwick Papers*, appearing in April 1837, Mr Pickwick and company meet Dowler as they travel to Bath. Dowler, as Percy Fitzgerald pointed out,[83] was partly based on Forster: the 'buttoned up' appearance, 'the fierce and peremptory air, which was very dignified', the readiness to 'direct' his friends, are genial reminders of Forster's manner. But central to the characterization is Dowler's quarrel with Mr Winkle. Mistakenly believing Mrs Dowler to be eloping with Mr Winkle, Dowler threatens vengeance only for the timid Mr Winkle to discover, when confrontation eventually occurs, that 'this blustering and awful personage was one of the most egregious cowards in existence'.[84] The reference is clear: during November 1836 Forster had been roundly abused by Charles Westmacott in the *Age*, had been very angry, had felt the appropriateness of a physical reaction, either horse-whipping or calling out, yet had prevaricated by 'consulting' one friend after another, notwithstanding urgings '*to do* something and do it determinedly and completely in regard to Mr. Westmacott', before tamely deciding to take 'no further notice'.[85] Six weeks later Forster met Dickens; three months after that came Dowler and a similar gap between anger and action.

Here was no genial reminder but the first expression of hostility – still submerged, at this stage – against a new dominating force. There followed occasions and letters in which Dickens ridiculed Forster no less frequently than he asserted his undying regard. Such feelings were communicated not only to old friends and confidants but also to comparatively slight acquaintances. That the journalist J. R. Robinson, never very close to Dickens and belonging to the younger generation, could recall Dickens's 'imitations of the interruptions, the forwardness, the assumptions of infallible knowledge of the biographer and essayist' and the fact that Dickens 'laughed at him ... and made boisterous fun of his pretensions',[86] does not argue much for Dickens's loyalty. Further, as with Dowler, the tone of these later references to Forster, to judge from those which appear in the letters, is not simply 'jovial' as Robinson states and Fitzgerald appears to confirm;[87] there is an unpleasant edge that even the early letters from Dickens to Ainsworth possess to some degree. For example:

> Our worthy friend the Mogul has been very unwell for some days, and has worn a dark and gloomy appearance in consequence. I found him yesterday, in company with a phial and a basin of mutton broth, but he is recovering. He has been in a very blaspheming and foaming condition in consequence of Westmacott's attacks upon him, but he is now greatly softened down – quite reasonable in fact.[88]

And:

> The Mogul is in the last agonies of procrastinated composition – hunted down by that prince of humbugs Lardner, baited by Longmans, and bullied by the Printers. He related dreadful and mysterious anecdotes of not having been in bed for a fortnight, and is reduced to such a fearful ebb of nervous exasperation that Mrs. Cooper has temporarily fled No. 58 and resigned her duties to a deputy who is under a course of violence.[89]

In the first letter Forster's illness and anger became sources of humour; in both extracts he receives little sympathy. In each instance the energy and exaggeration of the prose conveys a sense of Dickens's eagerness to capitalize on comic possibilities, an eagerness to make a butt of his friend that suggests almost a subconscious and hostile delight in Forster's discomfiture coupled with an awareness of Forster as an immensely powerful presence in his life.

This note of hostility reappears frequently, even in the middle of a business letter to Edward Chapman about passages in *American Notes*: 'Mr. Forster seems to have got it into his head (and the quantity of hair he wears, probably prevents it coming out again) that I mean to use them for a separate chapter',[90] and sharply, unjustifiably and, again, with a complete lack of sympathy, in Dickens's letter to Maclise about the death of Macready's infant daughter:

> It is impossible, I am sure, that any people can more truly

> sympathize with the affliction of others, than we do for the sorrows of those to whom we are so strongly and ardently attached – and so I know you will say and feel. But I vow to God that if you had seen Forster last night, you would have supposed our Dear Friend was dead himself – in such an amazing display of grief did he indulge, and into such a very gloomy gulf was he sunk up to the chin.[91]

The note persists in Dickens's later correspondence. To Bulwer, discussing projected amateur dramatics at Knebworth, Dickens wrote:

> I have not yet had conference with Forster, who has been sitting, since his return from you, with a touzled head, a dirty blouse, and extraordinarily dishevelled pantaloons, anathematizing Henry, in an equable state of distraction. The last time I saw him, his eyebrows were just visible above a dirty sea of proofs.[92]

Four years later in a letter to Georgina Hogarth, he writes: '[Catherine] is described in Mrs. Stowe's book; which Forster, in a languid state of rheumatico-calchico-hiccoughy-frowsy-aperient-medical mystery informed me yesterday he had "been obliged to assault dreadfully"'.[93]

Here is an additional factor, implicit in the evocation of the squalid. It would be going too far to describe Dickens's tone in these extracts as one of loathing or disgust but neither word is wildly inappropriate. The prose in each of the four letters has vitality and a sense of engagement; it reveals an attitude towards Forster of hostile attraction and defensive attack.

Coupled with this is the awareness that, despite all that brought and held the two men together, as the friendship developed so did basic differences in attitudes and opinions. To give only a few examples: in the 1850s Dickens became the editor of popular magazines as Forster abandoned weekly journalism for seventeenth-century historical scholarship. Dickens came to lose faith in Parliament; Forster presided over an *Examiner* that became less radical and more whiggish, and himself long cherished political ambitions.[94] Dickens responded violently to the reappearance of Maria Beadnell; Forster[95] could not comprehend the intensity of Dickens's feelings to an extent that highlights their increasing lack of emotional kinship.

But the basic work of literary advice and criticism and business management continued; Forster was always consulted when Dickens faced important decisions. Yet this last role, Forster as consultant, adds a final complication. Forster advised against Dickens taking the editorship of the *Daily News*, against separating from his wife, against making a public statement about the separation, against giving public readings, against the tour of America, against the inclusion of the Sikes/Nancy reading. In each case Dickens's response can be described in Forster's weary words from Ross as he prepared to urge upon Dickens strong objections to the second American visit: 'We are proceeding to the discussion immediately: but I fancy it can only end in one way: that he will fail in convincing me, that I shall not entirely fail in convincing him, but that he will go all the same.'[96] Forster's advice was always rejected.

Forster's position was consistent and, as has been said, straightforward. In his private life he became more and more sober and respectable. His advice sought to keep his friend on a 'moderate middle course'.[97] That is to say, Forster's private life, his wealthy marriage, paid government post as Commissioner of Lunacy, and affluent life-style became a model for the literary man desiring social acceptability and status; that advice sought to make others in his own image. Forster, in most of his friendships and particularly in that with Dickens, resembled a painter who sought to transform experience into a series of self-portraits eminently suitable for middle-class parlours; what made matters even worse for his friends was that he acted out of genuine affection for them.

Dickens needed Forster's practical help; he valued Forster's judgment; Forster was the closest of friends. Yet there seems little doubt that Forster's friendship was experienced by Dickens as a constant pressure that made him guiltily aware of his own faults and misguided conduct. Dickens responded with hostile ridicule and with the rejection of Forster's advice. But even though, comparatively speaking, they drifted apart, Dickens could never ignore Forster. Indeed, the main events that aggravated the rift – Forster's scholarly activities, his marriage, his wealth and respectability – would surely have strengthened Dickens's consciousness of his own very different position – separated from his wife, having an affair with an actress, reverting generally to a bachelor existence and surrounding himself with younger, more flashy companions. Certainly, from the 1850s onwards Wilkie Collins took Forster's place as boon companion, but it is also certain that amidst the desperate jollity and raffish facetiousness of Dickens's letters to the ever-eager Wilkie is a constant awareness of Forster's bulky existence. Writing to Collins during 1855 Dickens told him of his plans to read *The Lighthouse* and added, '"I am here" (to adapt Forster's last sonorous form of speech), for that purpose'.[98] In 1858: 'All day yesterday I was pursuing the Reading idea. Forster seems to me to be extraordinarily irrational about it. (I have a misgiving sometimes that his money must have got into his head.)'[99] Long letters in 1860 and 1862 described visits to Forster in Brighton and rearranged business to accept Forster's dinner invitations.[100] Forster had become for Dickens the baleful representative of middle-class values which Dickens did not altogether despise but found impossible to practise. Even Dickens's extreme expressions of affection indicate both his unspoken sense of the strength of Forster's position and subconscious compensation for his more hostile outbursts. The most hostile of all began in 1864 with the publication of *Our Mutual Friend* and the characterization of Podsnap.

The widely accepted version of the link between Forster and Podsnap is summed up by Edgar Johnson: 'All Forster's acquaintances recognized his mannerisms embedded in Podsnap – the indignant flush, the sweeping gesture of dismissal.'[101] The suggestion is that Dickens merely and perhaps mischievously made use of a few of Forster's external traits. But this is far too simple. Podsnap is the ultimate expression of Dickens's reaction to the reproving pressure of Forster's respectability and is based, though not completely yet fundamentally and in many points of detail, on the characteristics of Dickens's closest friend. That the following account does not include all aspects of Forster's personality may well reflect a lack of knowledge about Forster rather than the presence of purely fictional elements.

Podsnap makes seven main appearances in *Our Mutual Friend*:[102] he meets the Veneerings, quickly 'making himself quite at home', becomes their 'oldest friend' and in that capacity is both consulted about procedure at the Lammles's wedding and 'all but does the honours' at the wedding breakfast. Then follows a chapter in which 'Podsnappery' is described and the Podsnaps return hospitality by giving a dinner party for their daughter. Veneering then consults Podsnap about getting into Parliament and Podsnap plays a leading part in organizing the campaign. His next appearance gives further personal details, stressing his conceit, obstinacy and possessiveness. We encounter him as an aggressively intolerant member of 'A Social Chorus' and his even more extreme intolerance dominates the closing pages of the novel. From this last summary one can see how closely Podsnap's progress through the work follows the general pattern of Forster's friendships: the early dominance, the role of adviser, the energetic worker, the permanent fixture more and more concerned to impose his opinions. Leigh Hunt, Bulwer, Macready, Carlyle, and Dickens himself, could all testify to this.

The Podsnaps live 'in a shady angle adjoining Portman Square'; so did Forster, immediately after his marriage, at 46 Montagu Square. Forster, like Podsnap, was 'certain to dwell in the shade', surely an oblique reference to Forster's role as a background presence in the lives of his literary friends. Like Podsnap, Forster had 'married a good inheritance' and though, unlike Podsnap, Forster was not in marine insurance his brother Christopher had been; it is tempting to see even this choice of occupation, suggesting ideas of support in times of difficulty or disaster, as having a certain appropriateness. Podsnap's speedy translation into the godfather of the Veneering baby is another similarity, given Forster's godchildren in the families of Dickens, Macready, Elwin, Henry Morley and George Cattermole. The assertion that 'there was no youth (the young person always excepted) in the articles of Podsnappery' is a further quite direct reference to Forster, whose life was distinguished by his friendships with men much older than himself: Emerson and Whiteside in his law class, Hunt, Lamb, Bulwer, Macready and Landor, Carlyle and others.

Like Podsnap's, Forster's rudeness was extreme and proverbial. Like Podsnap Forster was, in Macready's words, constantly 'laying down his opinions (and upon subjects of which he...knows nothing) as if it were law'.[103] Podsnap's legalistic response to Mortimer's tale of the 'Man from Somewhere' looks to Forster's role as trustee (for the recently dead Landor) and trustee-designate (for Dickens, Bulwer and Carlyle). Podsnap's hesitant use of French recalls Dickens's jokes about Forster's visit to Boulogne;[104] the lengths to which Podsnap goes to correct the English of his foreign guest reminds us of Forster even correcting Macready's delivery of Shakespeare[105] and John Poole's early parody[106] of Forster's drama reviews with its reference to Forster correcting the actors' pronunciation.

As for Podsnap's more weighty views: he speaks in favour of the 'Constitution', of the 'charter of the land', as Forster did in 1860 in *The Debates on the Grand Remonstrance*, with its extended discussion of the nature and great influence of Magna Carta and the survival of England's 'civil constitution'.[107] Podsnap then describes the qualities of his countrymen: 'there is in the Englishman a combination of qualities, a modesty, an independence, a responsibility, a repose...which one would seek in vain among the Nations of the Earth'. Forster had written, in his well-known essay on Defoe, reprinted in 1860, of the 'inflexible constancy, sturdy dogged resolution, unwearied perseverance, and obstinate contempt of danger and of tyranny, [of] the great Middle-class English character'.[108]

Again:

> Podsnap always talks Britain, and talks as if he were a sort of Private Watchman employed, in the British interests, against the rest of the world. 'We know what Russia means, sir,' says Podsnap; 'we know what France wants; we see what America is up to; but we know what England is. That's enough for us.'

As Dickens wrote to Macready during the Crimean period:

> Forster ... appears to be troubled by the great responsibility of directing the whole War. He doesn't seem to me to be quite clear that he has got the ships into the exact order he intended, on the sea-point of attack, at Sebastopol.[109]

And, to Leigh Hunt, of 'Forster having to direct the whole war, and being troubled in his mind with doubts as to whether the ships have been as well brought into action before Sebastopol, as he intended'.[110]

The main 'articles of a faith and school' called 'Podsnappery' are similarly grounded in Forster's attitudes. Podsnap's patronage of foreigners ('he considered other countries ... a mistake') is only an extreme version of the nationalism revealed, for example, in Forster's work for the *Foreign Quarterly Review*. The Forster who, as editor, accepted articles that asserted, of the peace with China, that to England went 'the glory of having opened the way for European civilization to one-third of the human race',[111] the rest of the article suggesting that in this context 'European' meant 'English' and that the French, for one nation, might well look to the flaws in their institutions, and who himself advised America of the need to rid itself of corruption and infamous practices, remembering that they derived their best quality ('the attachment to True Freedom')[112] from the English, planted the seeds, if no more than the seeds, of Podsnap's prejudice.

Fitzgerald[113] confirms Forster's tendency to sweep aside difficulties and disagreeables; a Podsnappian complacency, at least about the English, is evident in the extracts already given. But at the centre of Dickens's description of Podsnappery is 'Podsnap's notions of the Arts';

> Literature; large print, respectfully descriptive of getting up at eight, shaving close at a quarter past, breakfasting at nine, going to the City at ten, coming home at half-past five, and dining at seven ...

Here we see the absurdly exaggerated result of Forster's concern for the dignity and social standing of the literary profession: a literature risking nothing, wholly acceptable, wholly respectable. Behind Podsnap's distortion of what literature should be lies Dickens's consciousness of Forster's pressure not only on his private life and business life but also directly on his fiction. Forster's desire for moderation in all things, summed up in his praise of Mrs Gaskell's *Ruth* ('I detect nothing false, nothing exaggerated. Every such temptation is forborne ...'),[114] his insistence on correctness of fact and of taste, the elimination of the over-sensational or all that might detract from a novel's morally exalting effect, was all designed, as Dickens well knew, to further the acceptability of the writer's work on the impeccable hearths of eminently respectable homes.

Linked to Podsnap's central statement on literature are further references to his obsession with dignity, typical of which is:

> Mr. Podsnap, as a representative man, is not alone in caring very particularly for his own dignity, if not for that of his acquaintances, and therefore in angrily supporting the acquaintances who have taken out his Permit, lest, in their being lessened, he should be.

Here also is a statement applicable to all Forster's literary friendships and there is some truth in this assertion that one of the reasons why Forster was concerned about the dignity of others was in order to preserve his own. There is no doubt that his constant agitation for the cause was the result not only of the influence of Hunt, Lamb and the others, but also a consequence of Forster's feelings of inferiority about his lowly upbringing, feelings that prompted a profound need for status and dignified position.

There is no evidence to show that Podsnap's wife was based on Eliza Colburn; what is known of Mrs Forster suggests otherwise. And in real life there was no young person; the Forsters died childless. But the invention of Miss Podsnap does allow Dickens to incorporate even more references to Forster. Remembering Stanfield's account of the depreciatory effect that being engaged to marry Forster had on Mrs Colburn,[115] and Renton's assertion that Forster was 'an exacting husband, a despot in his own house, one whose "word was law" for all who were in any way dependent upon him',[116] we can even see something of Forster's relationship with his wife in the idea of Miss Podsnap being 'crushed by the mere deadweight of Podsnappery'. Further, in the manner in which Podsnap sought to determine every aspect of his daughter's existence and thinking and, particularly, in the idea of her being 'restricted to companionship with not very congenial older persons', it seems permissible to detect an unkind allusion to Forster's friendship with and virtual guardianship of Bulwer's son, Robert Lytton.

More generally, the relationship between Podsnap and his daughter is a version of Forster's dominance of all his friends; that we are encouraged to think in this way is evident from the best-known of Podsnap's views: 'The question about everything was, would it bring a blush into the cheek of the young person?' In that first review by the young Forster of the 1828 editions of *The Keepsake* and *The Anniversary*, a review which he preserved carefully in his library for the rest of his life, he wrote of the taste of *The Keepsake*'s editor, Frederick Reynolds:

> Did Mr. R. consider that, in the course of a few weeks, his book would be in the hands of almost every family in the kingdom – does he consider that such passages ... would be apt to raise a blush on the cheek of a young English female becoming the pride of her purity?[117]

Viewing Podsnap as a reaction to the pressure that Dickens felt Forster exerted upon him, and the characterization as an opportunity for Dickens to work off his feelings about such pressure, highlights the faults in the presentation. Podsnap's reactions to the Lammles's insolvency and, in particular, to the Wrayburn/Lizzie Hexam marriage ('[my] gorge rises ... it offends and disgusts me ... it makes me sick'), show how Dickens's personal involvement with Podsnap blunted his sense of proportion and weakened the effect through over-reaction. This gives added weight and fortuitous biographical shrewdness to Edmund Wilson's[118] comment that Dickens was afraid of Podsnap and all that he represented.

That he had good cause for such fear is one of the points of *Our Mutual Friend*. Whilst the Lammles crash, the Veneerings totter and Lady Tippins prattles ineffectively, Podsnap emerges as evidence of the basic indestructability of the new order's prejudices. On the final page of the novel it is Podsnap who confronts Twemlow and, though we know where virtue lies, equally we are in no doubt of Podnap's eventual dominance.

There is no firm evidence that Forster perceived Podsnap's full meaning. Dickens fancied he did[119] but one can be sure that Forster only saw the presence of external mannerisms; no friendship could have survived more complete apprehension. As it was, their friendship continued until Dickens's death and Forster later considered Podsnap to have been one of the novel's few successes.[120]

Even at its most exaggerated the characterization never loses complete contact with its real-life model; although Podsnap is not Forster much of Forster is certainly in Podsnap. The characterization dramatizes Forster's main effect upon Dickens's life and work. It brings home to us not only the complex nature of their friendship but also the extent to which that work could serve as a safety-valve for violent reactions against repressive social bonds.

As for Forster: paradoxically our sense of his resemblance to Podsnap reminds us of the qualities that Dickens left out, amongst them a sincere concern for others, kindness, and courage. Podsnap's young person may remind us of Robert Lytton but excludes all that is implicit in Lytton's reaction to Forster's death: 'No man ever *had* such a friend as I had in him.'[121] That Dickens also thought this is seen in his continued need and desire for Forster's friendship. No greater compliment could be paid to Forster than this implicit assertion that his finer qualities were sufficient to counter even Podsnap and all that that monster represented.

CHAPTER 12 *Thomas Carlyle*

With the advantage of ironical hindsight it can now be seen that Thomas Carlyle prepared himself thoroughly for the inevitable Forsterian encounter. Leigh Hunt was his near neighbour and had become his friend; he had known Charles Lamb, though had thought little of him. Fonblanque, Landor, Maclise – who sketched him for *Fraser's Magazine* in 1832 – and B. W. Procter were all long-standing acquaintances. Carlyle and Jane Carlyle were regular readers of the *Examiner*; Carlyle had an abiding interest in the Commonwealth period. Above all, through *Sartor Resartus*, *The French Revolution* and successful public lectures regularly noticed and supported by the *Examiner*, Carlyle had become a literary lion. They first met early in 1839, when Carlyle was 43 and Forster was 26.

The meeting was a consequence of Carlyle's concern to found a lending library in central London. On 17 January 1839 he wrote his first letter to Forster asking for the *Examiner*'s support.[1] This he obtained in the form of space for 'a fierce blast',[2] reports of the project's progress, and other propagandizing. Forster himself took up the cause: he involved Bulwer, distributed prospectuses, and helped organize the public meeting held at the Freemason's Tavern on 24 June 1840.[3] Forster drew up advertisements for that meeting[4] and was elected to the committee formed 'to draw up rules and organise'[5] what became the London Library. It remained a common interest throughout their friendship; the Lacaita affair of the 1850s when Carlyle, supported by Forster and, eventually, by most of the committee, successfully opposed Gladstone's attempt to appoint the emigré Neapolitan, James Lacaita, as librarian is an example of the way that Library business deepened their relationship.[6] This continued to happen even as late as 1870; when Carlyle was offered the Library's presidency he accepted only after Forster 'had carefully prepared them all to acquiesce in'[7] the one condition on which Carlyle would agree to serve.

To quote Nowell-Smith: 'He accepted election as president on the specific understanding that he must never be asked to preside.'[8]

This is, of course, to move far away from the friendship's beginnings. In 1839 a further literary campaign brought the two men together: following the defeat of Talfourd's bill in 1837 there developed increasingly desperate agitation for copyright reform. On 7 April 1839 the *Examiner*, supporting this movement also, published 'The Claims of Authors to an Extension of Copyright', a hard-hitting article that included a petition to Parliament from Carlyle himself.[9]

Both copyright reform and the London Library, concerned as they were to benefit the literary profession, were dear to Forster's heart. Common intellectual ground and Carlyle's fame apart, Forster was naturally attracted to the central figure in such campaigns. For Forster, this friendship thus began as yet another expression of regard for the dignity of literature, that constantly recurring theme.

But whereas Forster was powerfully drawn to Carlyle that impulse was not at first reciprocated. Carlyle was much older than Forster, as were Leigh Hunt and Landor and as Charles Lamb had been. But the latter three needed Forster to impose order upon their personal chaos; Carlyle was never so disorganized and in 1839 had closer friends, more valued correspondents. He was simply glad of Forster's support. Had Forster not been available Fonblanque would doubtless have come up with *Examiner* space and many others could have drafted advertisements and distributed leaflets. In this beginning Forster was for Carlyle at worst an office-boy, at best a conveniently influential assistant, and was patronized accordingly: 'Tomorrow night I shall be at home, and very glad to see you', Carlyle wrote to W. D. Christie, the barrister who helped draft the Library's manifesto; 'Forster also would do no harm; at any rate, perhaps you could *see* him beforehand, and get out of him what news he had?'[10] At other times he was treated with wry amusement: when *Chevely* appeared, the 'scandalous novel'[11] read avidly by Jane Carlyle, Forster became 'Fuz' for both husband and wife and 'Fuz' he remained throughout the 1840s. He never wholly escaped this disrespectful tone though, years later, Carlyle tried to account for the initial uncertainty and concluded that Forster's more valuable qualities had resisted quick discovery: 'he was yet but a new untried acquaintance, and ... our tone towards or concerning him ... greatly improved itself, on the ample trial there was'.[12]

The improvement began with Forster's friendship with Jane Carlyle that became an important counter to her essential loneliness and to a frustration that was at least partly intellectual. Mazzini was her closest confidant: she wrote to him seriously and intimately of her domestic and marital problems.[13] Forster was different and began as 'one of those people who go about, that one likes, in moderation, without feeling them to be worth the pains of a particular study'.[14] Initially she valued him for his sociability: he called regularly and offered a line in good-humouredly malicious literary gossip that greatly appealed to her. There was, she told Forster, 'something *sunshiny* about you, that cheers my gloom'.[15] As the friendship developed it included dancing at parties, visits to theatres and to concerts and more unusually, in 1848, to observe Tothillfields prison.[16] Forster lent her books and she admired his own, reading his biography of Goldsmith with much appreciation.[17] Their correspondence quickly achieved a distanced confidentiality. 'Why do women marry?' she wrote to Forster during 1840, 'God knows, unless it be that, like the great Wallenstein, they do not find scope enough for their genius and qualities in an easy life.'[18] In 1841, returning from an Annandale holiday, she complained feelingly:

> Oh such a place! Now that I am fairly done with it I look back upon it all as a bad dream! Never shall I forget its blood-red, moaning sea – its cracked looking-glasses, its 'industrious fleas', its desolation and hugger-mugger such as hath not entered into the heart of man to conceive![19]

Implicit in both extracts was marital unhappiness hidden from Forster by wit and facetious drama. To this considerable extent – but only to this extent – was Forster allowed to be a serious correspondent. In his turn he played his part:

> Ah my dear Mrs. Carlyle – here you are again. You talk of being in a state of continual blue devils! Blue Angels you mean – for is not this note of yours the very example of that Blue Divinity in its left hand corner, that hath come winging her way this blessed morning to make me indeed and in verity 'Sunshiny' in this shady dullness of Lincolns Inn. The Lord do as much for you, and more also. …
> … Meanwhile & Ever & Ever, am I not, my dear Mrs. Carlyle, yours from the Crown to the toe & most in the heartiest part of me
>
> John Forster[20]

Such heavily comic posturing in itself ensured that the relationship was as Jane Carlyle desired it to be, one observing the period's strict proprieties and one that continued even after Forster's marriage when, though Forster called less, Jane Carlyle's friendship with Mrs Forster took her frequently to their home. Her birthday present for Forster in 1864, a 'pretty little gold seal',[21] indicates continuing respect and affection; in that same year she stayed briefly with the Forsters after returning to London from an unhappy convalescence at St Leonard's.[22]

But the true source of their friendship lay deeper than sociability and kindness and was described by Jane herself:

> For my part, I have always thought rather well of [Forster's] judgment; for, from the first, he has displayed a most remarkable clear-sightedness, with respect to myself; thinking me little short of being as great a genius as my husband. ...
>
> This man, then, has been taking counsel with me – me of all people that could have been pitched upon – how to give new life to a dying Review, 'The Foreign' ...[23]

The flippant irony only accentuates Jane Carlyle's pleasure at being taken seriously, at being asked for advice. Forster regularly visited Carlyle but he also talked to and listened to Jane. When he became editor of the *Foreign Quarterly Review* she was not only in his confidence to the extent of knowing that Thackeray had tried for the job but was also relied upon to gain Mazzini and John Sterling as contributors.[24] The high regard that Forster had for her impressed Carlyle who wrote to his wife when at her uncle's in Liverpool,

> Fuz came here the night before last, talked long, or was talked to, really not in a quite distracted manner, and passionately solicited and thankfully received your address. They – Dickens, he, and a squad of that sort – have decided to act a play ... It is actually to be on the 21st of next month, and it is an immense feature of it to Fuz that you are to be there. The excellent Fuz![25]

Carlyle's patronizing assumption of wonder that his wife should be so in demand does not altogether hide his own pleasure. The relationship between Forster and Jane Carlyle linked Forster and himself and strongly influenced Carlyle towards an increasingly favourable opinion of his new young friend.

To that influence he added his own developing appreciation of Forster's qualities. Though the friendship had begun with Forster's usefulness as contact and organizer Carlyle, like his wife and like Hunt, Lamb, Bulwer, Dickens, and Macready before her, was swift to prize his conviviality. In Forster's company life could be enjoyed; in Forster's company Carlyle found some relief from labours that could be dreadful. 'I will stay for you on Saturday', he informed Forster eagerly in 1847, '... A walk after that, thro' all the lanes, will be delightful.'[26] Again, an example from some years later: 'I will come riding', wrote Carlyle, 'and be off again before 9½ o'clock; – fortified with your instructions, and a "chop" *plus* two glasses (not more) from that hospitable bottle, the memory of which is dear to me.'[27] At Cheyne Row Forster was very much at home: David Masson recalled Forster's familiarity with Carlyle, how Forster even 'rallied' his host when Carlyle left a guest unserved, how Carlyle was 'genial' in Forster's company, that there was much agreement between them and that Forster 'had quite as much of the talk as Carlyle'.[28] At Lincoln's Inn Fields Carlyle often met visitors of consequence: in 1848 Emerson dined there with Carlyle, Dickens, and the jovial host and wrote later that 'it seemed the habit of the set to pet Carlyle a good deal, and draw out the mountainous mirth'.[29] Certainly he was given privileged status for Elwin remembered a dinner during 1862 when he and Carlyle were the only guests allowed to smoke.[30] Forster celebrated Carlyle's birthdays with dinner parties – that for his 70th, in 1865, gave Robert Browning his last glimpse of Jane Carlyle[31] – and it became Carlyle's habit to dine with Forster on Christmas Day. In 1864 he even deserted an indisposed Jane to appear at Forster's festive table.[32]

During the late 1850s and early 1860s when the burden of *Frederick the Great* threatened to crush Carlyle psychologically and physically he owed much to Forster's ready sociability. Froude noted that Carlyle 'was fixed to his garret room again, rarely stirring out except to ride, and dining nowhere save now and then with Forster, to meet only Dickens'.[33] Forster's company was a desperate requirement, with Carlyle anxious for 'the sound of your friendly voice again' that could seem like a 'melody striking into the wearied heart of me'.[34] Thus at this time and at others, though Carlyle would sometimes grumble at Forster's over-abundant hospitality, he was troubled when events prevented contact. 'Send me word again how you are;' he enquired when Forster lay ill, '– and let it be, that you are better, like a good fellow! I am alone here, these two weeks, and lead the most secluded, abstruse, silent and indescribable life.'[35] When bereavement kept Forster away Carlyle's sympathy could not wholly mask his continuing hunger for company: 'Next week, drive down to Chelsea any day, you will probably find us both; – or write (to my wife), and *appoint* some evening, with tea, either there or at L.I.F. – God bless you dear F.'.[36]

Such socializing was the friendship's fundamental activity. Out of it grew Carlyle's awareness of Forster's other attributes. 'This Forster is a most noisy man', he told John Sterling, 'but really rather a good fellow (as one gradually finds), and with some substance in his tumultuary brains.'[37] In late 1841 he said much the same to Forster himself: 'It has been a real pleasure to see you visibly growing in all kinds of strength and clearness of late years.'[38] Such growth made Forster the husband's confidant as well as the wife's but it did not make him the husband's equal. As these extracts show Carlyle always assumed superiority; he patted Forster's practical back but remained disinclined to shake him by the intellectual hand. Yet as confidant Forster was invaluable. Two extracts make the point, both from 1843 and about Carlyle's work on Cromwell: 'Today I am in the Cambridge Fens', he wrote to Forster,

> a most delectable position in such weather. The Gods alone know whether any Cromwell will ever be got out of me. The secret of him lies deep and ever deeper; deep as the foundations of the world. The man is not a *quack*; he rather seems to me a *god*: but how shall I ever convince *you* of that![39]

and

> if I get fairly into that Cromwell, I shall have to go on, incessant, as a short projectile, as a kindled fire, and not stop, – under penalty of going out altogether! On the other hand if I do not begin it, if I never get it begun? All that I have written hitherto has gone straight to the fire! – I begin to approach the verge of desperation ...[40]

Very clearly Carlyle needed to express his frustrations, to explore his feelings during gestatory periods. He needed a correspondent like Forster. As so often during this relationship, from Carlyle's point of view there was no clear line between Forster as friend and Forster as useful acquaintance.

As for Forster himself, in 1839 he responded not only to a famous man anxious to give practical help to literary men but also to one already well known for his support of the profession. 'At no former era', Carlyle had written in *Signs of the Times*, 'has Literature, the printed communication of Thought, been of such importance as it is now'[41] and in the same essay referred particularly to the power of journalism, that 'Fourth Estate, of Able Editors'[42] mentioned again in *The French Revolution*. General commendation combined with practical concern so that even Thackeray, usually hostile to movements for 'dignity', confessed to his mother that 'It is Carlyle who has worked more than any other to give [literature] its independence.'[43] In 1841 came *On Heroes and Hero-Worship*, first as public lectures then as printed book, with its long section on 'The Hero as Man of Letters' in which Carlyle described 'the writers of Newspapers, Pamphlets, Poems, Books' as 'the real working effective Church of a modern country'[44] and discussed how writers could best be rewarded, the example of Robert Southey and the uses of literary guilds and literary men, given the latter's search for truth and attempts to disseminate it. Such material found its way into Forster's biography of Goldsmith, in which Carlyle was quoted approvingly, and into his *Examiner* articles. The whole movement for the dignity of literature drew strength from Carlyle's commitment. In particular it strengthened Forster's eagerness to help his new friend.

This help differed from that given to Forster's other major friends in its selectivity; he did not, was not allowed to, plunge his finger into every Carlylean pie. When they first met Carlyle had begun reading for what became, firstly, the Cromwell section of *On Heroes and Hero-worship* and then, in 1845, *Oliver Cromwell's Letters and Speeches with Elucidations.* Forster's own *Cromwell* completed publication in the summer of 1839 and when Carlyle mentioned reading it Forster gave his new friend a set of *Lives of the Statesmen of the Commonwealth*[45] in which Forster had done what Carlyle had once thought of doing, written an account of the Commonwealth period by concentrating on major figures.[46] In addition Forster allowed Carlyle to draw upon his collection of historical materials and did so again in 1846 when a second edition of *Cromwell* included new documents.[47] In the 1850s, when Carlyle returned to large-scale historical writing with *Frederick the Great*, his 'abominable chaos (of Prussian sand and peat bog)',[48] Forster played a similar role, making Carlyle the subject of 'beneficient remembrance'[49] by finding him books.

Occasionally he became more than mere supplier. He offered anecdotes of Cromwell for Carlyle's lectures in the 'Heroes' series;[50] when Carlyle asked for Thurloe's works he added, 'what of him you advise'.[51] In 1854, acknowledging material on Frederick's meeting with Voltaire, Carlyle accepted suggestions about further reading: 'It increases my desire to see *Burney*. – I will come to you one of these days ... and have a bit of dialogue and consultation again.'[52] In 1861 Forster tried more weighty urging:

> I wanted also to add a word to a request I lately preferred to you – and which I hardly made strong enough, I fear.
>
> Don't think of completing 'Frederick' in two more volumes! You cannot do it in a manner fully worthy of what is already done – how, possibly, can you in the space you have left yourself! I am convinced that you cannot – and I woke the other morning in the midst of a violent argument of which the drift was to show that by attempting it you'd not only do wrong to a magnificent piece of work by huddling it up at the close, but would inflict upon yourself all kinds of harassments and worries and troubles still more to be regretted by those to whom nothing that even you can write is so valuable as You.

Do think of all this in good time, dear Carlyle, and determine at once to add another volume –[53]

Carlyle replied grandly: 'You need not fear my doing *Fried*[h] the way that is *easiest* for me!'[54] Two volumes had been published, four more were added. The exchange demonstrates Forster's understanding of the scope and range of Carlyle's materials and the way he encouraged Carlyle during difficult years. There were other helpers, such as Joseph Neuberg, and other book-providers, such as Robert Browning. Forster's influence on the two historical biographies can be indicated but hardly delineated with any precision. Up to a point this was a relationship between two historians and the fact that Forster's influence was essentially marginal even upon the biographies is a further reminder of his place in the partnership.

There is no evidence that Forster had the kind of access to Carlyle's manuscripts that he had to those of Bulwer, Dickens, and Hunt. To be sure Carlyle showed him 'The Life of John Sterling', but apologetically 'So soon as you have done with that *Mss.* (which must be very crabbed company, I think, if your eyes and your patience are like mine), please send it over to *me*.'[55] Forster was asked for no more than a general opinion of the finished work and Carlyle told his brother that Forster had 'pronounced it to be readable'.[56] As literary adviser to Chapman & Hall Forster would, of course, have read several of Carlyle's completed manuscripts; certainly he advised them about the biography of Sterling.[57] Again there is no evidence, and it seems improbable, that he interfered with them. He was most useful to Carlyle in more practical spheres, such as help for distressed literary folk[58] and, far more importantly, with negotiations with publishers and contractual concerns.

In 1839 Carlyle was much engaged in public lecturing that ended the following year with the series on 'Heroes and Hero-Worship'. He lectured because he needed the money. His publisher was James Fraser and Carlyle had published much in *Fraser's Magazine*. Fraser had not been generous: for *Sartor Resartus*, which appeared in *Fraser's Magazine* during 1833–4, he paid only 8 guineas a sheet instead of the normal 15 and the 20 received by Carlyle for earlier contributions.[59] In all Carlyle made £82 from *Sartor* and throughout the 1830s his work, even *The French Revolution*, continued to make very little money. When Forster met him Carlyle's career was about to take off financially: *The French Revolution* was yielding American royalties collected by Emerson,[60] 1839 saw the publication by Fraser of *Chartism* and *Critical and Miscellaneous Essays*, with second editions of each during 1840, and in 1841 Fraser brought out the first edition of *On Heroes and Hero-Worship*, the lectures in book form.

Forster's first act was to persuade Carlyle to move to Chapman & Hall. Carlyle thought little of Fraser who was, he told Forster, 'what one calls honest, but timid, egoist – attornyish, &c: I am too happy to have a couple of such eagles as Hall and Chapman to fly at him: let the two parties have the battle all between them'.[61] The result of that 'battle' was a meeting between Carlyle and William Hall on 12 May 1842 when Carlyle was given documents on which Forster's advice was to be sought. Carlyle was surprised 'to find certain hundreds of pounds due to me *now* and no books mine any longer'. He was anxious for Forster's 'Commentary then the Booksellers declare that they will pay'.[62] As negotiations proceeded Fraser died but he had tried to retain Carlyle and the nature of the latter's surprise indicates the need to assign copyright probably to compensate Chapman & Hall for the cost of acquiring Carlyle's copyrights and, possibly, stereotypes from Fraser's firm. That cost may also explain why Carlyle grumbled a little about his first agreement with Chapman & Hall. On 17 May 1842 they agreed to publish a second edition of *On Heroes and Hero-Worship*, to bear all the costs and to pay Carlyle £100 on publication,[63] whereas many years earlier Boyd of Edinburgh had paid him £250 for the second edition of the *Wilhelm Meister* translation.[64] Nonetheless, as Carlyle wrote to Forster, 'I am very glad to be out of *such* hands and into such other, even at a little loss'.[65] 'Chapman and Hall', he considered, 'seem to be of another fibre than poor Fraser was!'[66] He readily accepted the advice of the firm and of Forster that the second edition should have a large and inexpensive format and stipulated only that Robson, the master printer who had set his work for Fraser, should now set it for Chapman & Hall.[67]

In 1842 Carlyle received £200 for the first edition of *Past and Present* and the assignment of copyright to Chapman & Hall.[68] Terms became progressively better as his fame and sales increased and so were not wholly a consequence of Forster's advice. Certainly Carlyle conducted much of his business with his publishers without reference to Forster; despite some pretence at being careless of business he had, as he put it, a 'business-"conscience"'[69] and was well able to write a detailed and sharp business letter. Forster probably worked to a brief, though possibly to a less detailed one than that received, for example, from Dickens. In the later years of the friendship he had a freer hand and sufficient documentation has survived from that time to bring out his developing role as business adviser and to enable some basic conclusions to be drawn.

By 1858 Forster had 'beneficiently made the Bargain with Chapman'[70] for the first two volumes of *Frederick the Great*, agreeing £800 for 2,000 copies of each, with each volume to be not less than 400 pages.[71] Carlyle mislaid the original agreement and, when queries arose, was about to leave London. 'You cannot go against my judgment in it while you follow your own',[72] he told Forster and his friend tied up all loose ends so successfully that Carlyle would, as he put it, 'instead of an arithmetical-commercial intanglio, retain merely a pleasant thought of Forster'.[73] By the end of 1858 the volumes had netted Carlyle £2,800.[74] Seven years later as he finished *Frederick*, Carlyle remained concerned with details of the agreement. Publication date for the final volumes was to be 20 February and when it was put back to 1 March he wrote indignantly and despairingly to Forster: '*You*, like the Champ^{n} of Xtendom you have always been, will pin down these financial Demons to the place that belongs to them, & save an afflicted worn-out man from such cattle.'[75] The appeal clearly shows Forster's main function as Carlyle's representative.

In 1866 the Edinburgh publishers, Edmonston & Douglas, brought out Carlyle's inaugural lecture to Edinburgh University, 'On the Choice of Books', as a 46-page pamphlet, by agreement with Chapman & Hall. Carlyle received £10 per thousand copies, a sum arranged by Carlyle's brother in Edinburgh. Forster was not pleased: 'that seems small, but was it so?' was his reaction to the royalty; 'I was to have received a formal memorandum from your brother, after conference with the Edmonstons, but never had it'. If Carlyle wished to maximize his earnings he could not do without his knowledgeable negotiator. But given the arrangement, Forster then concerned himself with the accounts, badgering Frederick Chapman for notification that by March 1867 3,000 copies had been sold.

As the years passed and Carlyle became an old man, and particularly after the saddening death of Jane Carlyle in 1866, the practical expression of Forster's concern was much increased. In 1867 he examined Carlyle's accounts and assumed more control:

> From the latter [Frederick Chapman] I have requested that your general account of sales to the end of 1866 should be handed in to me; and upon it I find that upon reprints and use of stereotypes for 1500 copies of Sartor, and 1000 of each of the volumes of French Rev^{n}, Schiller, and Chartism, £385 is now due. F.C. tells me that it is unusual for him to give you *a bill* at 3 or 4 months: if so, this is now due. Shall I obtain it from him and forward it you – or (perhaps the better course) send it as a payment in his name to your bankers?

Elsewhere, Forster continued, there was 'nothing perhaps to which objection can be fairly taken' though further points would be made when the returns for *Frederick* became available. Chapman would in future make a stock return as well as half-yearly accounts. The stereotype plates were in Robson's charge and he should be made more accountable for them.[76] The exchange reveals that Forster had not previously been familiar with Carlyle's day-to-day business; it hardly needs stressing that also revealed are the clear thinking, brisk efficiency, and astonishing capacity for taking pains that made Forster such an invaluable support for literary men with commercial anxieties.

During the same year *Shooting Niagara* appeared and Forster assumed further powers. 'Don't be stingy upon him, tho' strict',[77] counselled Carlyle and Forster agreed with Chapman a royalty of £5 per 1,000 copies of the pamphlet that followed publication in *Macmillan's*.[78] Chapman was told firmly 'to furnish the number printed and the sum now payable – when he should have license to proceed'.[79] Half-yearly accounts were closely scrutinized and when Chapman settled the first with a bill for £140 due on 23 December 1867 Forster induced his principal to protest sharply and wryly: 'Mr Forster... says farther, "the correct way of paying was by Bill of *three months, dated 30 June*:" – let us be *correct* to the uttermost *in future*, and so gain some tolerat^{n} from him!'[80]

But the main negotiations in 1867 were for the Library Edition of all Carlyle's works, which Forster began in May on his own initiative. He told Chapman that Carlyle would refer the idea to him and that 'I should think well of the proposal, if [Chapman] would make it the opportunity of getting rid of the over-printed huge volumes of Frederick, and begin his experiment with a proper literary edition of that book'.[81] Chapman was not held to that and the 30 volumes of this collected edition appeared from 1869 to 1871. Forster advised on dividing Carlyle's work into volumes, encouraged him to revise the texts, commented on advertising and approved each volume as it reached the publisher's office.[82] Most importantly, Carlyle noted with satisfaction that Forster was 'getting up the most precise documentary *signed* settlements, etc., with Chapman and Robson'.[83] In 1870 there was a temporary alarm when Robson had financial problems and it was feared that Carlyle's stereotypes, still in the printer's possession, might be controlled by creditors, thus affecting the title to Carlyle's volumes if Robson continued to print. Forster wrote reassuringly to Carlyle, took further consoling legal opinion and such alarm proved false.[84] It was, in any case, dominated by the lucrative consequences of the settlements Forster had made. He reported to Carlyle the 'extreme satisfaction' of 'the "Traveller for the house" ',[85] received and checked the receipts, now in the form of royalties, and forwarded them to Carlyle.[86] This was done well into 1875, the last full year of his life, and well deserved the reward, the 30 volumes of the Library Edition inscribed to Forster by Carlyle as his 'ever-helpful friend – without *whom* this *Edition* and much else, had never been'.[87]

The reference to royalties prompts a first general conclusion about Forster's career as Carlyle's business agent and adviser. In 1839 Carlyle was used to agreements that either involved the sale of his copyright to the publisher, usually for a fixed term, or made him dependent upon a share in whatever profits might arise. At Forster's death Carlyle had long received a substantial income from royalties: in 1865, for example, volumes 5 and 6 of *Frederick the Great* yielded £1,675, £558 of which was paid in cash followed by two equal instalments of £558 via bills of exchange at six months and at nine months.[88] When Carlyle's own life ended he owned all his copyrights and stereotypes. In this acquisition of control over his own literary possessions and in the receipt of an income rather than of lump sums, it seems permissible to detect Forster's dignified hand.

Further, as Carlyle's career progressed he worked his copyrights to an ever-increasing extent. Works previously published by Fraser were given second editions by Chapman & Hall: *Chartism* in 1842, *On Heroes and Hero-Worship* in the same year, with a third edition in 1843. Earlier material was reissued with later, as when *The Life of Schiller* joined *The Life of John Sterling* in 1857 as a single volume. In 1855 came a selection with a memoir by Thomas Ballantyne, with a second edition in 1870. Above all, in 1857–8 the first collected edition appeared in 16 volumes, followed by the Library Edition from 1869. There were translations, particularly of *Frederick the Great* into German. The result was the expected one, a sustained and substantial income from work already done: for example, from May to July 1871 the Library Edition realized £758 6s. 8d. in bills of exchange, and £491 13s. 4d. during the period from May to August 1873.[89] Five volumes of translations included in the edition brought in five bills of £100 each from March to July 1874.[90] The similarity to Dickens and Bulwer, those other friends of Forster whose work had popular appeal, is very striking: here is yet another example of a professional writer becoming a middle-class man with an income from assets as a result of his association with Chapman & Hall and with John Forster.

But Forster not only brought Carlyle to Chapman & Hall and influenced the commercial shape of his friend's career; he was also able, as the editor of important publications, to provide other outlets for Carlyle. One such was the *Foreign Quarterly Review* which Forster edited from 1842 to 1843. Carlyle was struggling with Cromwell and reluctant to turn aside but Forster beat down all defensive excuses, from pressure of work and lack of knowledge of foreign writing to a low opinion of the books

Forster sent him to review. In the end Carlyle *had* to write, as Jane Carlyle put it, 'if he would not run the risk of Forster's hanging himself'.[91] The resultant article on the Paraguayan dictator Rodriguez Francia is another example of Forster's ability to draw work of importance from his friends. Francia was a ruthless, cruel and oppressive ruler but was admired by Carlyle as a kind of Cromwell, a true man amidst a Guacho population that was 'greedy, superstitious, vain'.[92] Francia's atrocities could not be condoned, Carlyle agreed, even though the evidence for many of them was doubtful at best, but they were outweighed by his sense of purpose, his awareness of the tasks before him and his capacity for ordering his own life as well as his country. The article is an important precursor of the ferocious authoritarianism of Carlyle's later work; it was written for a man who, then, took a very different and far less favourable view of Cromwell and similar figures. That Forster published it eagerly is an early indication of his at least entertaining the ideas of a reactionary friend and a further reminder that his early radicalism had strong conservative potential.

In 1847 Forster became editor of the *Examiner*. As Fonblanque's assistant he had obtained from Carlyle only the London Library appeal, the copyright petition and, in 1840, a short review of a translation of Burns.[93] During 1848 he published four substantial essays by his friend.[94] One was an obituary appreciation of Charles Buller, whom Carlyle had once tutored, with a sympathetic editorial introduction. Carlyle stressed the early end to a promising political career and how Buller's 'wit' and 'radiancy' combined with basic worth and seriousness. The piece reveals the quiet, compassionate Carlyle who later wrote the affectionate biography of John Sterling.

The other three essays are very different. The first, 'Louis-Philippe', celebrated fiercely and scornfully the French emperor's loss of his throne. Louis Philippe deserved his fate, cried Carlyle, because he abused his power. The 'Repeal of the Union' was equally fierce, a satirical attack on the foolish notion that Repeal would solve Ireland's problems. Carlyle argued for England's right to rule large parts of the world and to 'care for' its subjects. Ireland could not hope to withstand English power and moral authority and England was morally bound to sustain the Union. The consequences were clear: either the Irish became British in attitudes and behaviour or they might be treated like the Red Indians and exterminated. 'Legislation for Ireland' also addressed itself harshly to that country's problems. The 'Sale of Encumbered Estates Bill' should be delayed no longer by Parliament, wrote Carlyle, for it sought to assist landlords to improve or to sell Irish estates by freeing them from heavy debts or mortgages. Only the 'Governing Class, or rich aristocracy of Landlords' could help Ireland and there should be nothing to prevent them or their successors from discharging their proper responsibilities. Characteristically, Carlyle welcomed the Irish disasters of the 1840s: in bringing matters to a catastrophic head they ensured that something must be done.

These three political essays mark the start of Carlyle's most reactionary phase. They began his alienation from more liberal intellectual circles: Mill wrote angrily to the *Examiner* to repudiate 'Repeal of the Union',[95] Arnold linked them with similar pieces in the *Spectator* as the work of 'a moral desperadoe'.[96] Carlyle was undismayed and even had 'Legislation for Ireland' reprinted as a pamphlet; *Latter-Day Pamphlets* quickly followed.

Landor, too, published extreme views in the *Examiner* but whereas they could be importantly at odds with the newspaper's position Carlyle's work was accommodated with surprising ease. 'Louis-Philippe' followed a leader treating the same subject in similar fashion; the *Examiner* was strongly against Repeal and for the 'Encumbered Estates' bill. Forster asked for parts of the 'Louis-Philippe' essay to be toned down and refused to publish a second piece on that subject, but such objections seem to have been Fonblanque's, no longer editor but still the owner.[97] Otherwise Forster exercised no discernible editorial authority: neither surviving manuscripts nor proofs[98] show his hand at work and the published text varies from that of the corrected proofs only in its punctuation and here no more so than was probably required by the house style. The *Examiner* under Forster moved steadily away from its one-time radicalism, almost certainly in part because of Carlyle's influence.

That movement was not without its element of conflict and this emerges in the reviews of Carlyle's work. The *Examiner* usually noticed him. In 1837, before that first meeting, it had hailed *The French Revolution*, despite some stylistic oddities, as a work of 'unquestionable originality and genius'[99] that would, however, make its way only slowly. Through 1838 Leigh Hunt had reviewed Carlyle's lectures, week after week, as 'the highest evidences of a true Christian wisdom'.[100] He gave similar support to the series in 1839 on 'The Revolutions of Modern Europe' that established Carlyle 'as a man of large heart and profound understanding'.[101] From 1839 to 1847 Forster was 'Literary Examiner'; for the next nine years he was editor. During this period, apart from the odd omission of *On Heroes and Hero-Worship*, all Carlyle's new works received sustained attention. Only one of these reviews can be certainly attributed to Forster but, as with the *Examiner* reviews of Dickens, it can be confidently assumed that all appeared with Forster's concurrence.

That being the case they can surprise. The review of *Past and Present*[102] begins with a detailed summary then grapples as much with the reviewer's own uncertainty as with the problems of the work:

> Frankly we will say, that not a few passages have been unintelligible to us; but with equal frankness may add, that this fault is more probably our own, and that a little time, and more reflection, might have made matters plain enough. The style is wilder, more lawless, more outrageous than ever, but yet enriched with passages more stamped with rugged energy, strong original feeling, exquisite gentleness, surpassing beauty and tenderness – passages more graphic and picturesque, and at the same time substantial, significant, and of the good old Saxon homeliness and purity – than any other living man could have written.

Further:

> We find ourselves often opposed to Mr Carlyle; his perpetual settings forth of class against class, and not a few of his doctrines of property, and yearnings for a new feudal system, we strongly condemn; and if, as some hints would have us suppose, his ideal of a modern governor can get no farther than the Oliver Cromwell of two centuries back, we would rather take our place among the Dead Sea Apes, where Mr Carlyle would in that case infallibly place us, than in the file of such of Abbot Samson's worshippers.

Nonetheless, here was 'the book of a sincere man, of a man terribly in earnest', with 'rare and pure truth'.

The reviewer, almost certainly Forster, protested too much. The opposition to Carlyle's ideas is at least slightly strained and so at odds with the conditional form of much of the second quotation. Implicit in the reviewer's inability to dismiss Carlyle out of hand lay his basic need to reconcile a liberal/radical position, which was also that of the editor and the newspaper, with Carlyle's elitist and increasingly harsh condemnation of much contemporary life and of democratic solutions to its problems. The need arose because of the reviewer's obvious regard for Carlyle himself, a regard clearly demonstrated in Forster's review of *Oliver Cromwell's Letters and Speeches: with Elucidations*[103] and its odd sequel, the affair of the 'Squire Papers'. Forster was overwhelmed by Carlyle's ability to recreate history, 'the Great Figure thus educed for us from the mists and shadows of the Past', and by the moral and didactic force of that recreation: 'the whole of it set forth here, not to amuse an indolent languid hour, but, by its high and noble lessons, to reprove, to teach, and edify us all'. Forster wrote as a historian already admiring and about to be dominated:

> We will not say that to such a portraiture we have no exception to make; but we have a better duty than to make exceptions. We have to acknowledge the general truth and wisdom embraced in it, and, till other special truths make themselves known, to accept the contents of these volumes in earnest of their probable discovery.

He concluded with praise that was as much of the author as of the work: 'Meanwhile all honour and success to this earnest, able, manly book.'

Such hero-worship was never better illustrated than when, in 1847, Carlyle published what he believed to be newly-discovered letters from Oliver Cromwell but which proved to be written by the forger William Squire. Carlyle was wholly deceived and not simply by clever forgeries: Squire produced only copies of letters the originals of which he said he had himself destroyed. Forster not only accepted Carlyle's view of the documents' authenticity but arranged a public reply to the many who doubted. This reply was an anonymous review in the *Examiner*[104] of Carlyle's article in *Fraser's* publishing Squire's material. It seems likely that Forster instigated this for though Carlyle provided part of the review he did so shamefacedly, befitting a man who was secretly reviewing his own work: 'Do as you will; – only be seen to put it into another than my dialect!'[105] Forster then added the rest of the review, part of which, such as the stress on the essential 'insignificance' of the whole affair so far as Cromwell's character was concerned, carried out Carlyle's further instructions. Carlyle considered the whole review to be more Forster's than his own.

The attack on the letters quickly began in the *Examiner*'s correspondence columns.[106] Carlyle did not admit his mistake and neither did Forster. Indeed, in May 1849 when including the Squire Papers in an Appendix to the third edition of *Cromwell* Carlyle explained the inclusion as a result of the urging of 'friends who believe, like myself, in the fundamental authenticity of Squire'.[107] Forster may well have been one of those. His belief, if such he had, in the letters' genuineness may have resulted from his general attitude to historical evidence; he too, when writing his later biographies, destroyed originals and indulged in some marginal forgery. That speculation apart, Forster's support of Carlyle is a potent demonstration of the older man's magnetism.

In later reviews of *Latter-Day Pamphlets* and *The Life of John Sterling*[108] that magnetism dominated whatever reservations the *Examiner* and its editor still entertained. As the notice of the complete *Pamphlets* insisted,

> We have never been indiscriminate admirers of Mr. Carlyle's style, or implicit believers in the soundness of all his views ... [Yet] ... we have acknowledged the importance of truths he has asserted ... Even with his most *bizarre* exhibitions, some moral and imaginative beauty was sure to be connected; honest truthfulness, what we must call the dignity of downright sincerity, has helped to reconcile us to his most perverse and obstinate waywardness; and amidst even his harsh and wholesale denunciations we were never at a loss to detect the still loving and generous soul.

The review, once again, was probably written by Forster; it was certainly sanctioned by him. Its response to Carlyle's views may well be, here as earlier, less than dismissive; certainly those views are regarded as less important than their author's character. In this friendship of Forster's, more than in any other, the compelling personality of the friend was the main attraction. The willing subservience of 1839 was sustained by Forster's developing hero-worship and by Carlyle's opinion of him. For though Carlyle admitted that he came to think more of Forster than at first, though he prized his sociability, valued his practical expertise, thought him to be an able editor of the *Foreign Quarterly Review*, and felt affection and even some respect for him, yet, to repeat, Forster never broke through Carlyle's reservations into intellectual equality. After ten years' acquaintance Carlyle still considered that 'Forster was not a man who had any serious truth to proclaim, or any purpose in life which he laid to heart, but he was infinitely friendly, and entirely sincere in his attachments. A good upright man, one might confidently say.'[109] His congratulations on Forster's lunacy appointment were also partly a patronizing slap on the back: 'This thing, in the uncertainties of Literature and health, is altogether well and suitable, and comfortably closes the gap on the side of economic exigencies. Long may the good Forster live to enjoy this and the other blessings he has.'[110] Occasionally he seemed to praise:

> As a crown to all the modern Biographies of Cromwell, let us note Mr. Forster's late one: full of interesting original excerpts, and indications of what is notablest in the old Books; gathered and set forth with real merit, with *energy* in abundance and superabundance; amounting in result, we may say, to a vigorous decisive tearing-up of all the old hypotheses on the subject, and an opening of the general mind for new.[111]

Given that Carlyle thought little of other modern studies this praise might be thought to be guarded. In any case its apparent fulsomeness is evasively precise; Carlyle disagreed almost completely with Forster's view of Cromwell and here does little more than admire Forster's industry. Again, though he praised aspects of Forster's life of Goldsmith he remained critical of Forster's choice of subject. Only very rarely did Forster force genuine admiration from him:

> I have read your third volume of *Dickens* with continued interest and pleasures – and with a glad surprise, moreover, which heightens all these feelings. Surprise I say, for the narrative flows with limpid clearness, soft harmony, perfection of phrase and idea; not a trace in it anywhere of the horrid state of pain in which I too well know you to have been all the while.[112]

Even this is patronizing in its surprise and partly countered by the over-careful description of Volume One: 'It is a work of wonderful diligence friendliness & clearness of detail…everything is said too with perfect neatness graceful precision and propriety.'[113]

Forster's influence on Carlyle was general, peripheral, unquantifiable and partly undesirable. By supplying historical materials and advice and by organizing his business affairs Forster gave an aging man more time for creative activities. He helped mould, albeit imperceptibly, Carlyle's approach to the past and in encouraging him to revise for collected editions fostered his works' literary artistry. Carlyle greatly valued the support: 'If all readers were possessed of the sure and practical candour of Forster', he wrote in 1865, 'it would be a pleas^{t} thing to write big Books.'[114] In meetings and correspondence that candour was of the complimentary kind; during the 1840s, when Carlyle turned to more brutally extreme solutions to society's problems and needed words of warning more forceful than those of reviewers, it combined with the ready provision of journalistic platforms to fan polemical flames that scorched his reputation.

Forster had been brought up a Unitarian, had radical associations and was concerned to promote literature's general acceptability. Yet it is understandable that Carlyle's seemingly very different views made a strong appeal to him. For the Unitarian belief in personal worth and education implied the ability to change and was not essentially at odds with the radical's need to persuade people and force events into new ways and patterns, nor with the notion of improvement implicit in that promoting of acceptability and in helpful friendship. The desire to change not only oneself but one's society and colleagues was necessarily involved with the exercise of power and what might be called authoritarian persuasion. When accompanied, as Forster grew older, with an increasingly conservative notion of change such desires had obvious Carlylean potential and combined with Carlyle's magnetic personality to ensure Forster's susceptibility to the ideas of his friend. Two examples from Forster's letters illustrate their pervasive influence. The first he wrote to Carlyle in 1859, at the time of the Franco–Austrian war that was an expression of Louis Napoleon's territorial ambitions. In July 1859, having promised Cavour that Italy would be free, Napoleon made a settlement with Francis Joseph at Villafranca that gave Venetia to Austria, Lombardy to Piedmont, and restored the sovereigns of Modena and Tuscany. Feeling in Britain ran high, for many, including Russell and Palmerston, sided with Italy. Forster began his letter by describing his own summer activities and continued:

> ... one is at any rate (at least I hope) doing no harm – neither fighting at Solferino, nor peace-making at Villa Franca.
>
> Oh, Carlyle, come and set things straight for us! Would you undertake the affair if we put it in your hands? – Never was war so imminent as in these peace-making days, and we shall live to see the shouters for 'Neutrality' making long faces before all is over. How sick the world would have made Cromwell or Elizabeth! – Prussia is the next mark for the 'most sagacious prince in Europe' (as Mr. Disraeli calls L.N.), and, when Austria and Russia are rubbing their hands at *that*, one wonders what England would be doing.[115]

Fifteen years later Forster commented on a very different matter, the conversion of Lord Ripon to Roman Catholicism:

> Delane said that L[d] Ripon was led to his folly by his wife. But L[d] Shaftesbury tells me that she had striven hard for 3 years to turn him from his miserable purpose – and it seems that he had made over to her & his son all the Church livings he had.[116]

Both extracts have the hard edge of intolerance. The first, in its scorn and nostalgic desire for the heroic figure able to force events into an acceptable pattern is pervasively Carlylean. So, in its way, is the second, one of several such comments in Forster's later correspondence. James Whiteside commented shrewdly that Forster 'had been a burning liberal but ... conceived a deadly antipathy to Popery, and seemed to have imbibed the opinions of his old Puritan friend Carlyle'. But whereas Whiteside considered Carlyle's effect on Forster's 'opinions religious and political'[117] to have occurred only at the close of Forster's life it is evident that its first public manifestation was during his *Examiner* editorship in that newspaper's departure from the remnants of its radical tradition.

The 'Villa Franca' letter considers contemporary politics in terms of a contrast with the past. It demonstrates the extent to which Forster not only absorbed Carlyle's opinions of historical figures but also accepted his friend's thinking on the *uses* of history. The former resulted in Forster changing his mind about Cromwell, rewriting his study of Eliot and beginning a new version of his life of Strafford. The latter, together with his admiration of Carlyle as man and as historian, helps explain why Forster, having become Secretary to the Lunacy Commission in 1856, was so eager to turn to the writing of history and to the scholarly life necessary for its creation.

In turning to history he turned from and thought less of the imaginative literature to which he had given so much of his life. Once more Carlyle was greatly responsible. His contempt for the novel has been convincingly documented.[118] That it influenced Forster to doubt even his greatest enthusiasms is evident from a letter to Carlyle written only a few months after Bulwer's death:

> Robert is daily at work among his fathers papers, and has found *scores* of unfinished work of all kinds – a full dozen novels certainly, begun and laid aside; five completed, & as many incompleted, plays; and poems, essays, & translations endless. A life of prodigious labour, whatever otherwise the value of it.[119]

The bleak note of that closing phrase is, in a sense, echoed in what can seem to be the enthusiastic opening to *The Life of Charles Dickens* – 'Charles Dickens, the most popular novelist of the century, and one of the greatest humorists that England has produced' – in its blatant avoidance of references to literary worth. Carlyle's opinion of imaginative literature and of so many of its creators, including his low regard for Goldsmith, together with his general concern for biographical honesty, had the final effect of changing Forster's literary-biographical practice to accommodate deteriorating views of the literary character. In 1839 he was drawn to Carlyle as a champion of the dignity of literature so it is sadly ironic that their friendship helped turn the friend of literature into a doubtful supporter.

All such changes were consequences of a hero-worship that was not only an attitude to Carlyle but also a response to a personal need. Thus, though several of Forster's other friendships, such as those with Macready, Dickens, and Browning, had difficult final phases, his friendship with Carlyle became more intense in its closing years. For in those years Forster's illness and sadness increased his dependence, and reciprocation became an increasing psychological necessity for Carlyle after his wife's sudden death.

Jane Carlyle died in 1866. The facts are well known. Carlyle went to Edinburgh in April to give his Rectorship address and news of his triumph reached Mrs Carlyle when dining at Forster's. Her letter to her husband recorded Forster's pleasure at such success: 'Fuz, in his joy over you, sent out a glass of brandy to Silvester!' she noted excitedly.[120] Less than three weeks later, still savouring the news and while Carlyle was on holiday in Scotland, she died in her carriage after a drive in Hyde Park. Forster took command, suppressed an inquest, arranged the funeral and then her financial affairs.[121]

Carlyle was 70. Apart from 'Shooting Niagra: and After?' he wrote nothing else of consequence, though he revised earlier work for the Library Edition. Forster handled his business, including the assigning of Craigenputtock to Edinburgh University,[122] and became an executor of Carlyle's will. The sociability that had always been at the heart of their friendship now dominated more completely, and with Carlyle old and Forster old before his time, expressed itself increasingly through intimate correspondence.

Part was from Carlyle, solicitous about Forster's dreadful health, sometimes retailing gossip, occasionally, from the depths of age, offering some firm instruction: 'I clearly feel as if it were a pious duty on your part', he told Forster when Procter died, 'as if the good Procter really deserved some outline of his aspect and pilgrimage through this world, and as if you of all men were the best qualified to give it ... Do not forget this precept I have just laid upon you.'[123] Forster could not comply and was suitably apologetic[124] to an extent that reasserted the friendship's central inequality. That notwithstanding, Carlyle cherished Forster's letters as they came 'dropping in, each of them, like a little brief break of sunbeams, suddenly falling in through the dim mists external & internal & are very welcome to me'.[125] When they did not arrive, Mary Aitken told Forster, they were badly missed.[126]

Forster wrote often and compulsively. He too offered gossip and comments on current literary and political affairs; Dickens, about to depart for his second American visit, was 'farther removed himself from the cheerful than I have ever known him to be, notwithstanding the Dinner celebration'; Mill was 'pitiable' and concerned only with 'querulous fault-finding with the Government of the world'; the journals could disappoint: 'They sent me the "Quarterly", and I tried to read an article on Modern Culture: but such doleful rubbish I think I never encountered';

Gladstone was naive and confused, 'That he should have lived all these years before he found out what Popery really means!', his rival consumed with conceit: 'I see Dizzy at the Mansion sneering at Bismarck, and exalting the magnanimity and wisdom of the present Ruler of France!! "A mad world my masters!" '. He described his own health and his travels in search of it and wrote of his work as Lunacy Commissioner. Inevitably and emotionally he wrote of losing friends.[127]

He conveyed much about his feelings for Carlyle, for in his disillusionment about other literary friends this one was still commensurate with his persisting capacity for wonder. When Carlyle sent compliments they aroused delight. 'I can have no such pleasure and reward, dear Carlyle, as this intimation of your liking or approval gives',[128] he wrote in response to praise of *Walter Savage Landor*. And when Carlyle wrote his famous letter on *The Life of Charles Dickens*, comparing Forster to Boswell, the reply was ecstatic:

> Your letter sinks deep into my heart indeed!
>
> This is My 'Order'. With the advantage over Yours that it is what even Kaisers and Kings cannot give –
>
> I shall leave it as an instruction when I die that it be printed on a flyleaf before the book as long as my representatives have power to give such direction.[129]

A present of another kind drew a similar reaction. When Carlyle sent venison from Lord Luichart's estate that arrived coincidentally with some from Bulwer's, Forster was quick to assert his priorities: 'tomorrow morning there will go to Procter a full half of the Knebworth present – I could not consent to part with any of yours!'[130]

Such flattery was and continued to be shameless. He reported his wife's reading of Carlyle's books, his own re-reading of *Sartor*, and even recommended *Frederick the Great* to its author:

> I have been taking the taste of Mill out of my mouth by reading, in the Wonderful Book, of Frederick's death & what may be said of the 'saddest' of creeds when accompanied by a real nobleness. I should almost recommend you to try that book again ...[131]

In 1868 he commissioned a portrait of Carlyle from G. F. Watts and wrote to its subject that:

> the expectation with which I went was more than satisfied. All that your face contains is by no means there – want of softness – want of sweetness – of humour – many wants – But much that *is* there

> rendered very grandly indeed – a face as of a prophet – very sorrowful – very mournful – wanting the corrective I would have him give it in the refining and humanizing way – but certainly the material for the greatest picture of you that has ever been done.[132]

Perhaps most reassuringly of all for any septuagarian, Forster described a visit to Macready in Cheltenham and commented: 'poor dear old Macready. He is only two years older than you are, but you are twenty years younger than he is.'[133]

The heights of sincere flattery were reached *via* imitation, *via* the grim and vehement humour and bite that increasingly, in Forster's later correspondence, caught the approach and sometimes the tone and style of his master's voice. In 1867, visiting Cambridge during a lunacy circuit Forster closed:

> the Colleges were busy & thriving over the production doubtless of the due number of wranglers and wooden spoons – but considering that I had just visited an asylum in Norwich having a Senior Wrangler for one of its patients, I thought the question of which article was best worth turning out might not be an unfair one ...

On politics in 1871:

> Oh, dear Carlyle, how dismal the outlook seems – but as it turns out to be a choice between the little Queen and Gladstone – and a Republic with Dilke at the head of it – I think we must stick even to sweet William! Only we ought to insist on his reading better poetry than Bradlaughs. I have some notion of sending him Tupper.

On Scottish history:

> I went to the London Library to consult some publishing Society's Early Scotch Chronicles – but they were as stupid and silent as Mr Burton, the Distinguished Historiographer of Scotland; and if any ditch-water is duller than that man's first volume, I should like to see it as a natural phenomenon.

And, in 1875, on a fatal collision at sea and on contemporary notions of heroism:

> That Solent catastrophe was a startling interruption to the ditch-water-news-level, but how amazing it is that it hadn't come before in all these years. An express train going at full speed through the crowds of cabs and carts in Strand or Holborn, is the only parallel one can fancy to it. And now they are making a hero

> of the merchants mate that swam across the channel, and R. H. Horne (expositer of the False Medium who gave that surprizing additional practical exposition of it by leaving his wife to support herself and sending his photograph to console her) proposes that the hero should be knighted! The ribbon of the Bath I suppose. Another hero in spite of himself I see made by Ld Grantley's death, which hoists into the peerage that scapegrace half-idiot son of Mrs Norton, of whom Browning used to tell such wondrous tales, and who married the fish-girl of Capri, now a Baroness of England. Strange is the world we live in, dear Carlyle, and no wonder some philosophers should be found even among science-mongers at Bristol who declare that there may have been great men even before the now-existing Agamemnon![134]

Such letters are evidence of compulsion become obsession and an essentially moving demonstration of Forster's need to speak, to pour out his feelings, to be and have a friend. Despite his marriage there is much here that points to a sad and lingering loneliness, not least the fact that though he retained his sense of humour Forster rarely had a good word for the world in which he was dying.

When he could he heaped hospitality upon his friend. C. E. Norton, close to both in later years, recalled Carlyle's comment on Forster's entertaining: 'I was as prudent as man could be, but I did not get to sleep till six o'the clock the next morning'.[135] More importantly, Norton described the harmony of such occasions: 'It was a pleasant dinner, for Forster was in far better condition than in the early winter, and in one of his mild and simple moods. The effect that Carlyle has on him is always beneficial, and their humours played well together.'[136] As death came closer such a meeting became for Forster 'the little gleam of coming pleasure on which meanwhile I shall live'.[137]

During 1875 he helped David Masson prepare the tribute to Carlyle for his 80th birthday, a gold medal and an address from leading intellectuals. Forster suggested names, helped contact signatories and signed the list.[138] It was his last significant service.

When he died it was, Carlyle told his brother, 'the end of a chapter in my life, which had lasted, with unwearied kindness and helpfulness wherever possible on Forster's part, for above forty years.... The event is really a sorrowful one, and practically a very considerable loss.'[139] That controlled tone contrasts with Forster's effusiveness to remind us, again, that the friendship was not one of equal reliance. The significance of Carlyle's stress on Forster's practical help hardly needs emphasizing. What is in no doubt is the depth of Forster's feelings. During the last year of his life he wrote privately and movingly:

> Carlyle came – sat some time. Grand, good old man, kindest & best – Described being blown down the Embankment, like an egg-shell – so frail, yet so little susceptible of the bleak bitter cold –[140]

It seems no accident that such regard, as much as any Forster felt for anyone else, should be for a man who always kept him slightly at a distance and limited his spheres of influence. The most amicable of all Forster's friendships, the one that seems never to have been disturbed by an important difference of opinion let alone a violent quarrel, was the one in which Forster was refused a part in the central creative process. There is no evidence that he resented this and it is likely that he did not. As he told Carlyle, in words that bear repeating, 'nothing that even you can write is so valuable as You'.[141]

Part Four Man of Letters – iii Professional Concerns

CHAPTER 13 *Journalist*

The first half of the nineteenth century was a crucial period in the history of journalism. During the previous century, as Forster's work on Defoe, Steele, Swift, and Goldsmith made him only too aware, the press had a history of political apostasy, licentiousness and blackmail. Newspapermen were numbered among the more disreputable inhabitants of Grub Street. Even as late as the 1820s Scott considered that no-one but a 'blackguard' would be a journalist.[1]

In the 1830s and 1840s the press increased its power and influence as Reform developed political awareness and literacy spread. It began to attract more men of integrity and principle, Forster amongst them, and so to improve its reputation. But improvement was slow as undesirables lingered: in 1839 Forster considered Edward Moran, editor of the *Globe*, to be 'at once the dirtiest in appearance and most disreputable every way of the long list of such that disgrace "the press" '.[2] Old attitudes persisted, as Forster discovered in 1848 in his dispute with James Prior; in 1851, in a leader entitled 'Journalism – Its Claim to Respect', the *Examiner* under Forster's editorship regretted the continuing 'discrepancy which exists between the power exercised by a journalist, and the respect paid to his vocation'.[3]

He was a professional journalist for 24 years, beginning in 1832 as the *True Sun*'s drama critic and, apart from a few later notices, ending in 1856 as editor of the *Examiner*. But even when he became an editor and wrote political leaders he never relinquished his work as a weekly reviewer. Only a gifted ostrich could have remained unaware that the opprobrium attached to journalism as a whole was due in part to the deplorable reputation of reviewing. It had always attracted the charlatan, 'condemning books he never reads; and applauding the fidelity of translations, of the originals of which he understands not a syllable',[4] and the vicious egotist:

> the swaggering cut-and-slash critic, now gone much out of vogue,

> but whom I can well remember in a still rampant state when first I was connected with letters, disposing easily of all kinds of reputations, terrifying his readers into thinking him original by merely opening on them sluices of slang, and finding them more and more foolishly eager to wipe his shoes the dirtier and more slipshod he wore them.[5]

Reviewers were rarely trusted: 'The great difficulty in criticism nowadays', Forster admitted in 1846, 'is to make people believe that praise is sincere.'[6] The pressing need to set a shining example shaped and connected the various parts of his journalistic career.

Certainly that pressure had a profound effect upon his reviewing, which, after the *True Sun*, a few pieces for the *New Monthly Magazine*, some essays for the *Foreign Quarterly Review* and occasional contributions elsewhere, took place in the *Examiner*. This was mainly a political weekly, founded in 1808 by Leigh Hunt, the editor until 1821, and owned and edited from 1830 by Albany Fonblanque. Under the former it was radical, under Fonblanque it moved slowly to the right without breaking completely with radical and Benthamite sentiments. It was a serious and responsible newspaper read by intelligent men of affairs. Though political comment was always given priority four to five of its 16 pages were devoted to the arts and dominated by literary and drama reviews controlled by Forster in his twin capacities as 'Literary Examiner' and 'Dramatic Examiner'. All reviewing was anonymous but to judge from attributions during 1840 and 1841[7] Forster himself wrote reviews in at least two issues out of three and on almost every kind of literary work. The constraints of professional concern were thus combined with the inevitable bias of the paper's politics and the exigencies of general reviewing for a non-specialized and essentially non-literary readership.

Such factors make necessary a distinction between Forster the critic and Forster the reviewer. As his friends knew he was a man with much common sense, a practical critic in the fullest sense of the word; his main critical ideas were effectively expressed within his major friendships through the collaborative procedures of pruning, revising, rewriting, reorganizing and clarifying. As reviewer he not only wrote within the specialized contexts of profession and journal but in a manner that was more that of the literary evangelist than the collaborator. He was concerned not only for literature but also for his readers. The depth of his concern could make him seem like 'Pungent ... of the "Exterminator" '[8] but never made him unprincipled. All such considerations are clearly exhibited in his well-known review of Ainsworth's *Jack Sheppard*.[9]

This is generally a savage review but the most violent attacks feature in the first part of the notice and are directed against the publicity that the novel had received through constant 'puffing' and innumerable adaptations and dramatizations: 'the worst passages of a book ... are served up in the most attractive form to all the candidates for hulks and rope – *and especially the youthful ones* – that infest this vast city'. Such publicity was aided and abetted by Ainsworth and by George Cruikshank, his illustrator; Ainsworth, in particular, gave public approval to 'the very worst specimen of rank garbage thus stewed up at these places of amusement'. The net result was that 'the original insignificance of the thing is lost, in the pernicious influences that are set at work around it'.

The conduct of all who exploited the novel was indefensible yet Forster did not simply assert this but demonstrated it with compelling logic before turning to the novel itself. This he treated in terms of a broad contrast with previous masters of the novel and related genres and the way they handled similar subject matter. From Le Sage to Gay to Fielding to Hogarth low life and crime were subjected to an unambiguous moral scrutiny. 'Their immortal works' taught 'the invaluable lesson ... of what man ought to be from what men are' and distinguished further 'between the truth of our nature and the accidents of the world'. The 'naked and unqualified feelings of humanity, however vulgar they may be imagined or called are shown to be superior to wilful and heartless depravity, however lofty its position or refined its look'. But in *Jack Sheppard*

> The sentiments of the work are pretty constant to two great principles. The one is a slavish adulation of high birth and the more vulgar incidents thereto belonging. The other is a strong sense of the moral capabilities, nice emotions, and sensitive affections, which belong to thieves and murderers.

The extract not only completes the central contrast but does so with an irony that is not only a departure from the fiercely direct denunciation of the review's first part but also a further means of fostering an intellectual response. As Forster analysed the work and unravelled its dangerous moral progression the reader found that initial indignation modulating into a more implicit condemnation through contrast and irony, before reaching a vehement but still logical conclusion in which persisting irony and final negatives ensured that the reader's response was never simply an emotional one:

> But there is a climax still! – The lowest deep contains a lower! – So thoroughly has the writer identified *his* sympathies at least with the

> crime of his hero as a trifling peccadillo, and indeed with thieves and murderers in general as naughty but yet amusing people, that the *fatal rope* ... seems now in the nature of an unworthy if not unrighteous thing.

Readers should not be deceived, Forster warned; in real life Sheppard 'was of the very refuse of the rope'. The author should think again.

Ainsworth, for one, thought Forster's attack the result of jealousy of *Jack Sheppard*'s sales exceeding those of *Oliver Twist*.[10] Now such a review seems obviously expressive of Forster's strongest convictions. Its optimistic notion of basic humanity is a reminder of Forster's Unitarian beliefs and wholly consistent with the *Examiner*'s vestiges of mild radicalism. This last, to which Forster then subscribed, lay behind the attack on Ainsworth's snobbishness and was a recurrent feature of reviews during Forster's literary editorship. Biographies could be criticized for servility towards royalty, novels praised for their democratic spirit.[11] In practice this was support for middle-class progress and aspirations that made direct appeal to the *Examiner*'s readers. To such readers Forster offered intellectually persuasive guidance and a stress on the utility of literature that exhibited the reviewer as recognizably respectable. The whole review was redolent of the particular professional concern that was itself part of Forster's abiding general concern that the social value of the moral force of literature should not be undermined by the occasional renegade.

'It is not the subject we shrink from', Forster wrote of Ainsworth's outrage, 'the treatment is the paramount objection.' The review was at once indignant and didactic; it urged other writers to do otherwise. Such urgings were not only expressed in response to obvious infringements of literature's social rules, as Forster conceived of them, but were implicit in the central thrust of all his reviewing, the essential modification of the various effects upon him of Hunt, Lamb, Bulwer and Macready, and then Carlyle.

In part such modifying involved the Victorianizing of Romantic attitudes, in particular those of Leigh Hunt. During 1844 Hunt published *Imagination and Fancy* in which the introductory essay, 'What is Poetry', summarized his central and constant critical tenets. Forster's review was enthusiastic:

> That the Poet is an interpreter of the invisible; that Poetry subdues the shews of things to the desires of the mind; that the attempt man makes to render his existence harmonious is a form and an assertion

> of the Poetical Faculty; – Mr Hunt helps us to a clearer understanding on all these points ...[12]

Forster thus commended the imagination for its creative perception and understanding and for harmonizing the world. Years later he did so again in that synthesis of earlier thoughts and reviews, the critical sections of *The Life of Charles Dickens*. Then Forster recalled Hunt's description of the imagination as 'the feeling of the subtlest and most affecting analogies; the perception of sympathies in the natures of things, or in their popular attributes'[13] and combined it with Hunt's later insistence that humour reconciled 'incongruities of character and circumstance'.[14] Forster wrote that humour, as an expression of the imagination, 'involves the feeling of subtlest and most affecting analogies, and from which is drawn the rare insight into sympathies between the nature of things and their attributes or opposites'.[15] That was in 1873 and a final expression of the reviewer's abiding preoccupation with the transforming power of the literary imagination: 'The poet's home is not so near the earth as it is the modern fashion to think it', he wrote in a notice of Landor's *Hellenics*,[16] and in Mrs Gaskell's *Ruth* 'the town and even the milliner's room are presented to our minds in a form that associates properly with the poetical'.[17] More importantly, Hunt's description of the imagination as harmonizer led naturally to the concept of organic form. When Forster wrote of *In Memoriam* that it seemed 'to have grown up rather than to have been composed' and revealed in its progression

> an original and deeply reflective mind capable of enduring affection, and endowed at once with the imagination which broods upon some single and cherished vein of sentiment, and with the fancy which diverges from it into multitudinous brief and glorious flights

to become a poem unified by 'the pervading sentiment',[18] he reflected the concern with the shaping process of the imagination which was central to Hunt's thinking and given even stronger expression in Lamb's critical writing.

Such popular Romantic ideas were not absorbed uncritically. Forster responded to the transcending power of the imagination with the suspicion proper to one brought up in Unitarian rationality. He rejected the extreme consequence of Hunt's argument in *Imagination and Fancy*, the acceptance of a 'pure'[19] poetry or, as Hunt put it, '*poetry of the most poetical kind*',[20] in favour of firm links between the real and the ideal. Here was an important effect of his friendship with Bulwer. When the latter wrote that 'Art is that process by which we give to natural materials the highest excellence they are capable of receiving' and that though the 'great artist ... may take flesh and blood for his model, he throws into the expression of the figure a something which elevates the model into an idealised image',[21] he was pointing to the demands of verisimilitude as well as insisting on the need to idealize. So was Forster when he wrote of the characters of Bulwer's *King Arthur* that 'they are real, because drawn from the book of life; they are ideal, as reflecting in imaginative form the subtlest spirits of the age'.[22] That the need for such a relationship was profoundly a part of Forster's thinking is shown by the persistence of the idea: as late as *The Life of Charles Dickens* he rejected

> distinctions alleged between novelists who are assumed to be real, or ideal, in their methods of treatment. To any original novelist of the higher grade there is no meaning in these contrasted phrases.
>
> Neither mode can exist at all perfectly without the other. No matter how sensitive the mind to external impressions, or how keen the observation is to whatever can be seen, without the rarer seeing of imagination nothing will be arrived at that is real in any genuine artist-sense.[23]

The final stress on the imagination's 'rarer seeing' also recalls Bulwer, in particular his insistence that 'the real truthfulness of all works of imagination ... is so purely in the imagination'.[24]

Also modified was the notion of the organic nature of literature. Though this was common to both Hunt and Lamb's critical theories neither were much concerned with what Warren has described as '"structure" and total effect'.[25] Forster, however, wrote of Landor's *Hellenics*, in an observation that also returns us to Forster's uneasiness about 'pure' poetry, that 'of what is called the "quintessential" in poetry – the thing in its essence without regard to form – we could even consent to spare somewhat, if we saw a greater ambition to shape forth and build up worthily'.[26] He commended *King Arthur* because 'the classical finish of the artist is everywhere felt, even while emotions are portrayed as truthfully as if nature spoke, unfashioned to rule';[27] such controlling form was an essential counter to what he elsewhere referred to as a poem's 'wild current of romance'.[28] Tennyson's *The Princess*, though containing much of worth, was limited by structural defects,[29] for Forster believed that 'few productions, of the highest class ... [were] ... wanting in completeness of structure'.[30] In *Poems 1842* 'his imagery is less profuse ... His sense of the beautiful ... has become more chastened, more intellectual.'[31] That Unitarian-inspired approval of 'intellectual' control rather than imagistic emotionalism combined with Bulwer's insistence upon 'some harmonious unity of interest'[32] and Macready's obsession with overall effect to make Forster's reviewing advocate the imagination's curbing.

Though curbed it had distinct aims. Hunt's assertion that one of the 'ends' of poetry was 'exaltation'[33] was restated as 'earnest moral purpose'. Great works of literature gave 'practical lessons of life and history'[34] or 'lessons of morality or discipline'.[35] Great writers sought to imitate those in the past, such as Goldsmith and Fielding, who revealed 'what was good and beautiful in the homeliest aspects of humanity'.[36] Thus Dickens sought to 'discover the soul of goodness in things evil'[37] and Bulwer to get below the 'grotesque surface ... into the heart of love which beats and glows underneath'.[38] But a writer like Ainsworth glorified evil and Thackeray, particularly in *Henry Esmond*, showed clearly the

> defect in his mind which ... rendered it impossible for him to present pictures of life which we can regard as true copies. If Mr. Thackeray could have faith in the hidden spark of the divinity which few men or women lose out of their hearts, if he could see his neighbours really as they are and so describe them, if he could be brought to feel that there is fairer play in finding the good that is in evil things than in dragging out the evil that is in good things, – his hold upon a true fame, still for the present doubtful, would be assured and strong.[39]

Such a passage brings together not only, once again, Forster's Unitarian optimism but also Carlyle's insistence upon the 'imperishable dignity of man'. It tells us much about the main basis of Forster's value-judgments: we can see, for example, why Forster was troubled by Dickens's later work and consequently why he favoured writers like the early Dickens who sought to explain the presence of evil in terms of external circumstances. Hence, also, his approval of Mrs Gaskell's *Ruth* whose heroine's 'stain ... is from without not from within'.[40]

Forster advocated a decorous Romanticism expressive of social aspirations. The imaginative writer, like the gentleman, never forgot himself. The way such reviewing supported his practical advice is most clearly seen within his friendships. But even a literary 'enemy' like Thackeray was forced to acknowledge its pervasive influence. He wrote indignantly to Robert Bell of a review of *Vanity Fair* in which Forster expressed a disapproval similar to that of *Henry Esmond*.[41] In Chapter 14 of *The Newcomes* he sought to answer his critic directly as the novel as a whole succeeded in offering an implicit reaction. Thackeray's changed and more optimistic sense of human nature in *The Newcomes* now commanded Forster's approbation.

Forster was still a fledgling reviewer when he made his first sortie as editor in December 1832, as first head of the *Reflector*. It was a brief and minor disaster. Nine years later came a second venture when Chapman & Hall acquired the *Foreign Quarterly Review*, a conservative and moribund journal edited by Worthington. They sought to revitalize it and Forster, as the publisher's literary adviser, began to sound out contributors. Thackeray's offer of himself as editor, for 'a thousand a year',[42] was rejected and with the issue of July 1842 Forster assumed what was meant to be temporary command.[43] With that first issue he outlined the aims of the revamped periodical:

> to give an English interest to its treatment of general Foreign Literature; and, on every possible occasion, to introduce into its pages that popular character, wherein ... the FOREIGN QUARTERLY REVIEW has been always felt to be deficient.[44]

As a contemporary noted, Forster 'infused into [the *F.Q.R.*] a spirit which it never possessed before or afterwards'.[45] He increased the length by 20 pages a number and used most of this to introduce new features. He began a 'Table of Foreign Literature' series that in the first number offered a useful chronological table of the main Italian works and writers since 1703. He included 'Foreign Correspondence', general surveys of current literary and political issues; the first number had communications from Paris and Stockholm. Much more importantly, he brought in a glittering group of contributors, the first number, in particular, being a compelling demonstration of Forster's power and influence in the London literary world; it contained contributions by Bulwer, Landor, Thackeray, Robert Browning and John Sterling, with foreign correspondence from George Stephens in Stockholm. Landor and Thackeray became regular contributors, as did G. H. Lewes and T. A. Trollope. J. S. Blackie wrote for Forster's fourth issue and, for the fifth, Carlyle provided 'Dr. Francia'. All were generously rewarded: Carlyle received 16 guineas a sheet, the comparatively unknown Thackeray £13 7s., and Lewes on one occasion obtained £20.

Upon such independent and disparate writers Forster sought to impose common qualities. The *Review*'s new political stance was that of 'moderate, subtle, and pervasive'[46] liberalism and Forster worked hard to bring deviants into 'greater agreement with the general tone'. Even Bulwer, whose reputation was so important to the success of Forster's first issue that he was given pride of place, was not spared. Forster found it hard to accept his Tory view of 'The Reign of Terror', that mob rule should be unequivocally condemned: 'You cannot trample men out of humanity', he argued unavailingly, 'and expect them to continue human.'[47] But that article was a rule-proving major exception; a piece by George Stephens was accepted 'notwithstanding some differences of opinion, as to which I must be permitted to use the Editorial discretion of omitting certain expressions here and there.... The world has room for the artist of the spinning jenny as well as him of the song.'[48] The objections were obviously political, the changes presumably could not be made. The article never appeared.

The 'general tone' was not only 'consciously English'[49] because of its liberalism (Forster's attacks on American democracy[50] indicate the special English quality) but also because of its adoption of 'earnestness, healthiness, sincerity, right-mindedness, manliness, and practicality as literary and philosophical standards'.[51] Certainly it was moderate in its approach to foreign affairs, whether general, as when it praised the earnest virtues of the German character, political, in its urging 'conservative reform' of the relationships between German states to avoid Prussian or Austrian repression, or literary, in its objective concern to separate immorality from true artistry in French literature.[52] When it criticized foreigners it often did so with a humour that countered tendencies towards Podsnappery and which expressed the 'popular character' of that initial statement of intent. Thus, on France:

> A nation which can understand a language without knowing it, has advantages that other European people do not possess. She *is* the intellectual queen of Europe, and deserves to be placed at its head. There is no coming up to her: we don't start with the same chance of winning.[53]

On a work on European diplomats:

> M. Capefigue has selected nine, of whom we have already named seven ... Why there should have been nine, neither more nor less, we cannot divine. Perhaps the number of the muses inspired some mystical analogy; for, cold and colourless as is the painting of the bard of diplomacy, he is not free from the modern French cant about symbols, and ideas, and systems.[54]

Forster's own contributions were of two kinds. He wrote a series of scholarly articles on Greek philosophers, originally sections of an uncompleted book,[55] and vigorously argued attacks on the American press full of genuine and deeply-felt indignation at their professional atrocities. Scholarship, polemic, lively writing and journalistic responsibility made Forster's own work a microcosm of the *Foreign Quarterly Review* under his editorship. The issue of October 1843 was his last, at which point, despite sniping from the deposed Worthington at his lack of languages,[56] the *Review*'s reputation had never been higher. That it survived his departure for only three faltering years is no surprise.

During his two years with the *Foreign Quarterly Review* Forster had maintained his association with the *Examiner*. That continued after his resignation despite the fact that within only a few months of leaving the *F.Q.R.* he was involved by Dickens in the founding of the *Daily News*.[57] Forster not only took part in regular consultations but also recruited: he hired J. R. Lowell to contribute from America.[58]

The *Daily News* was founded upon strong and unexceptionable principles, as Forster recalled years later in *The Life of Charles Dickens*, in referring to Dickens's draft prospectus:

> The paper would be kept free, it said, from personal influence or party bias; and would be devoted to the advocacy of all rational and honest means by which wrong might be redressed, just rights maintained, and the happiness and welfare of society promoted.[59]

Such idealism, together with high salaries, attracted a number of leading journalists, several of whom, including Fonblanque, Eyre Evans Crowe, Douglas Jerrold, Dudley Costello and Forster himself, had links with the *Examiner*. W. J. Fox joined from the *Morning Chronicle* and Dickens himself brought in his father-in-law, his father to take charge of the reporters, and W. H. Wills. Dickens was in command and W. J. Fox, who shared the leader-writing mainly with Forster, dominant, so that the paper's approach, despite the prospectus, had a radical tone.

It began publication on 21 January 1846. By 27 January Forster was giving Dickens much help with the editor's work: Fox considered that 'the getting up, and general appearance and arrangement of the paper' of that date was 'a triumph of Forster's power'.[60] Here was an early indication of what soon happened. To quote Fox again: as editor Dickens 'broke down in the mechanical business'.[61] That, plus probable differences with other directors, forced his resignation on 9 February. Forster was his natural successor.

He began with great hopes and 'seemed elated with his position'.[62] Certainly he had a clear understanding of the needs of popular journalism. He wrote authoritatively to Lowell that 'in a daily paper ... the blow should be prompt and instantly felt; ... the subject, however in itself remote, should yet, by some point or phase in the treatment, be brought to us in a practical and present form'.[63] But as the months passed he became increasingly unhappy. His friendships' demands never lessened. The burden of the

Examiner not only continued but increased when Fonblanque's health deteriorated and Forster took over his work.[64] But pressures were not only external: he was a weekly journalist used to writing for a narrower, more intellectual readership and found it difficult to adjust to the demands of a popular daily. 'He stops to trim his sentences', wrote Fox, 'and sits costive in his composition. Such sharp practice has been out of his way, and suits his taste as little as his habits.'[65] Again, during the 1840s under Carlyle's influence Forster was moving away from his early and never less than respectable radicalism, so that he was invariably at odds with Dickens and Fox.[66] When he became editor the owners also made C. W. Dilke the newspaper's manager and so swung to the right. Fox remained as radical gadfly and became ever more angry at Forster's 'timidity, and narrowness and carefulness'. The new editor was not, Fox considered, the right man to head 'anything political and popular'.[67] Forster was caught between his friend 'remonstrating one way' and his own desire 'to please the proprietors another way'.[68] He was much harassed and not in good health. In October the proprietors raised the paper's price despite failing to sustain the quality of its news-gathering. This affront to his honesty was the last straw and Forster resigned in some disgust and with much relief.

He resigned to face the *Examiner*'s burgeoning demands. From the mid-1840s he was editor in all but name and contributing much political material,[69] though he did not take over officially until November 1847. Fonblanque was then short of money and Forster, as a friendly gesture, accepted the editorship for only £500 a year plus an understanding that in due course he was to have 'either a percentage on profits or an absolute share'; he agreed to continue literary reviewing for no additional remuneration. Forster hoped to get the ownership of the paper 'gradually & altogether into my own hands'. But this never came about and Fonblanque remained owner.

Though Forster had 'never felt so nervous or anxious about anything'[70] as he did about the new editorship he conducted the business with an energy and enthusiasm vividly recalled by his reading-boy:

> I have many times had to watch Mr. Forster when he was writing very fast, and flung the sheets of MS. about, and had to catch them, or pick them up off the great desk or the floor, and number them with a pencil, ready for the other boy who would come for them, and carry them up to the compositors to be put in type. …
>
> At first his penmanship was fairly good, and small, and straight, but as he warmed to his subject it became expansive. He would scrawl and split his pen, and throw it over his shoulder, when it

> sometimes hit me, and take up another, and write worse. Often he would use five or six pens on one article. Towards the end of his task he would make some words reach right across the paper, and if it were a long word he would bend it down towards the right-hand bottom corner, and all the other lines had to follow it. Sometimes there would not be fifty words on a folio of copy, and when it was all put together for the reader's convenience it made a pile, so that the galley-proof of type looked too short by ever so much.[71]

He had learned much from his stint on the *Daily News* and no longer trimmed his sentences. Henry Morley valued his insistence that a journalist should not 'rewrite his MS. for the press, but to put down straightway what he meant to stand'.[72]

The tone of that advice indicates that in his third major editorship Forster was forceful and autocratic. He demanded standards as high as his own. Morley, who admired him, wrote of Forster playing 'the old trick of giving me pen and paper in his rooms...gives a handful of materials, and expects me to get out the pith intuitively'. On Morley's work Forster demonstrated a variety of journalistic skills, toning down articles that were 'too plain-spoken' and altering unobtrusively to fit changing circumstances.[73] Here are reminders of how similar to Forster's practical criticism was his work as a revising editor. And, as always, his command of techniques was combined with an insistence on accuracy and honesty. 'I am in your hands for the perfect accuracy of all the statements here...Pray look it carefully through with that view',[74] he counselled a contributor in 1850; 'It will be best', he told the historian and lawyer, J. H. Burton, 'to word the allusion to the report as to state the truth – viz. that the article was in type before the report was written.'[75]

Energy, autocracy and principle did not make Forster's appointment the cue for drastic change. Since he had long been editor in all but name this was not to be expected. The *Examiner*'s earlier Benthamite radicalism had undergone, even under Fonblanque, 'a gradual moderation of tone and aim'.[76] Forster and Fonblanque had 'never had a difference beyond opinion – seldom that – never unfriendly'.[77] In 1847 it was a liberal paper with Whiggish leanings, a firm supporter of Lord John Russell, then in the middle of his first administration. Thus for Ireland the *Examiner* advocated a mixture of *laissez-faire* and humanitarianism: 'We bow to the calamity as a dispensation of Providence ...', it wrote in 1847 of the latest famine, 'In such extremities, to palliate and mitigate is the most that can be done.'[78] A poor law system was necessary but should be paid for by the Irish themselves. The Irish gentry should look to their responsibilities and not expect to be coddled by the government in London; the Encumbered Estates Bill was thus greatly favoured. All in all, on Ireland the *Examiner* was like a soft-edged Carlyle. Elsewhere it was for Free Trade, hated Louis Philippe and his territorial ambitions and, consequently, supported Palmerston's conduct in the 'Spanish Marriages' affair that eventually deposed the detested Frenchman. At home it was fierce on social questions: it attacked judicial leniency, supported capital punishment and was cautiously in favour of flogging recalcitrant sailors. When Forster became editor its only significant clash with Russell was over the new Factory Act that brought in the ten-hour day. Russell was a late convert but the *Examiner*, with what was, in a sense, a last flourish of Benthamite individualism and radical distrust of government combined with a sincere concern for workers' reduced earnings, derided the Act as a 'project to improve the factory people morally by making them poorer';[79] for any worker involved, it declared, it must seem like 'pouring water on the drowned rat'.[80]

Forster employed Eyre Crowe to write on foreign affairs; George Birkbeck contributed some leaders. J. H. Burton was brought in to write on Scottish affairs. Talfourd occasionally wrote reviews and John Oxenford helped with the drama notices.[81] Landor, of course, was a regular correspondent and contributor; during 1848 Carlyle wrote his important essays. Dickens had long written occasional articles; during 1848 and 1849 he wrote frequently before *Household Words* claimed most of his attention. Possibly, too, after 1849 Dickens may have found the *Examiner* politically less congenial.

The new editor and his staff worked within a format only slightly modified from the Fonblanque era. The paper was 'enlarged by more than one-fourth of its present size, without increase of price'[82] but this extra space was taken up by 'scissors-and-paste' columns of news extracts and quotations from newly published literature, together with a mildly satirical round-up of the week's news from home and abroad entitled 'Events of the Week'. Its appeal was to a comfortable, affluent, intelligent middle class, as was evident from its advertisements for books, cutlery, life insurance, patent medicines and opera subscriptions at 200 guineas a year.

Initially there was a strong sense of continuity. Forster's first leader, on Bank of England reform, continued a recurring theme of previous months. The second leader attacked leniency to criminals and further articles disapproved of French opposition to liberal forces in Switzerland and Austria. At the end of November 1847 came firm support of the Russell government's Free Trade principles and reluctance to give government aid to Ireland. Praise of Lord John continued: he belonged 'to the highest class of accomplished minds when exalted by sincerity and earnestness'.[83] The change of editor would have caused few cancelled subscriptions.

Carlyle considered, with some accuracy but less kindness, that as *Examiner* editor 'Forster for the most part advocated the theory of human affairs prevalent in fashionable Whig circles'.[84] From 1848 onwards he also sounded darker notes that Carlyle may well have recognized. The leader of 29 January 1848 discussed 'West Indian Grievances':

> European free labour is as productive as negro slave labour – even more so; but negro free labour is by no means as productive as negro slave labour. The energetic free European labourer works with skill and assiduity; the negro in freedom is still a listless barbarian, without skill or intelligence, and possessing none of the attributes of a good labourer, save animal strength and adaptation to climate. In the state of slavery, the compensations for skill and assiduity are European superintendence and the cart-whip.[85]

The *Examiner* was not against slavery, which it regarded as the inevitable consequence of social and economic conditions in the West Indies. Without slavery labour would be too expensive; when the population increased sufficiently labour would become cheaper and slavery fade away. Such harsh pragmatism was also applied to problems nearer home: a leader on 'Protection Against Tumult'[86] and partly concerned with unemployment riots in Glasgow, came out strongly for the whipping of ringleaders.

The *Examiner* was in favour of 'prudent progress'[87] towards extending the franchise, though with a splendid metropolitan arrogance it later argued against universal suffrage by stressing the unfitness to vote of most rural labourers. It began to support Peel. Only at a safe distance did it remain consistently liberal: in foreign affairs, in particular during the European revolutions, its heart stayed in the right place as it supported forces for change. Under Forster the *Examiner* gradually but inexorably became the unashamed defender of those who bought it:

> For the defence of order the middle classes of England are, in Homeric phrase, the bulwark of the war. To the virtue of our institutions we owe the existence of the most numerous and best-conditioned middle class in the world; and as they have been produced by virtue of our free institutions, so they become preservative of them in turn. There are many faults in our Government, but the mere fact of the existence of our middle classes as they are is decisive evidence of the balance of merit in it; and into

> these middle classes any industrious artizan can ascend, and thousands continually are ascending.[88]

Podsnap may lurk behind parts of this as he tends to lurk behind Forster's editorial chair but the paper's political shift is clearly marked both in this extract and in the persisting support of the Whiggish Russell. In the closing months of Forster's editorship he was even more firmly on Lord John's side when the latter resigned from Aberdeen's cabinet in protest at the refusal to allow a commission of inquiry into mismanagement of the Crimean War. Since the 1830s the shift had been substantial and was summed up acidly by Francis Espinasse:

> *The Examiner*'s radicalism used to be defined to be the radicalism of Bulwer and Ward, once M.P. for Sheffield. Where are these two gentlemen now? Ward is Commissioner at the Ionian Islands, and carries things with a high hand there. Bulwer is in Parliament, as a conservative member for Hertford. Curious![89]

Forster knew his readers, perhaps because they were like himself: a circulation of 4,400 in 1850 was improved to 4,800 in 1854, a period during which, for example, the *Spectator*'s readership declined.[90] In 1855 Crabb Robinson considered that 'the *Examiner* thrives under his management'.[91] It did, but not for long. Fonblanque had allowed few changes in the format: at Forster's resignation it was still 'an old-fashioned sheet, of which only two or three pages were spared for original articles, and the rest was occupied by Dudley Costello, the sub-editor, with extracts of news from the daily papers', and for that it charged 5d. Cheaper Sundays, such as *Lloyds Newspaper* at 1d., began to make inroads into its readership. The *Examiner* had long lost its radical constituency; its shift to the right forced it to compete with the new and brighter *Saturday Review*. After Forster it began to fade as the world of the press quickly changed.[92]

Forster did not, however, effect a clean break. 'Various temporary alternatives'[93] kept the paper going through 1856. Forster himself helped out with editorial duties until his marriage that autumn.[94] His reputation lingered longer. The *Globe* hailed his appointment to the Lunacy Commission as 'a tribute to the press which cannot fail to be appreciated by the whole fraternity of which he is so esteemed a member';[95] at his death the *World* stressed that 'by furnishing in his own person a model of accuracy, fulness, and precision'[96] he did much to enhance the status of the profession.

Forster's career as a journalist was thoroughly consistent. At a time of increasing professional respectability he supported the cause by reviewing with an acute social consciousness that sought to discipline imaginative literature, and editing at first with a matching political moderation then with the fierce and insecure Whiggery of the new middle class. By 1858 he had changed once more. He read the proofs of W. B. Jerrold's memoir of his father and responded angrily:

> It is quite true that I was 'long the literary and dramatic critic etc' but I was also, for the last *thirteen years* of my connection with it, the absolute Editor of that great paper and a large political writer in it – and simply to put forward the other matter just at present would not be agreeable to me, especially in connection with the allusion at p.188, which, if the first allusion stands, would make me responsible down to 1856 for theatrical criticism, which I had thus for many years wholly ceased to write.[97]

To have been a reviewer was now a source of shame; to have been an editor and a political commentator was still acceptable. To hide the former and stress the latter he offered to pay Jerrold for altered and cancelled pages. Twelve years later Forster's disillusionment was general as he recalled 'the decisive, peremptory, dogmatic style, into which a habit of rapid remark on topics of the day will betray the most candid and considerate commentator'.[98] Reviewing, all journalism, and possibly at least to some extent literary activity in general, had been the means to his social end. To the wealthy, saddened and fading Forster they were now no more than the abandoned stepping-stones of his long-dead and unlamented selves.

CHAPTER 14 *Historian*

The earliest public expression of Forster's fascination with the seventeenth century is, of course, his youthful play, *Charles at Tunbridge*, that ardently romantic view of hard-pressed cavaliers and a neglectful Charles II. Less than three years later, whilst reading law in London, that ardour was transferred to the commonwealth period and resulted in a series of articles in the *Englishman's Magazine* during 1831. Entitled 'Our Early Patriots' it began with a general essay that considered 'the circumstances by which the characters of the patriots were formed' by outlining 'the state of the times and of parties preceding the reign of Charles I'.[1] Short studies of John Pym, Sir John Eliot and Sir Henry Vane then followed.

The series appeared when Forster was only 19 and shows a young man's passion for the past being shaped by three powerful forces: his Christian faith, his enthusiasm for Reform, and his study of the law under Andrew Amos. The first, particularly because of its dissenting nature, drew him inexorably to the Puritans and away from Catholic kings. The second made him enraptured by those long-dead heroes who had led Parliament in its fight against despotism:

> It was at this stirring era that men of first rate education and talents abandoned the calm of private life for the service of their country; and with that quick apprehension of their liberties inherent in Englishmen, prepared themselves to encounter every peril, even the sacrifice of their own personal freedom, for the vindication of those old rights which they had received from their fathers, and which they were anxious to transmit unimpaired to posterity … [They were] … men, high-born and wealthy, distinguished by far-seeing political wisdom …[2]

Such men had been neglected because earlier historians 'have yet been too much occupied in the discussion of the great constitutional questions of the time' at the expense of 'private motives or ... personal histories'. Yet, Forster insisted, there was great value in considering 'attentively the character of these "first patriots," who vindicated the rights of Englishmen in an age far removed from our own, though not altogether dissimilar in the great interests which divided it'. The past was viewed in the light of present concerns and in a passage combining both piety and party the connection was stressed even more explicitly:

> In that age as, thank God, in our own time, fear and favour were alike exerted in vain against the determined spirit of the nation; and, undismayed by the influence arrayed against them, none were found base enough to unmake themselves and their posterity, by the sale of their own rights or the sacrifice of those of their children. A share in the representation of the country became at this crisis a leading object of ambition ...[3]

Here was the main influence of Andrew Amos, 'whose name I can never mention without confessing the warmest and most lasting obligations which a pupil can owe to his teacher'.[4] Amos was an authority on constitutional history: he was the editor of Fortescue, Henry VI's chancellor, whose writings in support of the rights of the people, illustrative of the extent to which the popular will modified monarchical authority, and against 'obscure and mystical definitions'[5] of the royal prerogative, were quoted by Forster in his introductory essay. And Amos was also a prominent liberal supporter of Reform, to the extent of standing for Hull as the Reform candidate. Forster's concern with 'the growth of the Commons in the state',[6] that is, with the long and heroic pedigree of the Reform movement of the 1830s, developed from his legal studies and was inspired by Andrew Amos into enthusiastic obsession.

'Our Early Patriots' attracted great attention and substantial sections were reprinted in *The Times*. Lardner's invitation to contribute to the *Cabinet Cyclopaedia* was a consequence of that recognition. The essays on Pym, Eliot, and Vane, together with a review of Lord Nugent's study of John Hampden which Forster published in the *New Monthly Magazine*, became preliminary sketches for *Lives of Eminent British Statesmen* (1836–9).

These began with *Sir John Eliot*, who championed Parliament against James I and his chief minister the Duke of Buckingham: Eliot 'opposed always, with watchful jealousy, any attempt to move from the constitutional usages of the house'.[7] As effective leader of the house under Charles I he asserted the people's rights against the growing despotism of the king and of Wentworth, the king's greatest ally. His impassioned advocacy of parliamentary authority and religious tolerance led to his imprisonment and death in the Tower. But he left to his countrymen inspiring memories of

> an unyielded purpose, an unquailing endurance, a still unmitigated hatred of oppression, [that] would teach them, at the same time, that these great qualities had victories of their own to achieve, in which no worldly power could foil them; and that, supposing the public struggles of the time attended with disastrous issue, it was not for man, with his inherent independence, to admit the possibility of despair.[8]

Eliot's public life reflected a private life of high moral quality; he served his country and the popular cause by raising 'the great question of the privilege of the house of commons, – the question, in point of fact, upon which the character of "the English constitution" altogether depended'.[9] 'His genius', Forster asserted, '...showed itself supreme in the purpose of rescuing a state from misgovernment.'[10] The strain of public life and his long imprisonment destroyed him yet his sufferings were 'redeemed'[11] by subsequent constitutional progress. His earlier imprisonment was 'the first of that series of open and undisguised outrages which brought Charles to the scaffold'.[12]

Eliot shared a volume with his enemy *Thomas Wentworth, Earl of Strafford*. In this second study Forster, with Browning, saw Strafford's life as illustrative of his 'aristocratic principle'.[13] All circumstances, his lineage, his role as eldest of twelve, his great wealth, his education, his public positions, seemed designed 'to foster that principle within him'. They

> contributed to produce a character ill fitted to comprehend or sympathise with 'your Prynnes, Pyms, Bens, and the rest of that generation of odd names and natures', who recognised, in the struggling and oppressed Man, those splendid dawnings of authority, which others were disposed to seek only in the One.[14]

Though he began parliamentary life as 'a great and valuable supporter of the popular cause'[15] this was only because he hated the 'court flies that buzzed around the monarch'.[16] He felt too superior to be a true parliamentarian and when he established direct links with Charles I the 'aristocratic' began its change to the 'despotic principle'.[17] The presidency of the North and then the 'government of Ireland'[18] saw him immensely successful in controlling areas of the country and in raising money for the king, and in the process power became 'the great law of Wentworth's being'.[19] In the king's name he set himself above the law: he waged war, subdued opponents and levied taxes without parliamentary approval. Parliament's reply, which the king could not prevent, was to impeach him for treason, and his subsequent trial was a key moment in British history: 'It was not the trial of an individual, but the solemn arbitration of an issue between the two great antagonist principles, liberty and despotism.'[20] Pym led for Parliament and dominated the court. The result was Strafford's execution.

It was all too easy for Strafford's career to be described in terms of melodramatic villainy and this Forster tried to avoid. 'I have felt very strongly', he wrote, 'that the truth lies... somewhere between the extreme statements that have been urged on either side, by the friends and the foes of Wentworth.'[21] The biography insisted upon Strafford's sincerity and that, even with absolute power, he was never a vain tyrant but always at least harshly just. Forster admired his 'mightiness of will',[22] his powers of leadership, and his administrative skills. But he was too much in love with 'conquest and superiority'[23] and so the 'Despotic Principle', like power, became 'the very law of his being'.[24] Ultimately, Forster concluded,

> A great lesson is written in the life of this truly extraordinary person. In the career of Strafford is to be sought the justification of the World's 'appeal from tyranny to God'. In him Despotism had at length obtained an instrument with mind to comprehend, and resolution to act upon, her principles in their length and breadth, – and enough of her purposes were effected by him, to enable mankind to see 'as from a tower the end of all'.[25]

Even here, as Strafford served the democratic cause by reminding many of the unacceptable alternative, the dignified prose and final image hinting at heroic power betray Forster's persisting and, as will be seen, significant admiration.

John Pym came next, the longest of the *Lives* apart from that of Cromwell and the most openly and consistently adulatory. For Pym continued what Eliot had begun:

> An attempt appeared to be in progress to check the impulses of the reformation, when terrible energies sprang from the rebound, and embodied themselves in the Eliots, the Pyms, the Hampdens, and the Vanes; and new passions and emotions were scattered abroad among the people, under the forms of the great original type of power and expression, to check the threatened retreat into bigoted faith and slavish obedience.[26]

Faced by Roman Catholic intolerance and despotic rule the Puritans looked to the Bible for authority and motivation. In particular they recalled the time when 'the free people of Israel, without a king, lived majestically'.[27] Pym was no fanatic seeking to create a new Israel on the Biblical model yet his career demonstrated that the Puritan revolution was a religious as well as a political movement:

> Let it always be recollected that, to him, a true political government *was* religion. His was that great capacity in which bad government and good faith, or good government and bigoted faith, could not co-exist. To be free in thought and in act; to secure responsibility in government, and security in the public liberties; was with him, to set up the true religion in its purity.[28]

Pym led the Commons when it sent its Grand Remonstrance to the king; he was one of the five members to arrest whom the king forced his way into the chamber. Unlike Eliot he lived beyond all hope of reconciliation between king and Parliament, and through the early months of the Civil War. His life drew Forster to the appealingly pious heart of the popular cause.

John Hampden was no more than a short 'outline'[29] that filled out the *John Pym* volume. Hampden was offered as an example of inspiring patriotism: 'It was Hampden who first dared to anticipate a broader field of warfare than the floor of the house of commons, and to prepare himself for a more real struggle.'[30] Having prepared he gave himself absolutely: 'Hampden himself was the first, in this great hour, to throw aside every relation save those in which he stood to his country; and upon the issue of the contest which had now arrived, he cheerfully ventured all.'[31] His death from wounds received at Chalgrove Field was, paradoxically, fatal for Charles I: in reviving the king's hopes it led him to continue the struggle and so made inevitable the final dreadful outcome.

Sir Henry Vane, 'the ever gallant and generous defender of the rights of faith and conscience',[32] followed *John Hampden* as a representative of the next generation of Puritan leaders. His genius was administrative, demonstrated firstly as governor of Massachusetts and then at home. He played a leading part in passing 'the self-denying ordinance'[33] that separated Parliament from the army and so allowed the latter to be commanded by professional soldiers, and worked to form the 'New Model'[34] Army whose plain dress and religious and moral resolutions supported their military discipline. The Parliamentarians' sweeping victory at Naseby 'was the first memorable result of Vane's great policy'.[35] The king's fortunes having declined, Vane turned to parliamentary reform and formulated proposals to extend the suffrage; he effected a wholesale and brilliant reorganization of the navy. But above all else he desired 'the administration of a state without the intervention of a sovereign and a court, and the free and full toleration of all modes of religious worship and opinion'.[36] As an avowed republican he found himself at odds with Cromwell's growing ambitions and so 'was driven from the government of the commonwealth by a traitorous usurper, because he proposed to strengthen it with new institutions, and replenish its languid veins with the vigorous blood of the people'.[37] On Cromwell's death Vane again became influential and helped force Richard Cromwell's abdication. But in the reign of Charles II his republican sentiments led to his arrest and execution for treason. Here was his final triumph: his death marked the beginning of that king's end.

Henry Marten, like *John Hampden*, was also no more than an outline. He was of Vane's generation and showed how Puritanism could have a particularly attractive human face. In Parliament

> His wit had been the ornament and relief of almost every debate; his graceful manner, and never failing good humour, had been perforce made acceptable to the sourest puritan there; and by his gallant and unflinching adherence to republican principles, by the respect his intellect and genius inspired, he had bound himself in the fastest friendship to Cromwell, to St. John, and to Vane.[38]

Marten was prominent in the Civil War and in moves to execute Charles I. He interested Forster partly because he refused to acknowledge Cromwell's growing authority; for a time he was even imprisoned by him for 'his great talents and still fearless republicanism'.[39] After the Restoration Marten, like Vane, was indicted for treason but, unlike Vane, he was sentenced to life imprisonment and to 'the now impenetrable obscurity of those melancholy years'.[40] In *Henry Marten* Forster celebrated 'the memory of a well-spent life'; Marten was remembered for 'exalting' the cause 'by his generous purpose as he graced it by his wit'.[41]

The *Lives* were completed with a two-volume biography of *Oliver Cromwell*. As in *Strafford* Forster sought a balanced assessment:

> Viewed in his separate qualities a greater man has probably never lived – a man with more eminent abilities for statesmanship – a more masterly soldier, judging him by the age in which he lived, and the objects he accomplished – a person more wonderfully gifted in all the attributes of subtlest thought, and of an intellect the most piercing and profound. The moral elevation, too, of his *courage* should be admitted by all, since in the days of his greatest danger,

> when assassins beset him round his bed and at his board, he gave way to no base thought of mere personal fear. His eminent and thoughtful sagacity has never been disputed, nor the vastness of his comprehension, nor the marvellous intrepidity of his purposes, nor the inexhaustible expedients and powers of his mind.

Yet such qualities were undermined by 'some rooted curse that lay in his nature deeper than them all...That curse was his WANT OF TRUTH.'[42] The biography's central point is that Cromwell's life was one of dissembling and scheming in pursuit of his despotic ambitions. Though he created a great army that 'trampled on all thought of danger in the grander thought of liberty' yet he was always the 'crafty soldier'. That craft became 'a bare image of tyranny and force' as he used his military power to subvert democracy. He packed the council of state with 'his creatures ... or creatures he could mould into his', and dissolved Parliament. Though he did not dare to become king the desire for kingship was 'the secret of his soul': as Lord Protector he assumed 'the majesty of a king'. His reign was one of religious oppression, censorship, and imprisonment without trial; he arranged for his son Richard to succeed him. But his health broke, his friends fell away, he became estranged even from his own family. The country was in uproar and 'even his own body-guard he could trust no longer'.[43] Only in death did he recapture former greatness as he recognized the errors of his life and was glad to die.

The *Lives* were reprinted in 1840 as *The Statesmen of the Commonwealth of England*, to which Forster added an introductory essay 'A Treatise on the Popular Progress in English History'. This progress began with *Magna Carta* and included suffrage extension under Henry III, Bolingbroke's attack on 'divine right', the rise of the Commons and the associated development of parliamentary privilege, and Parliament's decline under the Tudors until its revival with Elizabeth I. She also championed Protestantism, thus fostering two main elements of the Puritan movement. The Puritan revolution was thus, Forster argued, the result of a long accumulation of 'social, political and religious influences'[44] that received only a temporary check when the Stuarts succeeded Elizabeth.

The 'Treatise' is constitutional history and so a reminder of Amos's seminal inspiration. The *Lives* themselves, like 'Our Early Patriots', are history written by a young lawyer of great promise who, though he quickly turned to literature, never forgot his youthful studies. The commonwealth period had special legal interest; its principals were all law-makers and Eliot, Hampden, Cromwell, and possibly Pym, had read for the Bar.

Forster demonstrated a mastery of legal detail as when, for instance, he outlined the impeachment charges brought by Pym against Buckingham, and a sound grasp of parliamentary history and procedures. He had a lawyer's fascination for oratory, whether parliamentary or forensic: speeches in the House were quoted at length and detailed accounts supplied of the trials of Strafford, Eliot, Vane, and Marten. His main concern was his subjects' use of legislative power.

To a degree the *Lives* were defences. Forster defended Eliot against D'Israeli's attacks on his character, and against the 'desperate and unwearied spirit of misrepresentation'[45] that was invariably political in origin. On Pym's behalf he countered the 'spite of Lord Clarendon'[46] so evident, for example, in the latter's assertion that Pym had intrigued with Charles I to gain the chancellorship in return for moderating his criticism of the king. This, Forster showed, was only one of Clarendon's 'plain falsehoods'.[47] Others were directed against Hampden by both Clarendon and Lord Nugent who suggested that Hampden, though active in impeaching Strafford, craftily withdrew from the attainder proceedings the better to preserve his standing even with Parliament's opponents. D'Israeli's suggestion that Vane sought to prosecute Strafford because the families hated each other, Hume's charges of hypocrisy against Marten, were firmly rebuffed. Even Strafford's career had its share of mitigating circumstances. In each case evidence was reviewed and misinterpretations corrected. The *Lives* became substitutes for the courts so recently deserted by the lawyer turned man of letters.

When the *Lives* became *Statesmen* they were dedicated to Lord Holland 'in memory of his illustrious kinsman Charles James Fox'. Fox, of course, had been the superb parliamentary orator on behalf of the rights of the people, Holland remained the Whiggish supporter of Reform. Whereas 'Our Early Patriots' encouraged Reform, the *Lives* and *Statesmen* celebrated what had been achieved. Thus Vane's advocacy of suffrage extension was now 'rendered remarkable by events of our own day',[48] though the desires of Vane and of other Puritans for more truly representative government were not then met:

> Two centuries were allowed to pass, and a new settlement of the constitution and the crown was suffered to be made, before the simple, wise, and manly claims of these republican officers … were conceded to the English people![49]

The 1832 bill had become the most recent manifestation of the inexorable popular progress.

Forster's democratic fervour permeates these volumes; at its heart is a passion for Parliament most forcefully expressed in *Oliver Cromwell* in an eulogy of the Long Parliament that Cromwell had so violently dispersed. That parliament had upheld 'with unceasing dignity and spirit the national honour', had 'placed in their service men of the greatest genius, in various departments of the state, that, since their day, have been produced by our nation' and had 'distinguished themselves by indefatigable perseverance and unwearying toil'.[50]

Such praise was intensified by Forster's religious beliefs. The *Lives* were also a dissenter's history and coloured by the fierce morality of a pious young man. He wrote of Henry VIII:

> He had himself no regard for the truth in any thing he did. The gospel light as little beamed on him from Boleyn's laughing eyes when she was about to mount his bed, as from her serene and patient look when she was about to mount his scaffold. The gospel light has nothing to do with lust, has no sympathy for satisfied cruelty, takes no regard of personal interests, sheds no virtue upon ambitious passions, and could find in the huge bulk of Henry not a crevice or a corner into which it might cast even one of its diviner rays.[51]

As for Elizabeth: 'The glory of this extraordinary woman's reign was the final uprooting of the Roman catholic faith, and the establishment of protestantism.'[52]

Carlyle told Francis Espinasse that the *Lives* had been written in only eight months.[53] Certainly Forster had been pressed for time and this may well have been good for him: he wrote with a dash, verve and conviction not often found in his later work. And though he wrote with strong beliefs and much idealism he was not, in the context of the time, a religious or political extremist. His liking for Marten was strong evidence of his lack of sympathy with the grim side of Puritanism. More importantly, he was no republican. 'All the vices of the old kingly rule were nothing to what was now imposed upon her',[54] he wrote of the country under Cromwell's Protectorate. The monarchy was deserted only with reluctance:

> For, be it kept in mind, republicanism was of recent growth even in the breasts of these founders of the new republic. The most influential of them had not played the lofty part they did from any preconceived notion of the abstract excellence of that form of civil society. It has been abundantly shown in this work, that what such men as VANE sought, was popular and good government; embracing extensive representation, security for person and property, freedom

> of thought, freedom of the press, and entire liberty of conscience. It was only because they could not find these under a monarchy, that they became republicans; but under a monarchy they would have been content with these.[55]

Here is a further reminder of conservative potential in the youthful and attractive radicalism that enhanced the appeal of those early volumes. Up to and including the *Statesmen* and its 'Treatise' Forster's historical writings convey a radiantly attractive sense of the freshly passionate intellectual blissfully alive in his fascinating world.

After 1840 he wrote no more history for 16 years, until an essay on Cromwell in the *Edinburgh Review*. In 1858 this was reprinted with some additions and revisions, in *Historical and Biographical Essays*. The later version was itself reprinted two years later in *Biographical Essays*. The 1858 volumes also included 'The Debates on the Grand Remonstrance', reconstructed from Sir Simonds D'Ewes's 'A Journal of the Parliament', and 'The Plantagenets and Tudors: A Sketch of Constitutional History', an extended version of the 1840 'Treatise'. In 1860 came a detailed volume on *The Arrest of the Five Members*, and *The Debates on the Grand Remonstrance*, an extended version of the essay, prefaced by 'An Introductory Essay on English Freedom under Plantagenet & Tudor Sovereigns', extended from the version of 1858. An article on 'Strafford's Youth' appeared in 1861 as Forster began an extended biography of Thomas Wentworth that he was never to finish; at his death even the first sections had only become uncorrected proof-sheets.[56] His plan to publish an extensively revised edition of the *Statesmen* had even less success; Longmans reprinted them, unchanged, in 1862. Forster's last completed work was *Sir John Eliot*, first published in two volumes in 1864 and reprinted, with a few additions and corrections, in 1872.

Thus, throughout his life Forster worked and reworked the same historical subject, 'the popular movement against the Stuart princes in the seventeenth century'.[57] As he did so his emphases changed. He became more and more interested in constitutional history, particularly in the origins and history of Parliament, and much concerned to demonstrate his impressive grasp of the law's evolution, as if to satisfy his continuing yearning for the lawyer's career he had so rashly rejected. Necessarily his approach became specialized, more concerned with minutely detailed accounts, with facts for their own sake. He tended to bury the original conception beneath mounds of scholarship as another expression of his rejection of the 'popular', much as he did in his biographies of Goldsmith. Though he continued to regard the parliamentarians as men 'whom

Bishop Warburton truly characterised as the band of greatest geniuses for government that the world ever saw leagued together in one common cause',[58] and though Eliot remained 'THE MOST ILLUSTRIOUS CONFESSOR IN THE CAUSE OF LIBERTY WHOM THAT TIME PRODUCED',[59] it must be said that those scholarly mounds also buried the attractive qualities of the early work. A few final shovelfuls were supplied by new views and these came from Carlyle.

These can be detected in 1846 in Forster's review of *Oliver Cromwell's Letters and Speeches* and seen clearly in the *Edinburgh Review* essay of ten years later. In the latter, describing current interpretations of Cromwell's career, Forster outlined his own in the *Statesmen*: Cromwell had been a great and pure soul who 'thoroughly deceived himself' before deceiving others and whose 'final remorse is made to arise, not from treason to royalty, but from treason to liberty'.[60] But, Forster later confessed, Carlyle had induced him 'very greatly indeed to modify it',[61] to be persuaded by his friend's insistence that in the 'protest against popery' there

> broke forth the utterance of a true man, of a consistency of character perfect to a heroic degree; ... [This] Cromwell was no hypocrite or actor of plays, had no vanity or pride in the prodigious intellect he possessed, was no theorist in politics or government, was no victim of ambition, was no seeker after sovereignty or temporal power. That he was a man whose every thought was with the Eternal, – a man of a great, robust, massive mind, and of an honest, stout, English heart; subject to melancholy for the most part, because of the deep yearnings of his soul for the sense of divine forgiveness, but inflexible and resolute always, because in all things governed by the supreme law. ... [and who] ... believed God to have called him. ... That such a man could not have consented to take part in public affairs under any compulsion less strong than that of conscience. That his business in them was to serve the Lord, and to bring his country under subjection to God's laws. That if the statesmen of the republic who had laboured and fought with him, could not also see their way to that prompt sanctification of their country, he did well to strike them from his path, and unrelentingly denounce or imprison them.[62]

Forster the parliamentarian persists in the conditional mode of the final sentence: his changed views of Cromwell failed to shake the pedestals of his heroic statesmen. Neither could he bring himself to support the Long Parliament's dispersal: it was 'an interruption to the temperate wisdom which generally guided [Cromwell] ... because ... without it the supreme power must nevertheless have been his, unattended by the difficulties in which the consequences of that act involved him'.[63] This apart, Forster's account of Carlyle on Cromwell reflects in its neo-biblical cadences not only the effect of Carlyle's prose but also the strength of Forster's new commitment. When Carlyle wrote 'Very well indeed!' on the proof sheets of the *Edinburgh* essay[64] the exclamation mark perhaps suggests understandable self-satisfaction. Certainly the annotation demonstrates Carlyle's recognition of an interpretative accord.

In 1860, after reading and praising *The Arrest of the Five Members*, Carlyle began to change Forster's view of Strafford:

> I think you are too severe upon the poor Charles-First Party; and am sorry for their poor heads, going like eggs under your wheels. That is now the side to take ... but there is another side too, wh[h] will again claim to have the meaning of its views brought home to us, and justly *interpreted* on the new terms now possible. Take that Strafford Affair up, wh[h] you were speaking of; get fairly into the inside of Strafford, and make the eye of him alive again! That too wd be an admirable thing. Dare you?[65]

The first effect of such urging came later that year in *The Debates on the Grand Remonstrance* when Forster conceded that even though 'justice remained with the Parliament, I think not the less that high and noble qualities were engaged on the side of the King'.[66] Such qualities were exemplified, he continued, in Strafford's Irish administration. To be sure his government failed because it had insufficient regard for civil liberties but 'it also included much that had no unpopular aspect, for it was the design of a man of courage and genius'. Strafford, considered Forster,

> would have cleared the land, by foul means or fair, of the native possessors; he would have rooted out the idle, improvident, beggarly proprietor; and he would have planted everywhere English wealth and English enterprise. It is remarkable that a scheme which in its final development brought its author to well-merited ruin, should yet have involved so much that, in other hands, and with other ultimate aims, might have saved and regenerated Ireland. Every petty oligarchy would have been reduced by it to subjection before the monarchy, and it would have struck down all the tyrannies but its own.[67]

The similarity of Forster's contemptuous view of Ireland and the Irish to that of Carlyle's hardly needs stating. What should be stressed is Forster's new willingness to accept a benevolent despotism that moved him *towards* Carlyle's position.

'Strafford's Youth', written for Adelaide Procter's magazine *The Victoria Regia*, confirmed the shift. Strafford's upbringing was notable for his making and keeping valuable friends and for the young man's acquisition of learning. He gained early experience of Parliament and was 'hardly perhaps much gratified'[68] by that institution when, in 1614, he saw it capitulate to James I. Most significantly Forster abandoned the 'aristocratic principle' theme that in the biography had been the prelude to reprehensible despotism. Instead he inserted a single and less condemnatory reference to 'what force must have been given, by his early independence of controul, to that over-mastering sense of hereditary privilege and right which everything around him made intense and strong'.[69]

Carlyle had one other specific effect on Forster's historical writing. The essay of 1858 on 'The Debates on the Grand Remonstrance' began with Carlyle's work on D'Ewes's *Journal*: he wrote about it in 1844 before giving Forster his abstract of D'Ewes's notes.[70] Forster's essay was 'a capital stroke of Historical Investigation' that led Carlyle to urge Forster to transcribe the whole of D'Ewes's manuscript.[71] The result was the volume of 1860.

Carlyle's Strafford and Cromwell made strong appeal to Forster's piety and to the high regard for individual power implicit in his anti-republicanism. In particular, the new Cromwell, the man of God imposing personal will on historical circumstance, was an appropriate hero for the successful and essentially nonconformist Victorian middle class. It was not fortuitous that Forster's change of stress from 'popular progress', implying the inevitability of history's course, to the assertive individualism of Strafford and Cromwell was most firmly made at a time when his wealthy marriage and government appointment had confirmed his own middle-class status and given him greater independence. Neither was it chance that the appeal of Strafford and Cromwell increased as his regard for literature declined, for Forster never lost his capacity for hero-worship. Of that capacity Carlyle was, of course, a permanent beneficiary, to the detriment of Forster's historical work. For Carlyle's authoritative promptings, those regarding D'Ewes's *Journal* being typical, encouraged Forster's swamping specialization. And the tensions and uncertainties set up by Forster's failure wholly to reconcile new views of Strafford and Cromwell with persisting principles, such as his belief in parliamentary democracy, destroyed the clear lines and attractive idealism of his early writings on the period.

Such writings appeared at a key moment in the history of history. Before Forster were the examples of such Whiggish historians as his dedicatee, Charles Fox, and Henry Hallam. Fox had written of the seventeenth century out of the party passions of his own day; Hallam had to some extent viewed 'human evolution through a lawyer's spectacles'[72] and had attacked despotism with the authority of an expert on the constitution. In continuing the Whig tradition Forster demonstrated his affinity with Fox's age, in which 'there was no sense of the pastness of the past, of the otherness of the past, but rather of the sameness',[73] and with Hallam's legalistic approach. But he also wrote as a more 'objective', more 'scientific' idea of history was turning the historian from printed sources to primary materials. The Record Commission was reformed in 1838; Forster himself belonged to both the Camden and Chetham Societies that reprinted rare items. His work was the result of much original research.

This last he was quick to emphasize. The *Lives* were essentially new: four of them were 'written in a detached shape for the first time'.[74] *The Arrest of the Five Members* was based on material in the 'noble stores of our State collections'[75] newly available to Forster in the State Paper Office through the personal kindness of Sir John Romilly, Master of the Rolls. There followed the first painstaking transcription of D'Ewes's *Journal*, and the second version of *Sir John Eliot* extended through access to the Eliot family papers and the new resources of the Record Office. With the assumptions of the traditional historian Forster combined the habits of the modern.

The results, however, even in Forster's lifetime, had a mixed reception. Not surprisingly the early work was received rapturously by Forster's more radical friends. To Leigh Hunt, reviewing the first volume of *Lives*, Forster was 'an eloquent, and ... vehement biographer'.[76] To Dickens, reading *Henry Marten*, 'the biography was glorious'.[77] W. J. Fox considered that Forster's work 'held itself proudly and claimed the affinity of eternal truth and essential beauty, telling us of human collisions, what would bear to be read where there was nobody but God'.[78] But through later years, though the *Literary Gazette* described *Historical and Biographical Essays* as a 'brilliant cluster',[79] the *Leader* as 'masterly and fascinating volumes',[80] and though there was particular praise for the essays on 'The Debates' and on constitutional history, critical comment was also forthcoming.[81] Thus the *Guardian*, reviewing Forster's historical work up to 1858, was typical in its disapproval:

> Mr. Forster comes before us as the avowed unflinching exponent of the Puritan movement in its political and moral aspect. With him its

> chiefs have no faults ... When an intelligent man throws himself so unreservedly into a party view, he is worth listening to. The probability is so great that he is, on the whole, wrong, that he is not likely to mislead any but those who choose to be misled ...[82]

At Forster's death the same criticism was repeated by a much greater authority. In a shrewd obituary appreciation the historian Samuel Gardiner considered that Forster had been too stirred by

> the spirit which animated the Reformers who rose to power upon the ruins of the Tory party in 1830 ... He was an advocate, not a judge. ... He was deficient in that judicious scepticism with which an historian is bound to test his assertions, and he therefore frequently, in spite of his love of hard work and his constant reference to original authorities, made assertions which will not bear the test of serious investigation. ... [Yet his] portraits, too, have in them the life which springs from sympathy. From them the world learned, not quite all that Eliot and Pym and Hampden really were, but what they wished to be.[83]

Despite the charitable tone these were harsh words and Gardiner added to them in the preface to his *History of the Great Civil War* when he described Forster and Macaulay as historians who were too concerned to view the past in terms of present party positions.[84]

Forster's work never recovered from such attacks and was quickly superseded by more balanced accounts of the period, of which Gardiner's own work was the great example. His books fell out of print and references to them, let alone complimentary references, have become rare. Occasionally an omnivorous modern scholar reads through him *en route* to greater authorities and even more occasionally puts in a good word. Judson, for example, thinks Forster to have had 'real understanding of some aspects of Vane's career and thought'.[85] Brett[86] is more typical in listing the mistakes and inconsistencies to be found in *John Pym*. The modern editor of D'Ewes's *Journal* confirms what Gardiner had noticed years earlier, that Forster 'was so careless and so uncritical in the use of sources ... that historians cannot rely upon him for authentic details'.[87] The most crushing blow of all is delivered by the modern standard bibliography of seventeenth-century history: only *The Debates on the Grand Remonstrance* is cited as a main reference and then criticized for its 'strong parliamentary bias'. Of Forster's other volumes, *Sir John Eliot* and *Sir Henry Vane* receive cursory attention: the former is condemned as 'laudatory', the latter is valued only because it reprints one or two important documents.[88]

That the countless eye-straining hours of historical investigation, often sustained against the ardours of ill-health and the harassments of his busy life, should have yielded so little that has lasted is appalling but not surprising. Forster's histories derived too much of their life and most of their appeal from reflecting their author's character and changing circumstances rather than from their portrait of the past. It remains a sad irony that throughout his literary life and particularly after 1856 Forster sought to base his most serious and dignified claim to posthumous fame on what proved to be the most vulnerable of all his professional concerns.

CHAPTER 15 *Literary Biographer*

Forster's scholarly ambitions expressed themselves not only in the writing of history but in a series of literary biographies. During the 1830s he began a life of Goldsmith; it was published in 1848, followed by an extended version in 1854 and an abridged edition a year later. As this work proceeded he published essays on Dryden, Churchill, Defoe and Foote. 'Sir Richard Steele' appeared in 1855, when work also began on a biography of Swift originally envisaged as a paper for the *Quarterly Review*.[1] As a group these studies reveal a consistent approach shaped by several basic and familiar influences. Those of Charles Lamb, Leigh Hunt and Bulwer Lytton partly explain Forster's choice of subjects whilst associating them (and here Carlyle also played his part) with the idealization of writers and a concern for the dignity of literature. Further, the eighteenth-century studies reflect Forster's legal training and experience of the press: the lawyer-turned-journalist was skilled at undermining opposing points of view and presenting partial impressions. The tenor of the times, the numerous pressures on biographical truth, was the strongest force of all.

Thus, Forster's work is both aggressively polemical and judiciously slanted, the former quality seen at its most extreme in the essay on Churchill. This opens with a full-blooded attack on Churchill's editor, William Tooke: 'It would be difficult to imagine a worse biographer than Mr. Tooke ... But though Mr. Tooke is a bad biographer and a bad annotator, he is a worse critic. ... Whether he praises or blames, he has the rare felicity of never making a criticism that is not a mistake.'[2] Damning evidence is supplied and the attack extended to expose Tooke's factual and grammatical errors. Other targets are Boswell on Goldsmith; Scott and Hazlitt on Defoe; Macaulay on Foote, Steele, and Swift; Cooke on Foote; and Jeffrey and Johnson on Swift. Frequently Forster's work seems that of a biographically inclined Tom Cribb.

As for judicious slanting: this involves suppression, distortion, and – for us – revealing comparisons with modern authorities.[3] Many things are silently omitted from Forster's pages: Goldsmith's envy, coarseness in company, extravagant gambling, and failure to honour contracts; Churchill's hatred and harrying of Smollett and vindictive satirical attacks on the man who thwarted him of his father's living, his participation in the rites at Medmenham Abbey, the hedonism of his epitaph; Defoe's uncontrollable anger; Foote, fat and flabby, leaving his estate to his illegitimate sons; Steele's heavy drinking, homicidal duelling, mercenary marriage, illegitimate children, and flagrant dishonesty; Swift as absentee parish priest and congenital misanthrope.

Whitwell Elwin noted that Forster 'could scarcely bring himself to recognise that moral meannesses could co-exist with majesty of intellect, or that a man, who was a genius in his books, could out of his line be inferior to ordinary mortals';[4] Fonblanque wrote to Forster: 'Your office of righting wronged reputations is a noble one'.[5] Such comments point accurately to the nature of Forster's work, yet he did not write simple hagiography. Despite the suppressions, even the most favourable account, that of Defoe, does not quite 'extol his hero throughout':[6] Forster does indicate Defoe's imaginative limitations, such as his failure, often, to appreciate qualities that transcended 'the merely shrewd, solid, acute, and palpable'.[7] Churchill was given to 'violent extremes … carrying a hatred of hypocrisy beyond the verge of prudence … to the very borders of licentiousness'.[8] Steele was improvident; Foote, 'the heedless, light-hearted coxcomb',[9] often indulged in cruel public mimicry of the famous; Goldsmith was too often the dandy, too often impulsive, too often foolishly over-sensitive; Swift sometimes wrote coarsely and abusively.

But such faults, argued Forster, resulted either from spontaneity – Churchill and Swift splendidly carried away in the heat of literary and political battle, Foote enraptured by his own creativity, Steele and Goldsmith tempted by the good things of life or into ill-afforded kindness – or from unpropitious circumstances, the latter clearly seen in Forster's comment on Churchill: 'The stars do not more surely keep their courses, than an ill-regulated manhood will follow a misdirected youth.' Churchill's riotous life was the consequence of 'a marriage most imprudent – most unhappy', contracted too early in life as a reaction to parental pressure to enter the Church. Similarly, Defoe's limitations were linked to his 'Presbyterian breeding', and Goldsmith's faults further explained by reference to his unhappy childhood, the boy persecuted because of his ugliness and seeming stupidity: 'It was early to trample fun out of a child; and he bore marks of it to his dying day.' The insults and brutality of college life also cast a 'shadow…over his spirit, the uneasy sense of disadvantage which obscured his manners in later years'.[10] In contrast, faults that were both socially dishonourable and indicative of basic personal deficiencies, faults hard to excuse or condone and too often occurring when the spontaneous became the uncontrolled, were silently suppressed.

Forster's *selection* of material is also governed by recognizable principles. His eighteenth-century studies illustrate the Romantic fallacy that the nature of the work reflects the author's character: for example, Steele's *Tatler* 'could have arisen only to a fancy as pure as the heart that prompted it was loving and true',[11] and Forster wrote to Bulwer: 'I question... that effects declared to be almost universally good and even fascinating, and especially to the young, could possibly have been produced by a man who sat down with a "deliberately malignant" design. I don't believe it of any one – and especially I deny it of Swift'.[12] But though he considered that his subjects produced idealistic and morally sound literature, they were generally regarded as an unlikely band of paragons, the main biographical problem being clearly put in a letter from Procter: 'You must be so tired and perplexed with your labour, in trying to make out a good character for Mr. Jonathan Swift'.[13] The solution involved a concept of 'essential character', an inviolate core of innate goodness expressed by the author's works. Hence Forster's description of Goldsmith: 'His existence was a continued privation. ... But ... he passes through it all without one enduring stain upon the childlike purity of his heart', and frequent assertions that Goldsmith 'looked into his heart and wrote'.[14]

Closely allied to 'essential character' is Forster's idea of genius: 'to charming issues did the providence of Goldsmith's genius shape these rough-hewn times. It was not alone that it made him wise enough to know what infirmities he had, but it gave him the rarer wisdom of turning them to entertainment and to profit.... it lighted him to those last uses of experience and suffering which have given him an immortal name'.[15] And, from Forster's account of Dryden composing *The Fables*:

> It was thus amid the most grinding incidents of poverty, and in immediate contrast to the remorseless and close-shut coffers of the publisher, that the superabundant wealth of the poet's genius overflowed all restraints at last, and, regardless of such things as Tonsons in the world around it, poured itself freely forth to gladden future generations.[16]

Inviolate itself, literary genius transforms circumstances and reassures its possessor. Such ideas partly reflect the influence of Carlyle's lectures on

'The Hero as Man of Letters', which Forster, of course, attended and from which he quoted in the life of Goldsmith; Carlyle, like Forster, insists on the writer's 'inward sphere' of superior moral qualities expressed by his literary work. But there is one important difference: Carlyle's mystical rhetoric is absent from Forster's work. Whereas, for example, Carlyle envisages literary genius as 'continually unfolding the Godlike to men',[17] in Forster's scheme, to use only the quotations immediately above, it 'shaped' and 'overflowed'. Such words are more matter-of-fact than transcendental, for Forster's literary–biographical method associates the Romantic with, if not the ordinary, at least the socially desirable.

This latter is heavily stressed. Above all, Forster's writers are indomitable: Goldsmith 'shows to the last a bright and cordial happiness of soul, unconquered and unconquerable', Foote has 'a fulness and invincibility of *courage* ... which unfailingly warded off humiliation', Churchill a compelling fearlessness. They are men of integrity: what Forster wrote of Swift ('He had nothing in him of the hired scribe, and was never at any time in any one's pay')[18] applies to all his subjects. Despite intolerable financial pressures they wage ceaseless war against hypocrisy and corruption. Much is summarized by Forster's description of Defoe:

> He did not stand at the highest point of toleration, or of moral wisdom; but with his masculine active arm, he helped to lift his successors over obstructions which had stayed his own advance. He stood apart and alone in his opinions and his actions from his fellow men; but it was to show his fellow men of later times the value of a juster and larger fellowship, and of more generous modes of action. And when he now retreated from the world Without to the world Within in the solitariness of his unrewarded service and integrity, he had assuredly earned the right to challenge the higher recognition of posterity. He was walking toward History with steady feet; and might look up into his awful face with a brow unabashed and undismayed.[19]

Limitations and virtues are alike indicated, but the passage is most important as an example of the assertive, angular, muscular, almost uncouth language typical of these studies and embodying a main principle of Forster's approach. His writers *strive* and even though general recognition, let alone monetary reward, is rarely gained, yet such massive perseverance *forces* praise from the discerning contemporary and from posterity. Such work offers a literary–biographical equivalent to, say, the 'Epilogue to Asolando', or literary heroes fit for Samuel Smiles. They are also fit for Forster himself because he endows them with his own qualities of courage, integrity, and fierce determination to pursue literary fame and power. And whereas his contemporary relationships could become strained when he sought to transform friends into self-portraits, he was more successful with the dead.

The influence of Forster's mentors shows itself mainly in his stress on the socially commendable: his eighteenth-century studies present literary history from Dryden onwards in terms of the desire of writers for social acceptance and just rewards. Dryden was 'the first writer of any significance who composedly faced the world on the solid and settled basis of literary pursuits ... Literature was his trade: he not only lived upon its wages, but was never ashamed to own it. ... It was a man's own fault, after this, if he was thought disreputable because he wrote for bread.'[20] Defoe, Steele, and Swift represented the next stage:

> At the critical moment when the people were rising into the first importance, men who could best use the pen found themselves best able to influence and persuade them. Speakers to either Lords or Commons had no such influence, for the reporting of debates was unknown, and their speaking remained within their four walls. What the orator now is, the writer was then, with the world for his audience.[21]

Though Forster's fascination for 'the party of literary politicians'[22] of Queen Anne's time came naturally to one who at times sought to become a Victorian equivalent, it was not uncritical; he saw clearly that dependence upon the whims of politicians and the promises of office made literary men, despite their achievements, little better than slaves. And even though Defoe, Steele, and Swift were men of integrity, literary men as a class lost their reputation through associating with corrupt and scheming politicians.

For Foote, Churchill, and Goldsmith, matters did not improve: 'It was, in truth, one of those times of Transition which press hardly on all whose lot is cast in them. The patron was gone; and the public had not come. The seller of books had as yet exclusive command over the destiny of those who wrote them; and he was difficult of access; without certain prospect of the trade wind, hard to move.' Literary men had lost both high office and influence and were still slaves, though now controlled by the bookseller: 'the Man of Genius... must descend in the social scale' and, again despite exceptions, ' "man-of-letters" became the synonyme [*sic*] for dishonest hireling'.[23] Goldsmith's life of poverty and misery, chronologically the last of Forster's eighteenth-century studies, is offered as an example of how not to treat literary genius; here Forster departs from his biographical brief to argue that mid-Victorian England needed to recognize such genius without patronage or other degradation. This recognition was not a question of money, for 'The public have quite altered these matters since the days of Dryden. Their direct interference has placed upon a basis entirely different the whole question of literature and literary pursuits. A writer of any merit is now as little dependent on the generosity of a publisher, as on the more degrading charity of a patron.'[24] Rather, the concern was for social respectability, as is made clear by Dickens's reaction to Goldsmith: 'The gratitude of every man who is content to rest his station and claims quietly on literature, and to make no feint of living by anything else, is your due for evermore.'[25] The theme of 'dignity' unifies all Forster's literary–historical work.

In 1864 Landor's death recalled Forster from seventeenth-century history to literary biography. His reluctance to return was a product not only of ill-health, more compelling interests, and social inhibitions, given the scandals of Landor's life, but also of his knowledge of the constraints of the libel laws.[26] The biographical result was hardly satisfactory: much of *Walter Savage Landor* is very dull, and consists of arid summaries of Landor's works, long illustrative quotations, and extracts from correspondence offered without comment. But it is of interest for two reasons. Firstly, and for the first time, we see Forster applying his biographical principles to the life of a close friend. Polemical attacks on Landor's critics, suppression and falsification of material,[27] some attempt to explain Landor's faults in terms of his undisciplined childhood and early freedom from monetary cares, the basic pattern of struggle and worldly failure, part of Landor's works offered as evidence of 'the nobler part of his character', the attempt to stress socially acceptable qualities, all remind us of Forster's earlier studies – as does, also, the language of undaunted striving: 'To the end we see him as it were unconquerable. He keeps an unquailing aspect to the very close, has yielded nothing in the duel he has been fighting so long single-handed with the world, and dies at last with harness on his back.'[28]

But despite these similarities, there are crucial differences in Forster's approach. Even though he indicates Landor's good qualities, such as his ability to inspire affection and his 'pervading passion for liberty', Forster is now openly critical of the essential character both of his subject and his subject's literary works. Landor's failure properly to educate his children ('such nonsense ... Such a fool's paradise'), and his desertion of his family ('more for his own sake than for theirs') are condemned unequivocally as expressions of an extreme and damaging egotism and, even though libel laws prevented explicit mention of Landor's improprieties, such as the seduction of Nancy Jones and the old man's scandalous relationship with 16-year-old Geraldine Hooper, Forster does hint strongly at these. And in Landor's work he detects basic flaws, writing, for example, of *Gebir* that 'Impetuosity, want of patience, is as bad in literature as in life'.[29]

Further, and not only because of personal faults and literary defects, Landor was hard to associate with the 'dignity of literature' theme; 'Landor wrote without any other aim than to please himself', knew nothing of the hardships of the author by profession, and refused to write for pay. The biography's real hero is Southey, 'the representative man of letters of his day';[30] Forster prints his correspondence and eulogizes his character. The 'dignity' theme is thus carried into the nineteenth century but at the expense of Landor's reputation. Forster preserved his own by presenting himself, in *Walter Savage Landor*, as the man who furthered Landor's literary career and sought to keep his friend out of trouble; Landor was grateful but not always obedient; he begged Forster to be his biographer. Such treatment of himself is the predictable (because partial) reaction of Forster-as-Podsnap, a contrast to the treatment of Landor and to the more insistent fact that at that point in his life when Forster seemed more likely to purvey whitewashed distortion he began to incline towards honesty.

Walter Savage Landor appeared in 1869; in 1870 Dickens's death forced Forster to shoulder another massive biographical burden. His appalling health, the constant harassment of Lunacy business, his grief as friends died, made him despair of the new task before him. 'This book hangs over me now like a nightmare',[31] he wrote desperately to Carlyle. Certainly the state of Forster's 'Now' must have tempted him to sentimentalize the biographical 'Then'. The tendency to idealization of Forster's approach to literary subjects, the constraints of libel laws with many principals still alive, the wishes of Georgina Hogarth and Dickens's daughter Mamie, the early appearance of significant studies of Dickens by Hotten (blandly uncritical) and Sala (adulatory),[32] together with Forster's own affection for and admiration of his dead friend, and his own enhanced social position – all these seemed to make such temptation irresistible.

Most modern critics agree that Forster succumbed. Notable exceptions are the Leavises, who appear to assert the straightforward and candid nature of Forster's presentation: 'Forster … gives us the sense … of being really inward with Dickens's personality and character, and without being concerned to make out a case by "interpreting" his subject'.[33] The Leavises' views are enthusiastically restated by Elliot Engel who misleadingly suggests that they are widely accepted.[34] But other commentators divide into two groups. The first considers that Forster made an effort to tell the truth and achieved a certain truthfulness before idealizing pressures prevailed. Thus George H. Ford points to Forster's valuable insights into Dickens's complex character, yet concludes that Forster's desire 'to paint an accurate portrait of one of his closest friends' could not be and was not reconciled with the 'idealized conception of Dickens' character'[35] that dominates the biography. Sylvère Monod reminds us that Forster 'did not use a tone of uniform praise... Self-centredness, vein of hardness, intellectual limitations, are all there'; but, in the end, he 'said about as much as he thought he could say after his life-long friendship and with a good many of the family still around him'.[36]

The second group is less inclined to stress Forster's good intentions, and views him, more simply, as a successful idealizer. K. J. Fielding notes Forster's exclusion of uniquely personal reminiscence, considers that he evades such controversial issues as the separation and Dickens's relations with his wife, and sees the whole as the distorting 'biography of a friend'.[37] Gerald G. Grubb states that 'almost everything of any consequence which Forster omitted was the result of deliberate design, not of ignorance.... [to] keep alive the public idolatry of Dickens, and to please, insofar as possible, the conflicting elements of Dickens' own family'.[38] Madeline House and Graham Storey differ from Grubb only in their assessment of the nature of Forster's idealism: 'He was... concerned not simply with the public image... but with truth, as he conceived it. The *Life* contains numerous small distortions of fact, but paradoxically these distortions were in the interest of a larger, or ideal truth.'[39] Alec W. Brice makes much the same point but explains it in terms of a 'Romantic theory of biography': original materials were manipulated or altered so that, in F. R. Hart's words, quoted by Brice, they would 'accord more closely with...[the biographer's] intuitive grasp of his subject'.[40] This group is completed by Edgar Johnson and the implications of his massive biography: reminders of what Forster must have known but carefully suppressed.[41]

The Leavises' view, based as it is on the fallacious idea that only inept modern biographers offer 'interpretations' of their subjects, can be set aside, along with Engel's enthusiasm, as undiscriminating. This present account seeks to relate to other modern critics. Like them, it accepts that Forster idealizes; unlike them, it does not believe that this was his main aim. And whereas the most favourable commentators treat Forster as truthful and perceptive only up to a point, this account emphasizes that Forster does face the consequences of his perceptivity. In other words, in arguing that, despite so many pressures towards idealization, Forster sought valiantly to convey the truth, it aims to reverse the view of Ford and Monod. Or, to put matters in yet another way: modern critics, with their stress on Forster's 'deliberate design' in the interests of idealization, implicitly support a view of the *Life* as illustrative of the principles that govern Forster's eighteenth-century literary studies; but it is suggested here that the study of those latter, and of *Landor*, in relation to the *Life*, is the best way of demonstrating that, in the *Life*, Forster's biographical approach has changed.

The change is not absolute, however, for to an extent the *Life* is another work by a slanting polemicist and partial advocate. As is well known, Forster edited and falsified documents to stress the lively, sparkling side of Dickens, removed vulgarisms or the cutting response, and suppressed socially damaging facts such as Dickens's dandyism, the extent to which his family sponged on him, his antagonism towards the established church, and the depth of his pessimism about the condition of England.[42] Forster is again able to assert, more plausibly because of such suppressions, the Romantic relationship between author and work: much of the latter taught 'the invaluable lesson of what men ought to be from what they are' and reflected 'that inner life which essentially constituted the man'.[43] The associated concept of inviolate genius is, here, socialized by Forster to stress both Dickens's indomitable spirit and integrity, and those of his qualities attractive to hearth and home: Dickens the family man, the lover of regularity and order, and Dickens the hearty extrovert, never bookish, never highbrow, fond of riding and walking and amateur dramatics, irrepressible companion, good friend, philanthropist. To this extent Dickens is assimilated into Forster's 'composite literary man'.

But the *Life* reveals what *Landor* revealed, that whereas, when writing of the long-dead, Forster could impose ideas (about biography, literary men, personality) upon all his material, when writing of his friends the immediacy of their lives' truth drew him towards honest revelation, to a fundamental change of emphasis apparent in *Landor* and intensified in the *Life*. In the former Forster faced facts but had to draw back from complete disclosure; in the latter, despite some local bias and falsification, so far as the key incidents are concerned Forster not only faces facts but also seeks ways round obstacles to explicitness.

The contrast between the *Life* and Forster's earlier works shows the change in his principles. Such change is underlined when Forster's treatment of key topics is contrasted with the work of Hotten and Sala, the most important earlier biographers of Dickens. Thus, Hotten's treatment of Dickens's childhood and youth simply refers to his 'education at a good school' and his boyhood reading of 'the standard works of the best authors';[44] Sala is more certain but equally inaccurate: 'He had not been born in poverty, but in a respectable middle-class family. He had never known – save, perhaps, in early youth, the occasional "harduppishness" of a young man striving to attain a position – actual poverty....He had no terrible experiences to tell....From youth to age he lived in honour, and affluence, and splendour.'[45] Only Forster knew the truth, and Engel has skilfully shown, with special reference to Dickens's childhood and youth, that 'one way of understanding the value of Forster's work is to discover how much information about Dickens it revealed which was completely new to the Victorian reader'.[46] Even more impressive is the use Forster makes of this unique material. Dickens's autobiographical account is linked to the rags-to-riches theme of the *Life*, as the source of 'the fixed and eager determination, the restless and resistless energy, which opened to him opportunities of escape from many mean environments, not by turning off from any path of duty, but by resolutely rising to such excellence of distinction as might be attainable in it', it is also the beginning of a counter-theme, the relationship between early humiliations and Dickens's persisting and ultimately self-destructive faults of character: 'A too great confidence in himself, a sense that everything was possible to the will that would make it so, laid occasionally upon him self-imposed burdens greater than might be borne by any one with safety.'[47] The purely pathetic and sentimental potential of the account is manfully resisted.

This presence of theme and counter-theme supports Monod's and Ford's assertion that Forster's approach is not simply uncritical. But the consequences of such explicit statements, in particular the rigorous tracing of character flaws, are also faced with some frankness. And when sufficient frankness is not possible Forster resorts to a kind of fearless implication: documents are printed and arranged so that they seem to speak for themselves. We can see this in a minor way in, for example, Forster's treatment of Dickens's relations with Richard Bentley. Though Forster refrains from explicit condemnation of Dickens's lack of moral awareness in his disputes with the publisher, he does print the letter in which Dickens admits to having foolishly agreed the poor terms to which he was now objecting, refers to his (Forster's) 'no small difficulty in restraining him from throwing up the agreement altogether', thus implying where at least some right lay, before appealing, with slight ambiguity, for a 'considerate construction to be placed on every effort made by [Dickens] to escape from obligations incurred in ignorance of the sacrifices implied by them'.[48]

Again, without comment, Forster offers much quite startling evidence of the morbid side of Dickens's imagination: for example, he does not delete Dickens's thoughts of the drowned, in *The Old Curiosity Shop*, with 'the stars shining down upon their drowned eyes', or Dickens's description of his eagerness, when in America, to 'see the exact localities where Professor Webster did that amazing murder'. Forster retains Dickens's thoughts of Mary Hogarth, including his friend's reaction to Mrs Hogarth's death that meant he could no longer be buried next to her daughter Mary ('I cannot bear the thought of being excluded from her dust'), and Dickens's strange and emotional dream of Mary Hogarth's apparition urging Roman Catholicism upon him. The last incident draws from Forster direct reference to 'trying regions of reflection' that trouble men of genius, and to Dickens's 'disturbing fancies'.[49]

Forster allows such incidents to offer evidence of Dickens's obsessive and insensitive singlemindedness. This use of the frank and the implicit in developing the counter-theme is most clearly and importantly seen in his handling of two major topics, Dickens's marital troubles and the reading tours. Once more, we are helped to see the changed emphasis in Forster's work by contrasting it with Hotten and Sala. Hotten attempts to whitewash Dickens's marital troubles: brief references to the *Household Words* 'manifesto' and to 'a misunderstanding...betwixt Mr. and Mrs. Dickens, of a purely domestic character – so domestic – almost trivial, indeed – that neither law nor friendly arbitration could define or fix the difficulty sufficiently clear to adjudicate upon it. ... we trust the reader will think we act wisely in dropping any further mention of it'.[50] Sala is pompously vague:

> He chose ... to make the fact of his domestic troubles public; although into the circumstances thereof he did not enter. But he published...a vehement vindication of himself from some attacks, or some scandalous imputations so wildly improbable in their nature, and so obscure that their very existence was ignored by ninety-nine out of every hundred men and women who began to wonder at the passionateness of his defence. ... Nothing more need or can be said. ... Those who have a right to speak, have not spoken; and the world has no right to enquire into the mystery – if any mystery there be – nor will have, any time these fifty years.[51]

Forster is more candid. He illustrates Dickens's developing unhappiness, analyses his state of mind in 1858, and sees Dickens's inability properly to consider others and his impulsive and restless behaviour as manifestations of the too-great concern for self and the fierce determination to get what he wanted that were legacies of the early hardship: Forster criticizes the 'manifesto' and the writing of the 'violated letter', and states: 'Thenceforward he and his wife lived apart. The eldest son went with his mother, Dickens at once giving effect to her expressed wish in this respect;

and the other children remained with himself, their intercourse with Mrs. Dickens being left entirely to themselves.'[52] Forster writes with impressive compassion and events force from him the haunting phrase and some fine sentences: 'There was for him no "city of the mind" against outward ills, for inner consolation and shelter. It was in and from the actual he still stretched forward to find the freedom and satisfactions of an ideal, and by his very attempts to escape the world he was driven back into the thick of it.'[53] The moving imagery and rhythms appropriate in their anguished awkwardness suggest both Dickens's predicament and his biographer's sincere sadness. Nonetheless, Forster goes as far as the libel laws allowed *and* at the end of 'Volume the Third' he prints Dickens's will.

Hotten had remarked that 'After his [Dickens's] wishes had been put into legal form by his solicitors, he copied out the entire document in his own handwriting',[54] and then quotes Dickens's description of Georgina Hogarth as 'the best friend I ever had', his instructions for a quiet burial, and his expressions of religious faith. Forster, however, prints the will in its entirety, an inclusion almost certainly unique in Victorian biography. In doing so he is able to give Ellen Ternan due prominence as first legatee and recipient of a generous bequest, and is able to remind his readers of his own role as Dickens's 'dear and trusty friend' and an executor of the will. Further, the will provides a penetrating insight into Dickens's thinking and into his household arrangements by contrasting Georgina Hogarth, his children's 'ever useful self-denying and devoted friend',[55] with Mrs Dickens, the unhelpful beneficiary of Dickens's post-marital financial generosity. It is a cruel and bitter document, final suggestive testimony of those faults of character that aggravated the separation. Its inclusion circumvents libel laws and other pressures to demonstrate the strength of Forster's desire to tell the whole truth; it undermines such criticism as, for instance, that of K. J. Fielding that Forster offers only 'the vaguest outline'[56] of the separation. Even Edgar Johnson's detailed biography can offer little more on Dickens's domestic feelings at this time than can be deduced from the material Forster supplies.[57]

Finally, the reading tours: Hotten records without comment that, in 1858, Dickens began to read 'professionally, and as an avowed source of income',[58] and cites dates and subjects during his narrative. Sala's main concern is with the 'Sikes and Nancy' reading, questioning the 'taste and the usefulness of the display', criticizing Dickens for some overacting, and summing up: '[Dickens gained] by these performances many thousands of pounds, but losing, I am afraid, many years of the life which he might have reasonably hoped to attain'.[59] Forster begins with Dickens's request for his opinion, restates his opposition to the readings ('It was a substitution of lower for higher aims; a change to commonplace from more elevated pursuits; and it had so much of the character of a public exhibition for money as to raise, in the question of respect for his calling as a writer, a question also of respect for himself as a gentleman'),[60] and then, once again, ascribes Dickens's disregard of all arguments against the tours to the defects of character consequent upon his traumatic upbringing by repeating his earlier comments about Dickens's hard and aggressive confidence and fierce determination. Having expressed his disapproval, Forster then devotes over a quarter of 'Volume the Third' to descriptions of the tours, mainly in Dickens's own words, that exhibit significant changes of emphasis.

During the early days of the tours, Dickens's letters concentrate on places and people; there is nothing like the account of accounts in the chapter on the second series:

> On the 18th I finished the readings as I purposed. We had between seventy and eighty pounds *in the stalls*, which, at four shillings apiece, is something quite unprecedented in these times.... The result of the six was, that, after paying a large staff of men and all other charges, and Arthur Smith's ten per cent, on the receipts, and replacing everything destroyed in the fire at St. Martin's Hall (including all our tickets, country-baggage, cheque-boxes, books, and a quantity of gas-fittings and what not), I got upwards of £500. A very great result.

Succeeding references to 'Hunted Down', that 'its principal claim to notice was the price paid for it', and to 'Two brief extracts from letters of the dates respectively of the 8th of April and the 28th of June will *sufficiently describe* the London readings'[61] (the extracts referring exclusively to box-office takings and the possibility of taking more), show Forster suggesting forcefully that, for Dickens, money-making now came above all else. During the American tour Dickens's letters reduce people to numbers, are much obsessed with occurrences that might decrease takings, such as the activities of speculators, and crow over the eclipse of competition. At the end of that chapter Forster offers a detailed analysis of American takings and earnings before, only four pages later, quoting Dickens's own similarly detailed account of the great financial triumph. An account of the 'Last Readings' then follows, but now it is dominated by Dickens's dreadful ill-health.

As everybody's literary adviser Forster had a special talent for understanding popular taste and reaction. Because of this it is hard to accept G. H. Ford's opinion that 'Forster was simply overwhelmed by the difficulties of writing about a contemporary to whom he had been too closely attached',[62] particularly if we recall his controlled use of material in the eighteenth-century studies and his considered attempt at honesty in the life of Landor. It seems odd to deny that Forster, in the *Life*, knew exactly what he was doing when he reprinted the will and organized his documents to suggest that Dickens killed himself for money. It seems even odder, given Forster's own clear sense of purpose. As he told C. E. Norton,

> I was sorry to see a little remark in that paper you so kindly sent me, and which I read with so much satisfaction and pleasure – to the effect that it was eulogy 'gross and unmeasured'. But if the person who said this is a sincere man, & has merely overlooked indications very much to the contrary he might have seen in the 2 volumes published, he will not hesitate to atone for it *when he reads the third*.[63]

In *The Life of Charles Dickens* Forster is no longer the restorer of wronged reputations but the Carlylean biographer valuing integrity in the face of mealy-mouthed pressures.

This last is underlined as we recall Forster's own abiding obsession with the 'dignity of literature', and the unifying progress from Dryden through the essays to Goldsmith and on to Southey that seems, in the early stages of the *Life*, to be completed by Dickens:

> He would have laughed if, at this outset of his wonderful fortunes in literature, his genius acknowledged by all without misgiving, young, popular, and prosperous, any one had compared him to the luckless men of letters of former days, whose common fate was to be sold into a slavery which their later lives were passed in vain endeavours to escape from. Not so was his fate to be, yet, something of it he was doomed to experience.[64]

But the shining jewel of the literary profession, the man who, through the good influence of his books and the example of his life, seemed to be forcing 'writer' and 'gentleman' into permanent juxtaposition, not only began writing books that attacked the very foundations of the society whose acclaim Forster wished literary men to receive, but also took up with an actress half his age, separated from his wife, and made much money through non-literary, ungentlemanly, and obsessively self-destructive activities. Forster's chagrin must have been intense, yet, amidst disappointed hopes and crumbling theories, he sought valiantly and ingeniously to be truthful to life.

A final consequence of such seeking is Forster's treatment of his own role in Dickens's life. As is well known, he manipulated and falsified documents to emphasize Dickens's reliance upon him and to counter the fact that the two had been less close in later years.[65] There is, as G. H. Ford has shown, a long tradition of regarding the biography as an expression of Forster's egotism: 'The Autobiography of John Forster with Recollections of Charles Dickens'. Ford himself stresses that 'in the biography itself, it is the egotism which is especially evident'.[66] But the traditional view is too simple. Fielding notes that Forster sometimes suppressed complimentary references to himself in Dickens's letters;[67] Grubb concludes that, in the extant letters, Forster 'omitted or toned down most of the passages in which Dickens expressed his deep regard for his biographer, most of those in which he expressed his dependence upon him as a critic, most passages in which Dickens undertook to thank him for his services as a mediator'.[68] Forster could have said very much more about the overall effect he had on Dickens's work, and he says little or nothing about, for example, the platform and support he provided for Dickens in the *Examiner*, and the way he brought Dickens into London literary life. Self-aggrandizement is thus an inadequate description of his approach. We see further that Forster's treatment of himself is consistent with his treatment of Dickens: whereas, in treating his friend, a more localized idealizing is countered by a general emphasis on frankness and implicit revelation, so, in treating himself, a carefully controlled stress on his own importance is at least balanced by what can, perhaps, be called a policy of dissociation. It is hard to agree, for example, with the Leavises, that Forster was simply concerned 'to give himself greater importance in relation to Dickens in the eyes of his world',[69] when after the closeness and affection of the early relationship Forster is almost anxious to show how frequently Dickens ignored his advice. Forster advised against Dickens taking the editorship of the *Daily News*, against his separation from his wife, against making a public statement about the separation, against giving paid public readings, against the tour of America, against the inclusion of the Sikes/Nancy reading. We are allowed to see only too clearly that he might as well have kept silent. The resemblance to his role in *Walter Savage Landor* is considerable, but with this difference, again marking the changing emphasis, that Forster's treatment of himself in the *Life* is of a piece with the treatment of his subject.

In one sense Forster paid the price of his honesty, for contemporary reviewers were shrewd and accurate in their reading.[70] They were almost unanimous in praising the biography of Goldsmith for its advocacy of the worth of its central figure and of the wider claims of literature. In reviewing the collected eighteenth-century studies the *Literary Gazette* made a representative response in noting that Forster was

> always siding in heart and sympathy with the subject of his narrative. He raises Defoe in our estimation as a politician; he openly challenges Lord Macaulay's depreciatory estimate of Steele...; he brings into relief the manliness of Churchill, and all the brilliancy and amiable qualities of Foote.[71]

John Wilson, in the *Quarterly Review*, summed up the general opinion of *The Life of Jonathan Swift*, Volume One:

> The work ... will, we are confident, place Swift the man ... at least in a position to engage a larger share of human sympathy than has hitherto been accorded him by the common run of readers; a generation of whom it may be said, at the present day, that they know not Jonathan.[72]

Few thought Forster's Landor to have advanced literary men in the public's estimation. As for *The Life of Charles Dickens*, there was much agreement that Forster had harmed his friend's reputation by stressing his lowly background and lust for lucre. *The Times* was typical: Dickens had been 'uneasy in society, and... lacking, in a word, the manners of a gentleman'.[73] *Temple Bar* later concurred.[74]

Though Carlyle may well have influenced Forster against the popular literary world, as he had into franker biography, there can be no doubt that Forster still found the pursuit of truth to be a wretched one. It was, he told Longfellow, a task 'more painful and heavy to me than I could ever hope to convey to you'.[75] Nonetheless the aging, sick, and saddened man sought to reject all applicable biographical precedents, to tell much and when unable to tell more to imply much more. In this there was the kind of heroism, the undaunted attempts at obstacles, the striving towards commendable goals, that Forster had so often portrayed in his subjects. There is much to be said for Longfellow's opinion:

> To write the life of a dear friend just gone, must be a task almost too painful. How fearlessly and well you have done yours I need not say ... You give an exact portrait of Dickens, and have had the courage not to conceal some things that others might have hidden, but which make the likeness true and lifelike.[76]

Postscript

John Forster died at Palace Gate House on the morning of Tuesday, 1 February 1876, two months short of his 64th birthday. His health had been poor for so long that his friends had ceased to think of him as being in any danger. He died, as Whitwell Elwin put it, in 'an unexpected hour'.[1] Eliza Forster grieved, Robert Lytton broke down, Carlyle expressed controlled sadness, Browning regret,[2] Henry Rawlins, for whom Forster had obtained a clerkship in the Lunacy Commission, was 'stunned';[3] a sprinkling of condolences were offered to the widow. But though all who knew Forster were moved by his death comparatively few were now left to know him.

His death came 20 years after his main withdrawal from literary life and almost three years after the third volume of *The Life of Charles Dickens*, his final popular flourish. The world had moved on and so the obituaries were perfunctory: in London only *The Times* and the *Examiner* got much beyond listing Forster's posts and publications to pay tribute to his 'unflinching firmness and honesty of purpose ... real tenderness and sympathy',[4] and to his 'keen appreciation for obscure merit'.[5] More valuable but little known were the newspapers of his birthplace. The *Newcastle Weekly Chronicle* considered Forster to have 'a kind of talent which only just fell short of genius';[6] in the *Newcastle Daily Chronicle* W. Lockey Harle wrote an account of Forster when young that remains an important because perceptive biographical document based on Harle's personal knowledge of Forster's Newcastle upbringing.[7] The first flurry of short notices was followed only by a few reminiscing articles,[8] mainly anecdotal and, as with R. H. Horne's, occasionally malicious.

It follows that the funeral was small: 'an unplumed hearse, four mourning coaches, and two private carriages'.[9] They carried Carlyle and Robert Lytton (though not Robert Browning, nor Elwin, the latter because of illness), Dickens's children, Joseph Chitty, son of Thomas Chitty in whose chambers Forster had once impressed, Frederick Chapman, representing Chapman & Hall, Percy Fitzgerald, and a few others. Forster was buried beside his sister Elizabeth at Kensal Green Cemetery where, a year later, the tomb was inscribed with references to 'the warmth of his affections' and 'the lavish services in the midst of his crowded life/He rendered to friends',[10] a rare instance of an understated epitaph.

The timing of his death and the private nature of much of his achievement ensured that Forster did not receive the recognition he deserved, a situation compounded by his own closing gestures. These had begun in 1864 when shortly after moving into Palace Gate House he had started to put his private papers into order. His files contained many thousands of letters from leading literary, theatrical and political figures.[11] During these last years he weeded and destroyed. In 1874 he made his last will; it was a rich man's, 'sworn under £30,000'.[12] Most was left to Eliza Forster but a number of legacies showed his capacity for gratitude and for appreciative friendship. To Carlyle he gave the gold repeater watch left to him by Dickens, to Robert Lytton a painting by Maclise, to Elwin £2,000. The 'faithful' Rawlins and Forster's doctor, Richard Quain, were not forgotten. But he also left instructions about the disposal of his library and of his surviving letters and papers. At his widow's death the former was to go to the South Kensington Museum though, in the event, she allowed it to be given immediately. The letters and papers were first to be examined by Forster's executors and those that they 'may not direct to be destroyed, or as I myself may not have marked for destruction, may be bound in volumes for reference and not for publication, and may be placed ... among the manuscript collections of my library'. Forster added:

> generally it is my express wish that all letters coming under the denomination of merely private correspondence shall at once be destroyed, and I leave the decision of this absolutely to the judgment of my said executors ... on which judgment I also implicitly rely that such letters as shall ... be retained ... shall be those only which derive interest from the reputation and position of the writers, and which ... may properly be preserved.[13]

The executors were Whitwell Elwin, Joseph Chitty, and Robert Lytton. With Lytton in India Chitty handled legal and business matters whilst Elwin took charge of literary affairs. His main task was to examine the letters. Of the considerable number still extant at Forster's death some were swiftly reclaimed by correspondents, such as Robert Browning,[14] anxious to prevent their letters being made available to the public at South Kensington. Even then enough survived to fill several boxes which were sent to Elwin at Booton Rectory. Though he had been Forster's friend for 20 years Elwin did not have the highest opinion of him. He had always thought him far too impatient to publish and his later work to be of poor quality.[15] Oddly, Forster had never asked Elwin to be his executor and the clergyman, who disliked being under pressure, was mildly irritated by the discovery.[16] He was, besides, a reserved and cautious man, even more so than Chitty and Lytton. The result was his well-known act of literary vandalism: almost all Forster's papers were burned in the rectory garden and Elwin's son, Warwick, recalled, years later, roasting chestnuts in the ashes of the great.[17]

Meanwhile, Eliza Forster tried to sell Palace Gate House. It was auctioned in May 1876 but bought in at £17,300.[18] She stayed on in that 'large and gloomy'[19] house until her death in 1894. And she cherished Forster's memory. 'She lives only for one thing', Rawlins told Elwin in 1879, 'the realisation of Mr Forster's wishes as to the library at S.K. To this purpose she devotes all her time.'[20] Long after the Forster Collection had been received by the South Kensington Museum she continued to augment it from what remained at Palace Gate House. There her memories were sustained by what had survived successive holocausts and the gift to the nation: Forster's diary or, at least, its remains, and hundreds of letters.[21]

Elwin's pyromaniacal interpretation of Forster's instructions was to create great problems for would-be biographers. They were not solved by Mrs Forster's reluctance to allow access to the documents she had retained. Yet her active presence as custodian of the immortal memory must have been a main source of the uneasiness felt by Forster's surviving friends at their failure to recognize his achievements. 'The only thing that haunts me with a sense of incumbency as a thing yet to do', wrote Carlyle in 1877, 'is that of writing something about poor Forster ... but I find it extremely difficult, – owing considerably to my total want of *hand power*!'[22] Robert Lytton was in India and, as he told Mrs Forster, when he returned he hoped to write his father's biography.[23] By 1880 the need became pressing: the South Kensington Museum wished to publish a *Dyce and Forster Collections Handbook* that would include Forster's memoir of Dyce and one of Forster. Elwin seemed unable to work with sufficient speed[24] and Henry Morley eventually wrote the slight 'Biographical Sketch of John Forster' for the *Handbook*. Eight years later, with minimal help from Mrs Forster,[25] Elwin produced a suggestive but brief memoir for the Forster Collection catalogue. In the same year, 1889, appeared the *Dictionary of National Biography* article by Charles Kent that reflected in its blandness the protective influence of Forster's widow.[26]

Such an inadequate biographical fate provides a final irony. Forster's own acts of destruction, his executor's compliance, his widow's protective reserve, together expressed his abiding and influential concern for the dignity of literature that swiftly condemned him to an undeserved but long-lasting obscurity.

Abbreviations

Note: Places of publication are given only for works published outside the United Kingdom. In abbreviating titles of periodicals, the commonly accepted usage of, e.g., *J.* for *Journal*, *Rev.* for *Review* etc. has been adopted. Other abbreviations are listed below.

ABL Armstrong Browning Library, Baylor University, Waco, Texas

BL British Library

Diaries William Charles Macready, *Diaries*, ed. W. Toynbee (2 vols., 1912)

Dickens John Forster, *The Life of Charles Dickens* (3 vols., 1872–4)

DNB *Dictionary of National Biography*

FC Forster Collection, Victoria & Albert Museum Library

FC (Aux.) Forster Collection (Auxiliary), Victoria & Albert Museum Library. This contains material added since the receipt of the Forster Collection proper.

HL Huntington Library, San Marino, California

Landor John Forster, *Walter Savage Landor* (2 vols., 1869)

NLS National Library of Scotland

Pilgrim *The Letters of Charles Dickens*, ed. M. House, G. Storey, K. Tillotson *et al.* (Pilgrim edn, 1965—; in progress)

PMLA *Publications of the Modern Language Association*

TLS *The Times Literary Supplement*

For a list of sources, see the Bibliography, p. 297ff.

Notes

CHAPTER ONE
Newcastle to London

1. HL MS: part of Forster's diary entry for 12 Oct. 1860, transcribed by Mrs Forster.
2. W. L. Harle, 'John Forster: a sketch', *Monthly Chronicle of North-Country Lore and Legend*, II (1888), 50.
3. From a note by James Gilmore, repr. *ibid.*, 54.
4. *Ibid.*
5. HL MS: James Gilmore to Mrs Forster (13 Aug. 1877).
6. *Op. cit.*, 54.
7. HL MS: James Gilmore to Mrs Forster (13 Aug. 1877).
8. See *The Picture of Newcastle Upon Tyne, Containing A Guide to The Town and Neighbourhood* (1807); *The Picture of Newcastle Upon Tyne, Being a Brief Historical and Descriptive Guide* (1812).
9. Harle, *op. cit.*, 50.
10. R. V. Holt, *The Unitarian Contribution to Social Progress in England* (1938), 276.
11. W. E. Channing, *The Superior Tendency of Unitarianism to Form an Elevated Religious Character* (1827), 32, 34. I have used Forster's own copy in the Forster Collection.
12. *The Picture of Newcastle* ... (1807), and Turner's life in *DNB*.
13. See A. R. Laws, *Schola Novocastrensis* (2 vols., 1932); *Register of the Royal Free Grammar School of Newcastle upon Tyne*, ed. B. D. Stevens (1955).
14. HL MS: James Gilmore to Mrs Forster (13 Aug. 1877).
15. John Forster, *The Life of Charles Dickens*, ed. J. W. T. Ley (1928), xxiii.
16. Harle, *op. cit.*, 50.
17. See *A Historical Sketch of the Transactions of the Literary and Philosophical Society of Newcastle Upon Tyne* (1807); *Arranged Catalogue of the Library of the Literary and Philosophical Society of Newcastle Upon Tyne* (1819); *Twenty-Seventh Year's Report* (1820); *Twenty-Ninth Year's Report* (1822).
18. Harle, *op. cit.*, 50.
19. BL Add. MS 28510, f. 56: a biographical notice (c. 1860) corrected by Forster.
20. Harle, *op. cit.*, 50; HL MS: Mitchell to Forster (13 May 1828).
21. FC (Aux.) MS: *Ali Baba or The Forty Thieves*, annotated and interleaved by Forster (1814), 3.
22. FC (Aux.) MS: Miss Bennett to Mr Chitty (12 Sept. 1877). A copy.
23. FC (Aux.) MS: Forster to Mrs Bennett (20 June 1827).
24. FC (Aux.) MS.
25. FC (Aux.): a Newcastle press cutting, dated 17 May 1828, attached to the MS of the play.
26. Harle, *op. cit.*, 54 (Gilmore's note).
27. BL Add. MS 38109, f. 93: Forster to Mrs Leigh Hunt [c. 1830].
28. p. 51.
29. 'John Forster', *Forster Collection: a Catalogue of the Printed Books* (1888), viii.
30. 'Encouragement of Literature by the State', *Examiner* (5 Jan. 1850), 2.
31. H. H. Bellot, *University College London 1826–1926* (1929), 54 and *passim.* See also J. Maynard, *Browning's Youth* (Cambridge, Mass., 1977), chap. xi, *passim.*
32. K. J. Fielding and G. G. Grubb, 'New letters from Charles Dickens to John

Forster', *Boston University Studies in English*, II (1956), 149.
33. FC Newspaper Cuttings, xix, no. 381; *Globe* (5 Jan. 1856).
34. HL MS: Henry Rawlins to Whitwell Elwin (20 Dec. 1879).
35. *Op. cit.*, ix.
36. See R. Gettman, *A Victorian Publisher* (1960), 1–22; I. Jack, *English Literature 1815–32* (1963), 406–37; J. A. Sutherland, *Victorian Novelists and Publishers* (1976), *passim*; R. L. Patten, *Charles Dickens and His Publishers* (1978), 61.
37. FC Pamphlets, vol. 518. The review is dated 22 Nov. 1828.
38. pp. 28, 35.
39. HL MS: Mitchell to Forster (30 Jan. 1829).
40. Fielding and Grubb, *op. cit.*, 149.
41. *Ibid.*
42. Harle, *op. cit.*, 51.
43. Henry Morley, 'Biographical Sketch of John Forster', *The Dyce and Forster Collections* (1880), 57.
44. II (1831), 79–83.
45. I (1831), 351–6, 499–512, 623–37.
46. HL MS: Mrs Forster to Whitwell Elwin (18 Dec. 1879). Mrs Forster's italics.
47. HL MS: Forster to James Emerson (13 Apr. 1831).
48. HL MS: Forster to James Emerson (5 Mar. 1831). Mrs Forster's copy.
49. R. Renton, *John Forster and His Friendships* (1912), 17.
50. Identified by Halkett and Laing.
51. From 'Advice', 13–17.
52. Earl of Lytton, *The Life of Edward Bulwer, First Lord Lytton* (1913), I, 373.
53. *Ibid.*
54. Folger Library MS: Forster to J. P. Collier (12 June 1832).
55. Harle, *op. cit.*, 51.
56. H. G. Merriam, *Edward Moxon, Publisher of Poets* (New York, 1939), 35n.
57. J. H. Wiener, *The War of the Unstamped* (Ithaca, N.Y., 1969), 141; see also 30–2.
58. B. Jerrold, *The Life and Remains of Douglas Jerrold* (1859), 186.
59. *Diaries*, I, 88 (28 Dec. 1833).
60. BL Add. MS 38109, f. 93: Forster to Mrs Leigh Hunt [c. 1830].
61. Fielding and Grubb, *op. cit.*, 149.
62. HL MS: Henry Rawlins to Whitwell Elwin (20 Dec. 1879).
63. HL MS: Forster to James Emerson (5 Mar. 1831). Mrs Forster's copy.
64. Harle, *op. cit.*, 51.
65. J. S. Mill, *Autobiography*, Library of Liberal Arts edn (New York, 1957), 111.
66. Sir C. G. Duffy, *Conversations with Carlyle* (1896), 84.
67. Renton, *op. cit.*, 158.
68. *Diaries*, I, 36 (25 May 1833).

CHAPTER TWO
Leigh Hunt

1. L. A. Brewer, *My Leigh Hunt Library: the Holograph Letters* (Iowa, 1938), 248 (29 Aug. 1859).
2. BL Add. MS 38109, f. 93 [c. 1830].
3. Leigh Hunt, *Christianism* (1832), iii.
4. BL Add. MS 38109, f. 93.
5. E. Blunden, *Leigh Hunt* (1930), 185.
6. Brewer, *op. cit.*, 246 (19 June 1849).
7. *Christianism*, iv.
8. K. J. Fielding, 'Leigh Hunt and Skimpole' *Dickensian*, LXIV (1968), 8.
9. BL Add. MS 38109, fos. 93–4. Forster's italics.
10. ABL MS (23 Mar. n.y.).
11. ABL MS: Forster to J. W. Parker (31 Dec. 1857). Hunt's contribution was published as 'The Tapiser's Tale', *Fraser's Mag.*, LVII (1858), 160–3.
12. W. M. Phelps and J. Forbes-Robertson, *The Life and Life-Work of Samuel Phelps* (1886), 375ff.; BL Add. MS 38110, fos. 295–6: Forster to Hunt (6 Jan. 1849).
13. Leigh Hunt, *Poetical Works*, ed. H. Milford (1923), liii.
14. HL MS [May/June 1845].
15. Houghton Library MS: Forster to Davis [n.d.].
16. Leigh Hunt, *Correspondence*, ed. T. Hunt (1862), I, 281 (6 Jan. [1840]). Leigh Hunt's italics.
17. BL Add. MS 38110, fos. 320–1 (11 June 1849).
18. BL Add. MS 38524, f. 156 (7 Feb. 1840).
19. *New Monthly Mag.*, XXXIV (1832), 288.

20. *Examiner* (9 Feb. 1840), 85.
21. *Ibid.* (25 Oct. 1840), 677.
22. *Ibid.* (16 July 1842), 452.
23. *Ibid.* (28 Apr. 1855), 261.
24. *Ibid.* (13 Apr. 1844), 227.
25. *New Monthly Mag.*, XXXIV (1832), 289.
26. *Examiner* (9 Feb. 1840), p. 85.
27. Brewer, *op. cit.*, 249 [n.d.].
28. BL Add. MS 38524, f. 19 (4 Aug. 1849).
29. *Correspondence*, ed. Hunt, II, 83 (3 Aug. 1846).
30. Brewer, *op. cit.*, 253 [c. 1840]. Forster's italics.
31. See FC MS 278.
32. *Correspondence*, ed. Hunt, II, 74 (9 Dec. 1845).
33. Brewer, *op. cit.*, 247 (1850).
34. *Correspondence*, ed. Hunt, II, 108 (10 Sept. 1847).
35. BL Add. MS 38110, f. 350 (18 Feb. 1850). Forster's italics.
36. *Correspondence*, ed. Hunt, I, 263 (20 June 1831).
37. *Ibid.*, I, 280 [n.d.].
38. *Ibid.*, I, 282 [n.d.].
39. *Ibid.*, II, 176 (3 May 1855).
40. *Ibid.*, II, 75 (16 Feb. [1845]).
41. *Ibid.*, II, 92 (25 Feb. [1848]). The line is from Hunt's poem 'Ode to the Sun'.
42. BL Add. MS 38110, f. 182 (20 Feb. 1847).
43. *Gentleman's Mag.*, 240 (1876), 380.
44. *Dickens*, I, 75.
45. HL MS: Mrs Forster's transcript of Forster's diary entry for 29 Aug. 1859.
46. *Correspondence*, ed. Hunt, II, 78 (13 Aug. [1845]).
47. *Critical Essays on the Performers of the London Theatres* (1807), 72.
48. *Ibid.*, 210.
49. *Examiner* (5 Mar. 1837), 149.
50. W. Elwin, 'John Forster', x–xi.
51. 'What is poetry?', *Imagination and Fancy* (new edn, 1878), 1.
52. *Critical Essays*, 1.
53. 'What is poetry?', 33. Hunt's italics.
54. *Examiner* (9 Feb. 1840), 85.
55. BL Add. MS 38110, f. 229 (4 Dec. 1847).
56. Berg Collection MS (7 Dec. [1847]).
57. Brewer, *op. cit.*, 251 [Feb. 1840].

CHAPTER THREE
Charles Lamb

1. [John Forster], 'Charles Lamb: his last words on Coleridge', *New Monthly Mag.*, XLIII (1835), 199.
2. Charles and Mary Lamb, *Letters*, ed. E. V. Lucas (1935), III, 318 [Aug. 1831].
3. *Ibid.*, III, 350–1 [Jan. 1833].
4. *Ibid.*, III, 318 [Aug. 1831].
5. E. V. Lucas, *The Life of Charles Lamb* (5th edn, 1921), II, 830.
6. *Letters*, ed. Lucas, III, 364 [Apr. 1833].
7. *Ibid.*, III, *passim.*
8. Lucas, *op. cit.*, II, 798.
9. 'Charles Lamb: his last words on Coleridge', *New Monthly Mag.*, XLIII (1835), 198–206. Quotations in this and the next two paragraphs are taken from this article.
10. P. Fitzgerald, *The Life, Letters and Writings of Charles Lamb* (1876), I, 234.
11. HL MS: J. B. Payne to Forster (13 Oct. 1865).
12. Fitzgerald, *op. cit.*, I, 244.
13. *Letters*, ed. Lucas, III, 350–1.
14. *John Forster By One of His Friends* (1903), 5.
15. *Landor*, I, 497; II, 243.
16. *Lamb's Criticism*, ed. E. M. W. Tillyard (1923), 34–51. Unless otherwise stated all quotations from Lamb are from this edition of the essay.
17. *The Life and Times of Oliver Goldsmith* (3rd edn, 1855), 402.
18. *New Monthly Mag.*, XLI (1834), 218.
19. *Examiner* (4 Feb. 1838), 69.
20. *Ibid.* (5 Mar. 1837), 149.
21. *Ibid.* (21 Oct. 1838), 662.
22. See e.g. the last parallel, above.
23. *Biographical Essays* (3rd edn, 1860), 172–3.
24. A. M. Eastman, *A Short History of Shakespearian Criticism* (New York, 1968), 90.
25. *Examiner* (11 Oct. 1835), 644.
26. *Ibid.*, (6 Nov. 1836), 711.
27. *Landor*, I, 268–9.
28. *Examiner* (11 Oct. 1835), 644.
29. *Works*, ed. P. P. Howe (1930), IV, 200.

30. Quoted in F. E. Halliday, *Shakespeare and His Critics* (1949), 251.
31. 'On the Artificial Comedy of the Last Century', *The Essays of Elia* (World's Classics edn, 1951), 213.

CHAPTER FOUR
Bulwer

1. *Our Recent Actors* (1890), 25.
2. M. Sadleir, *Bulwer: a Panorama* (1931), 289–91. See also *The Wellesley Index to Victorian Periodicals*, ed. W. E. Houghton, III (Toronto and London, 1979), 166.
3. Sadlier, *op. cit.*, 21. A useful short account of Bulwer's life at this time is S. J. Flower, *Bulwer-Lytton* (1973).
4. Earl of Lytton, *The Life of Edward Bulwer, First Lord Lytton* (1913), I, 373.
5. *Miscellaneous Prose Works* (1868), I, 89. Bulwer's essay first appeared in *Edinburgh Rev.*, LXXXVIII (1848), 193–225.
6. Lytton MS, attached to Letters and Papers, vol. 15. The full tribute is as follows:

   John Forster, Author of the Lives of Statesmen, Life of Oliver Goldsmith, etc – A most sterling Man – with an intellect at once massive & delicate – Few indeed have his strong practical sense – & sound judgment – fewer still unite with such qualities – his exquisite appreciation of latent beauties in literary art – Hence in ordinary life, there is no safer adviser; in literature, especially poetry – no more refined critic. A large heart naturally accompanies so masculine an understanding. He has the rare capacity for affection which embraces many friendships without loss of depth or warmth in one. Most of my literary contemporaries are his intimate companions & their jealousies of each other do not diminish their trust in him – He has served more than any living critic to establish reputations. Tennyson & Browning owed him much in their earlier career. Me, I think, he served in that way, less than any of his friends. But indeed I know of no critic to whom I have been much indebted for any position I hold in letters. In more private matters I am greatly indebted to his counsels – His reading is extensive. What faults he has lie on the surface – He may be irritable sometimes bluff to rudeness – But these are trifling irregularities in a nature solid & valuable as a block of gold 1869

   It is perhaps revealing of Bulwer's professional vanity that, even here, he will not admit receipt of Forster's literary advice so amply illustrated in this present chapter.
7. See, e.g. Edward Lytton Bulwer, *England and the English*, ed. S. Meacham (Chicago and London, 1970). The work was first published in 1833.
8. Yale MS (18 Feb. 1846).
9. ABL MS [n.d.].
10. Earl of Lytton, *op. cit.*, II, 325.
11. Lytton MS, Letters and Papers, vol. 15 (2 May 1848).
12. Earl of Lytton, *op. cit.*, II, 325.
13. HL MS (19 Jan. 1873).
14. Lytton MS, Letters and Papers, vol. 15 (27 Nov. 1838).
15. Earl of Lytton, *op. cit.*, II, 73–4.
16. C. H. Shattuck, *Bulwer and Macready* (Illinois, 1958), 250.
17. Lytton MS, Letters and Papers, vol. 15; Forster to Bulwer (26 Sept. 1856).
18. *Ibid.* (27 July 1860).
19. CVIII (July–October 1860), 499–547.
20. Lytton MS, Letters and Papers, vol. 15: (Apr.–Aug. 1860, *passim*).
21. See n. 6 above.
22. Lytton MS, Letters and Papers, vol. 15: Forster to Bulwer (16 Nov. 1836).
23. Lytton MS, Box 103: Spence and Hawks to Forster (5 June 1865); A. B. Harlan, *Owen Meredith: a Critical Biography of Robert, First Earl of Lytton* (New York, 1946), 208; Lytton MS, Letters and Papers, vol. 15 (16 Nov. 1836 and 30 Oct. 1865).
24. Flower, *op. cit., passim.*
25. ABL MS: Forster to W. J. Fox (13 Apr. 1840).

26. *Ibid.*
27. Lytton MS, Letters and Papers, vol. 15 (9 Apr. 1839). 'F' is Fonblanque.
28. R. H. Super, *Walter Savage Landor* (New York, 1954), 308.
29. Lytton MS, Letters and Papers, vol. 15 (21 Mar. 1839).
30. See Lytton MS, Box 61 *passim.*
31. Berg MS: Forster to George Cattermole (2 Oct. 1850).
32. HL MS: Robert Lytton to Forster (16 Jan. 1866).
33. Harlan, *op. cit.*, 121. Dr Harlan's fine study, based as it is on a thorough study of the Lytton MSS, is a major source of material for this section on Robert Lytton.
34. HL MS: Robert Lytton to Forster (26 Dec. [c. 1855]).
35. Lytton MS, Letters and Papers, vol. 15: Forster to Bulwer (2 May 1848).
36. J. H. Wiener, *The War of the Unstamped* (Ithaca, N.Y., 1969), 51, 59–62.
37. See K. J. Fielding, 'Dickens and the Royal Literary Fund – I', *TLS* (15 Oct. 1954), 664, and 'Dickens and the Royal Literary Fund – II', *ibid.* (22 Oct. 1954), 680.
38. Shattuck, *op. cit.*, 33.
39. Earl of Lytton, *op. cit.*, II, 465.
40. Forster was consulted about *Duchesse de la Vallière* (1837) and *Richelieu* (1839), and closely involved in the writing of *The Sea Captain* (1839), revised in 1868 as *The Rightful Heir*, *Money* (1840), *Not So Bad As We Seem* (1851), *Walpole* (1869), a play in rhyming couplets that was published but never performed, and three other plays, 'Cromwell', 'Brutus', and 'Oedipus', that were neither performed nor published.
41. Lytton MS, Letters and Papers, vol. 15: Forster to Bulwer (28 Nov. 1869).
42. Shattuck, *op. cit.*, 39–40 (22 Sept. 1836).
43. *Ibid.*, 41 (28 Sept. 1836).
44. Lytton MS, Letters and Papers, vol. 15 (6 Jan. 1851).
45. *Ibid.* (21 Jan. 1851).
46. *Ibid.* (13 Jan. 1851).
47. Shattuck, *op. cit.*, 164 (28 Sept. 1840).
48. Lytton MS, Letters and Papers, vol. 15: Forster to Bulwer (particularly, 30 Oct. 1849, 27 Nov. 1869, Easter Monday 1851, 28 Nov. 1869).
49. *Ibid.* (28 Jan. 1850).
50. See n. 6 above.
51. J. A. Sutherland, *Victorian Novelists and Publishers* (1976), 57.
52. Lytton MS, Letters and Papers, vol. 15: Forster to Bulwer (18 Sept. 1854).
53. *Ibid.* (20 Dec. 1859). Quotations in the preceding paragraph are also from this letter.
54. *Ibid.* (18 Sept. 1854). Quotations from *St. Stephen's* are from *The New Timon and St. Stephen's* (Leipzig, 1860).
55. *Ibid.* (29 Jan. 1860).
56. *Ibid.* (18 Sept. 1854).
57. *Ibid.* (20 Dec. 1859).
58. *Ibid.* (18 Sept. 1854). Forster's italics.
59. *Ibid.* (3 Jan. 1860). Forster's italics.
60. *Ibid.* (17 June 1848).
61. Lytton MS, Box 61: Louden to Forster [n.d.]; Forster to Bulwer [n.d.]; Thomas Chitty to Forster ([n.d.] and 28 July 1840).
62. Lytton MS, Letters and Papers, vol. 15: Forster to Bulwer (27 Apr. 1857).
63. Lytton MS, Box 61: Forster to Bulwer (17 Oct. 1872). Forster's italics.
64. Lytton MS, Letters and Papers, vol. 15: Forster to Bulwer (Dec. 1861 to Feb. 1862). Forster's italics.
65. 'The absorbing tyranny of everyday life: Bulwer Lytton's *A Strange Story*', *Nineteenth-Century Fiction*, XVI (1961–2), 1–16.
66. On Forster's letter of 23 Jan. 1862.
67. Quotations are from *A Strange Story* (Knebworth edn, [n.d.]), 432 and 422–6.
68. 'The publication of collected editions of Bulwer Lytton's novels', *Publishing History*, III (1978), 46,
69. Lytton MS, Letters and Papers, vol. 15 (1 Oct. 1850).
70. Lytton MS (*passim*); Berg MS: Forster to R. Bentley (6 Sept. 1838; [Feb. 1839]; 13 Feb. 1839). See also Sutherland, *op. cit.*, *passim.*

71. Shattuck, *op. cit.*, 139: Webster to Bulwer (9 Oct. 1839).
72. See *Pilgrim*, III, 587; Lytton MS, Letters and Papers, vol. 15: Forster to Bulwer (26 Oct. 1850).
73. Lytton MS, Letters and Papers, vol. 15: Forster to Bulwer (9 Sept. 1869).
74. *Ibid.* (14 Mar. 1870).
75. Berg MS: Forster to R. Bentley [Feb. 1839].
76. Lytton MS, Letters and Papers, vol. 15 [1838].
77. *Ibid.* (15 Dec. 1849).
78. Sutherland, *op. cit.*, 31–2.
79. Lytton MS, Letters and Papers, vol. 15 (1 Jan. 1850).
80. *Ibid.* (10 Sept. 1840).
81. Lytton MS, Box 61: Forster to Bulwer [1838]. Forster's italics.
82. Lytton MS, Letters and Papers, vol. 15 (10 Sept. 1840).
83. *Ibid.* (1 Oct. 1850).
84. ABL MS: Bulwer to Charles Kean (2 Oct. 1850).
85. Lytton MS, Letters and Papers, vol. 15 [1850].
86. *Ibid.* (21 Nov. 1848).
87. *Ibid.* (26 Apr. 1862). Forster's italics.
88. Morgan MS: Bulwer to Chapman & Hall [1848].
89. *Examiner* (4 Mar. 1848), 147.
90. *Ibid.* (31 Mar. 1860), 196.
91. *Ibid.* (12 Dec. 1846), 789.
92. *Ibid.* (20 Oct. 1849), 661.
93. *Ibid.*, 659.
94. *Ibid.* (17 Jan. 1841), 35.
95. *Ibid.* (31 Mar. 1839), 197.
96. Earl of Lytton, *op. cit.*, II, 98.
97. *Ibid.*, II, 34.
98. See n. 6 above.
99. See, e.g., Lytton MS, Letters and Papers, vol. 15: Forster to Bulwer (30 May 1842).
100. See, e.g., *Examiner* (24 July 1847), 466–7; (7 Aug. 1847), 497; (16 Dec. 1848), 801; (23 Dec. 1848), 817–18.
101. Lytton MS, Box 61 (13 Dec. 1858).
102. Lytton MS, Letters and Papers, vol. 15 (21 Nov. 1848).
103. *Ibid.* (25 Oct. 1849).
104. W. A. Clark Library MS: Bulwer to Forster (6 Jan. 1832). Bulwer's italics.
105. See, e.g., Bulwer's 'Dedicatory Epistle' to *Zanoni* (1845), in which Bulwer writes of his novel: 'I love it not the less because it has been little understood, and superficially judged by the common herd.' (Knebworth edn, vi–vii.)
106. Quotations are from *Dramatic Works* (new edn, [n.d.]), 421, 416.

CHAPTER FIVE
Macready

1. *Diaries*, I, 71–2, 79 (20 Oct. and 20 Nov. 1833).
2. Basic biographical information about Macready is taken from or can be obtained from A. S. Downer, *The Eminent Tragedian: William Charles Macready* (Cambridge, Mass., and London, 1966).
3. Princeton University Library MS: Forster to Macready (3 Nov. 1834).
4. Berg MS: Forster to T. N. Talfourd (29 Apr. 1838).
5. *Examiner* (26 May 1849), 422, and (2 June 1849), 339.
6. Berg MS: Forster to Talfourd (29 Apr. 1838).
7. Fales Library MS: Forster to George Cattermole (7 May 1836).
8. *Diaries*, II, 92 (29 Oct. 1840).
9. Yale MS: Forster to Phelps (29 Jan. 1848).
10. *Diaries*, II, 100 (26 Nov. 1840).
11. ABL MS: Forster to W. J. Fox (3 Dec. 1840).
12. *Diaries*, II, 449–64, *passim* (Feb.–Apr. 1850).
13. Berg MS: Forster to Robert Browning (15 July 1858).
14. *Ibid.* (17 Apr. 1860). Forster's italics.
15. *Ibid.* (28 Dec. 1860). Forster's italics.
16. Morgan Library MS: Dickens to Macready (28 Sept. 1863).
17. *Diaries*, I, 72 (20 Oct. 1833).
18. *Ibid.*, 445 (27 Feb. 1838).
19. *Ibid.*, I, 97, (29 Jan. 1834).
20. *Ibid.*, II, 478 (1 Dec. 1850).
21. *Ibid.*, II, 481 (11, 12 Dec. 1850). Macready's italics.
22. *Ibid.*, I, 263 (25 Nov. 1835). Macready's italics.
23. ABL MS: Forster to W. J. Fox [n.d.].
24. *Diaries*, II, 295 (12 May 1845).

25. *Ibid.*, II, 300 (1 Aug. 1845); and see Downer, *op. cit.*, 275.
26. *Diaries*, II, 300 (7 Aug. 1845).
27. This paragraph and the next two are based on ABL MSS: Forster to Manby (14 July 1849 to 30 Oct. 1850), plus a copy of Manby to Forster (29 July 1849).
28. *Diaries*, II, 60–1 (21 May 1840).
29. S. C. Hall, *Retrospect of a Long Life* (1883), II, 259.
30. (31 Jan. 1842), 5.
31. Quoted in G. H. Lewes, 'Macready', in *Victorian Dramatic Criticism*, selected and introduced by G. Rowell (1971), 84.
32. *Ibid.*
33. *Examiner* (4 Feb. 1838), 69.
34. *Diaries*, I, 251 (1 Oct. 1835).
35. *Ibid.*, II, 306 (13 Oct. 1845).
36. *Examiner* (18 Mar. 1838), 165.
37. *Ibid.* (4 Feb. 1838), 70.
38. *Ibid.* (4 Oct. 1835), 629.
39. *Ibid.* (11 Oct. 1835), 644.
40. *Ibid.* (25 Oct. 1835), 676.
41. *Op. cit.*, xvi.
42. *Op. cit.*, 80.
43. 'Macready as Macbeth', *Victorian Dramatic Criticism*, ed. Rowell, 73.
44. Quotations here and in the preceding paragraph are from 'Mr Macready', *Examiner* (22 Feb. 1851), 117–18. Forster's italics.
45. pp. 76–7. Downer's italics.
46. F. Archer, *An Actor's Notebook* [n.d.], 158–9.
47. *Examiner* (26 Mar. 1842), 197.
48. *Ibid.* (8 Oct. 1837), 647.
49. *Ibid.* (26 Mar. 1842), 197.
50. FC (Aux). MS: Forster to Mrs Bennett (20 June 1827).
51. *Examiner* (8 Oct. 1837), 647.
52. *Ibid.* (26 Mar. 1842), 197.
53. 'Covent Garden and Drury Lane', *Examiner* (8 Oct. 1837), 646–7.
54. 'Mr Macready', 118.
55. *Examiner* (8 Mar. 1851), 152.
56. *Ibid.* (6 Nov. 1836), 711.
57. *Ibid.* (30 Oct. 1836), 695.
58. *Ibid.* (14 Jan. 1838), 20–1.
59. I, 146 (31 May 1834).
60. pp. 166–7.
61. *Diaries, passim.*
62. *Ibid.*, II, 33 (30 Nov. 1839). Macready's italics.
63. *Ibid.*, I, 478 (26 Nov. 1838).
64. *Ibid.*, 339 (25 May 1846). Macready's italics.
65. *Ibid.*, II, 392 (28 May 1848). Macready's italics.
66. *Ibid.*, I, 324 (3 June 1836).

CHAPTER SIX
Literature's Friend

1. *Op. cit.*, 50.
2. FC (Aux): Forster to Mrs Bennett [n.d.].
3. ABL MS [1842]. Forster's italics. See also ABL MSS, Forster to W. J. Fox (16 Jan. 1841 and 11 Sept. 1841), for further evidence of Forster's church attendance.
4. Berg MS (22 March [1842]).
5. ABL MS ([1840]).
6. HL MS: memoir by Henry E. Rawlins, Forster's servant and general factotum.
7. ABL MS (15 May 1855).
8. FC MS: Maclise to Forster (13 Oct. 1868).
9. R. H. Horne, 'John Forster; his early life and friendships', *Temple Bar*, XLVI (1876), 497.
10. Jane Carlyle, *Letters to Her Family*, ed. L. Huxley (1924), 169–70.
11. Horne, *op. cit.*, 493.
12. *Pilgrim*, IV (1977), 14.
13. *Dickens*, I, 159.
14. 'How I first met Charles Dickens', *Press News* (Dec. 1905), 27, 29.
15. Quoted in *Jarndyce Miscellany*, Catalogue xiv (1977), Item 423.
16. Horne, *op. cit.*, 501–2.
17. Thackeray, *Letters and Private Papers*, ed. G. N. Ray (1945), II, 248.
18. HL MS: Letitia Landon to Pickering [n.d.]. The preceding part of this paragraph is based on the *DNB* entry and the 'L.E.L.' letters held by the Morgan Library and the Huntington Library.
19. *Diaries*, I, 173 (18 Aug. 1834); Charles and Mary Lamb, *Letters*, ed. E. V. Lucas (1935), III, 350–1.
20. R. Renton, *John Forster and his Friendships* (1912), 10.
21. R. R. Madden, *The Literary Life and Correspondence of the Countess of Blessington* (1855), II, 395.

22. *Diaries*, I, 262 (20 Nov. 1835).
23. M. Sadleir, *Bulwer: a Panorama* (1931), 426.
24. B. Jerrold, 'John Forster', *Gentleman's Mag.*, XVI (1876), 318–19.
25. *Ibid.*
26. D. Maclise and W. Maginn, *A Gallery of Illustrious Literary Characters*, ed. William Bates (1873), 113.
27. *Diaries*, I, 262 (20 Nov. 1835).
28. HL MS: 'L.E.L.' to S. L. Blanchard [Aug.–Oct. 1838].
29. Maclise and Maginn, *op. cit.*, 113. See also Berg MS: F. Mahony ('Father Prout') to R. Bentley (3 Mar. [1866]).
30. (9 Aug. 1845), 500.
31. *Examiner* (19 Aug. 1848), 532.
32. BL Add. MS 38110, f. 268 (16 Sept. 1848).
33. HL MS [n.d.]. Forster's italics.
34. Lytton MS, Letters and Papers, vol. 15 [1849]. Forster's italics.
35. *Ibid.* (15 Dec. 1849). See my article, 'John Forster at the Mannings' execution', *Dickensian*, LXVII (1971), 12–15.
36. Mrs Gaskell, *Letters*, ed. J. A. V. Chapple and A. Pollard (1966), 83.
37. D. Parker and M. Slater, 'The Gladys Storey Papers', *Dickensian*, LXXVI (1980), 4.
38. HL MSS (16 Mar. 1839; 7 Nov. 1843).
39. ABL MSS (19 Feb. 1845; 29 Aug. 1848).
40. *Diaries*, I, 279 (24 Feb. 1836).
41. *Pilgrim*, IV (1977), 246.
42. HL MS (transcribed by Mrs Forster).
43. Lytton MS, Letters and Papers, vol. 15 (24 Sept. 1853).
44. For this paragraph see, respectively: ABL MS [6 Nov. 1839]; HL MS: Rawlins's memoir, and Folger MS: Forster to Mrs Kemble (15 May 1852); R. and E. Garnett, *The Life of W. J. Fox* (1910), 284; E. Johnson, *Charles Dickens: His Tragedy and Triumph* (1953), II, 736; Lytton MS, Letters and Papers, vol. 15: Forster to Bulwer (8 Nov. 1851); Manchester Public Library MS: Forster to Sir John Potter (1 June 1852) (dictated); Thackeray, *Letters and Private Papers*, ed. Ray, III, 231, 341; Berg MS: Forster to R. Bentley (12 Sept. 1852); Houghton Library, Harvard University MS: Forster to C. C. Felton (3 June 1853), Forster's italics; *Pilgrim*, IV, 285.
45. HL MS: Rawlins's memoir.
46. R. L. Patten, *Dickens and His Publishers* (1978), 464.
47. For this paragraph see, respectively: *Diaries*, I, 98; R. H. Barham, *The Garrick Club* (1896), 30; Johnson, *op. cit.*, II, 610; Leigh Hunt, *Correspondence*, ed. T. Hunt (1862), II, 90; BL Add. MS 38109, f. 255: Forster to Hunt (11 Aug. 1839), for Holland House; *Diaries*, I, 326; Jerrold, *op. cit.*, 317.
48. *Dickens and Crime* (1962), 178.
49. Lytton MS, Letters and Papers, vol. 15 (21 Jan. 1850).
50. C. Tennyson, *Alfred Tennyson* (1949), 244.
51. *Letters and Private Papers*, ed. Ray, III, 127.
52. *Diaries*, II, 75 (20 Aug. 1840).
53. Barham, *op. cit.*, 30–1. Text follows the MS front-piece.
54. For this paragraph see, respectively: 'Theatre Royal Little Pedlington', *The Times* (5 Apr. 1837), 7; *Diaries*, I, 427 (24 Nov. 1837); Folger MSS (12 June 1832, 21 Jan. 1841, 1 May 1846); *Pilgrim*, III, 213n.; G. N. Ray, *Thackeray: The Uses of Adversity* (1955), 287. 'JL' is John Leech.
55. (3 June 1848), 375–6. For Forster's reply: *Literary Gazette* (17 June 1848), 407–8.
56. *Ibid.* (29 July 1848), 505. Prior's italics.
57. ABL MS: Forster to Peter Cunningham (2 Feb. 1854).

CHAPTER SEVEN
Friendship's Variations 1834–55

1. To this point the paragraph is based on HL MS: Rawlins's memoir.
2. For Procter, see Charles and Mary Lamb, *Letters*, ed. E. V. Lucas (1935), III, 399, and R. W. Armour, *Barry Cornwall: a Biography of Bryan Waller Procter* (Boston, Mass., 1935), 105 and *passim*; see also p. 82, above.

3. For Cunningham, see ABL MSS: Forster to Peter Cunningham (21 Sept. 1847, 20 Mar. 1850, 25 Nov. 1853).
4. For Knowles, see *Diaries*, I, 184, 411, 456, 464.
5. B. Jerrold, *The Life and Remains of Douglas Jerrold* (1859), 187.
6. For Lady Blessington, see Berg MS: Lady Blessington to Forster (9 Oct. 1848) (copy), and M. Sadleir, *Blessington-D'Orsay: a Masquerade* (1933), 284.
7. Bristol Central Library MS: Forster to Thomas Hood (14 Aug. 1843).
8. W. M. Phelps and J. Forbes-Robertson, *The Life and Life-Work of Samuel Phelps* (1886), 381, 384; Yale University Library MS: Forster to Samuel Phelps (27 Nov. 1848).
9. Berg MS: Forster to R. Bentley (10 June 1846).
10. D. A. Wilson, *Carlyle at His Zenith (1848–53)* (1927), 133.
11. Berg MS: Forster to Richard Bentley (12 Sept. 1852).
12. Berg MS: Forster to T. N. Talfourd (26 Sept. 1852).
13. For Morley, see H. S. Solly, *The Life of Henry Morley*, LL.D. (1898), *passim*, and 154.
14. C. Tennyson, *Alfred Tennyson* (1949), 176.
15. In the *True Sun* (19 Jan. 1833), 3.
16. Lincoln Central Library MS: Tennyson to Forster [1838].
17. Yale University Library MS (18 Feb. 1846).
18. *Examiner* (8 Jan. 1848), 21.
19. Herodotus Smith [Francis Espinasse], 'The Examiner', *Critic* (1 Sept. 1852), 442.
20. Lincoln Central Library MS. Tennyson to Forster (22 June 1850).
21. *Ibid.* (24 Apr. 1851).
22. Yale University Library MS (9 Dec. 1854).
23. *Examiner* (10 Jan. 1846), 20.
24. Yale University Library MS. This letter to Tennyson undermines all previous accounts of the 'New Timon' incident by demonstrating, with some conclusiveness, that though Forster appears to have chosen *Punch*, he was carrying out and, of course, encouraging for reasons of principle, Tennyson's own desire to publish. Further and more importantly, 'The New Timon, and the Poets' was published with Tennyson's concurrence and not because Forster took matters into his own hands: see J. B. Jones, 'Tennyson, Forster, and the *Punch* connection', *Victorian Periodicals Newsletter*, II (1978), 118–21; J. A. Davies, '"Tennyson, Forster, and the *Punch* connection": a reply', *Victorian Periodicals Rev.*, XIII (1980), 64–6; Jones, 'The *Punch* connection II; or, *et tu*, Tennyson?', *ibid.*, 66–9; Davies, '"Tennyson, Forster, and the *Punch* connection": again', *ibid.*, 103–5.
25. (24 Mar. 1849), 180. This was later subtitled, 'After Reading a Life and Letters'.
26. Respectively: (31 Jan. 1852), 67, (7 Feb. 1852), 85, *ibid.*, 86, (14 Feb. 1852), 99.
27. 'Suggested by Reading an Article in a Newspaper', l. 87.
28. (9 Dec. 1854), 780.
29. Houghton Library, Harvard University MS (4 Feb. [1852]).
30. Lincoln Central Library MS: Tennyson to Forster (7 Dec. 1854). Emily Tennyson's postscript.
31. Lincoln Central Library MS: Tennyson to Forster (6 Dec. 1854). Emily Tennyson's postscript.
32. Lincoln Central Library MSS: corrected proofs.
33. Lincoln Central Library MS: Tennyson to Forster (9 Dec. 1854).
34. Yale University MS (9 Dec. 1854).
35. Charles Tennyson, *op. cit.*, 288.
36. See *Pilgrim*, III, *passim.*
37. *Ibid.*, III, 335, 343; *Diaries*, II, 185; E. Johnson, *Charles Dickens: His Tragedy and Triumph* (1953), I, 435–6.
38. FC MS: Longfellow to Forster (28 Feb. 1843).
39. Houghton Library, Harvard University MS: Forster to Longfellow (4 June 1843).
40. XXXII (1844), 291–324.
41. Houghton Library, Harvard University MS: Forster to Longfellow (18 Nov. 1851); FC MS: Longfellow to Forster (7 Dec. 1851).

42. W. Gérin, *Elizabeth Gaskell* (1976), 82.
43. A. B. Hopkins, *Elizabeth Gaskell: Her Life and Works* (1952), 87.
44. ABL MS: Forster to Peter Cunningham (14 Jan. 1854).
45. Respectively: Mrs Gaskell, *Letters*, ed. J. A. V. Chapple and A. Pollard (1966), 92, 829; *Examiner* (20 May 1854), 309–10.
46. Brotherton Library, University of Leeds, transcript (19 Feb. 1851).
47. Mrs Gaskell, *Letters*, ed. Chapple and Pollard, 205.
48. *Ibid.*, 281.
49. Brotherton Library, University of Leeds, transcript (21 Nov. 1853).
50. *Dickens*, II, 423; III, 33.
51. Brotherton Library, University of Leeds, transcripts (21 Nov. 1853).
52. *Ibid.* (21 Dec. 1852).
53. *Ibid.* (17 Jan. 1853).
54. *Ibid.* (13 Mar. 1852).
55. *Ibid.* (7 Dec. 1851).
56. *Letters and Private Papers*, ed. G. N. Ray (1945), II, 252.
57. Respectively: R. W. Emerson, *Letters*, ed. R. L. Rush (New York, 1939), IV, 55, 66; L. Stevenson, *Dr. Quicksilver: The Life of Charles Lever* (1939), 205; FC MS: Longfellow to Forster (28 Feb. 1843).
58. *Pilgrim*, III, 515n.
59. Hopkins, *op. cit.*, 87. 'Lily' was Mrs Gaskell.
60. A. Waugh, *A Hundred Years of Publishing* (1930), 27, 29.
61. R. Gettman, *A Victorian Publisher* (1960), 191.
62. Waugh, *op. cit.*, 70. Chapman & Hall's early records, on which Waugh presumably based his remarks, were destroyed during the Second World War.
63. ABL MS (4 Dec. 1854).
64. Respectively: *Diaries*, I, 348; ABL MS: Forster to W. J. Fox [Sept. 1838].
65. *Pilgrim*, III, 527ff.
66. *Ibid.*, II, 39.
67. For Blanchard, see L. A. Brewer, *My Leigh Hunt Library: the Holograph Letters* (Iowa, 1938), 243; Lytton MS, Letters and Papers, vol. 15: Forster to Bulwer (15 Mar. 1845); *Pilgrim*, IV, 305. *Pilgrim*, IV, 275, has a good account of the efforts of Blanchard's friends.
68. Respectively: D. A. Wilson, *Carlyle on Cromwell and Others (1837–48)* (1925), 166; C. Knight, *Passages from a Working Life* (1865), III, 176; D. A. Wilson, *Carlyle at Three-Score-and-Ten (1853–65)* (1929), 161.
69. Dickens, *Speeches*, ed. K. J. Fielding (1960), 40, 123, 137, 138.
70. Respectively: *Pilgrim*, III, 264n.; *Diaries*, II, 485ff.; R. and E. Garnett, *The Life of W. J. Fox* (1910), 223; W. Jerdan, *Autobiography* (1852–3), 368–74.
71. *Diaries*, I, 505.
72. *Diaries*, II, 34; Knight, *op. cit.*, III, 38.
73. Houghton Library, Harvard University MS: Forster to J. P. Collier (3 Feb. 1852).
74. *Dickens*, II, 363; R. B. Knowles, *The Life of James Sheridan Knowles* (1872), 136.
75. *Examiner* (28 Apr. 1849), 267.
76. ABL MSS: Forster to Peter Cunningham, *passim*; R. Renton, *John Forster and his Friendships* (1912), 120–3.
77. Wilson, *Carlyle on Cromwell and Others*, 99, 337. Forster's work for the London Library led to his friendship with Carlyle. A fuller account is given in Chapter 12, below.
78. See pp. 43–4, above.
79. Johnson, *op. cit.*, I, 383–4.
80. *Pilgrim*, III, 491–2.
81. Respectively: Johnson, *op. cit.*, I, 571, 572; *Dickens*, II, 340ff., 363.
82. For a full account of Forster's acting see A. Burton, 'Forster on the stage', *Dickensian*, LXV (1974), 171–84.
83. *Diaries*, II, 304, 365.
84. C. and M. Cowden Clarke, *Recollections of Writers* (1878), 335.
85. 'John Forster', *Temple Bar*, 498.
86. R. and E. Garnett, 200.
87. W. Elwin, 'John Forster', *Forster Collection: a Catalogue of the Printed Books* (1888), xxvii.
88. B. Jerrold, 'John Forster', *Gentleman's Mag.*, XVI (1876), 313.
89. Johnson, *op. cit.*, II, 723–4. For Forster and the Royal Literary Fund, see [K. J. Fielding], 'Dickens and the Royal Literary Fund – I',

TLS (15 Oct. 1954), 664, and 'Dickens and the Royal Literary Fund – II', *ibid.* (22 Oct. 1954), 680.

90. *Dickens*, II, 77.
91. S. M. Ellis, *William Harrison Ainsworth and His Friends* (1911), I, 341.
92. *Pilgrim*, I, 231n.
93. Ellis, *op. cit.*, I, 300.
94. *Ibid.*, I, 330.
95. *Pilgrim*, I, 637.
96. Ellis, *op. cit.*, I, 346ff.
97. *Pilgrim*, I, 530.
98. HL MS [Apr. 1839].
99. *Pilgrim*, I, 531n.
100. Lytton MS, Letters and Papers, vol. 15 (3 Feb. 1840).
101. Berg MS: Forster to R. Bentley (3 June 1839).
102. *Pilgrim*, I, 538n.
103. (3 Nov. 1839), 691.
104. Respectively: *Pilgrim*, II, 170–1; HL MS (27 Jan. 1842); HL MS [Mar. 1842]; HL MS (14 Jan. 1843); Manchester Public Libraries MS (31 May 1845).
105. Ellis, *op. cit.*, II, 283.
106. *Diaries*, II, 488. See *Quarterly Rev.* LXXXVIII (Dec.–Mar. 1850–1), 197–247.
107. *Examiner* (18 Jan. 1851), 33–4.
108. *Diaries*, I, 159.
109. G. N. Ray, *Thackeray: The Age of Wisdom* (1958), 87.
110. Berg MS (31 Oct. [1855]).
111. Ray, *Thackeray: the Uses of Adversity*, 321.
112. Berg MS: Thackeray to Forster (31 Oct. [1855]).
113. *Letters and Private Papers*, ed. Ray, II, 815.
114. *Ibid.*, III, 47.
115. Ray, *Thackeray: the Uses of Adversity*, 321.
116. *Letters and Private Papers*, ed. Ray, II, 296.
117. K. J. Fielding, 'Thackeray and the "Dignity of Literature" – I', *TLS* (19 Sept. 1958), 536.
118. (5 Jan. 1850), 2.
119. See Ray, *Thackeray: the Age of Wisdom*, 137.
120. *Examiner* (19 Jan. 1850), 35.
121. *Letters and Private Papers*, ed. Ray, II, 781.
122. *Examiner* (5 July 1851), 422.
123. (12 July 1851), 433–4.
124. *Letters and Private Papers*, ed. Ray, II, 792.
125. HL MS. Mrs Forster's copy.
126. ABL MS (1 June 1853).
127. Renton, *op. cit.*, 123.
128. Collins, *op. cit.*, 178.
129. ABL MS (25 Feb. 1854).
130. Lytton MS, Letters and Papers, vol. 15 (9 July 1850).
131. HL MS: Rawlins's memoir.
132. *Ibid.*
133. See BL Add. MSS 34624–6 *passim.*
134. T. B. Macaulay, *Letters*, ed. Thomas Pinney, IV (1977), 329.
135. I, vii.
136. ABL MS: Forster to Peter Cunningham (30 Nov. 1852).
137. For Crossley, see FC MS: James Crossley to Forster [1837]; Ellis, *op. cit.*, I, 339, 341, 344, 416–17; Manchester Public Library MSS: Forster to Crossley, *passim.*
138. ABL MS (18 Feb. 1854).
139. ABL MS (14 Jan. 1854).
140. Robert Lytton, *Personal and Literary Letters*, ed. Lady Betty Balfour (1906), I, 18.
141. Houghton Library, Harvard University (18 Nov. 1851).
142. Lytton MS, Letters and Papers, vol. 15 (6 Jan. 1854).
143. Elwin, *op. cit.*, xiv.
144. HL MS: Forster's Diary. Mrs Forster's copy.
145. *Ibid.*
146. HL MS: copy of extracts from James Whiteside's diaries.

CHAPTER EIGHT
Withdrawal and Return

1. BL Add. MS 28510, f. 56. The phrase is one of Forster's corrections of a biographical notice due to appear in 1860.
2. Here, and elsewhere in this chapter, information on the Lunacy Commission is taken from K. Jones, *Lunacy, Law, and Conscience 1744–1845* (1955) and *idem*, *Mental Health and Social Policy 1845–1959* (1960).

3. BL Add. MS 38524, fos. 77–8: Forster to Leigh Hunt (9 Apr. 1857).
4. E. Johnson, *Charles Dickens: His Tragedy and Triumph* (1953), II, 857.
5. R. Renton, *John Forster and his Friendships* (1912), 148.
6. ABL MS: Forster to Peter Cunningham (30 Nov. 1852).
7. Renton, *op. cit.*, 94. Boxall's sketch appears opposite p. 96.
8. NLS MSS: Jane Welsh Carlyle to Mrs Forster, *passim.*
9. *Op. cit.*, 94.
10. A. B. Harlan and J. L. Harlan (eds.), *Letters from Owen Meredith (Robert, First Earl of Lytton) to Robert and Elizabeth Barrett Browning* (Waco, Texas [1936]), 172. Lytton's italics.
11. L. and E. Hanson, *Necessary Evil* (1952), 472.
12. NLS MS. Jane Welsh Carlyle to Mrs Forster ([30 Aug. 1864]). Jane Carlyle's italics.
13. NLS MS ([19 Dec. 1861]). Jane Carlyle's italics.
14. NLS MS (30 Oct. 1862).
15. Berg MS (20 Oct. 1856).
16. Johnson, *op. cit.*, II, 864.
17. *Landor*, I, 325.
18. Lincoln Central Library MS: Emily Tennyson to Forster (31 Oct. 1858). See also J. S. Hagen, *Tennyson and His Publishers* (1979), 108–9.
19. For this paragraph, see Dickens, *Speeches*, 227–8, K. J. Fielding, 'Dickens and the Royal Literary Fund – II', *TLS* (22 Oct. 1854), *passim*, and *idem*, 'Dickens and the Royal Literary Fund – 1858', *Rev. English Studies*, n.s. VI (1955), 383–94.
20. K. J. Fielding and G. R. Grubb, 'New Letters from Charles Dickens to John Forster', *Boston Univ. Studies in English*, II (1956), 142.
21. Lytton MS, Letters and Papers, vol. xv. Forster to Bulwer (12 Jan. 1860).
22. K. J. Fielding, 'Thackeray and the "Dignity of Literature" – II', *TLS* (26 Sept. 1958), 552.
23. Lytton MS. Letters and Papers, vol. 15: Forster to Bulwer (12 Jan. 1860; 20 Jan. 1860).
24. Lytton MS, Letters and Papers, vol. 15: Forster to Bulwer (16 Feb. 1862; 18 Feb. 1862).
25. Dickens, *Speeches*, ed. K. J. Fielding (1960), 349–52; *Dickens*, III, 450.
26. See above, p. 485, for Forster's post-1855 contributions. Henry Morley's much-quoted remark that, after resigning as editor, Forster 'never wrote another line' in the *Examiner* ('A Biographical Sketch of Mr. Forster', *The Dyce and Forster Collections, Handbook* (1880), 69) is simply not true. For a reference to proof-vetting, see Lytton MS, Letters and Papers, vol. 15: Forster to Bulwer (10 Feb. 1865).
27. *Dickens*, III, 145.
28. Thackeray, *Letters and Private Papers*, ed. G. N. Ray (1945), IV, 58, 61.
29. ABL MS (10 June [1857]).
30. R. and E. Garnett, *The Life of W. J. Fox* (1910), 333. See also ABL MS: Forster to Mrs Bridell (3 Feb. 1866).
31. R. H. Super, *Walter Savage Landor* (New York, 1954), *passim.*
32. ABL MS: Forster to Peter Cunningham (21 Feb. 1857).
33. A. B. Harlan, *Owen Meredith: a Critical Biography of Robert, First Earl of Lytton* (New York, 1946), 135.
34. BL Add. MS 38898, f. 175 (17 May 1863).
35. Johnson, *op. cit.*, II, 556–7.
36. *Ibid.*, II, 867.
37. A. Waugh, *A Hundred Years of Publishing* (1930), 123.
38. *Letters and Private Papers*, ed. Ray, III, 552.
39. Lincoln Central Library MS (18 Jan. [1856]).
40. Lytton MS, Letters and Papers, vol. 15 (9 Dec. 1862).
41. Respectively: ABL MS (14 Aug. 1857); ABL MS: Forster to Peter Cunningham (22 May 1857); A. B. and J. L. Harlan (eds.), *op. cit.*, 178; ABL MS: Forster to Peter Cunningham (19 Dec. 1857); ABL MS: Forster to Mr Ellis (4 Jan. 1860); Lytton MS, Letters and Papers, vol. 15 (27 Sept. 1862); *ibid.* (9 Dec. 1862); *The Times* (11 May 1876), 11.

42. Lytton MS, Letters and Papers, vol. 15: Forster to Bulwer (13 Dec. 1863).
43. Whitwell Elwin, *Some XVIII Century Men of Letters*, ed. W. Elwin (1902), I, 251.
44. P. Fitzgerald, *The Life of Charles Dickens as Revealed in His Writings* (1905), I, 245.
45. B. Jerrold, 'John Forster', *Gentleman's Mag.*, XVI (1876), 316.
46. Quoted in Dickens, *Speeches*, ed. Fielding, 227–8.
47. HL MS: Forster to W. B. Jerrold (1 Dec. 1858).
48. HL MS: entry for 12 Oct. 1860. Mrs Forster's copy.
49. ABL MS (1 Jan. 1858).
50. FC MS (10 July 1859).
51. Yale University Library MS: Forster to Mr Broderip (8 July 1857).
52. Pforzheimer Library MS: Forster to Panizzi (11 July 1859).
53. FC MS: Carlyle to Forster (10 July 1859).
54. Fitzgerald, *op. cit.*, I, 243.
55. ABL MS (11 Aug. 1861).
56. Free Library of Philadelphia MS (5 Mar. 1862).
57. Lytton MS, Letters and Papers, vol. 15: Forster to Bulwer (9 Dec. 1862).
58. BL Add. MS 43901, f. 194: Forster to C. W. Dilke (20 Dec. 1862).
59. Lytton MS, Box 61: Forster to Bulwer (14 Mar. 1859).
60. BL Add. MS 38986. f. 381: Forster to A. H. Layard (11 June 1860).
61. ABL MS: Forster to Spring Rice (5 Oct. 1862).
62. Lytton MS, Letters and Papers, vol. 15: Forster to Bulwer (5 May 1860).
63. D. Woolley, 'Forster's *Swift*', *Dickensian*, LXX (1974), 191–204.
64. E. B. de Fonblanque, *The Life and Labours of Albany Fonblanque* (1874), 64.
65. HL MS: Forster's diary. Mrs Forster's copy. Nothing came of such consideration.
66. Lytton MS, Letters and Papers, vol. 15 (2 June 1864). Forster's italics.
67. For this paragraph, respectively: *ibid.*: Forster to Bulwer (31 Dec. 1866); S. Nowell-Smith, 'Carlyle and the London Library', *English Libraries 1800–1850* (1958), 76; FC MS 366: Longfellow to Forster (12, 20 July, 10 Aug., 6 Sept., 11 Oct. 1868). And see C. Gohdes, 'Longfellow and his authorized British publishers', *PMLA*, LV (1940), 1165–79; FC MS 366: Longfellow to Forster (12 July 1868); ABL MS (28 Jan. 1865); ABL MS (16 Nov. 1869); Fitzgerald, *op. cit.*, *passim.*
68. HL MS: Forster to Charles Kent (20 Oct. 1867).
69. ABL MS: Forster to Carlyle (26 May 1867).
70. Lytton MS, Letters and Papers, vol. 15 (9 Apr. 1868).
71. Morgan MS, Dickens to Macready (27 Dec. 1868). Dickens's italics.
72. Fales Library MS: Forster to John Bruce (12 Dec. 1865).
73. ABL MS: Forster to Carlyle (4 Dec. 1867).
74. Lytton MS, Letters and Papers, vol. 15: Forster to Bulwer (21 Sept. 1868).
75. HL MS: Georgina Hogarth to Annie Fields (12 Nov. 1869).
76. Lytton MS, Letters and Papers, vol. 15 (10 Feb. 1865).
77. NLS MS (18 Dec. 1869).
78. *Dickens*, III, 277.
79. ABL MS: Forster to Carlyle (11 Oct. 1868).
80. Berg MS.
81. HL MS (8 May 1869).
82. Lytton MS, Letters and Papers, vol. 15 (31 Dec. 1866). Forster's italics. For an account of these events see J. Y. LeBourgeois, 'Swinburne, Lord Lytton, and John Forster', *Notes & Queries*, XIX (1972), 417–19.
83. ABL MS (19 Jan. 1867).
84. Houghton Library, Harvard University MS (29 Mar. 1869).
85. ABL MS: Forster to Carlyle (16 May 1869).
86. Houghton Library, Harvard University MS (22 June, 1870).
87. Free Library of Philadelphia MS: Mrs Forster to Mrs Tindall (31 July [1870]).
88. ABL MS (11 July 1870).
89. Free Library of Philadelphia MS: Mrs Forster to Mrs Tindall (8 July [1870]). Mrs Forster's italics.

90. Elwin, *op. cit.*, I, 280–1.
91. NLS MS (22 Oct. 1870).
92. NLS MS: Forster to J. H. Burton (17 Dec. 1870).
93. Lytton MS, Box 61 (4 Dec. 1870).
94. For the deaths of friends: Houghton Library MSS: Forster to Norton (23 Feb. 1872), Forster to Longfellow (7 May 1873); ABL MS: Forster to Carlyle (6 Oct. 1874).
95. For Forster's health see HL MS: Georgina Hogarth to Annie Fields (13 May 1874); W. H. Dunn, 'Carlyle's last letters to Froude', *Twentieth Century*, CLX (1956), 242; NLS MS: Forster to J. H. Burton (14 Dec. 1875).
96. ABL MS (5 Nov. 1874).
97. For Forster's enemies, see T. W. Reid, *The Life, Letters and Friendships of Richard Monckton Milnes, First Lord Houghton* (1890), II, 249–50; J. B. Castieau, 'The fictions of Forster', *Dickensian*, XII (1916), 268.
98. HL MS: Robert Lytton to [Fleetwood Wilson] (10 Dec. 1872).
99. For Forster's marriage, see ABL MSS, *passim*. In this paragraph I quote from Forster's letters to Carlyle of 29 Aug. 1870, 10 Aug. 1869, 12 Dec. 1872, 23 July 1869, and 10 Oct. 1874, respectively.
100. ABL MS: Henry Forster Morley to J. Lee Harlan (4 Jan. 1938).
101. ABL MS: Forster to Mrs Morley (28 June 1872).
102. FC MS 184: C. L. Dodgson to Forster (13 Jan. 1872).
103. Lytton MS, Box 61: Forster to Bulwer (30 Jan. 1872).
104. Houghton Library, Harvard University MS: Forster to Mr Agassiz (18 May 1869).
105. *The Times* (6 May 1872), 10.
106. HL MSS: Lord Shaftesbury to Forster, *passim*.
107. ABL MS: Forster to Carlyle (21 Aug. 1871). Forster's italics.
108. Houghton Library, Harvard University MS (3 Sept. 1870).
109. ABL MS (5 July 1874).
110. ABL MS: Forster to Carlyle (4 Aug. 1875).
111. ABL MS (25 Feb. 1874). And see, e.g., Ray, Thackeray, *The Uses of Adversity*, 287.
112. ABL MS (13 Dec. 1875).
113. ABL MS (2 Feb. 1875).
114. NLS MS (11 Jan. 1876).

CHAPTER NINE
Robert Browning

1. See W. H. Griffin and H. C. Minchin, *The Life of Robert Browning* (3rd edn, 1938), *passim* and 74, and J. Maynard, *Browning's Youth* (Cambridge, Mass., 1977), chap. xi, *passim*.
2. *Diaries*, I, 267.
3. Griffin and Minchin, *op. cit.*, 75–6.
4. *Examiner* (6 Sept. 1835), 563.
5. 'Evidences of a new genius for dramatic poetry (No. 1)', *New Monthly Mag.*, XLVI (Jan.–Apr. 1836), 289–308.
6. p. 565.
7. p. 308.
8. *Diaries*, I, 272 (1 Feb. 1836).
9. *Diaries*, I, 277 (16 Feb. 1836).
10. *Ibid.*
11. According to Browning's son, HL MS: R. B. ('Pen') Browning to Mrs Forster (27 Feb. 1893).
12. *Ibid.*, and *Diaries*, I, 279.
13. The account that follows is based on S. Monod, 'John Forster as a literary biographer' (University of Paris Thèse Complémentaire, 1952), 238–73. This is the most detailed and convincing attempt to distinguish between the contributions made by each collaborator. Professor Monod's conclusions about internal evidence concur with mine and are supported by many more examples than are quoted here. Unlike most writers on this topic Professor Monod and I are able to approach the problem with a knowledge of Forster's style and procedures. The summary offered here is probably as far as can now be gone, unless new evidence turns up.
14. *Lives of Eminent British Statesmen* (1836), II, 183.
15. *Ibid.*, II, 228.
16. *Ibid.*, II, 375.
17. Monod, *op. cit.*, 256–7.
18. *Lives of Eminent British Statesmen*, II, 391. Mountnorris was one of Strafford's Irish victims.

19. *Ibid.*, II, 404.
20. Copy now in ABL.
21. Robert Browning, *New Letters*, ed. W. C. DeVane and K. L. Knickerbocker (1951), 76; Berg MS: Forster to R. Browning (18 Feb. 1860).
22. *The Letters of Robert Browning and Elizabeth Barrett 1845–6*, ed. E. Kintner (Cambridge, Mass., 1968), II, 763.
23. ABL MS. See *Cymbeline*, II. 4. 15–17, and *Hamlet*, V. 2. 33–4.
24. *Diaries*, I, 385 (5 Apr. 1837). The *Diaries* for January–May 1837 remain the best account of the preparation of the play.
25. *Ibid.* (7 Apr. 1837).
26. *Ibid.*, I, 392 (2 May 1837).
27. W. C. DeVane, *A Browning Handbook* (2nd edn, 1955), 61–2.
28. *Examiner* (7 May 1837), 294–5.
29. *Diaries*, I, 393 (7, 9 May 1837).
30. *Ibid.*, II, 143 (26 Sept. 1841).
31. Browning first knew of Dickens's reaction 31 years later when Forster printed Dickens's letter in *Dickens*, II, 25.
32. DeVane, *op. cit.*, 138–41. See also J. W. Reed, 'Browning and Macready: the final quarrel', *PMLA*, LXXV (1960), 597–603.
33. *Diaries*, I, 383, 390–1 (30 Mar., 28 Apr. 1837). Longman did.
34. S. M. Ellis, *William Harrison Ainsworth and His Friends* (1911), I, 289. See also HL MS: Forster to W. H. Ainsworth [n.d.].
35. *Learned Lady: Letters from Robert Browning to Mrs. Thomas Fitzgerald 1876–1889*, ed. E. C. McAleer (Cambridge, Mass., 1966), 104. For Browning's review, see *Examiner* (4 Sept. 1836), 563.
36. Robert Browning, *Letters*, coll. T. J. Wise, ed. T. L. Hood (1933), 7.
37. *Foreign Q. Rev.*, XXIX (Apr.–July 1842), 465–83. For a full discussion see *Browning's Essay on Chatterton*, ed. D. Smalley (Cambridge, Mass., 1948).
38. Respectively: *Examiner* (2 Oct. 1841), 628–9; (26 Nov. 1842), 756; (15 Nov. 1845), 723; (25 Apr. 1846), 260.
39. Respectively: *Examiner* (2 Apr. 1842), 212; (22 June 1855), 389.
40. DeVane, *op. cit.*, 49.
41. W. Irvine and P. Honan, *The Book, the Ring, and the Poet* (1974), 77. See *Sordello*, I, 693–7; II, 788–801, 821.
42. Griffin and Minchin, *op. cit.*, 119–21.
43. *Examiner* (5 Oct. 1844), 628.
44. A. Hayter, *A Sultry Month* (1965), 163.
45. *Letters of Robert Browning and Elizabeth Barrett Browning*, ed. Kintner, I, 135.
46. *Diaries*, I, 402.
47. R. and E. Garnett, *The Life of W. J. Fox* (1910), 277.
48. Respectively: ABL MS: Forster to W. J. Fox (21 Sept. 1839); *Letters of Robert Browning and Elizabeth Barrett Browning*, ed. Kintner, I, 245.
49. S. Allen, *Samuel Phelps and Sadler's Wells Theatre* (Middletown, Conn., 1971), 280. See *Examiner* (9 Dec. 1848), 789.
50. Griffin and Minchin, *op. cit.*, 167.
51. *Letters*, ed. Hood, 30. The reference is to Elizabeth Barrett Browning, *Poems* (1850), her first collected edition.
52. *New Letters*, ed. DeVane and Knickerbocker, 77.
53. Morgan Library MSS.
54. Respectively: Humanities Research Centre, University of Texas at Austin MS: Forster to Mr Mosley (28 Sept. 1859); Berg MSS: Forster to E. B. Browning (17 Apr. 1860, 20 Oct. 1856).
55. Respectively: Berg MSS (1 Nov. 1859, 15 July 1858, 18 Feb. 1860).
56. Berg MS (18 Feb. 1860).
57. Respectively: *Browning to His American Friends*, ed. G. R. Hudson (1965), 44–6; *Letters*, ed. Hood, 52; Hudson (ed.), *op. cit.*, 44; Berg MSS: Forster to R. Browning (18 Feb. 1860, 1 Nov. 1859).
58. Respectively: *New Letters*, ed. DeVane and Knickerbocker, 62; *ibid.*, 76; *ibid.*, 137–40.
59. *Examiner* (8 Sept. 1849), 565.
60. *Examiner* (6 Apr. 1850), 213.
61. *Examiner* (1 Dec. 1855), 757.
62. Berg MS (16 Oct. 1855).
63. Morgan MS: R. Browning to Chapman & Hall [n.d.].
64. Griffin and Minchin, *op. cit.*, 179.

65. DeVane, *op. cit.*, 241.
66. A. B. and J. L. Harlan (eds), *Letters from Owen Meredith (Robert, First Earl of Lytton) to Robert and Elizabeth Barrett Browning* (Waco, Texas, 1936), 183, 185, 186.
67. Irvine and Honan, *op. cit.*, 387.
68. R. W. Armour, *Barry Cornwall: a Biography of Bryan Waller Procter* (Boston, Mass., 1935), 192.
69. Berg MS: Forster to R. Browning (13 Oct. 1862).
70. Berg MS (1 May 1863).
71. Berg MS (25 Dec. 1868).
72. Berg MSS (13 Jan. 1869, 4 Feb. 1869).
73. Berg MSS: Julian Fane to Forster (24 July 1869), Forster to R. Browning (28 July 1869).
74. C. R. Sanders, 'The Carlyle–Browning correspondence and relationship', *Bull. John Rylands Univ. Library*, LVII (1974–5), 455.
75. Griffin and Minchin, *op. cit.*, 292.
76. Berg MS (1 Dec. 1875).
77. *New Letters*, 229–30.
78. *Ibid.*, 231–2.

CHAPTER TEN
Walter Savage Landor

1. *Landor*, II, 273.
2. p. 757.
3. (13 June 1835), 181.
4. *Examiner* (27 Mar. 1836), 196.
5. *Ibid.* (3 Apr. 1836), 212.
6. R. H. Super, *Walter Savage Landor* (New York, 1954), 247–8.
7. *Landor*, I, 16.
8. 47 (May–Aug. 1836), 342–58, and 48 (Sept.–Dec. 1836), 200–8.
9. *Examiner* (3 Dec. 1837), 772.
10. *Ibid.* (20 June 1846), 387.
11. *Ibid.* (15 Sept. 1839), 581.
12. *Ibid.* (20 June 1864), 387.
13. *Ibid.* (1 Feb. 1851), 69.
14. *Ibid.* (22 Nov. 1851), 743.
15. For a list of Landor's contributions to all periodicals see T. J. Wise and S. Wheeler, *A Bibliography of the Writings in Prose and Verse of Walter Savage Landor* (1919), *passim.*
16. *Examiner* (21 July 1849), 450–1.
17. *Ibid.* (25 Aug. 1849), 432.
18. *Ibid.* (24 Nov. 1849), 739–40.
19. *Ibid.* (1 Dec. 1849), 759.
20. *Ibid.* (25 Mar. 1848), 196.
21. p. 193.
22. p. 196.
23. ABL MS: Forster to W. J. Fox (27 Oct. 1840).
24. HL MS [20 Mar. 1851].
25. *Landor*, II, 361.
26. *Ibid.*, II, 362.
27. *Ibid.*, II, 445.
28. Super, *Walter Savage Landor*, 351, 413.
29. *Ibid.*, 476–7.
30. *Landor*, II, 450.
31. Information from a description of that volume in Catalogue No. 12 [n.d.] issued by Charles Cox, Crediton, Devon: item 213.
32. Super, *Walter Savage Landor*, 353.
33. University of Chicago MS [1837].
34. Super, *Walter Savage Landor*, 353.
35. For this paragraph, see R. H. Super, *The Publication of Landor's Works* (1954), 88; *idem, Walter Savage Landor*, 303, 351–2 and 581, 371, respectively.
36. Berg MS [1839].
37. Super, *Walter Savage Landor*, 414. The standard account of Landor's relations with publishers is Super, *The Publication of Landor's Works.*
38. HL MS [17 June 1839].
39. HL MS [24 Apr. 1848].
40. See *Examiner* (29 Apr. 1848), 278. v.6 finally appeared as 'First actor in the world's first scene', which suggests either Forster's rejection of Landor's correction or, more probably, a further revision, by Landor, of the corrected line.
41. *Landor*, II, 447.
42. *Ibid.*, II, 455–6.
43. Super, *Walter Savage Landor*, 400.
44. Cox, *Catalogue*, item 213.
45. University of Chicago MS [1845].
46. *Dickens*, III, 454.
47. IV (July–Dec. 1846), 141–52.
48. 'Landor's *Collected Writings* – new *Imaginary Conversations*', *Edinburgh Rev.*, LXXXIII (Apr. 1846), 486–511.
49. Super, *Walter Savage Landor*, 363, 583–4. See also BL Add. MS 34626: Forster to Macvey Napier, *passim.*
50. *Landor*, I, 52.
51. *Ibid.*, II, 595–6.

52. See *Landor, passim*; Super, *Walter Savage Landor, passim.* Two letters arranging visits and showing Forster's affection for Landor are Berg MS: Forster to George Cattermole [n.d.], and Folger Library MS: Forster to J. P. Collier (20 Apr. 1850).
53. *Landor*, II, 477–8.
54. HL MS: Landor to Forster [Jan. 1848].
55. Berg MS: John Forster, *The Life and Adventures of Oliver Goldsmith* (1848). Inscribed by Forster: 'Walter Savage Landor. With affectionate admiration and regard.' The quoted annotations are on pages 178 and 689, respectively.
56. II, 449.
57. Super, *The Publication of Landor's Works*, x.
58. *Landor*, II, 317.
59. Super, *Walter Savage Landor*, 405.
60. *Ibid.*, 309.
61. HL MS [4 Nov. 1852].
62. *Walter Savage Landor*, 443–59.
63. *Ibid.*, 455.
64. Berg MS (15 July 1858).
65. HL MS (19 Aug. 1858).
66. Super, *Walter Savage Landor*, 461–2.
67. ABL MS (25 Aug. 1858).
68. Super, *Walter Savage Landor*, 476–7.
69. Yale University Library MS (4 June 1860).
70. Super, *Walter Savage Landor*, 477.
71. *Ibid.*, 497.
72. *Ibid.*, 474.
73. *Landor*, II, 587–8.
74. William Allingham, *A Diary*, ed. H. Allingham and D. Radford (1907), (entry for 10 June 1888).

CHAPTER ELEVEN
Charles Dickens

1. *Dickens*, I, 96.
2. *Examiner* (11 Dec. 1836), 792.
3. J. Grant, *The Great Metropolis* (2nd edn, 1837), II, 226.
4. *Pilgrim*, I, 210.
5. *Dickens*, I, 206
6. *The Life and Adventures of Oliver Goldsmith* (1848), 79.
7. *Dickens*, I, 51–4.
8. *Pilgrim*, I, 212.
9. *Dickens*, I, 96–7.
10. *Ibid.*, III, 472.
11. *Ibid.*, I, 162n.
12. *Pilgrim*, IV, 33–4.
13. W. E. Buckler, 'Dickens's success with *Household Words*', *Dickensian*, XLVI (1949–50), 198.
14. See, e.g., R. L. Patten, *Charles Dickens and His Publishers* (1978), 161.
15. E. Johnson, *Charles Dickens: His Tragedy and Triumph* (1953), II, 1007.
16. Patten, *op. cit.*, 27. The account that follows owes much to Patten's fine study.
17. *Pilgrim*, I, 269–70.
18. *Pilgrim*, II, 482. William Chapman's italics.
19. *Ibid.*, II, 487.
20. *Ibid.*, II, 365–6.
21. *Dickens*, II, 50.
22. Berg MS (6 Oct. 1838).
23. *Ibid.* (8 Nov. 1838).
24. *Ibid.* ([24 Oct. 1839]).
25. *Pilgrim*, I, 223–4n.
26. p. 260.
27. Patten, *op. cit.*, 86.
28. *Dickens*, I, 105.
29. Noted by S. Monod, *Dickens the Novelist* (Norman, Okla., 1969), 202.
30. *Pilgrim*, II, 127n.
31. *Dombey and Son* (Clarendon edn, ed. A. Horsman, 1974), xlvi.
32. *Little Dorrit* (Clarendon edn, ed. H. P. Sucksmith, 1979), xlviii.
33. *Dickens*, I, 185. See also *Pilgrim*, II, 167n.
34. *Dickens*, I, 215.
35. FC MS. See also Monod, *op. cit.*, 208, and *Pilgrim*, II, 253n.
36. FC MS. See also *Pilgrim*, II, 275n.
37. *Dickens*, I, 216.
38. *Dickens*, II, 135.
39. See *Pilgrim*, IV, 209n. A full discussion of Forster's part in the composition of *The Chimes* is in M. Slater, 'Dickens (and Forster) at work on *The Chimes*', *Dickens Studies*, II (1966), 106–40.
40. *Dickens*, II, 315. For Forster and *Dombey and Son* see *Dombey and Son*, ed. Horsman, *passim*, and *Pilgrim*, IV and V, *passim.*
41. *Dickens*, I, 131.
42. *Dickens*, I, 188.

43. Yale University Library MS ([15/16 Jan. 1841]).
44. *Pilgrim*, II, 188.
45. *Dickens*, I, 217.
46. *Ibid.*, II, 13.
47. *Ibid.*, II, 54–5.
48. *Ibid.*, II, 59.
49. *Ibid.*, II, 134–5. See Dickens, *The Christmas Books* (Penguin edn, ed. M. Slater, 1971), I, 247–52, for a full discussion and list of passages deleted as a consequence of Forster's objection.
50. Again, for the next three paragraphs see *Dombey and Son*, ed. Horsman, *passim*. See also *Pilgrim*, IV and V, *passim*, and J. Butt and K. Tillotson, *Dickens at Work* (1957), chap. 5, *passim*.
51. *Dickens*, II, 404.
52. Dickens, *Letters* (Nonesuch edn, ed. W. Dexter, 1938), I, 817.
53. *Examiner* (2 July 1837), 421–2.
54. *Ibid.* (23 Sept. 1838), 596.
55. *Ibid.* (27 Oct. 1839), 677.
56. *Ibid.* (4 Dec. 1841), 773.
57. *Ibid.* (14 Dec. 1850), 798.
58. *Ibid.* (2 July 1837), 422.
59. *Ibid.* (27 Oct. 1839), 677.
60. *Ibid.* (18 Nov. 1838), 723).
61. *Ibid.* (23 Dec. 1843), 804.
62. *Ibid.* (21 Dec. 1844), 803.
63. *Ibid.* (25 Nov. 1838), 740.
64. *Ibid.* (9 Sept. 1854), 568.
65. *Ibid.* (30 May 1846), 340.
66. *Ibid.* (28 Oct. 1848), 692.
67. *Edinburgh Rev.*, LXXXI (1845), 181.
68. *Examiner* (25 Nov. 1838), 740.
69. *Ibid.* (28 Oct. 1848), 692.
70. *Ibid.* (8 Oct. 1853), 644.
71. For a convenient listing, see *Pilgrim*, V, 710–11.
72. K. J. Fielding and A. W. Brice, '*Bleak House* and the Graveyard', in *Dickens the Craftsman*, ed. R. B. Partlow, Jr (Carbondale and Edwardsville, 1970), 120.
73. *Dickens*, II, 416–22. See also P. Fitzgerald, *Memories of Charles Dickens* (1913), chap. 8, *passim.*
74. See, e.g., *Pilgrim*, I, 243, and the dedication, in 1858, to the Library Edition of Dickens's works.
75. *Pilgrim*, I, 503.
76. *Dickens*, I, 99.
77. *Ibid.*, I, 202–3n.
78. *Ibid.*, II, 155n.
79. *Ibid.*, I, 241.
80. *Ibid.*, I, 337.
81. *Ibid.*, I, 387.
82. *Pilgrim*, III, 244.
83. *Pickwickian Studies* (1899), 89–90.
84. All quotations are from *The Pickwick Papers* (Penguin edn, ed. R. L. Patten 1972), 579, 589, 631.
85. *Diaries*, I, 357–8 (7–10 Nov. 1836). Macready's italics.
86. *Fifty Years of Fleet Street*, comp. and ed. F. M. Thomas (1904), 203.
87. *Memories of Charles Dickens, passim.*
88. *Pilgrim*, I, 325.
89. *Ibid.*, I, 359.
90. *Ibid.*, III, 324.
91. *Ibid.*, II, 158.
92. *Letters*, ed. Dexter, II, 224.
93. *Ibid.*, II, 570.
94. Lytton MS, Letters and Papers, vol. 15: Forster to Bulwer (9 July 1850).
95. *Dickens*, I, 72.
96. ABL MS: Forster to Carlyle (29 Sept. 1867).
97. *Dickens*, III, 164.
98. Morgan MS (11 May 1855).
99. *Ibid.* (1 Mar. 1858).
100. Respectively: Morgan MSS (24 Oct. 1860; 4 Jan. 1862).
101. Johnson, *op. cit.*, II, 1053.
102. Book I, chapters 2, 10, 11; Book II, chapters 3, 4; Book III, chapter 17; Book IV, chapter 17. All subsequent quotations are from these chapters.
103. *Diaries*, II, 142.
104. See, e.g., *Letters*, ed. Dexter, II, 488.
105. S. C. Hall, *Retrospect of a Long Life* (1883), II, 260.
106. 'Theatre Royal Little Pedlington', *The Times* (5 Apr. 1837), 7.
107. p. 420.
108. *Biographical Essays* (3rd edn, 1860), 142.
109. Morgan MS (1 Nov. 1854).
110. *Letters*, ed. Dexter, II, 606.
111. 'The newspaper press of France', *Foreign Q. Rev.*, XXX (1842–3), 493.
112. 'Newspaper literature of the United States', *Foreign Q. Rev.*, XXX (1842–3), 214.
113. P. Fitzgerald, *The Life of Charles Dickens as Revealed in His Writings* (1905), II, 123–4.

114. Brotherton Library, University of Leeds, transcript: Forster to Mrs Gaskell [n.d.].
115. See above, pp. 110–11.
116. R. Renton, *John Forster and His Friendships* (1912), 114.
117. 'Remarks on two of the annuals', *Newcastle Mag.* (1829), 33–4.
118. *The Wound and the Bow* (New York, 1947), 78.
119. Or rather, Johnson, *op. cit.*, II, 1053, fancied that Dickens fancied Forster did, on the evidence of HL MS: Dickens to G. Hogarth (28 July 1864). The evidence is not conclusive.
120. *Dickens*, III, 344.
121. A. B. Harlan, *Owen Meredith: a Critical Biography of Robert, First Earl of Lytton* (New York, 1946), 216.

CHAPTER TWELVE
Thomas Carlyle

1. FC MS.
2. Carlyle to John Carlyle (5 Feb. 1839). Quoted in F. Harrison, *Carlyle and the London Library* (1907), 7. For the 'blast' itself see 'Appeal for London Library', *Examiner* (27 Jan. 1839), 53–4.
3. Harrison, *op. cit.*, 48, 50.
4. *Ibid.*, 60.
5. *Ibid.*, 71. For a report of the meeting and details of the committee see 'The proposed London Library', *Examiner* (28 June 1840), 408.
6 Thomas Carlyle, *New Letters*, ed. and annotated by Alexander Carlyle (1904), II, 127–30. See also S. Nowell-Smith, 'Carlyle and the London Library', *English Libraries 1800–1850* (1958), 70–2.
7. ABL MS: Forster to Carlyle (25 July 1870).
8. p. 76.
9. pp. 214–15.
10. Morgan Library MS [1840].
11. *New Letters*, I, 159.
12. *Letters and Memorials of Jane Welsh Carlyle*, ed. J. A. Froude (1883), I, 134.
13. L. and E. Hanson, *Necessary Evil: The Life of Jane Welsh Carlyle* (1952), 272, and *passim.*
14. *Ibid.*, 261–2.
15. *Ibid.*, 262.
16. Jane Welsh Carlyle, *Letters to Her Family, 1839–1863*, ed. L. Huxley (1924), 313.
17. FC MS: Carlyle to Forster (26 Nov. [1847]).
18. *Letters and Memorials,* ed. Froude, I, 118.
19. L. and E. Hanson, *op. cit.*, 265.
20. NLS MS [n.d.].
21. ABL MS: Forster to Mrs Carlyle (4 Apr. 1864).
22. Thomas Carlyle, *Reminiscences*, ed. C. E. Norton (Everyman's University Library edn, 1972), 153–4.
23. *Letters and Memorials,* ed. Froude, I, 135.
24. *Ibid.*, I, 135–7.
25. J. A. Froude, *Thomas Carlyle: A History of His Life in London 1834–1881* (1884), I, 356.
26. FC MS (20 Aug. 1847).
27. FC MS (26 Apr. 1857).
28. D. Masson, *Memories of London in the 'Forties* (1908), 70–2.
29. R. W. Emerson, *Letters*, ed. R. L. Rusk (New York, 1939), IV, 66.
30. W. Elwin, *Some XVIII Century Men of Letters*, I, 251.
31. C. R. Sanders, 'The Carlyle–Browning correspondence and relationship: II', *Bull. John Rylands Univ. Library*, LVII (1974–5), 452.
32. *Letters and Memorials*, ed. Froude, III, 241.
33. Froude, *op. cit.*, II, 243.
34. FC MS (31 Jan. 1861).
35. FC MS (15 July 1853).
36. FC MS (29 Sept. 1853).
37. *Letters of Thomas Carlyle to John Stuart Mill, John Sterling and Robert Browning*, ed. A. Carlyle (1923), 250.
38. *New Letters*, I, 242–3.
39. FC MS [n.d.].
40. FC MS [n.d.].
41. *Critical and Miscellaneous Essays* (Centenary edn, [n.d.]), II, 77.
42. Centenary edn (1896), I, 235.
43. *Letters and Private Papers*, ed. G. N. Ray (1945), I, 396.

44. Centenary edn (1907), 162.
45. Houghton Library MS: Forster to Carlyle [1839].
46. *The Collected Letters of Thomas and Jane Welsh Carlyle* (Duke-Edinburgh edn, 2: Durham, North Carolina, 1970), 94.
47. FC MSS: Carlyle to Forster (17 Sept. 1840, 4 May 1844, 20 Jan. 1846) and *passim.*
48. FC MS: Carlyle to Forster (7 Nov. 1854).
49. FC MS: Carlyle to Forster (18 July 1854).
50. FC MS: Carlyle to Forster [n.d.].
51. FC MS: [n.d.].
52. FC MS: (18 July 1854).
53. ABL MS (11 Aug. 1861).
54. FC MS: (17 Aug. 1861).
55. FC MS: (17 Apr. 1851).
56. *New Letters*, II, 110.
57. FC MS: (17 Apr. 1851).
58. See above, p. 95.
59. *Froude's Life of Carlyle*, abr. and ed. J. Clubbe (1979), 284.
60. *Reminiscences*, ed. Norton, p. 77.
61. FC MS [n.d.].
62. FC MS (12 May 1842).
63. HL MS.
64. *Froude's Life of Carlyle,* ed. Clubbe, 150–1.
65. FC MS [n.d.].
66. FC MS [n.d.].
67. FC MS [n.d.].
68. HL MS: receipt dated 3 May 1843.
69. FC MS: Carlyle to Forster (9 June 1858).
70. *Ibid.*
71. FC MS: Carlyle to Forster (11 June 1858).
72. FC MS: Carlyle to Forster (17 June 1858).
73. D. A. Wilson, *Carlyle to Three-Score-and-Ten* (1929), 316.
74. According to the *DNB.*
75. FC MS (6 Feb. 1865).
76. ABL MS: Forster to Carlyle (9 Mar. 1867). The preceding paragraph is also based on this letter.
77. FC MS (23 Sept. 1867).
78. HL MS: Carlyle to Chapman & Hall (31 Oct. 1867).
79. ABL MS: Forster to Carlyle (29 Sept. 1867).
80. HL MS: Carlyle to Chapman & Hall (31 Oct. 1867).
81. ABL MS: Forster to Carlyle (26 May 1867).
82. See, e.g., FC MS: Carlyle to Forster (6 May 1868); ABL MSS: Forster to Carlyle (7 May 1868, 15 Aug. 1868, 17 Jan. 1869).
83. *New Letters*, II, 251–2.
84. ABL MSS: Forster to Carlyle (31 July 1870, 29 Aug. 1870).
85. ABL MS (13 Aug. 1872).
86. ABL MSS: Forster to Carlyle (1 Feb. 1874), 4 Mar. 1875, 9 Mar. 1875).
87. Now part of the Forster Collection.
88. HL MS: receipt dated 15 Feb. 1865.
89. HL MS: receipts dated 23 May, 3 June, 7 July 1871, and 30 July 1873.
90. HL MS: undated receipt for bills for royalties for March–July 1874.
91. *Letters to Her Family*, ed. Huxley, 135.
92. *Foreign Q. Rev.*, XXXI (Apr.–July 1843), 570.
93. (27 Sept. 1840), 612–13.
94. 'Louis-Philippe' (4 Mar. 1848), 145–6; 'Repeal of the Union' (29 Apr. 1848), 275–6; 'Legislation for Ireland' (13 May 1848), 308; 'Death of Charles Buller' (2 Dec. 1848), 771.
95. (13 May 1848), 307–8.
96. *Letters to Arthur Hugh Clough*, ed. H. F. Lowry (1932), 111.
97. FC MS: Carlyle to Forster (5 Mar. 1848).
98. FC MSS.
99. (17 Sept. 1837), 596.
100. (20 May 1838), 310.
101. (5 May 1839), 278.
102. (29 Apr. 1843), 259–61.
103. (13 Dec. 1845), 787–9.
104. (15 Jan. 1848), 35–7. Identified by K. J. Fielding. See *idem*, 'A new review (of himself) by Carlyle: the Squire Papers', *Carlyle Newsletter* (forthcoming), for further discussion and references.
105. FC MS [n.d.]; see also FC MS: Forster to Carlyle (7 Jan. 1848).
106. e.g. (22 Jan. 1848), 54 and (12 Feb. 1848), 102.
107. Centenary edn (1897), II, 341.
108. Respectively, (29 June 1850), 404–6 and (18 Oct. 1851), 659–61.
109. C. G. Duffy, *Conversations With Carlyle* (1892), 84.

110. FC MS (2 Jan. 1856).
111. *Oliver Cromwell's Letters and Speeches With Elucidations* (Centenary edn, 1897), I, 19.
112. FC MS (16 Feb. 1874).
113. FC MS (22 Nov. 1872).
114. FC MS (29 Mar. 1865).
115. ABL MS (15 July 1859).
116. ABL MS (17 Sept. 1874).
117. HL MS: copy of extracts from James Whiteside's Journals.
118. See, e.g., G. H. Ford, 'Stern Hebrews Who Laugh: further thoughts on Carlyle and Dickens', in *Carlyle Past and Present*, ed. K. J. Fielding and R. L. Tarr (1976), 112–26.
119. ABL MS (29 June 1873).
120. *Letters and Memorials*, ed. Froude, III, 318.
121. ABL MS: Forster to Carlyle (22 June 1866).
122. NLS MS: Carlyle to Forster (16 June 1867).
123. FC MS (26 Oct. 1874).
124. ABL MSS: Forster to Carlyle (26 Oct., 31 Oct. 1874).
125. FC MS: Carlyle to Forster (19 Nov. 1874).
126. ABL MS: Forster to Carlyle (13 Sept. 1875).
127. Respectively: ABL MSS: Forster to Carlyle (5 Nov. 1867, 24 Oct. 1874, 14 Nov. 1874, 11 Aug. 1861, 16 May 1869, 27 Oct. 1874).
128. ABL MS (27 May 1869).
129. Berg MS (18 Feb. 1874).
130. ABL MS (17 Oct. 1869).
131. ABL MS (31 Oct. 1874).
132. ABL MS (29 July 1868). Sittings dragged on and Carlyle hated them and the portrait. He wrote on Forster's letter to him of 12 Oct. 1868 (ABL MS): 'Watts's Blotch-Portrait ("last sitting" to *be*, Friday next, 2½ p.m. to end at 4 *forever*). – So distracted a monster of Painting I have never seen before: cross bet[n] a Lunatic & an Imposter: no feature of me recognisible in it. Fie!'
133. ABL MS (26 Mar. 1871).
134. Respectively: ABL MSS (9 Mar. 1867, 19 Nov. 1871, 15 Feb. 1872, 30 Aug. 1875). See also p. 127 above.
135. S. Norton and M. A. DeWolfe Howe, 'English friends: from letters and journals of Charles Eliot Norton', *Scribners* (1913), 775.
136. *Ibid.*, 781.
137. ABL MS: Forster to Carlyle (21 Dec. 1875).
138. NLS MSS: Forster to Masson (19 Nov., 22 Nov., 24 Nov., 27 Nov., 29 Nov. 1875).
139. *New Letters*, II, 325–6.
140. HL MS: copy of extract (19 Feb. 1875) from Forster's diary.
141. ABL MS (11 Aug. 1861); quoted on p. 190 above.

CHAPTER THIRTEEN
Journalist

1. See A. Aspinall, 'The social status of journalists at the beginning of the nineteenth century', *Rev. English Studies*, XXI (1945), 216–32, and John O. Hayden, *The Romantic Reviewers 1802–1824* (1969), *passim*.
2. Lytton MS, Letters and Papers, vol. 15: Forster to Bulwer (21 Mar. 1839).
3. (22 Nov. 1851), 739.
4. John Forster, *Biographical Essays* (1860), 411.
5. *Landor*, II, 518
6. *Examiner* (20 June 1846), 387.
7. See K. Tillotson and N. Burgis, 'Forster's reviews in the *Examiner*, 1840–1841', *Dickensian*, LXVIII (1972), 105–8.
8. He was parodied as such in G. H. Lewes, *Ranthorpe* (1847), 32–3.
9. *Examiner* (3 Nov. 1839), 691–3. Forster's italics.
10. S. M. Ellis, *William Harrison Ainsworth and his Friends* (1911), I, 358.
11. See, e.g., *Examiner* (6 Feb. 1847), 84 and (13 Mar. 1847), 164–5.
12. *Ibid.* (23 Nov. 1844), 740.
13. *Imagination and Fancy* (new edn, 1878), 26.
14. *Wit and Humour* (new edn, 1878), 10.
15. *Dickens*, III, 295.
16. *Examiner* (22 Jan. 1848), 53.
17. *Ibid.* (22 Jan. 1853), 52.

18. *Ibid.* (8 June 1850), 356.
19. See A. H. Warren, Jr, *English Poetic Theory 1825–1865* (Princeton, N. J., 1950), 98.
20. *Imagination and Fancy*, v. Hunt's italics.
21. 'On art in fiction', *Pamphlets and Sketches* (Knebworth edn, vol. 34, 1874), 318. The essay was first published in 1838.
22. *Examiner* (4 Mar. 1848), 147.
23. *Dickens*, III, 347.
24. *Miscellaneous Prose Works* (1868), III, 355.
25. *Op. cit.*, 98.
26. *Examiner* (22 Jan. 1848), 53.
27. *Ibid.* (4 Mar. 1848), 147.
28. *Ibid.* (17 Mar. 1855), 164.
29. *Ibid.* (8 Jan. 1848), 20.
30. *Landor*, I, 78.
31. *Examiner* (28 May 1842), 340.
32. *Miscellaneous Prose Works*, III, 372.
33. *Imagination and Fancy*, 1.
34. *Examiner* (27 Jan. 1849), 52.
35. *Ibid.* (20 Oct. 1849), 659.
36. *The Life and Times of Oliver Goldsmith* (3rd edn, 1855), 236.
37. *Dickens*, I, 138.
38. *Examiner* (20 Oct. 1849), 659.
39. *Ibid.* (13 Nov. 1852), 72.
40. *Ibid.* (22 Jan. 1853), 51.
41. *Letters and Private Papers*, ed. G. N. Ray (1945), II, 424.
42. *Letters and Memorials of Jane Welsh Carlyle*, ed. J. A. Froude (1883), II, 137.
43. BL Add. MS 38110, f.48: Forster to Leigh Hunt (11 Nov. 1843).
44. Quoted from E. M. Curran, '*The Foreign Quarterly Review* (1827–1846)' (unpublished Ph.D. thesis, Cornell University, 1958), 117. In the account that follows I have drawn further on this thesis and on the *Wellesley Index*, vol. II.
45. Herodotus Smith [Francis Espinasse], '*The Examiner*', *Critic* (1 Sept. 1852), 442.
46. Curran, *op. cit.*, 119.
47. Lytton MS, Letters and Papers, vol. 15 (30 May 1842).
48. Kungliga Biblioteket Stockholm MS: Forster to George Stephens (9 Feb. 1843).
49. Curran, *op. cit.*, 118.
50. 'Newspaper literature of the United States', *Foreign Q. Rev.*, XXX (Oct. 1842–Jan. 1843), 197–222.
51. *Wellesley Index*, II, 135.
52. Curran, *op. cit.*, 132–6, 207.
53. XXXII (July–Oct. 1843), 232.
54. *Ibid.*, 190.
55. ABL MS: Forster to W. J. Fox [20 Sept. 1843].
56. Curran, *op. cit.*, 119.
57. For part of the account that follows I have drawn upon *Pilgrim*, IV, *passim*.
58. Houghton Library, Harvard University MS: Forster to J. R. Lowell (3 Nov. 1845).
59. *Dickens*, II, 192.
60. R. and E. Garnett, *The Life of W. J. Fox* (1910), 282.
61. *Ibid.*, 283.
62. *Diaries*, II, 321.
63. Houghton Library MS, Harvard University (3 June 1846).
64. HL MS: Forster to Chapman & Hall [n.d.].
65. R. and E. Garnett, *op. cit.*, 283.
66. *Ibid.*, 282.
67. *Ibid.*, 284.
68. *Ibid.*
69. HL MS: Forster to W. B. Jerrold (1 Dec. 1858).
70 Lytton MSS: Forster to Bulwer (27 Oct. 1847; 1 Nov. 1847).
71. J. G. [J. Gibbs], 'How I first met Charles Dickens', *Press News* (Dec. 1905), 28.
72. H. S. Solly, *The Life of Henry Morley LI.D.* (1898), 160.
73. To this point in the paragraph: Solly, *op. cit.*, 201–2, 175, 161.
74. Yale University Library MS: Forster to My Dear Sir (15 Nov. 1850).
75. NLS MS [1849].
76. [Espinasse], *op. cit.*, 442.
77. E. B. de Fonblanque, *The Life and Labours of Albany Fonblanque* (1874), 64.
78. *Examiner* (23 Jan. 1847), 49.
79. *Ibid.* (20 Mar. 1847), 177.
80. *Ibid.* (22 May 1847), 321.
81. To this point in the paragraph: HL MS: Rawlins's memoir; NLS MSS; Berg MS: Forster to Talfourd (26 Sept. 1852).
82. *Examiner* (18 Dec. 1847), 801.
83. *Ibid.* (18 Dec. 1847), 802.
84. Sir C. A. Duffy, *Conversations with Carlyle* (1892), 83.
85. p. 65.

86. (11 Mar. 1848), 161.
87. (25 Mar. 1848), 193.
88. (15 Apr. 1848), 241.
89. [Espinasse], *op. cit.*, 442.
90. J. D. Vann and R. T. Van Arsdel, *Victorian Periodicals: A Guide to Research* (New York, 1978), 171, 173.
91. *Henry Crabb Robinson on Books and Their Writers*, ed. E. J. Morley (1938), II, 755.
92. H. R. Fox Bourne, *English Newspapers* (1887), II, 227–53, *passim.*
93. Solly, *op. cit.*, 226.
94. Yale University Library MS: Forster to W. J. Linton (4 Feb. 1856); NLS MS: Forster to J. H. Burton (11 Aug. 1856).
95. FC Newspaper Cuttings, xix, no. 381: *Globe* (5 Jan. 1856), no p. no.
96. *Ibid.*, xxxiii, nos. 355–8: *World* (5 Jan. 1876), 5.
97. HL MS: Forster to W. B. Jerrold (1 Dec. 1858).
98. *Dickens*, III, 457.

CHAPTER FOURTEEN
Historian

1. *Englishman's Mag.*, 1 (Apr.–Aug. 1831), 351.
2. pp. 353–4.
3. pp. 351–3
4. 'A Treatise on the Popular Progress in English History', *Statesmen of the Commonwealth of England* (1840), I, xxviii.
5. *Op. cit.*, 355n. Forster is quoting from Amos's explication in Sir John Fortescue, *Fortescue de laudibus legum Angliae*. With Notes. By A. Amos (1825).
6. *Op. cit.*, 351.
7. *Sir John Eliot* (1836), 20.
8. p. 105.
9. p. 102.
10. p. 123.
11. p. 123.
12. p. 46.
13. *Thomas Wentworth, Earl of Strafford* (1836), 181.
14. p. 194.
15. p. 222.
16. p. 227.
17. p. 275.
18. p. 260.
19. p. 299.
20. p. 381.
21. p. 191.
22. p. 369.
23. p. 283.
24. p. 275.
25. p. 411.
26. *John Pym* (1837), 197.
27. p. 197.
28. p. 198.
29. *John Hampden* (1837), 306.
30. p. 337.
31. p. 345.
32. *Sir Henry Vane* (1838), 25.
33. p. 91.
34. p. 95.
35. p. 102.
36. p. 131.
37. p. 162.
38. *Henry Marten* (1838), 256.
39. p. 333.
40. p. 358.
41. p. 360.
42. *Oliver Cromwell* (1839), I, 190–1.
43. Respectively: I, 151, II, 12, 51, 54, 164, 228, 379.
44. 'Treatise on the Popular Progress in English History', 5.
45. *Sir John Eliot*, p. 11.
46. *John Pym*, p. 152(n.).
47. p. 203.
48. *Sir Henry Vane*, 159.
49. p. 288.
50. *Oliver Cromwell*, II, 120–3.
51. 'Treatise on the Popular Progress in English History', xlvii.
52. p. lvi.
53. F. Espinasse, *Literary Recollections and Sketches* (1893), 114.
54. *Oliver Cromwell*, II, 305.
55. II, 3.
56. FC MSS.
57. *Sir John Eliot* (2nd edn, 1872), I, vii.
58. *The Debates on the Grand Remonstrance* (1860), 421.
59. (2nd edn, 1872), I, xii.
60. 'The Civil Wars and Cromwell', *Edinburgh Rev.* 103 (Jan.–Apr. 1856), 14.
61. *Historical and Biographical Essays* (1858), I, 282n.
62. 'The Civil Wars and Cromwell', 15–16.
63. p. 34.
64. FC MS.

65. FC MS: Carlyle to Forster (13 Apr. 1860).
66. p. 149.
67. pp. 150–1.
68. *The Victoria Regia* (1861), 253.
69. pp. 239–40.
70. *Historical and Biographical Essays*, I, 6.
71. FC MS: Carlyle to Forster (28 Aug. 1858).
72. G. P. Gooch, *History and Historians in the Nineteenth Century* (1920), 284.
73. M. Peckham, 'Afterwards: Reflections on historical modes in the nineteenth century', in *Victorian Poetry*, ed. M. Bradbury and D. Palmer (1972), 279.
74. 'Treatise on the Popular Progress in England', lxxviii.
75. *The Arrest of the Five Members*, 3.
76. 'Reflections on some of the great men of the reign of Charles the First', *New Monthly Mag.*, XLVII (1836), 214.
77. *Pilgrim*, I, 370.
78. R. and E. Garnett, *op. cit.*, 199.
79. (10 July 1858), 45.
80. (15 May 1858), 473.
81. See, e.g., FC Newspaper Cuttings, vol. 20, which includes the reviews quoted in this paragraph.
82. p. 524.
83. *Academy* (1876), 122.
84. Quoted by R. C. Richardson, *The Debate on the English Revolution* (1977), 70.
85. M. A. Judson, *The Political Thought of Sir Henry Vane the Younger* (Philadelphia, 1969), 82.
86. S. R. Brett, *John Pym 1583–1643* (1940), 93–4.
87. W. H. Coates (ed.), *The Journal of Sir Simonds D'Ewes* (New Haven, 1942), xxv.
88. M. F. Keeler (ed.), *Bibliography of British History: Stuart Period, 1603–1714* (1970), 122, 59, 140.

CHAPTER FIFTEEN
Literary Biographer

1. Respectively: *The Life and Adventures of Oliver Goldsmith* (1848); *The Life and Times of Oliver Goldsmith* (2nd edn, 2 vols., 1854); 'John Dryden and Jacob Tonson', *The Pic Nic Papers*, ed. Charles Dickens (Philadelphia, 1841), I, 46–62; 'Charles Churchill', *Edinburgh Rev.*, LXXXI (Jan.–April 1845), 46–88; 'Daniel De Foe', *Edinburgh Rev.*, LXXXII (July–Oct. 1845), 480–532; 'Samuel Foote', *Q. Rev.*, XCV (June–Sept. 1854), 483–548; 'Sir Richard Steele', *ibid.*, XCVI (Dec. 1854–Mar. 1855), 509–68; *The Life of Jonathan Swift*, I (1875). Only the first volume of Swift was published and this not until after *The Life of Charles Dickens*, but the collection of materials and most of the preparatory work was completed by 1860 (see D. Woolley, 'Forster's *Swift*', *Dickensian*, LXX, 1974, 196); in its approach to literary character, also, it belongs with Forster's earlier work.
2. 'Charles Churchill', 46–7.
3. I have consulted R. M. Wardle, *Oliver Goldsmith* (Kansas, 1957); C. Churchill, *Poetical Works*, ed. D. Grant (1956); J. R. Moore, *Daniel Defoe, Citizen of the Modern World* (Chicago, 1958); C. Winton, *Captain Steele* and *Sir Richard Steele M.P.* (Baltimore, 1964 and 1970); S. Trefman, *Sam. Foote, Comedian, 1720–1777* (New York, 1971); S. N. Bogorad, 'Samuel Foote: the prospects for a life and works', *Restoration and Eighteenth Century Theatre Research*, VI (1967), 11–13; I. Ehrenpreis, *Swift: the Man, His Works, and the Age*, I and II (1962, 1967); L. Landa, *Swift and the Church of Ireland* (1954); J. Swift, *Journal to Stella*, ed. H. Williams (2 vols., 1948); J. Swift, *Correspondence*, ed. H. Williams (3 vols., 1963–5).
4. 'John Forster', *Forster Collection: a Catalogue of the Printed Books* (1888), xvii.
5. E. B. de Fonblanque, *The Life and Labours of Albany Fonblanque* (1874), 58.
6. Macvey Napier, *Selections from the Correspondence*, ed. M. Napier (1879), 508. The comment is Francis Jeffrey's.
7. 'Daniel De Foe', 498.

8. 'Charles Churchill', 61–2.
9. 'Samuel Foote', 500.
10. Respectively: 'Charles Churchill', 52, 53; 'Daniel De Foe', 498; *The Life and Times of Oliver Goldsmith* (1848), 5, 26.
11. 'Sir Richard Steele', 529.
12. Lytton MS, Letters and Papers, vol. 15 (26 Apr. 1862).
13. R. W. Armour, *Barry Cornwall: a Biography of Bryan Waller Procter* (Boston, 1935), 266.
14. *The Life and Times of Oliver Goldsmith* (1848), viii, 540.
15. *Ibid.*, 30–1.
16. 'John Dryden and Jacob Tonson', 61.
17. *On Heroes, Hero-Worship, and the Heroic in History* (World's Classics edn, 1950), 205.
18. Respectively: *The Life and Times of Oliver Goldsmith* (1848), 117; 'Samuel Foote', 490; *The Life of Jonathan Swift*, 131.
19. 'Daniel De Foe', 528.
20. 'John Dryden and Jacob Tonson', 46.
21. *The Life of Jonathan Swift*, 130.
22. BL Add. MS 34626, f. 148: Forster to Napier (20 Apr. 1846).
23. *The Life and Times of Oliver Goldsmith* (1848), 69–70, 71.
24. 'John Dryden and Jacob Tonson', 61–2.
25. *Letters*, ed. W. Dexter (1938), II, 83.
26. So far as Forster's period is concerned, three points can be made. Firstly, since Fox's Libel Act of 1792 the jury, and not the judge, decided what was defamatory; thus general middle-class standards prevailed, well understood by Forster the literary adviser with legal training. Secondly, Campbell's Act of 1843 laid down that 'The fact that the matter published was true and for the public benefit was to be a defence to a prosecution' (Sir W. Holdsworth, *A History of English Law*, ed. A. L. Goodhart and H. G. Hanbury, 1965, XV, 150). But 'this is seldom relied on in practice because the defendant must prove the entire statement complained of to be true in substance and in fact, and if he fails, this merely aggravates the damages' (*Halesbury's Statutes of England*, ed. Sir R. Burrows, 2nd edn, 1949, XIII, 150). Such aggravation had occurred in 1863 (Caulfield *v.* Whitworth), even as Forster was writing *Landor*. Thirdly, even though 'prior to the passing of the Slander of Women Act, 1891, no action lay, without proof of special damage, for words imputing unchastity or adultery to a woman' (Sir H. Fraser, *Principles and Practice of the Law of Libel and Slander*, ed. A. P. Fachiri, 6th edn, 1925, 61), where 'special damage' meant any *provable* loss or damage, the rigorous moral climate of the time would have made it comparatively easy to demonstrate such loss and hard to prove the truth of libellous statements. The libel laws must have strongly reinforced the Victorian biographer's tendency towards reticence.
27. See Super, *Walter Savage Landor*, *passim*, and *idem*, 'Forster as Landor's literary executor', *Modern Language Notes*, LII (1937), 504–6.
28. Respectively: *Landor*, II, 594; II, 593.
29. Respectively: *ibid.*, II, 595; II, 234; II, 310; I, 181.
30. Respectively: *ibid.*, I, 3; II, 408.
31. ABL MS (12 Aug. 1872).
32. Respectively: G. A. Sala, *Charles Dickens* (1870); [J. C. Hotten], *Charles Dickens: the Story of His Life* [n.d.].
33. F. R. Leavis and Q. D. Leavis, *Dickens the Novelist* (1970), ix–x.
34. 'Dickens's obscure childhood in pre-Forster biography', *Dickensian*, LXXII (1976), 3.
35. G. H. Ford, *Dickens and His Readers* (Princeton, N.J., 1955), 160.
36. Respectively: S. Monod, 'John Forster's "Life of Dickens" and literary criticism', *English Studies Today – Fourth Series* (Rome, 1966), 359–60; G. H. Ford, E. Johnson, J. H. Miller, S. Monod, N. C. Peyrouton, *Dickens Criticism* (Cambridge, Mass., 1962), 32.
37. '1870–1900: Forster and reaction', *Dickensian*, LXX (1970), 91. See also K. J. Fielding, *Charles Dickens* (British Council Pamphlet, rev. edn, 1963), 9.
38. K. J. Fielding and G. R. Grubb, 'New letters from Charles Dickens to John

Forster', *Boston Univ. Studies in English*, II (1956), 153.

39. *Pilgrim*, I, xi. Engel uses this passage to support his statement that 'Madeline House and Graham Storey comment on the amazing objectivity of Forster's volumes' ('Dickens's obscure childhood', 3). But the reference to 'ideal' would seem to indicate Engel's misreading.
40. F. R. Hart, *Lockhart as Romantic Biographer* (1971), 43. See A. W. Brice, 'The compilation of the critical commentary in Forster's *Life of Charles Dickens*', *Dickensian*, LXX (1974), 188–9.
41. E. Johnson, *Charles Dickens: His Tragedy and Triumph* (1953), *passim.*
42. See *Pilgrim*, I, xi–xvii. And compare Johnson, *op. cit.*, *passim.*
43. Respectively: *Dickens*, I, 138, III, 441.
44. pp. 19–20.
45. p. 45.
46. 'Dickens's obscure childhood', 5.
47. *Dickens*, I, 51–2.
48. Respectively: *ibid.*, I, 113; I, 139; I, 139.
49. Respectively: *ibid.*, I, 183; III, 368; I, 264; II, 125.
50. p. 244.
51. pp. 96–7.
52. *Dickens*, III, 175.
53. *Ibid.*, III, 164.
54. p. 330.
55. *Dickens*, III, 517.
56. *Charles Dickens* (British Council Pamphlet), 6.
57. Johnson (*op. cit.*, II, 1110–11) treats Dickens's will as a revealing biographical document. Victorian readers would have reacted similarly; and were meant to do so.
58. p. 243.
59. pp. 65, 92.
60. *Dickens*, III, 165.
61. Respectively: *ibid.*, III, 229 (Dickens's italics), III, 224–5, III, 239 (my italics).
62. *Dickens and his Readers*, p. 161.
63. Houghton Library, Harvard University MS (15 Dec. 1873). Forster's italics.
64. *Dickens*, I, 99–100.
65. See *Pilgrim*, i, xi–xvii.
66. Ford, *op. cit.*, p. 161.
67. *Charles Dickens: a Critical Introduction* (2nd edn, 1965), 31.
68. Fielding and Grubb, *op. cit.*, 155.
69. F. R. and Q. D. Leavis, *op. cit.*, ix.
70. See FC Newspaper Cuttings, vols. VIII, XI, XIX–XXI, XXXI–XXXIII, *passim.*
71. (10 July 1858), 46.
72. 141 (1876), 80.
73. (26 Dec. 1871), 4.
74. 43 (1874–5), 168–80.
75. Houghton Library, Harvard University MS (7 May 1873).
76. FC MS: Longfellow to Forster (18 June 1873).

Postscript

1. 'John Forster', *Forster Collection: a Catalogue of the Printed Books* (1888), xxv.
2. Robert Browning, *New Letters*, 231.
3. HL MS: Henry Rawlins to Whitwell Elwin (10 Feb. 1876).
4. *The Times* (2 Feb. 1876), 10.
5. *Examiner* (5 Feb. 1876), 148.
6. (5 Feb. 1876), 4.
7. (15 Feb. 1876), 4. Reprinted in *Monthly Chronicle of North-Country Lore and Legend*, II (1888), 49–54.
8. e.g. R. H. Horne, 'John Forster; his early life and friendships', *Temple Bar*, XLVI (1876), 491–505, and B. Jerrold, 'John Forster', *Gentleman's Mag.*, XVI (1876), 313–19.
9. *The Times* (7 Feb. 1876), 5.
10. The full inscription is conveniently found in R. Renton, *John Forster and His Friendships* (1912), 269.
11. For details see K. J. Fielding and G. R. Grubb, 'New letters from Charles Dickens to John Forster, *Boston Univ. Studies in English*, II (1956), 145–7.
12. *The Times* (7 Apr. 1876), 10.
13. This paragraph is based on Forster's will, probate granted 22 March 1876.
14. Fielding and Grubb, *op. cit.*, 143.
15. D. Woolley, 'Forster's *Swift*', *Dickensian*, LXX (1974), 198, 203.
16. *Ibid.*, 198.
17. Whitwell Elwin, *Some XVIII Century Men of Letters*, ed. Warwick Elwin (1902) I, 308.
18. *The Times* (11 May 1876), 11.

19. HL MS: Georgina Hogarth to Annie Fields (23 June 1877).
20. HL MS: Henry Rawlins to Whitwell Elwin (15 Dec. 1879).
21. To judge from what Mrs Forster's niece, Fanny Crosbie, sold at Sotheby's on 23 July 1935. As for Forster's diary, when Whitwell Elwin asked after it in 1879 Mrs Forster told him that her husband had 'so sadly cut [it] up ... that it is all in bits – very difficult to refer to – and after all perhaps the best pieces were used with the MS of the Dickens Life – and are not to be found' (HL MS [11 Dec. 1879]). Certainly she did not then let Elwin see it but sent him extracts copied into a small exercise book (HL MS). Warwick Elwin referred to the diary when writing the memoir of his father as part of *Some XVIII Century Men of Letters* (1902) but it cannot be assumed that he saw any more than further extracts perhaps supplied to him by Fanny Crosbie. The rest is silence.
22. *New Letters,* ed. A. Carlyle (1904), II, 333.
23. HL MS: Robert Lytton to Dearest Friend (Mrs Forster) (25 Feb. 1880).
24. *Ibid.*
25. Elwin, *op. cit.*, I, 339–40.
26. HL MS: Charles Kent to Mrs Forster (18 June 1888).

Bibliography

1. FORSTER'S PUBLICATIONS

A. BOOKS AND PAMPHLETS

Rhyme and Reason (privately printed, 1832).

Lives of Eminent British Statesmen, II (*Sir John Eliot; Thomas Wentworth, Earl of Strafford*) (Longman, Orme, Brown, Green & Longmans, 1836). *Lardner's Cabinet Cyclopaedia*, XLIV.

Lives of Eminent British Statesmen, III (*John Pym; John Hampden*) (Longman, Orme, Brown, Green & Longmans, 1837). *Lardner's Cabinet Cyclopaedia*, XLV.

Lives of Eminent British Statesmen, IV (*Sir Henry Vane, the Younger; Henry Marten*) (Longman, Orme, Brown, Green & Longmans, 1838). *Lardner's Cabinet Cyclopaedia*, XLVI.

Lives of Eminent British Statesmen, VI–VII (*Oliver Cromwell*) (Longman, Orme, Brown, Green & Longmans, 1839). *Lardner's Cabinet Cyclopaedia*, XLVIII–XLIX.

The Statesmen of the Commonwealth of England. With a treatise on the popular progress in English history. (5 vols., Longman, Orme, Brown, Green & Longmans, 1840.)
  Reprinted 1862.
  Another edn, ed. J. O. Choules (Harper & Brothers, New York, 1846).

A Treatise on the Popular Progress in English History (Longman, Orme, Brown, Green & Longmans, 1840).

The Life and Adventures of Oliver Goldsmith (Bradbury & Evans, 1848). Subsequent editions are entitled *The Life and Times of Oliver Goldsmith.*
  2nd edn (2 vols., Bradbury & Evans, 1854).
  New (abridged) edn (Bradbury & Evans, 1855).
  4th edn (Chapman & Hall, 1863).
  Another edn, ed. G. T. Bettany (Ward, Lock & Co., 1890).
  Another edn, ed. R. Ingpen (Hutchinson & Co., 1903).

Daniel De Foe and Charles Churchill (Travellers' Library, 1855).

with C. W. Dilke and Charles Dickens, *The Case of the Reformers of the Royal Literary Fund* (privately printed, 1858).

with C. W. Dilke and Charles Dickens, *Royal Literary Fund. The Answer to the Committee's Summary of Facts* (privately printed, 1858).

Historical and Biographical Essays (2 vols., John Murray, 1858).
  Rev. and enlarged edn (2 vols., John Murray, 1860).

Biographical Essays, 3rd edn (John Murray, 1860).

The Arrest of the Five Members by Charles I (John Murray, 1860).

The Debates on the Grand Remonstrance, November and December, 1641. With an introductory essay on English freedom under the Plantagenet and Tudor sovereigns (John Murray, 1860).

Sir John Eliot: a Biography (2 vols., Longman, Green, Longman, Roberts & Green, 1864).
  2nd edn (1872).

Walter Savage Landor (2 vols., Chapman & Hall, 1869).
  Another edn (Fields, Osgood & Co., Boston, 1869).
  Rev. and abridged edn (Chapman & Hall, 1876). *The Works and Life of Walter Savage Landor* (Chapman & Hall, 1876), I.

The Life of Charles Dickens (3 vols., Chapman & Hall, 1872–4).
Another edn (3 vols., J. B. Lippincott & Son, Philadelphia, 1872–4).
Library edn (2 vols., Chapman & Hall, 1876).
Rev. and abridged George Gissing (Chapman & Hall, 1903).
Another edn, ed. B. W. Matz (2 vols., Chapman & Hall, 1911).
Everyman's Library edn, intro. G. K. Chesterton (2 vols., J. W. Dent & Sons, 1927).
Another edn, ed. J. W. T. Ley (Doubleday, Doran & Co., New York, 1928).
Another edn, ed. A. J. Hoppé (2 vols., J. M. Dent & Sons, 1966).
Everyman's Library edn, ed. A. J. Hoppé (2 vols., Dent, 1970).

The Life of Jonathan Swift. Volume the First: 1667–1711 (John Murray, 1875).

with G. H. Lewes, *Dramatic Essays*, ed. W. Archer and R. W. Lowe (Walter Scott, 1896).

B. EDITIONS

JOHN FLETCHER, *The Elder Brother*. Adapted for Modern Representation [by John Forster]. (Bradbury & Evans, 1846.)

JOHN EVELYN, *Diary and Correspondence. To which is Subjoined the Private Correspondence.*, ed. W. Bray. New edn corrected, revised, and enlarged [by John Forster] (4 vols., H. Colburn, 1854).

ROBERT BROWNING, *Selections*, ed. J. Forster and B. W. Procter (Chapman & Hall, 1863).

WALTER SAVAGE LANDOR, *Works* (7 vols., Chapman & Hall, 1876).

C. ARTICLES AND REVIEWS

This list is far from complete. It restricts itself to those of Forster's mainly anonymous writings that can be positively identified. I have accepted and included the attributions made by Kathleen Tillotson and Nina Burgis (see 2d, below).

'Remarks on two of the annuals', *Newcastle Mag.* (1829), 27–38.

'Our early patriots', *Englishman's Mag.*, I (Apr.–Aug. 1831), 351–6.

'Our early patriots – John Pym', *Englishman's Mag.*, I (Apr.–Aug. 1831), 499–512. Part reprinted as 'John Pym', *The Times* (9 July 1831), 3.

'Our early patriots – Sir John Eliot', *Englishman's Mag.* I (Apr.–Aug. 1831), 623–37.

'Sir Henry Vane's scheme of parliamentary reform', *Englishman's Mag.*, II, no. 1 (Sept. 1831), 1–13. Reprinted *The Times* (5 Sept. 1831), 7.

'Prodigious!', *Englishman's Mag.*, II, no. 1 (Sept. 1831), 79–83.

'John Hampden', *New Monthly Mag.*, XXXIV (1832), 121–30.

[Leigh Hunt, *Sir Ralph Esher*], *New Monthly Mag.*, XXXIV (1832), 288–9.

[Tennyson, *Poems*], *True Sun* (19 Jan. 1833), 3.

'*King Lear*, "As Shakespeare Wrote It"', *New Monthly Mag.*, XLIV (1834), 218–23.

[D. Jerrold, *Beau Nash*], *New Monthly Magazine*, 41 (1834), 514–16.

[Ainsworth, *Rookwood*], *Examiner* (18 May 1834), p. 308.

[Landor, *Citation and Examination of William Shakespeare*], *Examiner* (30 Nov. 1834), 756–8.

'Charles Lamb. His last words on Coleridge', *New Monthly Mag.*, XLIII (1835), 198–206.

'Charles Lamb: an autobiographical sketch', *New Monthly Mag.*, XLIII (1835), 499–501.

[Wordsworth, *Yarrow Revisited*], *Examiner* (26 Apr. 1835), 259–60.

[Browning, *Paracelsus*], *Examiner* (6 Sept. 1835), 563–5.

[Macready as Macbeth], *Examiner* (4 Oct. 1835), 629–30.

[Macready as Hamlet], *Examiner* (11 Oct. 1835), 644–5.

[Macready as Othello], *Examiner* (25 Oct. 1835), 676–7.

'Evidences of a new genius for dramatic poetry. No. I', *New Monthly Mag.*, XLVI (1836), 289–308.

'Evidences of a new genius for dramatic poetry. No. II', *New Monthly Mag.*, XLVI (1836), 342–58.

[Landor, *Pericles and Aspasia*], *Examiner*

(27 Mar. 1836), 196–8; and (3 Apr. 1836), 212.
'Evidences of a new genius for dramatic poetry. No. III', *New Monthly Mag.*, XLVIII (1836), 200–8.
[Talfourd, *Ion*], *Examiner* (29 May 1836), 341.
[Forrest as Othello], *Examiner* (30 Oct. 1836), 694–5.
[Forrest as Lear], *Examiner* (6 Nov. 1836), 711–12.
[Ainsworth, *Crichton*], *Examiner* (27 Nov. 1836), 755–7.
[Dickens and Hullah, *The Village Coquettes*], *Examiner* (11 Dec. 1836), 791–2.
[J. Prior, *The Life of Goldsmith*], *Examiner* (25 Dec. 1836), 819–22; and (1 Jan. 1837), 5–6.
[Forrest as Macbeth], *Examiner* (12 Feb. 1837), 101–2.
[*Abel Allnutt*. By the Author of 'Hajji Baba'.], *Examiner* (19 Feb. 1837), 117–18.
[Forrest as Richard III], *Examiner* (5 Mar. 1837), 148–9.
[*Bentley's Miscellany*, No. 3], *Examiner* (12 Mar. 1837), 165–6.
[Browning, *Strafford*], *Examiner* (7 May 1837), 294–5.
[Ainsworth, *Crichton*], *Metropolitan Mag.*, XIX (May 1837), 9–11.
[Dickens, *Pickwick Papers*, No. 15], *Examiner* (2 July 1837), 421–2.
[Moncrieff, adaptation of *Pickwick Papers*], *Examiner* (16 July 1837), 454–5.
[Leigh Hunt, *The Monthly Repository*], *Examiner* (6 Aug. 1837), 500–1.
[Dickens, *Oliver Twist*], *Examiner* (10 Sept. 1837), 581–2.
'Covent Garden and Drury Lane', *Examiner* (8 Oct. 1837), 646–7.
[*Bentley's Miscellany*, Nov.], *Examiner* (19 Nov. 1837), 740.
[Landor, *Pentameron*], *Examiner* (3 Dec. 1837), 772.
[Kean as Hamlet], *Examiner* (14 Jan. 1838), 20–1.
'Macready's Lear', *Examiner* (4 Feb. 1838), 69–70.
[Bulwer, *The Lady of Lyons*], *Examiner* (18 Feb. 1838), 101–2; and (25 Feb. 1838), 118.
[Macready's Coriolanus], *Examiner* (18 Mar. 1838), 165–6.
[T. B. Browne, *Thoughts of the Times*], *Examiner* (18 Mar. 1838), 164.
[Macready's *Tempest*], *Examiner* (21 Oct. 1838), 662–3.
[*Bentley's Miscellany*, Mar.], *Examiner* (3 Mar. 1839), 133–4.
[Bulwer, *Richelieu*], *Examiner* (31 Mar. 1839), 197–8.
[Landor, *Andrea of Hungary* and *Giovanni of Naples*], *Examiner* (15 Sept. 1839), 580–2.
'*Twelfth Night* at the Haymarket', *Examiner* (22 Sept. 1839), 598–9.
[Ainsworth, *Jack Sheppard*], *Examiner* (3 Nov. 1839), 691–3.
[J. S. Knowles, *Love*], *Examiner* (10 Nov. 1839), 709–10.
[Defoe's *Works*], *Examiner* (22 Dec. 1839), 804–5.
[Leigh Hunt, *A Legend of Florence*], *Examiner* (9 Feb. 1840), 85; and (16 Feb. 1840), 102.
[Thackeray, *The Paris Sketch Book*], *Examiner* (19 July 1840), 451–2.
[*Stradling Correspondence*, ed. J. M. Traherne], *Examiner* (23 Aug. 1840), 533–4.
[Bulwer, *Paul Clifford*], *Examiner* (30 Aug. 1840), 550.
[R. M. Milnes, *Poetry for the People*; F. H. Doyle, *Miscellaneous Verses*], *Examiner* (30 Aug. 1840), 549.
[Bulwer, *Eugene Aram*], *Examiner* (6 Sept. 1840), 566.
[Horace Smith, *Oliver Cromwell: an Historical Romance*], *Examiner* (20 Sept. 1840), 595–6.
[Knowles, *Bride of Messina*], *Examiner* (27 Sept. 1840), 613–14.
[Leigh Hunt, *Dramatic Works of Sheridan*], *Examiner* (4 Oct. 1840), 629.
[John Bowring, *Report on Egypt*], *Examiner* (18 Oct. 1840), 661–2.
[Leigh Hunt, *Dramatic Works of Wycherley, Congreve, etc.*], *Examiner* (25 Oct. 1840), 676–7.
[Bulwer, *Money*], *Examiner* (13 Dec. 1840), 790–1.
[Richard Cattermole, *The Great Civil War of Charles the First and the Parliament*], *Examiner* (20 Dec. 1840), 805–6.
[J. S. Knowles, *Dramatic Works*], *Examiner* (20 Dec. 1840), 806–7.
'John Dryden and Jacob Tonson', *The Pic Nic Papers* (1841), I, 46–62.

[Landor, *Fra Rupert*], *Examiner* (3 Jan. 1841), 4–5.

[Thackeray, *The Second Funeral of Napoleon and The Chronicle of the Drum*], *Examiner* (17 Jan. 1841), 37.

[Bulwer, *Night and Morning*], *Examiner* (17 Jan. 1841), 35–7.

[George Darley, *Ethelstan*], *Examiner* (7 Feb. 1841), 83–4.

[R. H. Dana, *Two Years Before the Mast*], *Examiner* (7 Feb. 1841), 85.

[Sarah Flower Adams, *Vivia Perpetua*], *Examiner* (14 Feb. 1841), 99–100.

[Ignace Moscheles, *The Life of Beethoven*], *Examiner* (14 Feb. 1841), 100–1.

[[Catherine Crowe], *The Adventures of Susan Hopley*], *Examiner* (28 Feb. 1841), 132.

[Lord Jocelyn, *Six Months with the Chinese Expedition*], *Examiner* (14 Mar. 1841), 164–5.

[D. C. Moylan (ed.), *The Opinions of Lord Holland*], *Examiner* (28 Mar. 1841), 197–8.

[T. Hook, *The French Stage and the French People*], *Examiner* (4 Apr. 1841), 211–12.

[T. Hook, *Fleury's Memoirs*], *Examiner* (11 Apr. 1841), 229–30.

[W. D. Cooley, *The Negroland of the Arabs*], *Examiner* (18 Apr. 1841), 243–5.

[John Sterling, *The Election*], *Examiner* (25 Apr. 1841), 259–60.

[Sarah Austin, *Fragments from German Prose Writers*], *Examiner* (9 May 1841), 292.

[J. and H. Buller, *A Winter in the Azores*], *Examiner* (6 June 1841), 354–5.

[Laman Blanchard, *Life and Literary Remains of L.E.L.*], *Examiner* (13 June 1841), 371–2.

[[W. Cooke Taylor], *The Bishop*], *Examiner* (20 June 1841), 387–8.

[[Lady Charlotte Bury], *The History of a Flirt*], *Examiner* (26 June 1841), 405–6.

[N. L. Beamish, *The Discovery of America by the Northmen*], *Examiner* (24 July 1841), 468–9.

[C. M. Sedgwick, *Letters from Abroad*], *Examiner* (24 July 1841), 469.

[I. D'Israeli, *The Amenities of Literature*], *Examiner* (7 Aug. 1841), 501–2.

[Isabella F. Romer, *Sturmer*], *Examiner* (21 Aug. 1841), 532–3.

[Harriet Martineau, *The Playfellow*], *Examiner* (4 Sept. 1841), 565–6.

[J. A. Manning (ed.), *Memoirs of Sir Benjamin Rudyerd*], *Examiner* (18 Sept. 1841), 595–6.

[Henry Spicer, *Lost and Won*], *Examiner* (18 Sept. 1841), 596–7.

[Browning, *Pippa Passes*[, *Examiner* (2 Oct. 1841), 628–9.

[J. W. Marston, *The Patrician's Daughter*; G. Catlin, *Letters and Notes on ... the North American Indians*; P. Macgregor, *The Genuine Remains of Ossian*], *Examiner* (9 Oct. 1841), 644–6.

[G. Catlin, *Letters and Notes on ... the North American Indians*], *Examiner* (16 Oct. 1841), 661.

[A. M. Maxwell, *A Run Through the United States*], *Examiner* (30 Oct. 1841), 692–3.

[Schiller, *The Maid of Orleans*], *Examiner* (6 Nov. 1841), 709.

[Lady Blessington, *The Keepsake for 1842*], *Examiner* (13 Nov. 1841), 725.

[Dickens, *Barnaby Rudge*, *The Old Curiosity Shop*, *Master Humphrey's Clock*], *Examiner* (4 Dec. 1841), 772–4.

[C. Edwards Lester, *The Glory and the Shame of England*; J. P. Collier, *Reasons for a New Edition of Shakespeare's Works*; C. Knight, *Postscript to the Sixth Volume of the Pictorial Edition of Shakespeare*], *Examiner* (11 Dec. 1841), 787–90.

[Thomas Murray (ed.), *Letters of David Hume*], *Examiner* (18 Dec. 1841), 803–4.

[C. G. Addison, *The History of the Knights Templars*; [Sir Arthur Helps], *Essays Written in the Intervals of Business*], *Examiner* (25 Dec. 1841), 820–2.

[Bulwer, *Zanoni*], *Examiner* (26 Feb. 1842), 132–3.

[G. Griffin, *Gisippus*], *Examiner* (26 Feb. 1842), 133–4.

'Drury Lane', *Examiner* (26 Mar. 1842), 197.

[Browning, *King Victor and King Charles*], *Examiner* (2 Apr. 1842), 211–12.

[Tennyson, *Poems*], *Examiner* (28 May 1842), 340–1.

[Leigh Hunt, *The Palfrey*], *Examiner* (16 July 1842), 452.

[Macready's King John], *Examiner* (29 Oct. 1842), 693.
[Lady Blessington, *The Book of Beauty*], *Examiner* (19 Nov. 1842), 741–2.
[Browning, *Dramatic Lyrics*], *Examiner* (26 Nov. 1842), 756–7.
[The First Philosophers of Greece], *Foreign Q. Rev.*, XXX (Oct. 1842–Jan. 1843), 61–92.
[Newspaper Literature of America], *Foreign Q. Rev.*, XXX (Oct. 1842–Jan. 1843), 197–222.
[Socrates and the Sophists of Athens], *Foreign Q. Rev.*, XXX (Oct. 1842–Jan. 1843), 331–68.
[Browning, *A Blot on the 'Scutcheon*], *Examiner* (18 Feb. 1843), 101.
[The Answer of the American Press], *Foreign Q. Rev.*, XXXI (Apr.–July 1843), 250–81.
[The Dialogues of Plato], *Foreign Q. Rev.* XXXI (Apr.–July 1843), 471–501.
[Thackeray, *Irish Sketchbook*], *Examiner* (13 May 1843), 292–3.
[John Sterling, *Strafford*], *Examiner* (12 Aug. 1843), 499–500.
'American poetry', *Foreign Q, Rev.*, XXXII (Oct. 1843–Jan. 1844), 291–324.
[Leigh Hunt, *Poetical Works*], *Examiner* (13 Apr. 1844), 227.
[Browning, *Colombe's Birthday*], *Examiner* (22 June 1844), 388–9.
[E. B. Barrett, *Poems*], *Examiner* (5 Oct. 1844), 627–9.
[A. P. Stanley, *The Life and Correspondence of Thomas Arnold*], *Examiner* (12 Oct. 1844), 644–5.
[R. Chambers, *Vestiges of the Natural History of Creation*], *Examiner* (9 Nov. 1844), 707.
[Leigh Hunt, *Imagination and Fancy*], *Examiner* (23 Nov. 1844), 740–1.
[Charles Churchill], *Edinburgh Rev.*, LXXXI (Jan. 1845), 46–88.
'*The Chimes*, by Mr Dickens', Edinburgh Rev., LXXXI (Jan. 1845), 181–9.
[H. Walpole, *Memoirs of the Reign of George the Third*], *Examiner* (1 Feb. 1845), 67–9.
[Daniel De Foe], *Edinburgh Rev.*, LXXXII (Oct. 1845), 480–532.
[Browning, *Dramatic Romances and Lyrics*], *Examiner* (15 Nov. 1845), 723–4.
[Carlyle, *Oliver Cromwell's Letters and Speeches*], *Examiner* (13 Dec. 1845), 787–9.
[Bulwer, *The New Timon*, Part I], *Examiner* (20 Dec. 1845), 803–4.
[Bulwer, *The New Timon*, Part II], *Examiner* (10 Jan. 1846), 20.
[Leigh Hunt, *Stories from the Italian Poets*], *Examiner* (7 Feb. 1846), 83–5.
[H. Melville, *Typee*], *Examiner* (7 Mar. 1846), 147–8.
'Landor's *Collected Writings* – new *Imaginary Conversations*', *Edinburgh Rev.*, LXXXIII (Apr. 1846), 486–511.
[Browning, *Luria; and A Soul's Tragedy*], *Examiner* (25 Apr. 1846), 259–60.
[Landor, *Works*], *Examiner* (20 June 1846), 387–8.
'Killing no murder', *Examiner* (29 Aug. 1846), 546–7.
[Bulwer, *Lucretia*], *Examiner* (5 Dec. 1846), 771–3; and (12 Dec. 1846), 788–9.
[Thackeray, *Mrs Perkin's Ball*], *Examiner* (19 Dec. 1846), 864–5.
[Lady Blessington, *Marmaduke Herbert*], *Examiner* (22 May 1847), 324–5.
[Leigh Hunt, *Men, Women and Books*], *Examiner* (5 June 1847), 355–6.
[Landor, *Hellenics*], *Examiner* (11 Dec. 1847), 788.
'Books for Christmas', *Examiner* (18 Dec. 1847), 804; and (25 Dec. 1847), 820–1.
[Tennyson, *The Princess*], *Examiner* (8 Jan. 1848), 20–1.
[Landor, *Hellenics*], *Examiner* (22 Jan. 1848), 53–4.
[Bulwer, *King Arthur*, Part I], *Examiner* (4 Mar. 1848), 147–8.
[Letter to Editor], *Literary Gaz.* (17 June 1848), 407–8.
[Letter to Editor], *Literary Gaz.* (29 June 1848), 506–7.
'Drury Lane', *Examiner* (15 July 1848), 453–4.
[Thackeray, *Vanity Fair], Examiner* (22 July 1848), 468–70.
[Mrs Gaskell, *Mary Barton*], *Examiner* (4 Nov. 1848), 708–9.
[Bulwer, *King Arthur*], *Examiner* (27 Jan. 1849), 52–4.
[Leigh Hunt, *A Book for a Corner* and *The Town*], *Examiner* (9 June 1849), 357–9.
'Death of the Countess of Blessington', *Examiner* (9 June 1849), 358.

[German Socialism], *North British Rev.*, XI (Aug. 1849), 406–35.
[Browning, *Poems*], *Examiner* (8 Sept. 1849), 565.
[Bulwer, *The Caxtons*], *Examiner* (20 Oct. 1849), 659–61.
'The trial of the Mannings', *Examiner* (3 Nov. 1849), 691.
[Southey, *Life and Correspondence*], *Examiner* (10 Nov. 1849), 708–9.
'Mr Charles Phillips and the *Examiner*', *Examiner* (24 Nov. 1849), 737–9.
'What we have not done, and what Mr Charles Phillips has done', *Examiner* (8 Dec. 1849), 769–70.
'Encouragement of literature by the state', *Examiner* (5 Jan. 1850), 2.
'The dignity of literature', *Examiner* (19 Jan. 1850), 35.
[Alexander Dyce (ed.), *Works of Marlowe*], *Examiner* (19 Jan. 1850), 36–8.
[Browning, *Christmas-Eve and Easter Day*], *Examiner* (6 Apr. 1850), 211–13.
'Francis Jeffrey', *Household Words* (27 Apr. 1850), 113–18.
'New life and old learning', *Household Words* (4 May 1850), 130–2.
[Tennyson, *In Memoriam*], *Examiner* (8 June 1850), 356–7.
'Water supply', *Examiner* (6 July 1850), 444–5.
[Beddoes, *Death's Jest-Book*], *Examiner* (20 July 1850), 461–3.
'Southey and the *Quarterly Review*', *Examiner* (18 Jan. 1851), 33–4.
[Landor, *Popery: British and Foreign*], *Examiner* (1 Feb. 1851), 68–9.
'Mr. Macready', *Examiner* (22 Feb. 1851), 117–18.
'Mr. Macready's farewell', *Examiner* (1 Mar. 1851), 134.
'Mr. Thackeray's lectures', *Examiner* (24 May 1851), 325–6; (31 May 1851), 342–3; (14 June 1851), 374–5; (21 June 1851), 390–1; (5 July 1851), 422.
'Ill-requited services', *Examiner* (12 July 1851), 433–4.
[Beddoes, *Poems*], *Examiner* (27 Sept. 1851), 611–14.
'The representative of Hungary', *Examiner* (15 Nov. 1851), 721–2.
'Count D'Orsay', *New Monthly Mag.*, XCVI (1852), 112–26.
'The reason why', *Household Words* (30 Oct. 1852), 155–6.
[Thackeray, *Henry Esmond*], *Examiner* (13 Nov. 1852), 723–6.
'Chip: the reason why', *Household Words* (20 Nov. 1852), 233–4.
[Mrs Gaskell, *Ruth*], *Examiner* (22 Jan. 1853), 51–3.
'Seventy-eight years ago', *Household Words* (5 Mar. 1853), 1–6; and (16 Apr. 1853), 157–63.
[E. Arnold, *Poems*], *Examiner* (16 Apr. 1853), 245–6.
[Thackeray, *English Humourists*], *Examiner* (11 June 1853), 372–3.
'The power-loom', *Household Words* (9 July 1853), 440–5.
[Anon. *Margaret*], *Examiner* (22 Oct. 1853), 677–8.
[Memoir of the Author], in G. N. T. Grenville (Baron Nugent), *Some Memorials of John Hampden* (3rd edn, 1854).
[W. H. Smyth, *The Mediterranean*], *Examiner* (8 Apr. 1854), 212.
[Landor, *Letters of an American*], *Examiner* (1 July 1854), 410.
[Harriet Beecher Stowe, *Sunny Memories of Foreign Lands*], *Examiner* (22 July 1854), 455–6.
[Samuel Foote], *Q. Rev.*, XCV (Sept. 1854), 483–548.
[Sir Richard Steele], *Quarterly Review*, XCVI (Mar. 1855), 509–68.
[Owen Meredith, *Clytemnestra and Other Poems*], *Examiner* (17 Mar. 1855), 163–4.
[Leigh Hunt, *Stories in Verse*], *Examiner* (28 Apr. 1855), 261.
'Lord John Russell', *Examiner* (21 July 1855), 449–50.
[Tennyson, *Maud and Other Poems*], *Examiner* (4 Aug. 1855), 483–4.
[Browning, *Men and Women*], *Examiner* (1 Dec. 1855), 756–7.
[The Civil Wars and Cromwell], *Edinburgh Rev.*, CIII (Jan. 1856), 1–54.
[New Magazines: Edmund Yates's *The Train*, No. 1], *Examiner* (12 Jan. 1856), 22.
[Bulwer, *St. Stephen's*], *Examiner* (31 Mar. 1860), 196–7.
'Strafford's youth', *The Victoria Regia* (1861), 227–53.
'The death of Mr. Thackeray', *Examiner* (26 Dec. 1863), 817–18.
'A word on Alexander Dyce', *Fortnightly Rev.*, n.s. XVIII (1875), 731–46.

Reprinted as 'Alexander Dyce: a biographical sketch', in *Catalogue of the Dyce Collection in the South Kensington Museum* (1875).

2. GENERAL

A. MANUSCRIPTS

I have consulted Forster material held by the following libraries:

Austin, Texas – Humanities Research Centre, University of Texas
Bergen, Norway – University Library
Bristol – Central Library
Cambridge, Mass. – Houghton Library, Harvard University
Chicago – University of Chicago Library
Edinburgh – National Library of Scotland
Leeds – Brotherton Collection, University of Leeds
Lewes, Sussex – East Sussex County Record Office
Lincoln – Tennyson Research Centre, Central Library
Liverpool – Public Library
London – British Library – Dickens House – Forster Collection, Victoria & Albert Museum Library – Dr Williams' Library
Los Angeles – William Andrews Clark Memorial Library, U.C.L.A.
Manchester – John Rylands University Library – Public Library
New Haven. Conn. – Yale University Library
New York – Berg Collection, New York Public Library – Fales Library, New York University – J. P. Morgan Library – Pforzheimer Library
Oxford – Bodleian Library
Philadelphia – Free Library
Princeton – Princeton University Library
San Marino, Cal. – Huntington Library
Stevenage, Herts. – Lytton Papers, Hertfordshire County Record Office
Stockholm – Kungliga Biblioteket
Urbana – Champaign – University of Illinois Library
Waco, Texas – Armstrong Browning Library, Baylor University
Washington, D.C. – Folger Library
Wisbech – Townshend Collection, Wisbech & Fenland Museum

B. PRINTED BOOKS PAMPHLETS, THESES

ANON., *Arranged Catalogue of the Library of the Literary and Philosophical Society of Newcastle Upon Tyne* (1819).
—*A Historical Sketch of the Transactions of the Literary and Philosophical Society of Newcastle Upon Tyne* (1807).
—*Jarndyce Miscellany*, Catalogue 14 (1977).
—*The Picture of Newcastle Upon Tyne* (1807).
—*The Picture of Newcastle Upon Tyne* (1812).
—*Reports of the Literary and Philosophical Society of Newcastle Upon Tyne* (1820ff.).
[E.H.A.], *Scholae Novocastrensis Alumni* (1870).
A. A. ADRIAN, *Georgina Hogarth and the Dickens Circle* (1957).
—*Mark Lemon, First Editor of Punch* (1966).
SHIRLEY S. ALLEN, *Samuel Phelps and Sadler's Wells Theatre* (Middletown, Conn., 1971).
S. A. ALLIBONE, *A Critical Dictionary of English Literature and English and American Authors* (1858), I.
WILLIAM ALLINGHAM, *A Diary*, ed. H. Allingham and D. Radford (1907).
R. D. ALTICK, *Lives and Letters* (New York, 1966).
A. ANDREWS, *The History of British Journalism* (2 vols., 1859).
F. ARCHER, *An Actor's Notebook* [n.d.].
R. W. ARMOUR, *Barry Cornwall: a Biography of Bryan Waller Procter* (Boston, Mass., 1935).
MATTHEW ARNOLD, *Letters to Arthur Hugh Clough*, ed. H. F. Lowry (1932).
W. H. ARNOLD, *Ventures in Book Collecting* (New York, 1923).
R. H. BARHAM, *The Garrick Club* (1896).

T. L. BEDDOES, *Letters*, ed. E. Gosse (1894).

H. HALE BELLOT, *University College London 1826–1926* (1929).

A. BLAINEY, *The Farthing Poet: a Biography of R. H. Horne* (1968).

E. BLUNDEN, *Leigh Hunt: a Biography* (1930).

—*Charles Lamb and His Contemporaries* (1933).

—*Charles Lamb: His Life Recorded by His Contemporaries* (1934).

H. R. FOX BOURNE, *English Newspapers* (2 vols., 1887).

J. W. BRAYMER, 'The literary biographies of John Forster' (Ph.D. thesis, University of Tennessee, 1977).

S. REED BRETT, *John Pym 1583–1643* (1940).

L. A. BREWER, *Some Letters from My Leigh Hunt Portfolios* (Cedar Rapids, Iowa, 1929).

—*My Leigh Hunt Library: the Holograph Letters* (Cedar Rapids, Iowa, 1932).

A. W. C. BRICE, 'John Forster as a critic of fiction' (Ph.D. thesis, University of Edinburgh, 1972).

A. M. BROADLEY, *Chats on Autographs* (1910).

E. B. BROWNING, *Letters*, ed. F. G. Kenyon (2 vols., 1897).

ROBERT BROWNING, *Prose Life of Strafford*, intro. C. H. Firth (1892).

—*Letters*, coll. T. J. Wise, ed. T. L. Hood (New Haven, 1933).

—*New Letters*, ed. W. C. DeVane and K. L. Knickerbocker (New Haven, 1951).

—*Browning to His American Friends*, ed. G. R. Hudson (1965).

—*Learned Lady: Letters to Mrs Thomas Fitzgerald*, ed. E. C. McAleer (Cambridge, Mass., 1966).

—*Complete Works* (Baylor–Ohio edn, I—: Athens, Ohio, 1970—; in progress).

ROBERT BROWNING and ELIZABETH BARRETT BROWNING, *Letters 1845–6*, ed. Elvan Kintner (2 vols., Cambridge, Mass., 1968).

—*Letters to George Barrett*, ed. P. Landis (Urbana, Ill., 1958).

J. H. BUCKLEY, *The Triumph of Time* (1967).

SIR R. BURROWS (ed.), *Halesbury's Statutes of England* (2nd edn, 1949).

J. BUTT and KATHLEEN TILLOTSON, *Dickens at Work* (1957).

JANE WELSH CARLYLE, *Letters and Memorials*, ed. J. A. Froude (3 vols., 1883).

—*New Letters and Memorials*, ed. A. Carlyle (2 vols., 1903).

—*Letters to Her Family*, ed. L. Huxley (1924).

—*Letters to Joseph Neuberg 1848–1862*, ed. T. Scudder (1931).

THOMAS CARLYLE, *Rescued Essays*, ed. P. Newberry [1892].

—*New Letters*, ed. A. Carlyle (2 vols., 1904).

—*Letters to John Stuart Mill, John Sterling and Robert Browning*, ed. A. Carlyle (1923).

—*Letters to His Brother Alexander*, ed. Edwin W. Marrs, jr (Cambridge, Mass., 1968).

—*Reminiscences*, ed. C. E. Norton, intro. by Ian Campbell (Everyman's edn, 1972).

—*Works* (Centenary edn, 30 vols., 1896–1901).

—*On Heroes, Hero-Worship, and the Heroic in History* (World's Classics edn, 1950).

THOMAS and JANE WELSH CARLYLE, *Collected Letters*, ed. C. R. Sanders, K. J. Fielding *et al.* (Duke-Edinburgh edn, vols. I—: Durham, N.C., 1970—; in progress).

MARY CALLISTA CARR, 'John Forster: a literary biography to 1856' (Ph.D. thesis, Yale University, 1956).

B. CHAMPNEYS, *Memoirs and Correspondence of Coventry Patmore* (2 vols., 1900).

W. E. CHANNING, *The Superior Tendency of Unitarianism to Form an Elevated Religious Character* (1827).

CHARLES CHURCHILL, *Poetical Works*, with a Memoir by J. L. Hannay & Copious Notes by W. Tooke, F.R.S. (2 vols., 1866).

—*Poetical Works*, ed. D. Grant (1956).

C. and M. COWDEN CLARKE, *Recollections of Writers* (1878).

J. L. CLIFFORD (ed.), *Biography as an Art* (1962).

JOHN CLUBBE (ed.), *Froude's Life of Carlyle* (1979).

WILLSON HAVELOCK COATES (ed.), *The Journal of Sir Simonds D'Ewes* (New Haven, 1942).

PHILIP COLLINS, *Dickens and Crime* (1962).
—(ed.), *Dickens: the Critical Heritage* (1971).
EILEEN MARY CURRAN, 'The *Foreign Quarterly Review* (1827–1846)' (Cornell University Ph.D. thesis, 1958).
JAMES A. DAVIES, 'Aspects of the literary achievement of John Forster' (University of Wales (Swansea) Ph.D. thesis, 1969).
W. C. DEVANE, *A Browning Handbook* (2nd edn, New York, 1955).
CHARLES DICKENS, *Letters* (Nonesuch edn, ed. W. Dexter; 3 vols., 1938).
—*Letters to Angela Burdett-Coutts 1841–1865*, ed. E. Johnson (1963).
—*Letters* (Pilgrim edn, ed. M. House, G. Storey, K. Tillotson *et al.*, vols. I—, 1965—; in progress).
—*Speeches*, ed. K. J. Fielding (1960).
—*Oliver Twist*, ed. K. Tillotson (1966).
—*The Christmas Books* (Penguin edn, ed. M. Slater, 2 vols., 1971).
—*Dombey and Son*, ed. A. Horsman (1974).
—*Little Dorrit*, ed. H. P. Sucksmith (1979).
A. DOWNER, *The Eminent Tragedian* (1966).
SIR CHARLES GAVAN DUFFY, *Conversations with Carlyle* (1892).
A. M. EASTMAN, *A Short History of Shakespearian Criticism* (New York, 1968).
L. EDEL, *Literary Biography* (1957).
I. EHRENPREIS, *Swift: the Man, His Works, and the Age* (2 vols., 1962, 1967).
GEORGE ELIOT, *Letters*, ed. G. S. Haight (7 vols., New Haven, 1954–6).
S. M. ELLIS, *William Harrison Ainsworth and His Friends* (2 vols., 1911).
M. ELWIN, *Victorian Wallflowers* (1934).
WHITWELL ELWIN, *Some XVIII Century Men of Letters*, ed. Warwick Elwin (2 vols., 1902).
R. W. EMERSON, *Letters*, ed. R. L. Rusk, vol. I (New York, 1939).
—*Journals and Miscellaneous Notebooks*, ed. M. M. Sealts, Jr (vols. 5 and 6, Cambridge, Mass., 1965).
D. E. ENFIELD, *L.E.L.: A Mystery of the Thirties* (1928).
F. ESPINASSE, *Literary Recollections and Sketches* (1893).
K. J. FIELDING, *Charles Dickens*, Writers and Their Work: No. 37 (rev. edn, 1963).
—*Charles Dickens: a Critical Introduction* (2nd edn, 1966).
K. J. FIELDING and RODGER L. TARR (eds.), *Carlyle Past and Present* (1976).
P. FITZGERALD, *The Life, Letters and Writings of Charles Lamb* (6 vols., 1876).
—*Pickwickean Studies* (1899).
—*John Forster By One of His Friends* (1903).
—*The Life of Charles Dickens as Revealed in His Writings* (2 vols., 1905).
—*Samuel Foote* (1910).
—*Memories of Charles Dickens* (1913).
SIBYLLA JANE FLOWER, *Bulwer Lytton* (1973).
E. B. de FONBLANQUE, *The Life and Labours of Albany Fonblanque* (1874).
G. H. FORD, *Dickens and His Readers* (Princeton, N.J., 1955).
G. H. FORD etc., *Dickens Criticism* (Cambridge, Mass., 1962).
SIR H. FRASER, *Principles and Practice of the Law of Libel and Slander,* ed. A. P. Fachiri (6th edn, 1925).
[J. HAIN FRISWELL], *Charles Dickens* (1858).
J. A. FROUDE, *Thomas Carlyle: a History of His Life in London 1834–1881* (2 vols., 1884).
R. and E. GARNETT, *The Life of W. J. Fox* (1910).
E. GASKELL, *Letters,* ed. J. A. V. Chapple and A. Pollard (1967).
WINIFRED GÉRIN, *Elizabeth Gaskell* (1976).
R. A. GETTMAN, *A Victorian Publisher* (1960).
G. P. GOOCH, *History and Historians in the Nineteenth Century* (1920).
K. GRAHAM, *English Criticism of the Novel 1865–1900* (1965).
W. J. GRAHAM, *English Literary Periodicals* (New York, 1930).
[JAMES GRANT], *The Great Metropolis* (2nd edn, 2 vols., 1837).
JAMES GRANT, *The Newspaper Press* (3 vols., 1871).
W. H. GRIFFIN and H. C. MINCHIN, *The Life of Robert Browning* (1910).

S. GWYNN and G. M. TUCKWELL, *The Life of the Rt. Hon. Sir Charles Dilke* (2 vols., 1917).

J. S. HAGEN, *Tennyson and His Publishers* (1979).

J. R. HALE (ed.), *The Evolution of British Historiography* (1967).

S. C. HALL, *A Book of Memories* (1871).

—*Retrospect of a Long Life* (2 vols., 1883).

F. E. HALLIDAY, *Shakespeare and His Critics* (1949).

LAWRENCE and ELIZABETH HANSON, *Necessary Evil: The Life of Jane Welsh Carlyle* (1952).

AURELIA BROOKS HARLAN, *Owen Meredith: a Critical Biography of Robert, First Earl of Lytton* (New York, 1946).

AURELIA BROOKS and J. LEE HARLAN, Jr (eds.), *Letters from Owen Meredith (Robert, First Earl of Lytton) to Robert and Elizabeth Barrett Browning* (Waco, Texas, 1936).

FREDERIC HARRISON, *Carlyle and the London Library* (1907).

F. R. HART, *Lockhart as Romantic Biographer* (1971).

J. O. HAYDEN, *The Romantic Reviewers 1802–1824* (1969).

A. HAYTER, *A Sultry Month* (1965).

WILLIAM HAZLITT, *Works*, ed. P. P. Howe, vol. IV (1930).

SIR W. HOLDSWORTH, *A History of English Law*, ed. A. L. Goodhart, H. G. Hanbury, vol. XV (1965).

KEITH HOLLINGSWORTH, *The Newgate Novel* (Detroit, 1963).

R. V. HOLT, *The Unitarian Contribution to Social Progress in England* (1938).

A. B. HOPKINS, *Elizabeth Gaskell: Her Life and Works* (1952).

[JOHN CAMDEN HOTTEN], *Charles Dickens: The Story of His Life* [1870].

LORD HOUGHTON, *Monographs Personal and Social* (2nd edn, 1873).

SUSANNE HOWE, *Geraldine Jewsbury: Her Life and Errors* (1935).

W. D. HOWE, *Charles Lamb and His Friends* (Indianapolis, 1944).

LEIGH HUNT, *Critical Essays on the Performers of the London Theatres* (1807).

—*Christianism* [1832].

—*Correspondence*, ed. Thornton Hunt (2 vols., 1862).

—*Imagination and Fancy* (new edn, 1878).

—*Wit and Humour* (new edn, 1878).

—*Autobiography*, ed. R. Ingpen (2 vols., 1903).

—*Poetical Works*, ed. H. S. Milford (1923).

—*Dramatic Criticism*, ed. L. H. and C. W. Houtchens (1950).

—*Literary Criticism*, ed. L. H. and C. W. Houtchens (New York, 1956).

WILLIAM IRVINE and PARK HONAN, *The Book, the Ring, and the Poet* (1974).

IAN JACK, *English Literature 1815–1832* (1963).

WILLIAM JERDAN, *Autobiography* (4 vols., 1852–3).

B. JERROLD, *The Life and Remains of Douglas Jerrold* (1859).

EDGAR JOHNSON, *Charles Dickens: His Tragedy and Triumph* (2 vols., 1953).

KATHLEEN JONES, *Lunacy, Law, and Conscience* (1955).

—*Mental Health and Social Policy 1845–1959* (1960).

MARGARET A. JUDSON, *The Political Thought of Sir Henry Vane the Younger* (Philadelphia, 1969).

MARY FREAR KEELER (ed.), *Bibliography of British History: Stuart Period, 1603–1714* (1970).

P. M. KENDALL, *The Art of Biography* (1965).

F. G. KITTON, *Charles Dickens By Pen and Pencil* (1895).

C. KNIGHT, *Passages of a Working Life* (3 vols., 1864–5).

R. B. KNOWLES, *The Life of James Sheridan Knowles* (1872).

CHARLES LAMB, *Works*, ed. E. V. Lucas (6 vols., 1912).

—*Literary Criticism*, ed. E. M. W. Tillyard (1923).

CHARLES and MARY LAMB, *Poems, Letters and Remains*, ed. W. C. Hazlitt (1874).

—*Letters*, ed. E. V. Lucas (3 vols., 1935).

LOUIS LANDA, *Swift and the Church of Ireland* (1954).

WALTER SAVAGE LANDOR, *Letters*, ed. S. Wheeler (1899).

L. LANDRE, *Leigh Hunt* (2 vols., Paris, 1936).

A. R. LAWS, *Schola Novocastrensis* (1932).
A. H. LAYARD, *Autobiography and Letters* (2 vols., 1903).
F. R. and Q. D. LEAVIS, *Dickens the Novelist* (1970).
J. W. T. LEY, *The Dickens Circle* (1918).
JACK LINDSAY, *Charles Dickens* (1950).
London University Magazine, I–II (1829–30).
S. LONGFELLOW, *The Life of Henry Wadsworth Longfellow* (2 vols., Boston, 1886).
E. V. LUCAS, *The Life of Charles Lamb* (5th edn, 2 vols., 1921).
SIR EDWARD BULWER LYTTON, *Eugene Aram* (1831).
—*England and the English*, ed. Standish Meacham (Chicago, 1970).
—*The Sea-Captain* (1839).
—*The New Timon & St. Stephen's* (Leipzig, 1860).
—*The Lost Tales of Miletus* (1866).
—*Miscellaneous Prose Works* (3 vols., 1868).
—*The Rightful Heir* (1868).
—*Walpole* (1869).
—*Pamphlets and Sketches* (Knebworth edn, 1874).
—*King Arthur* (rev. edn, 1875).
—*Complete Novels* (28 vols., 1877–8).
—*Dramatic Works* (1887).
ROBERT LYTTON, *Lucile* (1860).
—*Poems by Owen Meredith* (2 vols., Boston, 1869).
—*Personal and Literary Letters*, ed. Lady Balfour (2 vols., 1906).
EARL of LYTTON, *The Life of Edward Bulwer, First Lord Lytton* (2 vols., 1913).
THOMAS BABINGTON MACAULAY, *Literary Essays* (Oxford edn, 1913).
—*Five Essays* (1914).
—*Letters*, ed. Thomas Pinney, vol. IV (1977).
E. MACKENZIE, *A Descriptive and Historical Account of the Town and Country of Newcastle upon Tyne*, vol. I (1827).
D. MACLISE and W. MAGINN, *A Gallery of Illustrious Literary Characters*, ed. William Bates (1873).
W. C. MACREADY, *Reminiscences and Selections from His Diaries and Letters*, ed. Sir. F. Pollock (2 vols., 1875).
—*Diaries*, ed. W. Toynbee (2 vols., 1912).
R. R. MADDEN, *The Literary Life and Correspondence of the Countess of Blessington* (3 vols., 1855).
L. A. MARCHARD, *The Athenaeum* (Chapel Hill, N.C., 1941).
L. MARDER, *His Exits and His Entrances: the Story of Shakespeare's Reputation* (1964).
W. MARSTON, *Our Recent Actors* (1890).
DAVID MASSON, *Memories of London in the 'Forties* (1908).
JOHN MAYNARD, *Browning's Youth* (Cambridge, Mass., 1977).
H. G. MERRIAM, *Edward Moxon, Publisher of Poets* (New York, 1939).
J. S. MILL, *Autobiography* (Library of Liberal Arts edn, New York, 1957).
BETTY MILLER, *Robert Browning: a Portrait* (1952).
J. F. MOLLOY, *The Life and Adventures of Edmund Kean, Tragedian* (2 vols., 1888).
SYLVÈRE MONOD, 'John Forster as a literary biographer' (University of Paris Thèse Complémentaire, 1952).
—*Dickens the Novelist* (Norman, Oklahoma, 1968).
J. R. MOORE, *Daniel Defoe, Citizen of the World* (Chicago, 1958).
S. P. MOSS, *Poe's Literary Battles* (Durham, N.C., 1963).
M. NAPIER, *Selections from the Correspondence*, ed. By His Son (1879).
ALLARDYCE NICOLL, *A History of Early Nineteenth Century Drama 1800–1850*, vol. I (1930).
H. NICOLSON, *The Development of English Biography* (1927).
G. C. D. ODELL, *Shakespeare from Betterton to Irving* (2 vols., 1921).
ROBERT L. PATTEN, *Charles Dickens and His Publishers* (1978).
THOMAS PRESTON PEARDON, *The Transition in English Historical Writing 1760–1830* (New York, 1933).
W. M. PHELPS and J. FORBES-ROBERTSON, *The Life and Life-Work of Samuel Phelps* (1886).
H. POTTER, *An Historical Introduction to English Law and Its Institutions* (1932).
T. POWELL, *The Living Authors of Britain* (New York, 1851).
T. J. POWYS, *Poems* (1891).

JOHN PREST, *Lord John Russell* (1972).
SIR J. PRIOR, *The Life of Oliver Goldsmith* (2 vols., 1837).
—*A letter accusing ... John Forster ... of having pirated the Life of O. Goldsmith by J. Prior* (1849).
CHARLES L. PROUDFIT (ed.), *Landor as Critic* (1979).
THOMAS de QUINCEY, *Collected Writings*, ed. D. Masson, vol. IV (1890).
GORDON N. RAY, *Thackeray: the Uses of Adversity* (1955).
—*Thackeray: the Age of Wisdom* (1958).
J. W. REED, Jr, *English Biography in the Early Nineteenth Century* (New Haven, 1966).
J. C. REID, *Thomas Hood* (1963).
T. WEMYSS REID, *The Life, Letters, and Friendships of Richard Monckton Milnes* (2 vols., 1890).
RICHARD RENTON, *John Forster and His Friendships* (1912).
R. C. RICHARDSON, *The Debate on The English Revolution* (1977).
H. CRABB ROBINSON, *On Books and Their Writers*, ed. E. J. Morley, vol. II (1938).
—*Diary, Reminiscences and Correspondence*, sel. and ed. T. Sadler (2nd edn, 3 vols., 1869).
J. R. ROBINSON, *Fifty Years of Fleet Street*, ed. F. M. Thomas (1904).
KENNETH ROBINSON, *Wilkie Collins* (1951).
GEORGE ROWELL, *The Victorian Theatre* (1956).
—(ed.), *Victorian Dramatic Criticism* (1971).
R. L. RUSK, *The Life of Ralph Waldo Emerson* (New York, 1949).
M. SADLEIR, *Bulwer: a Panorama* (1931).
—*Blessington-D'Orsay: a Masquerade* (1933).
G. A. SALA, *Charles Dickens* (1870).
C. SAWYER and F. DARTON, *Dickens versus Barabbas: Forster Intervening* (1930).
EDGAR F. SHANNON, Jr, *Tennyson and the Reviewers* (Cambridge, Mass., 1952).
J. G. SHARPS, *Mrs. Gaskell's Observation and Invention* (1970).
C. H. SHATTUCK, *Bulwer and Macready* (Urbana, Ill., 1958).
—*Mr. Macready Produces* As You Like it (Urbana, Ill., 1962).
—*William Charles Macready's* King John (Urbana, Ill., 1962).
G. B. SHAW, *Our Theatres in the Nineties*, II (1932).
W. TEIGNMOUTH SHORE, *Charles Dickens and His Friends* (1909).
DONALD SMALLEY (ed.), *Browning's Essay on Chatterton* (Westport, Conn., 1970).
H. S. SOLLY, *The Life of Henry Morley Ll.D.* (1898).
SOTHEBY & CO., *Sales Catalogues for 1935*.
A. C. SPRAGUE, *Shakespearian Players and Performances* (1954).
J. F. STANFIELD, *An Essay on the Study and Composition of Biography* (1813).
R. STANG, *The Theory of the Novel in England 1850–1870* (1959).
B. D. STEVENS, *Register of the Royal Grammar School Newcastle Upon Tyne* (1955).
L. STEVENSON, *Dr. Quicksilver: the Life of Charles Lever* (1939).
J. H. STONEHOUSE (ed.), *Catalogue of the Library of Charles Dickens from Gadshill* (1935).
HARVEY PETER SUCKSMITH, *The Narrative Art of Charles Dickens* (1970).
R. H. SUPER, *The Publication of Landor's Works* (1954).
—*Walter Savage Landor* (New York, 1954).
J. A. SUTHERLAND, *Victorian Novelists and Publishers* (1976).
JONATHAN SWIFT, *Works*, with Notes and a Life of the Author by Sir Walter Scott, vol. I (1814).
—*Journal to Stella*, ed. H. Williams (2 vols., 1948).
—*Correspondence*, ed. H. Williams (3 vols., 1963–5).
A. SWINBURNE, *Letters*, ed. Cecil Y. Lang, vols. I–IV (New Haven, Conn. 1959–60).
G. B. TAPLIN, *E. B. Browning: a Critical Biography* (1957).
W. G. TARRANT, *The Story and Significance of the Unitarian Movement* (1910).
JEREMY TAYLOR, *Works*, ed. R. Heber, vol. VIII (1828).

ALFRED, LORD TENNYSON, *Poems*, ed. Christopher Ricks (1969).
SIR CHARLES TENNYSON, *Alfred Tennyson* (1949).
W. M. THACKERAY, *Letters and Private Papers*, ed. G. N. Ray (4 vols., 1945).
—*The English Humourists and The Four Georges* (Everyman's Library edn, 1949).
GEOFFREY TILLOTSON and DONALD HAWES, *Thackeray: the Critical Heritage* (1968).
KATHLEEN TILLOTSON, *Novels of the Eighteen-Forties* (1954).
S. TREFMAN, *Sam. Foote, Comedian, 1720–1777* (New York, 1971).
A. TROLLOPE, *Letters*, ed. B. A. Booth (1951).
J. DON VANN and ROSEMARY T. VAN ARSDEL, *Victorian Periodicals: A Guide to Research* (New York, 1978).
J. A. VENN, *Alumni Cantabrigienses*, Part 2, vol. II (1944).
R. M. WARDLE, *Oliver Goldsmith* (Kansas, 1957).
A. H. WARREN, *English Poetic Theory 1825–1865* (Princeton, N.J., 1950).
A. WAUGH, *A Hundred Years of Publishing* (1930).
R. WELFORD, *Men of Mark 'Twixt Tyne and Tweed*, vol. II (1895).
JOEL H. WIENER, *The War of the Unstamped* (1969).
D. A. WILSON, *Carlyle on Cromwell and Others (1837–48)* (1925).
—*Carlyle at His Zenith (1848–53)* (1927).
—*Carlyle to Three-Score-and-Ten (1853–65)* (1929).
D. A. WILSON and D. W. MCARTHUR, *Carlyle in Old Age (1865–81)* (1934).
EDMUND WILSON, *The Wound and the Bow* (New York, 1947).
C. WINTON, *Captain Steele: the Early Career of Richard Steele* (Baltimore, 1964).
—*Sir Richard Steele M.P.: the Later Career* (Baltimore, 1970).
THOMAS J. WISE and STEPHEN WHEELER, *A Bibliography of the Writings in Prose and Verse of Walter Savage Landor* (1919).
WILLIAM and DOROTHY WORDSWORTH, *Letters: the Later Years*, arr. and ed. E. de Selincourt, vol. II (1939).
EDMUND YATES, *His Recollections and Experiences* (1885).
G. M. YOUNG (ed.), *Early Victorian England* (2 vols., 1934).

C. VICTORIAN PERIODICALS

(i) In addition to specific references elsewhere in this bibliography and in notes to chapters I have examined the following complete files:

Daily News – 1846
Examiner – 1833–56
Foreign Quarterly Review – 1842–4
Reflector – 1832
True Sun – 1832–3

(ii) I have also drawn upon Forster's own large collection of newspaper cuttings (FC, Victoria & Albert Museum Library), mainly reviews of his own work.

D. ARTICLES

ANON., 'The *Examiner* examined', *Scottish Temperance Rev.* (1 Dec. 1849), 554–5.
—'Dinner to Mr. Macready', *Examiner* (8 Mar. 1851), 9–11.
—'Obituary of Henry Colburn', *Gentlemen's Mag.*, XLIV (Nov. 1855), 547–8.
—'Miscellaneous: Notes on books, recent book sales, etc.', *Notes and Queries*, 2nd ser., III (1857), 458–9.
—'Royal Academy Banquet May 4, 1872', *The Times* (6 May 1872), 10.
—'Bulwer and Dickens. A contrast', *Temple Bar*, XLIII (1874–5), 168–80.
—'Obituary', *The Times* (2 Feb. 1876), 5.
—'Death of Mr. John Forster', *Newcastle Daily Chronicle* (2 Feb. 1876), 2.
—[Obituary], *Newcastle Daily J.* (2 Feb. 1876), 3.
—[Note by 'J.H.'], *Newcastle Daily Chronicle* (4 Feb. 1876), 2.
—'Death of Mr. John Forster', *Newcastle Courant* (4 Feb. 1876), 6.
—'Literature, art, and the drama', *Newcastle Weekly Chronicle* (5 Feb. 1876), 4.
—'Obituary', *Annual Register* (1876), 134.

—[Forster's funeral], *The Times* (7 Feb. 1876), 5.

—[Forster's will], *The Times* (7 Apr. 1876), 10.

—[Attempted sale of Palace Gate House], *The Times* (11 May 1876), 11.

—'The beginning of a great friendship', *Dickensian*, XXXIII (1936–7), 187–90.

G. S. AITKEN, 'James Ballantine and his correspondents', *Glasgow Herald* (22 Jan. 1910), 13.

OLIVE ANDERSON, 'The political uses of history in mid nineteenth-century England', *Past & Present*, XXXVI (Apr. 1967), 87–105.

A. ASPINALL, 'The social status of journalists at the beginning of the nineteenth century', *Rev. English Studies*, XXI (1945), 216–32.

FELIX AYLMER, 'John Forster and Dickens's Book of Memoranda', *Dickensian*, LI (1954–5), 19–23.

G. L. BARNET, 'A critical analysis of the Lucas edition of Lamb's letters', *Modern Language Q.*, IX (1948), 303–14.

F. S. BOAS, 'Charles Lamb and the Elizabethan dramatists', *Essays and Studies*, XXIX (1943), 62–81.

S. N. BOGORAD, 'Samuel Foote: the prospects for a Life and Works', *Restoration and Eighteenth Century Theatre Research*, VI (1967), 11–13.

DARWIN F. BOSTICK, 'An account of the *Examiner*', *Victorian Periodicals News.*, XI (1978), 19–21.

JOHN W. BRAYMER, '"The Role of John Forster in Victorian Letters": Forster at the MLA', *John Forster Newsl.*, I no. 2 (1979), 42–8.

ALEC W. BRICE, 'Reviewers of Dickens in the *Examiner*: Fonblanque, Forster, Hunt, and Morley', *Dickens Studies Newsl.*, III (1972), 68–80.

—'The compilation of the critical commentary in Forster's *Life of Charles Dickens*', *Dickensian*, LXX (1974), 185–90.

W. E. BUCKLER, 'Dickens's success with *Household Words*', *Dickensian*, XLVI (1949–50), 197–203.

MICHAEL A. BURR, 'Browning's note to Forster', *Victorian Poetry*, XII (1974), 343–9.

ANTHONY BURTON, 'Forster on the stage', *Dickensian*, LXX (1974), 171–84.

—'Some recent work on the Forster Collection', *John Forster Newsl.*, I no. 1 (1978), 11–20.

—'The Forster Library as a Dickens Collection', *Dickens Studies Newsl.*, IX (1978), 33–7.

BRUCE S. BUSBY, 'A note to the editor of *Thomas Wentworth, Earl of Strafford*', *Studies in Browning and His Circle*, V (1977), 65–70.

IAN M. CAMPBELL, 'Portrait of Carlyle', *Scotsman* (12 Aug. 1967), 3.

W. J. CARLTON, 'Postscripts to Forster', *Dickensian*, LVIII (1962), 87–92.

—'Dickens or Forster? Some *King Lear* criticisms re-examined', *Dickensian*, LXI (1965), 133–40.

—'Dickens studies Italian', *Dickensian*, LXI (1965), 101–8.

ALEXANDER CARLYLE, 'Correspondence between Carlyle and Browning', *Cornhill Magazine*, n.s. XXXVIII (Jan.–June 1915), 642–69.

JOHN B. CASTIEAU, 'The fictions of Forster', *Dickensian*, XII (1916), 264–9.

PHILIP COLLINS, 'Dickens's self-estimate: some new evidence', in *Dickens the Craftsman*, ed. R. B. Partlow (Carbondale and Edwardsville, Ill., 1970), 21–43.

WILMOT CORFIELD, 'The wisdom of Forster', *Dickensian*, XIII (1917), 12–13.

G. CRABBE [letter to John Forster], *Athenaeum* (18 Feb. 1832), 114.

M. CRAMER, 'Browning's friendships and fame before marriage (1833–46)', *PMLA*, LV (1940), 207–30.

ENGELINA DAVIDS, 'Forster: "Not the Slightest Comprehension". A letter by Dickens's secretary', *John Forster Newsl.*, I no. 1 (1978), 3–9.

JAMES A. DAVIES, 'Leigh Hunt and John Forster', *Rev. English Studies*, n.s. XIX (1968), 35–50.

—'John Forster at the Mannings' execution', *Dickensian*, LXVII (1971), 12–15.

—'Forster and Dickens: the making of Podsnap', *Dickensian*, LXX (1974), 145–58.

—'Charles Lamb, John Forster, and a Victorian Shakespeare', *Rev. English Studies*, n.s. XXVI (1975), 442–50.

—'Forster research: a progress report', *John Forster Newsl.*, I no. 1 (1978), 21–30.

—'Striving for honesty: an approach to Forster's *Life*', *Dickens Studies Annual*, VII (1978), 34–48.
—'Edgar Johnson's biography of Dickens and Forster research', *John Forster Newsl.*, I no. 2 (1979), 50–5.
—' "Tennyson, Forster, and the *Punch* Connection": A Reply', *Victorian Periodicals Rev.*, XIII (1980), 64–6.
—' "Tennyson, Forster, and the *Punch* Connection": Again', *Victorian Periodicals Rev.*, XIII (1980), 103–5.
W. DEXTER, 'The reception of Dickens's first book', *Dickensian*, XXXII (1935–6), 43–50.
J. P. D. DUNRABIN, 'Oliver Cromwell's popular image in nineteenth-century England', *Britain and the Netherlands*, V (1975), 141–63.
WALDO H. DUNN, 'Carlyle's last letters to Froude', *Twentieth Century*, CLIX (1956), 591–7; CLX (1956), 240–6.
A. EASSON, '*The Old Curiosity Shop*: from manuscript to print', *Dickens Studies Annual*, I (1970), 93–128.
WHITWELL ELWIN, 'John Forster', *Forster Collection: a Catalogue of the Printed Books* (1888), vii–xxvii.
ELLIOT ENGEL, 'Dickens's obscure childhood in pre-Forster biography', *Dickensian*, LXXII (1976), 3–12.
K. J. FIELDING, 'The MS. of the "Cricket on the Hearth" ', *Notes & Queries,* CXCVII (1952), 324–5, 329.
—'Dickens and the Royal Literary Fund – I', *TLS* (15 Oct. 1954), 664.
—'Dickens and the Royal Literary Fund – II', *TLS* (22 Oct. 1954), 680.
—'Dickens and the Royal Literary Fund – 1858', *Rev. English Studies*, n.s. VI (1955), 383–94.
—'Skimpole and Leigh Hunt again', *Notes & Queries*, CC (1955), 174–5.
—'Thackeray and the "Dignity of Literature" – I', *TLS* (19 Sept. 1958), 536.
—'Thackeray and the "Dignity of Literature" – II', *TLS* (26 Sept. 1958), 552.
—'Leigh Hunt and Skimpole: another remonstrance', *Dickensian*, LXIV (1968), 5–9.
—'1870–1900: Forster and reaction', *Dickensian*, LXVI (1970), 85–100.
—'Carlyle and Dickens or Dickens and Carlyle?', *Dickensian*, LXIX (1973), 11–18.
—'Forster: critic of fiction', *Dickensian*, LXX (1974), 159–70.
K. J. FIELDING and ALEC W. BRICE, 'Charles Dickens on "The Exclusion of Evidence" ', *Dickensian*, LXIV (1968), 131–40.
K. J. FIELDING and G. R. GRUBB, 'New letters from Charles Dickens to John Forster', *Boston Univ. Studies in English*, II (1956), 140–93.
J. FLEECE, 'Leigh Hunt's Shakespearian criticism', in *Essays in Honour of Walter Clyde Curry* (Nashville, Tenn., 1954), 181–96.
S. F. FOGLE, 'Skimpole once more', *Nineteenth Century Fiction*, VII (1952–3), 1–18.
J. I. FRADIN, 'The absorbing tyranny of everyday life: Bulwer Lytton's *A Strange Story*', *Nineteenth Century Fiction*, XVI (1961–2), 1–16.
SAMUEL R. GARDINER, 'Mr. John Forster', *Academy* (5 Feb. 1876), 122.
J. G. [J. GIBBS], 'How I first met Charles Dickens', *Press News* (Dec. 1905), 27–9.
CLARENCE GOHDES, 'Longfellow and his authorized British publishers', *PMLA*, LV (1940), 1165–9.
W. FORBES GRAY, 'Carlyle and John Forster: an unpublished correspondence', *Q. Rev.*, CCLXVIII (1937), 271–87.
WILLIAM LOCKEY HARLE, 'John Forster: a sketch', *Newcastle Daily Chronicle* (15 Feb. 1876), 4. Reprinted in *Monthly Chronicle of North-Country Lore and Legend*, II (1888), 50–4.
F. R. HART, 'Boswell and the Romantics: a chapter in the history of biographical theory', *English Literary History*, XXVII (1960), 44–65.
R. HAVEN, 'The Romantic art of Charles Lamb', *English Literary History*, XXX (1963), 137–46.
HEATHER HENDERSON, '"To You Only ...": Forster to C. E. Norton on Dickens's death', *John Forster Newsl.*, I no. 2 (1979), 32–40.
R. H. HORNE, 'John Forster; his early life and friendships', *Temple Bar*, XLVI (1876), 491–505, and *Appleton's J.*, XV (1876), 467–9, 500–3.

G. HOUGH, 'Coleridge and the Victorians', in *The English Mind*, ed. H. S. Davies and G. Watson (1964), 175–92.

LEIGH HUNT, 'Reflections on some of the great men of the reign of Charles the First', *New Monthly Mag.*, XLVII (1836), 207–18.

RICHARD J. HUTCHINGS, 'Dickens at Bonchurch', *Dickensian*, LXI (1965), 79–100.

ELIZABETH JAMES, 'The publication of collected editions of Bulwer Lytton's novels', *Publishing History*, III (1978), 46–60.

B. JERROLD, 'John Forster', *Gentleman's Mag.*, XVI (1876), 313–19.

JOHN BUSH JONES, 'Tennyson, Forster, and the *Punch* connection', *Victorian Periodicals Newsl.*, XI (1978), 118–21.

—'The *Punch* connection II; or *et tu*, Tennyson', *Victorian Periodicals Rev.*, XIII (1980), 66–9.

PHILIP KELLEY, 'Greek Slave mystery', *Notes & Queries*, CCII (1967), 194.

CHARLES KENT, 'John Forster', *DNB* (1889), XX 16–19.

GEORGE P. LANDOW, 'Some new Thackeray letters', *English Language Notes*, X (1973), 279–81.

JOHN Y. LeBOURGEOIS, 'Swinburne, Lord Lytton, and John Forster', *Notes & Queries*, XIX (1972), 417–19.

G. H. LEWES, 'Dickens in relation to criticism', *Fortnightly Rev.*, XVII (1872), 141–54.

J. W. T. LEY, 'The "Harbitrary Gent": John Forster's friendships', *Dickensian*, IX (1913), 12–15.

ANNE LOHRLI, 'Greek Slave mystery', *Notes & Queries*, CCXI (1966), 58–60.

W. J. McCORMACK, 'J. Sheridan Le Fanu: letters to William Blackwood and John Forster', *Long Room*, no. 8 (Autumn 1973), 29–36.

W. C. MACREADY [letter to the Editor], *The Times* (31 Jan. 1842), 5.

B. W. MATZ, 'John Forster', *Dickensian*, VIII (1912), 119–23.

SYLVÈRE MONOD, 'John Foster's "Life of Dickens" and literary criticism', *English Studies Today* (Rome, 1966), 357–73.

P. F. MORGAN, 'On some letters of Charles Lamb', *Notes & Queries*, CCI (1956), 531–2.

—'Alexander Dyce on Charles Lamb', *Notes & Queries*, CCII (1957), 124.

HENRY MORLEY, 'Biographical sketch of John Forster', *Dyce and Forster Collections Handbook* (1880), 53–73.

SARAH NORTON and M. A. DeWOLFE HOWE, 'English friends: from letters and journals of Charles Eliot Norton', *Scribners* (1913), 500–11, 567–80, 775–86.

S. NOWELL-SMITH, 'Carlyle and the London Library', in *English Libraries 1800–1850* (1958), 59–78.

PANSY PAKENHAM, 'The Memorandum Book, Forster and *Edwin Drood*', *Dickensian*, LI (1954–5), 117–21.

DAVID PARKER and MICHAEL SLATER, 'The Gladys Storey Papers', *Dickensian*, LXXVI (1980), 3–16.

MORSE PECKHAM, 'Afterword: reflections on historical modes in the nineteenth century', in *Victorian Poetry*, ed. M. Bradbury and D. Palmer, Stratford-Upon-Avon Studies 15 (1972), 276–300.

WILLIAM S. PETERSON, 'A re-examination of Robert Browning's *Prose Life of Strafford*', *Browning Newsl.*, no. 2 (Apr. 1969), 12–22.

J. S. R. PHILLIPS, 'The growth of journalism', *Cambridge History of English Literature*, XIV (1916), 167–204.

[J. POOLE], 'Theatre Royal Little Pedlington', *The Times* (5 Apr. 1837), 7.

SIR J. PRIOR, [letter to the Editor], *Literary Gaz.* (3 June 1848), 375–6.

—[letter to the Editor], *Literary Gaz.* (29 July 1848), 504–6.

J. W. REED, Jr, 'Browning and Macready: the final quarrel', *PMLA*, LXXV (1960), 597–603.

CHARLES RICHARD SANDERS, 'Carlyle's letters', *Bull. John Rylands Library*, XXXVIII (1955–6), 199–224.

—'Carlyle's letters to Ruskin', *Bull. John Rylands Library*, XLI (1958–9), 208–38.

—'Carlyle and Tennyson', *PMLA*, LXXVI (1961), 82–97.

—'The correspondence and friendship of Thomas Carlyle and Leigh Hunt: the early years', *Bull. John Rylands Library*, XLV (1962–3), 439–85; 'The later years', *ibid.*, XLVI (1963–4), 179–216.

—'Some lost and unpublished

Carlyle/Browning correspondence', *J. English and Germanic Philology*, LXII (1963), 323–35.
—'The Carlyles and Thackeray', in *Nineteenth-Century Literary Perspectives*, ed. Clyde de L. Ryals (Durham, N.C., 1974), 161–200.
—'The Carlyle–Browning correspondence and relationship', *Bull. John Rylands Library*, LVII (1974–5), 213–46, 430–62.
MICHAEL SLATER, 'Dickens (and Forster) at work on *The Chimes*', *Dickens Studies*, II (1966), 106–40.
C. E. SMITH, 'John Forster', *Procs. Massachusetts Historical Soc.*, XLIV (1911), 502–5.
HERODOTUS SMITH [FRANCIS ESPINASSE], '*The Examiner*', *Critic* (1 Sept. 1852), 441–2.
E. SPENDER, 'The life and opinions of Walter Savage Landor', *London Q. Rev.*, XXIV (1865), 171–206.
L. C. STAPLES, 'Dickens and Macready's *Lear*', *Dickensian*, XLIV (1948), 78–80.
G. D. STOUT, 'Leigh Hunt's Shakespeare: a "Romantic" concept', in *Studies in Memory of F. M. Webster* (St Louis, 1951), 14–33.
R. H. SUPER, 'Forster as Landor's literary executor', *Modern Language Notes*, LII (1937), 504–6.
—'Landor's "Dear Daughter", Eliza Lynn Linton', *PMLA*, LIX (1944), 1059–85.
P. V. THOMPSON, 'An unpublished letter from Swift', *Library*, XXII (1967), 57–66.
JAMES THOMPSON (B.V.), 'A note on Forster's *Life of Swift*', in *The Speedy Extinction of Evil and Misery*, ed. W. Schaefer (Berkeley and Los Angeles, 1967), 278–83.
KATHLEEN TILLOTSON and NINA BURGIS, 'Forster's reviews in the *Examiner*, 1840–41', *Dickensian*, LXVIII (1972), 105–8.
HUGH TREVOR-ROPER, 'Thomas Carlyle's historical philosophy', *TLS* (26 June 1981), 731–4.
SYLVANUS URBAN, 'Table talk', *Gentleman's Mag.*, XVI (1876), 378–82.
ROSEMARY VALLANCE, 'Forster's *Goldsmith*', *Dickensian*, LXXI (1975), 21–9.
J. CUMING WALTERS and J. W. T. LEY, 'The fictions of Forster: two views', *Dickensian*, XII (1916), 285–9.
H. H. WATTS, 'Lytton's theories of prose fiction', *PMLA*, L (1935), 274–89.
H. WILLIAMS, 'Deane Swift, Hawkesworth, and "The Journal to Stella"', in *Essays on the Eighteenth Century Presented to David Nichol Smith* (New York, 1963), 33–48.
DAVID WOOLLEY, 'Forster's *Swift*', *Dickensian*, LXX (1974), 191–204.

Index

Smith, Arthur, 255